Communication Assessment of the Bilingual Bicultural Child

Communication Assessment of the Bilingual Bicultural Child
Issues and Guidelines

Edited by

Joan Good Erickson, Ph.D.
Assistant Professor of Speech and Hearing Science
Midwest Organization for Materials Development
University of Illinois

and

Donald R. Omark, Ph.D.
Assistant Professor of Education
Midwest Organization for Materials Development
University of Illinois

University Park Press
Baltimore

UNIVERSITY PARK PRESS
International Publishers in Science, Medicine, and Education
300 North Charles Street
Baltimore, Maryland 21201

Copyright © 1981 by the Board of Trustees of the University of Illinois

Typeset by Maryland Composition Company, Inc.
Manufactured in the United States of America by
The Maple Press Company.

All rights, including that of translation into other languages, reserved. Photomechanical reproduction (photocopy, microcopy) of this book or parts thereof without special permission of the publisher is prohibited.

The activity which is the subject of this report was supported in whole or in part by the U.S. Office of Education, Department of Health, Education, and Welfare. However, the opinions expressed herein do not necessarily reflect the position or policy of the U.S. Office of Education, and no official endorsement by the U.S. Office of Education should be inferred.

Library of Congress Cataloging in Publication Data

Main entry under title:

Communication assessment of the bilingual, bicultural child.

Bibliography: p.
Includes index.
1. Education, Bilingual—United States—Addresses, essays, lectures. 2. Language arts—Ability testing—Addresses, essays, lectures. 3. Bilingualism—United States—Addresses, essays, lectures. 4. Biculturalism—United States—Addresses, essays, lectures. I. Erickson, Joan Good. II. Omark, Donald R.
LC3731.C623   371.97'0973   80-21398
ISBN 0-8391-1599-7

Contents

Contributors ... vii
Preface ... ix

chapter one
Communication Assessment of the Bilingual Bicultural Child
An Overview
Joan Good Erickson ... 1

chapter two
Concepts in Bilingualism and Their Relationship to Language Assessment
Pamela A. McCollum ... 25

chapter three
Issues and Procedures in the Analysis of Syntax and Semantics
Linda Locke ... 43

chapter four
Considerations in Phonological Assessment
Janet I. Anderson ... 77

chapter five
Conceptualizations of Bilingual Children
Testing the Norm
Donald R. Omark ... 99

chapter six
Evaluating Language Assessment Tests
Some Practical Considerations
Elizabeth M. Leemann ... 115

chapter seven
Discrete Point Language Tests of Bilinguals
A Review of Selected Tests
E. Catherine Day, Pamela A. McCollum, Valerie A. Cieslak, and Joan Good Erickson ... 129

chapter eight
Quasi-integrative Approaches
Discrete Point Scoring of Expressive Language Samples
Pamela A. McCollum and E. Catherine Day 163

chapter nine
Assessing Communicative Competence
Integrative Testing of Second Language Learners
E. Catherine Day 179

chapter ten
Pragmatics and Language Assessment
Kamal K. Sridhar 199

chapter eleven
The Role of Contextual Factors in Language Use and Language Assessment
Joel Walters 221

chapter twelve
Pragmatics and Ethological Techniques for the Observational Assessment of Children's Communicative Abilities
Donald R. Omark 249

appendix A
Suggestions for Interviewing Children
Joan Good Erickson 285

appendix B
Rules for Calculating Mean Length of Utterance in Morphemes for Spanish
Nicolás Linares 291

appendix C
An Annotated Bibliography on the Communication Assessment of the Bilingual Child
Kathryn Kutz Scott 297

Index 359

Contributors

Janet I. Anderson, Ph.D.
Department of English
Iowa State University
Ames, Iowa 50011

Valerie A. Cieslak, M.A.
Franciscan Hospital Rehabilitation
  Center
Rock Island, Illinois 61201

E. Catherine Day, Ph.D. Cand.
Office of Multicultural Bilingual
  Education
University of Illinois at Urbana-
  Champaign
Champaign, Illinois 61820

Joan Good Erickson, Ph.D.
Department of Speech and Hearing
  Science
University of Illinois at Urbana-
  Champaign
Champaign, Illinois 61820

Elizabeth M. Leemann, Ph.D. Cand.
French Department
Dahlhousie University
Halifax, Nova Scotia

Nicolás Linares, Ph.D.
Departamento de Trastornos
  Comunicológicos
Universidad de Puerto Rico
San Juan, Puerto Rico 00936

Linda Locke, Ph.D. Cand.
Department of Linguistics
University of Illinois at Urbana-
  Champaign
Champaign, Illinois 61820

Pamela A. McCollum, Ph.D.
Office of Multicultural Bilingual
  Education
University of Illinois at Urbana-
  Campaign
Champaign, Illinois 61820

Donald R. Omark, Ph.D.
Los Amigos Research Associates
7035 Galewood
San Diego, California 92120

Kathryn Kutz Scott, Ph.D.
Parkland Community College
Champaign, Illinois 61820

Kamal K. Sridhar, Ph.D.
Program in Linguistics
SUNY-Stony Brook
Stony Brook, New York 11794

Joel Walters, Ph.D.
Department of Educational
  Psychology
University of Illinois at Urbana-
  Champaign
Champaign, Illinois 61820

Preface

This book started as a project within the Midwest Organization for Materials Development, Office of Multicultural Bilingual Education, University of Illinois at Urbana-Champaign. Language testing had become and remains a salient issue as bilingual programs develop across the country in response to litigation and attempts to improve the education of language minority children. The initial goal of the project was to examine and critique the available instruments designed for testing the language of bilingual, limited-English, and non-English-speaking children and adults. As our examinations of evaluation materials continued, it became obvious that widely varying approaches were being used to assess communicative competence. There also appeared to be a discrepancy between the theoretical basis for most commercially available measurements and current linguistic theory which suggests that communicative ability is of a complex nature.

The question arose, *Why the diversity in assessment approaches?* It seemed that the more discrete-point type of instruments were based upon earlier linguistic approaches where concentration was on the form of language. In contrast, more integrative tests attempted to consider both the form and the function of language. This led to the next question: *Why use discrete-point tests to evaluate the language understanding and production of bilingual children?* One could answer that an approach that samples various predetermined lexical and syntactic-morphological items is easier to develop and score. But that did not seem to be a sufficient rationale for ignoring whether or not children could effectively communicate with others. Also, an approach that suggests that language testing should measure parts of a whole rather than the synergistic process introduces a potential risk in that limited information can lead to spurious decisions in the educational placements of children.

Even assuming that tests had positive reliability and validity reviews, a third question arose: *What standard should be used when assessing the communicative ability of a bilingual population?* Inferred in this question was the notion that there is a standard against which all children should be measured, or, for that matter, a standard language form upon which language professionals could agree. One might also suggest that attempts to sample surface structures based on a preconception of what is "standard" may be elitist if not racist. Furthermore, sociolinguists have long

ix

espoused the fact that language use varies according to context, a phenomenon which discrete-point sampling of surface structures does not consider. In addition, tests of this type do not usually deal with lexical variation or the constraints of the testing environment.

As these *issues* become more apparent, there is an obvious need to provide *guidelines* for choosing among assessment approaches. These guidelines are necessary for the professionals responsible for teacher training, for administrators who select the instruments, and for front-line practitioners, all of whom affect the lives of bilingual children. Therefore, the major point of this book, if it is to have any effect on the language testing of bilingual children, is to move the tester away from discrete point tests and toward integrative tests, to discourage the use of relatively quick, easy, and perhaps statistically questionable tests which sample language forms, and to encourage the assessment of language within a functional framework. What is important, especially in bilingual education, is not only an examination of whether a child knows certain lexical or syntactic-morphological forms, but whether he or she can communicate with teachers, parents, peers, and others in various communicative environments.

The text first provides basic information in the areas of communicative assessment, bilingualism, and the effects of second language learning on the phonological, semantic, and syntactic-morphological system. Next, information on concepts in testing and various assessment approaches are presented. The final chapters focus on assessing language in context and its relationship to bilingual children. These chapters emphasize the importance of viewing language function as the rubric for attaining communicative competence in second as well as first language usage. The appendices include further information on language sampling and an annotated bibliography of relevant literature.

Our thanks are owed to Dr. Henry Trueba, who initiated and supported this project, and Drs. Sridhar and Hastings, who saw it through to completion. Efforts of supportive personnel at the Midwest Organization for Materials Development and numerous faculty and graduate students who provided comments on the chapters are also acknowledged.

To the children we have worked with over the years and especially to those closest to us who provided numerous insights into how young children acquire language—Kristin, Kenneth, and Michael John (J. G. E.) and Karin and Anika (D. R. O.).

Communication Assessment of the Bilingual Bicultural Child

chapter one

Communication Assessment of the Bilingual Bicultural Child
An Overview
Joan Good Erickson

This introductory chapter 1) provides a historical overview of various approaches to testing language, 2) clarifies the issues that are both causing and complicating the assessment of the communicative competence of bilingual populations, and 3) proposes several approaches to solving the problem of language assessment in the educational environment. Succeeding chapters discuss many of the issues in depth and provide evaluations of tests as well as suggestions for assessing the communication of bilingual, limited English-speaking (LES), or non-English-speaking (NES) children.[1] Language specialists from several disciplines share their viewpoints with the readers from equally varied backgrounds. These specialists include teachers of English as a Second Language (ESL), speech-language pathologists, bilingual educators, linguists, and ethologists, all of whom are interested in appropriate and meaningful assessment of the target population.

Tests are an objective and standardized measure of a sample of behavior (Anastasi, 1976). The term *assessment* is used to imply a broader approach to the measurement of behavior and include information derived from tests and/or observation, although this information is still only a sample of an individual's behavior. Furthermore, those who are charged with the difficult task of sampling this behavior may not share a common definition of the general behavior to be assessed. Different theoretical perspectives, definitions, foci, and samples of behavior, as well as different assessment procedures, suggest different results.

---

[1] The text uses the terminology LES in contrast to LESA (limited English-speaking ability). The current terminology is non-English proficient (NEP). Terms change over time. Perhaps in the future, the term will be LCCE (limited communicative competence in English).

Inherent in the assessment of bilingual bicultural children is the diversity of definitions and theories on how first and second languages are acquired. Definitions and descriptions of what constitutes bilingualism are pendulous at the least and polar at the most (see McCollum, Chapter 2, this volume). Following is a discussion of how first and second language acquisition studies relate to assessment of a child's communication ability. The reader may become aware of the circular phenomena that how one views language is reflected in how it is measured, which is reflected in how it is taught, which is reflected in how it is viewed, ad infinitum. With this awareness, it is not surprising that testing or assessing the communication of first language (L_1), as well as second language (L_2), learners is fraught with problems.

HISTORICAL PERSPECTIVES

Historically language was seen from a structuralistic viewpoint. Linguists were interested primarily in writing the grammar of a language. Information on language acquisition was based on descriptive information regarding syntactic rules, parts of speech, size of vocabulary, and length of response, all of which were consistent with the structuralistic theory of the time. What a person heard or spoke was considered at face value to represent language ability, and there was limited concern regarding the process of language acquisition and its effect upon that apparent ability.

With the cognitive orientation proposed by Chomsky (1957, 1965), there was a reinterpretation of the nature of language. His transformational-generative point of view suggested that an individual has an elaborate set of rules or knowledge that underlies the generative nature of language performance. This basic competence, or capacity to use a language, was thus differentiated from the performance, or actual application, although the latter implies the former.

Other researchers (Bloom, 1970; McNeil, 1970; Slobin, 1971; Brown, 1973) extended the psycholinguistic interpretation into such discussions as the cognitive view of linguistic structures, the existence of language universals, and the notion that children are born with a language acquisition device that predisposes them to language learning. Insight into the areas of semantics, or the meaning of words and sentences, was offered by researchers such as Katz (1972) and Clark (1973).

There has also been an expansion of both philosophical and experimental reports on the *function* of language in contrast to *form*. The early writings of Austin (1962) and later of Grice (1967) and Searle (1969) prompted interest in speech acts and pragmatics. Some schemes discuss this topic in relationship to intentionality and emotional content, while other views of language function are couched in grammatical analysis. Researchers who are interested in the relationship of syntactic constructions to speech acts point out that, for the most common direct speech acts used by speakers, the structures are designed for the act. For example, when the purpose is to tell, declaratives are used; for a command, imperatives are used. Speakers, however, also develop the use of indirect speech acts which are supported by an extensive repertoire of grammatical forms (Clark and Clark, 1977). Additional research activity focuses on conversational rules and other aspects of discourse analysis (Halliday, 1973; Bates, 1976; Ervin-Tripp and Mitchell-Kernan, 1976; Hatch, 1978). The current thrust, therefore, is to view language in a contextual framework.

Meanwhile, the field of teaching English as a second langauge has been experiencing its own professional growth cycle. Contrasting the phonological and syntactic patterns of the native and target langauges initially provided the framework for testing and teaching second language learners. By the 1970s, the analysis of the errors made by the speaker in the second language was viewed as a more viable procedure (Richards, 1975). Other changes in thinking on second language learning indicated that L_2 acquisition may be similar in process to L_1 acquisition (Ervin-Tripp, 1974, and others) and that it shared the same "creative construction" attribute (Dulay and Burt, 1972, 1974).[2] Research on code mixing and code switching and the effects of the intra- versus interlanguage phenomenon added to the metamorphosis of the field of learning/teaching English as a second language. Chapters by Locke and Anderson discuss these points further.

Thus, a sociological orientation to both first and second language learning has developed. Researchers have become increasingly concerned with the importance of the social setting, interactors, and topic of discussion (Cazden, 1970, 1972a, 1972b), especially in regard to minority dialects and bilingualism (Fishman, 1972; Labov, 1972). In this volume, the chapters by Sridhar and Walters provide a review of the literature related to language in context. The focus of the entire volume is on the importance of assessing communication within an appropriate contextual framework.

---

[2] Recently an extensive test of syntax normed on the deaf, The Test of Syntactic Abilities (Quigley et al. 1978), has been used experimentally with bilingual populations. Just as the L_1–L_2 acquisition process has been shown to be related, the language of hearing impaired and learners of English as a second language show similar errors in syntax (C. King, 1979, personal communication).

From this brief look at various theoretical and research foci one can see changes in how the behavior of *speech, language,* or *communication* is viewed.[3] It is also apparent that many disciplines are involved in the study of language in general and bilingualism in particular. For these reasons, one finds differences in terminology usage. In some instances, two different fields use the same term but refer to different phenomena. For example, *fluency* has a different meaning in ESL than it has in speech-language pathology. There is also variability in usage of terminology when referring to integrative testing, language context, and speech acts, all of which depend upon the philosophical and/or theoretical foundation inferred as well as the discipline that uses the term. Readers are cautioned to recognize their own biases in definitions along with the various authors' biases when reading this and succeeding chapters.

PERSPECTIVES RELATED TO ASSESSING ENGLISH AS A FIRST OR SECOND LANGUAGE

Most measures of language available to educational specialists do not consider contemporary theory on communication nor first and second language acquisition data. Furthermore, they frequently do not reflect an awareness of the complex process and numerous variables related to assessment. One wonders how this problem occurred and what options are available for assessing communication. This section explores how those who are interested in assessing the communication of bilingual, LES, and NES children have found themselves in a problematic area. Perspectives on assessing the language of children who acquire English as a first language and those who acquire it as a second language are presented. Current testing approaches are summarized since each of these topics is discussed in depth in succeeding chapters.

Language tests developed before the Chomskyan revolution naturally reflected the thinking that language was a series of separate or discrete points which, when added up, made the whole. Language was not viewed as a synergistic and social phenomenon. From this structuralistic viewpoint one would measure vocabulary with instruments such as the Peabody Picture Vocabulary Test (Dunn, 1965) or syntax with the Northwestern Syntax Screening Test (Lee, 1969). Some tests measured

---

[3] Terms that describe various other aspects of communication include *diexis, kinesics, proxemics,* and *semiotics,* but it is beyond the scope of this volume to provide a discussion of these areas.

several discrete points. For example, the Michigan Picture Language Inventory (Lerea, 1958) evaluated vocabulary and syntax as well as the understanding and production of other structural relationships such as singulars, plurals, prepositions, present and past tense of verbs, possessive pronouns, comparatives, and superlatives. In addition to reflecting a structuralistic view of language, most of the discrete point tests also have limited or questionable statistical support, especially in regard to their use with minority children.

In the field of English as a second language, assessment approaches frequently have been based on a structuralistic viewpoint. Measures usually focused on testing for errors on specific forms without recognizing the developmental or functional aspects of second language learning. As the above examples indicate, discrete point tests of English were also available, so it is not surprising to find that discrete point tests in languages other than English or with "parallel" English forms continue to be developed. Examples of these types of tests include the Test of Auditory Comprehension of Language (Carrow, 1973), the Del Rio Language Screening Test (Toronto et al., 1975) and the James Language Dominance Test (James, 1975), which have Spanish and English forms for testing a child's lexical and syntactic ability. Most tests have normative data, but often these data were developed on local populations. Some authors warn examiners against generalized use of their test beyond the population on which it was normed. Others (Nelson-Burgess and Meyerson, 1975) do not distribute the test beyond their geographical area for this reason. For further discussion of discrete point tests see Day et al., Chapter 7, this volume.

A discrete point approach to testing has not been without criticism, however. Several authors (Jakobovits, 1970; Briere, 1972; Oller, 1973) have suggested using methods that more closely reflect contemporary linguistic thinking, i.e., assessing communicative competence or functional language ability. Furthermore, as with any evaluation attempt, it behooves a test user to recognize the importance of the statistical data and existence of various reviews of the tests. Several of the following chapters provide information that, it is hoped, will assist the reader in doing so.

In the midst of an era where changes in theory were not necessarily followed by changes in assessment of English as a first or second language, came the sudden necessity to evaluate the language of large numbers of bilingual bicultural, LES, and NES children in this country. School districts were faced with implementing federal legislation in two areas: bilingual education and special education. Educators became aware of the incorrect placement of some children as a result of the use of inappropriate testing approaches. Adequate assessments for these students were needed in order to provide appropriate programs for them and to ensure fair assessment of minority and/or LES or NES children. Thus, in spite of the fact that the shift to testing language as a synergistic, social phenomenon had not yet been made, educational institutions were faced with the task of providing a meaningful approach to assessing these children in their native language and in English. With a lack of resources upon which to draw in contrast to very real and immediate needs of practitioners, several problems developed during well-meaning attempts to assess this population.

What were some of these problems? In a panic approach to developing language assessment tools (such as tests of language dominance or of native language proficiency), tests in English were translated into other languages. This procedure obviously violated the statistical support for the tests, which may have been statistically weak from the beginning. In addition, the cultural and linguistic relevancy of items often became inappropriate. Haphazardly developed non-English and bilingual measures also sprouted up to meet immediate needs. These tests usually had a weak theoretical base and lacked reliability and validity data. In some instances, procedures originally designed to measure the language proficiency of adult second language learners were borrowed to satisfy the demand for assessing children. In other instances, attempts to evaluate English proficiency of bilingual children utilized tests designed for other purposes such as for evaluating reading or achievement. The use of available language measures for the bilingual bicultural child was further complicated by the fact that even if the normative data of English-speaking/reading/writing ability measures were appropriate to use, these norms were based on a white middle-class population (see Omark, Chapter 5).

There were further conditions that contributed to the lack of adequate/available language tests and also impeded their development. In addition to the changing theoretical foundations in second language learning, there was a lack of cohesiveness to the research being done. Furthermore, the amount of data available on the acquisition of languages other than English or on bilingual acquisition was not as extensive as was the information on English. Some information is more recent and readily available (i.e., texts by Ferguson and Slobin, 1973; McLaughlin, 1978; Ritchie, 1978), whereas other needed developmental information often tends to be in dissertations and fugitive literature. For this reason,

Afendras and Pianarosa (1975) are continuing to catalogue worldwide information on bilingualism and second language learning.[4]

ASSESSING COMMUNICATION

This section discusses general considerations in language assessment and is followed by suggestions for implementing an assessment model. The model is based on some commonly held assumptions regarding language that have prevailed or, at least, have met minimal challenge. These assumptions, listed below, do not appear to be used by most developers of discrete point tests.

1. Language is a symbolic, generative process that does not lend itself easily to formal assessment.
2. Language is synergistic, so that any measure of the part does not give a picture of the whole.
3. Language is a part of the total experience of a child and is difficult to assess as an isolated part of development.
4. Langauge use (quality and quantity) varies according to the setting, interactors, and topic.

The assessment approach to be described samples communication in a natural setting and obtains supportive information from integrative testing and interviews, including probes into specific functions and forms of language use. It is a model that encourages the use of criterion-referenced testing, and, when indicated, norm-referenced testing based on local data.

Assessment Considerations

While recognizing the formidable task of assessing a child's language, one is also faced with the necessity of doing so. It is hoped that appropriate approaches that take into account the language(s) and the culture(s) of the child will be used. At present the options for planning a language assessment approach require choosing between available instruments or developing new approaches. Either option necessitates evaluating reliability and validity of the approach (see Leemann, Chapter

---

[4] For a perspective on the limited, albeit burgeoning, information in this field, a quick comparison of the current number of journal and fugitive documents in the ERIC system was done. Descriptors in the abstracts (narrowed to children) showed the following possible hits: reading, 5,984; handicapped, 4,066; language, 1,036; in contrast to bilingualism, 589; language dominance, 36; and second language acquisition, 530. (See Scott, Appendix C, this volume, for an annotated bibliography of language assessment references.)

6, this volume). When using commercial tests or preparing new approaches for language assessment, one must ask the following questions:

1. What is the purpose of the evaluation (placement for bilingual programs, planning second language learning strategies, identification of communication handicaps in L_1)?
2. How extensive will the evaluation be (screening, diagnosis)?
3. What symbol media will be evaluated (written, spoken, both)?
4. What verbal and nonverbal channels of communication will be assessed (comprehension, expression, both)?
5. What environments (home, neighborhood, school) with what interactors (peers, adults) will be evaluated?
6. What surface structures will be evaluated (syntax, lexicon, morphology, phonology)?
7. How extensive will the analysis of verbal interactions/discourse be (communicative style, intent, conversational rules)?
8. What method (elicited, naturalistic) will be used to evaluate the child?

Thus, when planning an approach to language assessment of the bilingual bicultural child, one should not only decide why, how, and what language ability will be assessed, but also be very clear as to what one intends to do with the information once it is obtained. The more extensive the ramifications of the judgments and decisions being made, the more extensive the assessment should be.

All of the considerations that arise in planning an assessment of the language of a monolingual child are relevant to assessing the bilingual child. In addition, the assessment approach should consider the fact that the testing process itself may be culturally unfamiliar to a child. What is familiar to one child of one cultural or socioeconomic group, such as paper and pencil tests or talking about a picture, may not be a familiar task to a child from another cultural or economic group. Certain linguistic factors are also important to consider in assessing a bilingual bicultural child since phonological, syntactic, or semantic forms may vary between languages and cultures. For example, there may be a variance in the frequency of occurrence of specific constructions, a culture-specific use of familiar forms, or a lack of existence of certain concepts (e.g., pet). Locke (Chapter 3, this volume) presents an in-depth discussion of the significance of these differences in regard to semantics and syntax, and Anderson (Chapter 4) discusses them in regard to phonology. Dialect differences within a langauge (e.g., between Mexican-American,

Cuban, and Puerto Rican Spanish or nonstandard and standard English) also need to be considered because of lexical, syntactic, and phonological variations.

In order for any assessment of communication of the bilingual bicultural child to be meaningful, it should:

1. Be based on contemporary psycholinguistic and sociolinguistic theory
2. Relate to the particular model (transitional, maintenance) of bilingual education being used in the educational setting
3. Reflect the nature of the communicative process in the natural environment
4. Be an ongoing process that reflects a child's changing communicative needs and abilities
5. Emphasize what a child can do rather than what he or she cannot do

The following section presents a multifaceted approach to assessment which, in varying ways, satisfies these criteria. The most difficult criterion to fullfill when choosing from available tests is the first, which suggests that measures be based on contemporary theory. As is apparent from discussion in this chapter and throughout the book, there is a divergence between the "ideal" test and currently available tests, as well as a disparity between the *theory* and the methodology available to apply that theory. As a result of these disparities, dilemmas[5] are encountered when one attempts to plan any assessment program. It is the purpose of this book to provide several options to the practitioner for solving these dilemmas.

General Model for Assessment

Hard questions are never easily answered and certainly asking how to solve the assessment dilemma falls in that category. However, the necessity of attempting to reach an answer is obvious. Since most of the currently available tests reflect structural linguistic theory rather than more current psycholinguistic and sociolinguistic theory, it becomes important to turn to other approaches. The focus of assessment should be

---

[5] The one dilemma the author has often challenged is the statement frequently made by practitioners that they do not have time to do in-depth evaluations because they are so busy teaching. One can only wonder how confident these practitioners can be in what they are teaching if they do not know the linguistic ability of the child with whom they are working. A child's communicative ability cannot be determined from a 10- or 20-minute test. Thus, it is necessary to devote quality time to evaluation throughout the school year in order to achieve quality teaching and learning.

on language function or evaluation of a child's communicative competence. This does not mean it is necessary to "throw out" syntax like the proverbial "baby with the bathwater." Instead it is suggested that an assessment approach be *refocused* from sampling discrete points of the form of language to assessing the function of language, and then using the information on form in a supportive manner. If one were to speak for a child, the message would be, "Please listen to what I'm trying to tell you, to what I mean, rather than only to how I say it."

The importance of evaluating and teaching language to the child within situational contexts has been proposed by many (Cazden, 1972a, 1972b; Spolsky, 1973; Upshur, 1973; Burt and Dulay, 1975; Fishman and Cooper, 1978). Thus, a language assessment approach should indeed reflect the nature of the communication process and evaluate the major use of language, that of a verbal/social communicative interaction in a natural setting. Because an evaluator may not obtain all of the information needed from a natural setting, it may be necessary to use quasi-experimental and, in some cases, more formal approaches in addition to observation.

The proposed assessment model is a multi-informational approach that uses various types of analyses, data-gathering methods, and settings/informants. Several of the methods are discussed in depth in other chapters of this volume. Those professionals responsible for obtaining a meaningful assessment of the communication skills of bilingual, LES, and NES children could use a reasonable combination of the various methods as appropriate for their educational setting or purpose. For a discussion of psychometric consideration in developing various types of language testing procedures used by second language learners, see Clark (1978).

In general, several types of analyses can be done with data obtained from multiple sources. First, a communication sample (an expressive language sample with contextual information) can be obtained by observing a child in various settings with various interactors. Additional communication samples may be obtained from a clinical interview. Although communication samples from these two sources will focus on language function, they serendipitously provide information for analysis of the child's comprehension and expression of language form. Communication samples will, therefore, yield information on a child's 1) functional language use (speaker, listener, and contextual analysis which considers speech acts and conversational styles), and 2) surface structures (such as mean length of utterance). Inferences can also be made about a child's understanding of spoken language. For further information one can use integrative tests (see

Day, Chapter 9, this volume) or extensions of available tests (see Sridhard, Chapter 10, this volume). During a clinical interview one can use probes that tap verbal comprehension and expression of syntax, semantics, and morphology and various speech acts (see Walters, Chapter 11, and Appendix A, this volume). This information can then be compared with and embellish the communciation sample obtained in the natural setting.

ASSESSING LANGUAGE FUNCTION

The current research focus on pragmatics/speech acts/discourse analysis is reflected in proposals for assessing communication in context or using integrative testing. At this point, a digression to discuss the terms *integrative, functional, pragmatic* or *contextual* assessment procedures is necessary. Meaning diverges depending on the discipline using the terms, the type of test being referenced, and the specific interpretation of a term. For example, if the testing of second language learners was usually in written form, one could suggest that a test would be integrative if it added a verbal component. If context is defined within a written framework but exclusive of the typical structural type tests, one might view a cloze test (i.e., filling in every *n*th word) as a pragmatic or contextual task. Integrative tests could also be interpreted as those that require the person to write answers from oral dictation or tests that sample all areas of listening, speaking, reading, and writing. Recently, Oller (1978) provided a description of the manner in which he differentiates between the various testing approaches. He defines pragmatic tests as:

> ... that class of integrative tests meeting two requirements: first, they must require the pragmatic mapping of utterances (or their surrogates) onto extralinguistic context. This can be termed the *meaning* requirement. Second, they must require the processing to take place under temporal constraints. This may be termed the *time* requirement. Integrative tests, on the other hand, are a much broader class of tests defined as the antithesis of discrete-point tests (p. 57).

Several chapters in this volume provide further information on the topic.

A broader interpretation of context along with a focus on the functional use of native and/or target languages suggests another approach to communicative assessment. This view is based on the notion that a definition of context includes various interactors, topics, and situations, and that, consequently, it is necessary to analyze a child's communication according to several dimensions from samples obtained in several contexts. An excellent discussion on describing children's communication samples is provided by Bloom and Lahey (1978):

> Perhaps the most important single factor in obtaining evidence of child language and development is that what children do and what else goes on in the context is at least as important as what children say and what they hear. If only the child's utterances are recorded or transcribed, then it might be possible to describe something of what the child knows about language form, but the important interactions among content/form/use would be missed (p. 21).

In addition to suggesting that these samples be collected in a natural setting, Bloom and Lahey provide suggestions on how to develop a model for interpretations.

Collecting Communication Samples

This section offers suggestions on how to collect a communication sample for eventual analysis and later discusses how interview probes and integrative tests can provide additional information. When collecting communication samples, the settings, interactors, and informants should be variable enough to give adequate information about the child's communicative skills. *Settings* should include home, school, and other places such as stores. The *interactors* should include peers and adults of varying status to the child. Various *informants* should be involved in data collection including language specialists, teachers, paraprofessionals, and parents.

Support for teachers using pragmatic rather than morphological/syntactic criteria for language referrals is presented by Damico and Oller (n.d.). Fifty-four regular elementary school teachers (K-5) received in-service training in identifying children with communication problems. One group was trained to use traditional surface structure criteria and the other to use pragmatic criteria. Children who were referred during the year by the two groups of teachers received an in-depth evaluation to determine whether they indeed had a communication disorder. Results indicated that the pragmatic-trained teachers not only identified more cases but were also more accurate in their judgments than were the teachers trained in looking for surface structure disorders. In a study of young children's syntax, Prutting, Gallagher, and Mulac (1975) found subjects spontaneously used some syntactic forms that were failed on a discrete point test. These findings speak well for assessing language in context *and* for using the opinions of informed classroom teachers.

There are also definite advantages to having parents involved in language sample collection for they know their child well. Although results vary in studies that compare language samples obtained in the home versus a clinical situation, Kramer, James, and Saxman (1979) found home samples yielded higher scores on two surface structure measures used with their preschool subjects. Sociolinguistic and psycholinguistic literature is replete with evidence that shows a relationship between variation in language use and listener/setting (e.g., parent/home). Furthermore, the responsibility of collecting language samples provides parents with an active role in the education of their child. If the parents are not literate, they can be supplied with a tape recorder to either record their child directly or repeat the information as a sort of "oral diary" of language samples.

Analyzing Samples

There are several existing frameworks from which to draw when developing a system for analyzing communication samples. These systems can be used for analyzing a language corpus according to form and function. Prutting (1979) provides an extensive outline for evaluating pragmatic as well as other language development areas. Walters (Chapter 11, this volume) reviews the research on situational variables in language learning and presents a methodology for assessment that uses puppets and a script to elicit communication samples of bilingual children. He also suggests that this technique can be used to probe several language functions that may not be easily observed. Omark (Chapter 12, this volume) provides sample observational techniques based on ethological theory. In general, analysis of a child's communication samples according to speech acts can be based on models derived from 1) philosophical orientations, or 2) theoretical frameworks that are sociologically oriented.

In an attempt to provide a system for recording/categorizing children's speech acts, Cole et al. (1978, p. 73) suggest that neither a philosophical nor a sociological model ". . . in isolation, is useful for describing the function of each utterance as a linguistic act or for describing how specific kinds of social 'episodes' are created by speakers through their choice of utterance forms." The authors thus developed a coding system "to describe the influence of social settings, educational and interactional tasks on children's speech performance." The coding system allows one to evaluate conversational acts, which the authors term C-acts, according to organization devices (i.e., those that regulate conversational interaction), responses, requests, acknowledgments, descriptions, statements, performatives, and miscellaneous codes. Extensive explanations and subcategorizations are provided in their model, which evolved from analysis of preschoolers' conversational interactions in various settings.

The application to the educational setting is apparent, and this type of framework is usable for analyzing information obtained from observing bilingual bicultural children.

A less complicated analysis of communication interactions that may be more readily used by parents or professionals who have a limited background in linguistics is presented in the appendix to this chapter. The form has been piloted with parents of monolingual and bilingual clients of the University of Illinois Speech and Hearing Clinic. This suggested guideline for organizing data from ongoing communication samples can be used for collecting data on both the native language and target language.

Ideally, parents, teachers, and language specialists would record communication samples. In this way the multisourced data bank would more appropriately reflect the communicative ability of a child. Any recording source/informant who uses the form should be encouraged to report a broad spectrum of communication samples. In the author's experience, even when the data from a "nonlinguist" provided an inaccurate example of a particular speech act, the information still shed light on other areas of the child's linguistic performance. The focus of this observational guide is on 1) the function of the utterance, and 2) the conversational styles a child is capable of using. The expressive language sample obtained can then also be analyzed for its relevant syntactic support and other aspects of the child's linguistic facility.

ASSESSING LANGUAGE FORM

This section discusses various readily available and easily executed approaches to surface structure analysis of English, as well as similar measures in Spanish. Considerations for assessing children who speak other non-English languages are also presented.

Counting the length of utterances along with the various parts of speech has long been used as a method of assessing English language development. Since the early 1900s the average number of words in children's utterances was viewed as an appropriate unit to measure (for historical reviews see Linares-Orama, 1975, and Shriner, 1969). Various normative data on the mean length of response (MLR) indicated that as children grew older, their responses (as measured by word count) grew longer. The MLR was also shown to be one of the best predictors of a preschool child's language level amidst a cadre of discrete point measures of surface structures available in the 1960s (Shriner, 1967). Further research on the language acquisition of young children brought another approach that examined a child's mean length of utterance (MLU) and longest utterance or upper bound level (Brown, 1973). As part of the psycholinguistic research being conducted on child first language acquisition, a scoring system based on counting the number of morphemes in each utterance was developed for analyzing language samples. Brown provides various guidelines for crediting full versus partial utterances, diminutives, and auxiliaries. Support for this scoring system is indicated with:

> When I say the indices have served us well I mean simply that two children marked for MLU are much more likely to have speech that is, on internal grounds, at the same level of constructional complexity than are two children of the same chronological age (p. 55).

Thus, at least for young children acquiring English as their first language, MLU became a way of viewing the language level of a child. It was described as "an excellent simple index of grammatical development because almost every new kind of knowledge increases length" (p. 53).

Using the principle of measuring utterance length according to morpheme count (Brown, 1973), Linares-Orama (1975) developed a system for scoring Spanish (Puerto Rican) utterances. His system for scoring an expressive language sample according to MLU in Spanish is presented in Appendix B of this volume. Although norms are not provided, one can use the information for plotting the progress of a child or as part of a criterion-referenced educational approach.

The same approach may or may not be appropriate for use with other languages in that utterance length may reflect other aspects of communication used by a child. In addition, this system is not apt to be an effective indicator with older children (Cazden, 1972a; Shriner, 1967) or in poorly conducted cultural interactions (Labov, 1972). However, if L_2 acquisition is characterized by a developmental process similar to that of L_1, MLU could suggest a child's language progress/ability in English. Scoring systems, therefore, must appropriately reflect the nature of the language, the age of the child, and the communicative interaction.

Recognizing the limitations of a measure of length only, Templin (1957) suggested the use of weighted scores for crediting the structural complexity (e.g., simple, compound, complex sentences) of a child's utterances. Later, other investigators (Shriner and Sherman, 1967; Miner, 1969) combined the notion of utterance length with measures of a speaker's syntactic sophistication. Thus emerged the scoring approach entitled the Length-Complexity Index (LCI) for analyzing surface structures. Tyack and Gottsleben (1974) also proposed a system for analyzing expressive language samples of English. Their scoring system considered surface structures used, obligatory forms omitted, and word-morpheme counts.

Another system for analyzing the English surface structures used by children was developed by Lee (1974). Her method of scoring early utterances (Developmental Sentence Types) as well as sentence usage (Developmental Sentence Scoring) provided language specialists with another tool for evaluating young children's verbal output. In an approach similar to Lee, Toronto (1976) developed a method for scoring the sentence usage of Spanish-speaking children ages 3 years, 0 months to 6 years, 11 months. Weighted scores are given in the following syntactic categories: indefinite pronouns, noun modifiers, personal pronouns, primary verb, secondary verbs, conjunctions, and interrogative words. Other surface structure scoring systems that are outgrowths of specific research questions are also available (Cazden, 1972a, 1972b).

Recently developed tests such as the Bilingual Index of Natural Language (Herbert, 1977), the Bilingual Syntax Measure (Burt, Dulay, and Hernandez, 1975), and Oral Language Evaluation (Sivarolli and Maynes, 1975) similarly use elicitation of language samples that are then scored according to various syntactic categories. These tests are an effort to develop specific scoring systems within a "natural language" framework, in spite of the fact that they do not allow for interpreting the richness and versatility of a child's language use. In-depth discussions on this point are provided by Sridhar, Chapter 10, and by McCollum and Day, Chapter 8, this volume.

SUMMARY AND CONCLUSIONS

A communication assessment model that includes an analysis of function along with supportive information on form can satisfy the evaluation criteria of reflecting contemporary theories as well as the nature of the communicative process. Whether communication samples are obtained in a natural setting or through interview probes, they can be analyzed within a contemporary theoretical framework. This evaluation should relate to the bilingual education model of the community and be an ongoing process rather than only a pre- and posttest approach.

Information from the assessment has direct pedagogical application. If used in a positive manner, it will stress what a child can do. In other words, one can recognize what forms or functions a child is using rather than *not* using. For example, the cumulative data would mean a teacher could say, "Kristin has shown the abilility to request information, label objects, and give directions" rather than "Kristin doesn't make plurals right" or "Kristin doesn't know her colors." Furthermore, language assessment in a natural environment that focuses on language function will encourage professionals to use the same approach to language teaching/development.

The proposed communication assessment model has the further advantage of providing developmental information on an individual child and the potential for local norms that take into account dialect differences. This approach also allows for criterion- rather than norm-referenced testing, a more appropriate approach for minority children.

The question one may now ask is, "Who is qualified to do this type of assessment?" There are two components to the approach: the collection and recording of the data, and the analysis of the data. It would be ideal to have a bilingual data collector who could also score communication samples from all informants. This communication diagnostician would have the responsibility of coordinating the multi-informational assessment of a reasonable case load of bilingual bicultural, LES, and NES children. Data collection and analysis along with consultation regarding the communication status, progress and program planning of the target children would be his or her major responsibility. Collecting information on a child in both languages would allow the communication diagnostician to differentiate among children who are handicapped in their native language and need special education or speech-language therapy from those who are developing satisfactorily. In addition, he or she can make meaningful recommendations for bilingual classroom placements of children and, if necessary, indicate points at which transitional placements may be made.

Recognizing that the professional category of communication diagnostician may not be a viable option, other possibilities are proposed. Depending on pre-service or in-service training which would qualify various individuals, the data collectors could be different personnel from the data analyzers. Indeed, if the native language of the child is used by a limited number of cohorts, then parents, older siblings, and/or adult volunteers from that ethnic/linguistic community will be the primary resources. These cohorts, it is hoped, would be readily available since the school system had included them all along in an advisory capacity for developing their bilingual bicultural program. The professionals charged with the responsibility of data analysis would have the option of using various levels of sophistication when undertaking the communication analysis within the multi-informational approach.

In sum, the assessment of the communicative ability of the bilingual bicultural child is provocative and challenging. It is an issue that cannot be separated from the issues of pluralism and assimilation in American society. Therefore, communication must be looked at in a broad perspective. As Kjolseth (1972) points out, language is not school and school is not the only dimension in the life space of an individual. Professionals must keep this in mind when planning and conducting a relevant, ongoing, culturally and linguistically meaningful approach to assessing the communcative ability of bilingual bicultural, LES, and NES children.

REFERENCES

Afendras, E. A., and Pianarosa, A. 1975. Child Bilingualism and Second Language Learning: A Descriptive Bibliography. Les Presses de l'Université Laval, Quebec.
Anastasi, A. 1976. Psychological Testing. 4th Ed. Macmillan Publishing Co., New York.
Austin, J. L. 1962. How to Do Things with Words. Oxford University Press, Oxford.
Bates, E. 1976. Language and Context: The Acquisition of Pragmatics. Academic Press, New York.
Bloom, L. 1970. Language Development: Form and Function in Emerging Grammars. MIT Press, Cambridge, Mass.
Bloom, L. and Lahey, M. 1978. Language Development and Language Disorders. John Wiley & Sons, New York.
Briere, E. 1972. Are we really measuring proficiency with our foreign language tests? In: B. Spolsky (ed.), The Language Education of Minority Children: Selected Readings. Newbury House Publishers, Rowley, Mass.
Brown, R. 1973. A First Language: The Early Stages. Harvard University Press, Cambridge, Mass.
Burt, M. K., and Dulay, H. C. (eds.), 1975. New Directions in Second Language Learning, Teaching, and Bilingual Education. TESOL, Washington, D.C.
Burt, M., Dulay, H., and Hernandez, E. 1975. Bilingual Syntax Measure. Harcourt Brace Jovanovich, New York.
Carrow, E. 1973. Test for Auditory Comprehension of Language. Learning Concepts, Austin, Tex.
Cazden, C. 1970. The situation: A neglected source of social class differences in language use. J. Soc. Iss. 26:35-60.
Cazden, C. B. 1972. Child Language and Education. Holt, Rinehart & Winston, New York.
Cazden, C. B. 1972b. Language in Early Childhood Education. National Association for the Education of Young Children, Washington, D.C.
Chomsky, N. 1957. Syntactic Structures. Mouton Publishers, The Hague.
Chomsky, N. 1965. Aspects of the Theory of Syntax. The MIT Press, Cambridge, Mass.

Clark, E. V. 1973. What's in a word? On the child's acquisition of semantics in his first language. In: T. E. Moore (ed.), Cognitive Developments and the Acquisition of Language. pp. 65–110. Academic Press, New York.

Clark, H. H., and Clark, E. V. 1977. Psychology and Language: An Introduction to Psycholinguistics. Harcourt Brace Jovanovich, New York.

Clark, J. L. D. 1978. Psychometric considerations in language testing. In: B. Spolsky (ed.), Advances in Language Testing, Series 2. Center for Applied Linguistics, Arlington, Va.

Cole, M., Dore, J., Hall, W. S., and Dowley, G. 1978. Situational variability in the speech of preschool children. In: M. Ebinara and R. Gianutsos (eds.), Papers in Anthropoly and Linguistics, Ann. N.Y. Acad. Sci. 318:65–105.

Damico, J., and Oller, J. W., Jr. n.d. Pragmatic versus morphological/syntactic criteria for language referrals. Unpublished manuscript.

Dulay, H. C., and Burt, M. K. 1972. Goofing: An indicator of children's second language learning strategies. Lang. Learn. 2:235–252.

Dulay, H. C., and Burt, M. K. 1974. A new perspective on the creative construction process in child second language acquisition. Lang. Learn. 24:253–278.

Dunn, L. M. 1965. Peabody Picture Vocabulary Test. American Guidance Service, Inc., Circle Pines, Minn.

Ervin-Tripp, S. 1974. Is second language learning like the first? TESOL Q. 8:111–127.

Ervin-Tripp, S., and Mitchell-Kernan, C. (eds.), 1976. Child Discourse. Academic Press, New York.

Ferguson, C. A., and Slobin, D. I. 1973. Studies of Child Language Development. Holt, Rinehart & Winston, New York.

Fishman, J. A. 1972. Language in Sociocultural Change. Stanford University Press, Stanford, Cal.

Fishman, J. A., and Cooper, R. L. 1978. The sociolinguistic foundations of language testing. In: B. Spolsky (ed.), Advances in Language Testing, Series 2. Center for Applied Linguistics, Arlington, Va.

Grice, H. P. 1967. William James Lectures. Harvard Univerity, Cambridge, Mass. Published in part in: P. Cole and J. L. Morgan (eds.), 1975. Syntax and Semantics, Vol. 3: Speech Acts. Seminar Press, New York.

Halliday, M. A. K. 1973. Explorations in the Functions of Language. Edward Arnold, London.

Hatch, E. M. (ed.). 1978. Second Language Acquisition. Newbury House Publishers, Rowley, Mass.

Herbert, C. H. 1977. Basic Inventory of Natural Language, Checpoint Systems, San Bernardino, Calif.

Jakobovits, L. A. 1970. Foreign Language Learning. Newbury House Publishers, Rowley, Mass.

James, P. 1975. James Language Dominance Test, Second Edition. Learning Concepts, Austin, Tex.

Katz, J. J. 1972. Semantic Theory. Harper & Row, New York.

Kjolseth, R. 1972. Bilingual education programs in the United States: For assimilation or pluralism. In: B. Spolsky (ed.), The Language Education of Minority Children: Selected Readings. Newbury House Publishers, Rowley, Mass.

Kramer, C. A., James, S. L., and Saxman, J. H. 1979. A comparison of language samples elicited at home and in the clinic. J. Speech Hear. Disord. 44:321–329.
Labov, W. 1972. Language in the Inner City. University of Pennsylvania Press, Philadelphia.
Lee, L. 1969. Northwestern Syntax Screening Test. Northwestern University Press, Evanston, Ill.
Lee, L. 1974. Developmental Sentence Analysis. Northwestern University Press, Evanston, Ill.
Lerea, L. 1958. Assessing language development. J. Speech Hear. Res. 1:75–85.
Linares-Orama, N. 1975. The language evaluation of preschool Spanish-speaking Puerto Rican children. Unpublished doctoral dissertation, University of Illinois, Urbana, Ill.
McLaughlin, B. 1978. Second Language Acquisition in Childhood. Lawrence Erlbaum Associates, Hillsdale, N.J.
McNeil, D. 1970. The Acquisition of Language: The Study of Developmental Psycholinguistics. Harper & Row, New York.
Miner, L. 1969. Scoring procedures for the length-complexity-index: A preliminary report. J. Commun. Disord. 2:224–240.
Nelson-Burgess, S. A., and Meyerson, M. 1975. MIRA: A concept in receptive language assessment of bilingual children. Lang. Speech, Hear. Serv. Schools 6:24–28.
Oller, J. W. 1973. Discrete point tests versus tests of integrative skills. In: J. W. Oller and J. C. Richards (eds.), Focus on the Learner: Pragmatic Perspectives for the Language Teacher. pp. 184–199. Newbury House Publishers, Rowley, Mass.
Oller, J. W. 1978. Pragmatics and language testing. In: B. Spolsky (ed.), Advances in Language Testing, Series 2. Center for Applied Linguistics, Arlington, Va.
Prutting, C. A., Gallagher, T. M., and Mulac, A. 1975. The expressive portion of the NSST compared to a spontaneous language sample. J. Speech Hear. Disord. 40:40–48.
Prutting, C. A. 1979. Process prä|,ses\n: The action of moving forward progressively from one point to another on the way to completion. J. Speech Hear. Disord. 44:3–30.
Quigley, S., Steinkamp, M., Power, D., and Jones, B. 1978. Test of Syntactic Abilities. Dormac, Inc. Beaverton, Ore.
Richards, J. C. 1975. The context for error analysis. In: M. K. Burt and H. C. Dulay (eds.), New Directions in Second Language Learning, Teaching and Bilingual Education. pp. 70–79. TESOL, Washington, D.C.
Ritchie, W. C. 1978. Second Language Acquisition Research: Issues and Implications. Academic Press, New York.
Searle, J. R. 1969. Speech Acts. Cambridge University Press, Cambridge, Mass.
Shriner, T. 1967. A comparison of selected measures with psychological scale values of language development. J. Speech Hear. Res. 10:828–835.
Shriner, T. 1969. A review of mean length of response as a measure of expressive language development in children. J. Speech Hear. Disord. 34:57–68.
Shriner, T., and Sherman, D. 1967. An equation for assessing language development. J. Speech Hear. Res. 10:41–48.

Sivarolli, N. J., and Maynes, J. O., Jr. 1975. Oral Language Evaluation. D. A. Lewis, Associates, Clinton, Md.

Slobin, D. I. 1971. Psycholinguistics. Scott, Foresman & Co., Glenview, Ill.

Spolsky, B. 1973. What does it mean to know a language, or how do you get someone to perform his competence? In: J. W. Oller and J. Richards (eds.), Focus on the Learner: Pragmatic Perspectives for the Language Teacher. pp. 164–176. Newbury House Publishers, Rowley, Mass.

Templin, M. 1957. Certain Language Skills in Children: Their Development and Interrelationships. University of Minnesota Press, Minneapolis.

Toronto, A. S. 1976. Developmental assessment of Spanish grammar. J. Speech Hear. Disord. 41:150–169.

Toronto, A. S., Leverman, D., Hanna, C., Rosenweig, P., and Maldonado, A. 1975. Del Rio Language Screening Test (English/Spanish). National Educational Laboratories Publishers, Austin, Tex.

Tyack, D., and Gottsleben, R. 1974. Language Sampling, Analysis and Training: A Handbook for Teachers and Clinicians. Consulting Psychological Press, Palo Alto, Calif.

Upshur, J. A. 1973. Context for language testing. In: J. W. Oller and J. C. Richards (eds.), Focus on the Learner: Pragmatic Perspectives for the Language Teacher. pp. 200–213. Newbury House Publishers, Rowley, Mass.

APPENDIX

Parent/Teacher Observation of Functional Language Ability

Name_____ Language_____ Observer_____ Observation Period_____

Please record the child's utterances and the other information that will help the language specialist understand the child's communication ability. Try to record what the child says as accurately as possible. It is often easier to keep samples in a convenient place and transfer them to this form later. If you are not sure where to place an example on the form, put it in the category called "other." The information needed concerns the child's ability to 1) carry on a conversation and 2) express a variety of reasons behind what is being said.

Conversational Styles

Communication ability	Language samples	Interactors, situation, and comments
Started a conversation		
Showed listening behavior		
Took turns back and forth in a conversation		
Interrupted or changed topics within a conversation		
Appropriately ended a conversation		
Stayed on topic for at least three utterances		
Made inappropriate responses or irrelevant comments		
Other		

Communication Functions

Include examples of utterances in which a child says something directly as in "I want that cookie" and indirectly as in "That cookie looks good," which in context is a request.

Reason for making the statement	Language sample	Interactors, setting, and comments
Labeled things when requested to do so		
Labeled things spontaneously		
Described things or actions upon request		
Described things or actions spontaneously		
Gave information upon request		
Gave information spontaneously		
Asked for things		
Asked for action		
Asked for information		
Asked for permission		
Promised		
Agreed		
Threatened		
Apologized		
Warned		
Protested/argued		
Tried to convince the listener		
Showed humor or teased		
Other		

Observer Impressions

1. List the things that seem to help the child get his or her point across to a listener in this language. ─────────────
   ─────────────────────────────────

2. List the things that seem to interfere with the child getting his or her point across to a listener in this language. ─────────────
   ─────────────────────────────────

3. What communication situations/topics do you think the child does best in?
   ─────────────────────────────────

4. What communication situations/topics do you think the child does poorest in? ─────────────────
   ─────────────────────────────────

5. With whom does the child seem to communicate most effectively?
   ─────────────────────────────────

6. With whom does the child seem to communicate least effectively?
   ─────────────────────────────────

chapter two

Concepts in Bilingualism and Their Relationship to Language Assessment
Pamela A. McCollum

The literature on bilingualism is extensive and has come from many disciplines. For this reason, it is difficult for one who wishes to study bilingualism to find a single source that presents definitions and explanations of the basic concepts related to bilingualism. The purpose of the first part of this chapter is to consolidate the major theories describing bilingualism, while the second part of the chapter provides background that will help the reader approach the assessment of bilingualism and serves as an introduction to subsequent chapters in this volume.

As a consequence of the Saussurian dichotomy of *la langue* and *la parole*, the importance of language use (la parole) in relation to the structure of language (la langue) was traditionally ignored until recently in the field of American linguistics. One exception to this generalization is the study of bilingualism. Early works, such as *Languages in Contact* by Weinreich (1953) and *The Norwegian Language in America* by Haugen (1969), studied bilingualism in linguistic and sociological terms. For the most part, these are descriptive studies of linguistic change resulting from languages in contact. While they are extremely thorough in describing the results of languages in contact, they do not offer much analysis of the linguistic parameters of bilingualism, nor do they discuss how these parameters might be assessed.

Other early works on bilingualism (Arsenian, 1937; Leopold, 1939–49; Darcy, 1953; Osgood and Sebeok, 1954; Kolers, 1968) dealt with the relationship of bilingualism to intelligence, the psychological factors that were involved in language processing, and the interference of the first language (L_1) upon the second language (L_2). This research, which formed the groundwork for the study of bilingualism, ignored the bilingual's use of language within the speech community, the sociological factors that determine usage, and the speaker's motivation for using one language over another in a particular social situation. All of these considerations have implications in defining bilingualism, in identifying what characteristics are typical of a bilingual individual within a particular speech community, and in determining how bilingual proficiency is to be assessed.

Before reviewing various linguistic theories regarding the nature of bilingualism, Mackey's definition of biligualism should be noted: "Bilingualism is not a phenomenon of language but of the message. It does not belong to the domain of 'langue' but to the domain of 'parole'" (Mackey, 1962, p. 51). This view opens the door to the consideration of bilingualism as not just a purely linguistic phenomenon but rather as one that has sociological, political, and psychological ramifications as well.

DESCRIPTIONS OF BILINGUALISM

Theories that describe the bilingual individual may be placed on a continuum between what linguists consider strong and weak interpretations of bilingualism. The use of the terms *strong* and *weak* does not imply the relative superiority or inferiority of one version over another. Instead, they refer to the strictness of interpretation of a particular theory.

The strong version of bilingualism has been advanced by Bloomfield (1933), who considers a bilingual to be one who has native-like control of two languages. The weak version may be ascribed to Halliday and Strevens (1964), who extend bilingualism to persons who speak only one language but who switch registers, styles, and functionally differentiated language varieties to coincide with place, topic, interlocutor, and appropriate situational contexts of language.

Between the strong and weak theories of bilingualism lie other descriptions of the bilingual individual. In this chapter, these descriptions are presented in an order that reflects a movement away from the strong Bloomfieldian theory of bilingualism. This movement is characterized by an increasing number of sociological considerations which are seen as necessary to describe bilingualism adequately.

Weinreich (1953) defines a bilingual as one who is able to use two languages alternately. While Weinreich describes some bilingual speakers who are more proficient in one area of language than another, the difficulty is viewed in terms of interference between the first language (L_1) and the second language (L_2). Weinreich does not explain if alternate use of two languages includes receptive or productive language skills or both. He also does not specify whether alternate use of single words in an L_2 qualifies one as a bilingual. One is left wondering what the minimum qualifications are for classification as a bilingual.

The definition of bilingualism given by Haugen (1969) is a bit more specific. According to Haugen, a bilingual is one who can produce meaningful sentences in an L_2. This version implies that a speaker who has control of the syntax of an L_2 is bilingual, but it does not address the issue of the state of the speaker's use of L_2 phonology. While it would be an extreme case, a speaker of an L_2 could conceivably control the syntax of a language but still be unintelligible to a native speaker of that language because of extreme distortion of the phonological system.

The possession of at least one of the language skills—listening, speaking, reading, or writing—in a second language even to a minimal degree, is Macnamara's (1967) definition of bilingualism. He urges that bilingualism must be viewed as existing on a continuum or a series of continua which vary amongst individuals along a varitey of dimensions. Again, there would appear to be no minimal point at which one becomes bilingual.

The term *incipient bilingualism* was introduced to help clarify the problem of differentiating these minimal aspects of language use. *Incipient bilingualism* refers to the initial learning stages of an L_2 (Diebold, 1961). The speaker in this state is not yet able to make complete meaningful utterances in a second language. Competency may be limited only to passive knowledge of an L_2 or include varying degrees of lexical competence. Diebold developed the term after working with Mexican Indians who were excluded from census data as bilinguals because of their inability to make complete meaningful utterances in Spanish. Such a limited definition of bilingualism served to produce data that did not reflect the actual linguistic or social situation. He suggested that minimum bilingual skill be defined as "contact with possible models in a second language and the ability to use these in the environment of the native language" (p. 111).

Bilingualism is defined by Mackey (1962) as the alternate use of two or more languages by the same individual. "It is a behavioral pattern of mutually modifying linguistic practices varying in degree, function, alternation, and interference" (p. 53). Mackey's view of bilingualism is considerably broader than those previously presented:

> The point at which a speaker of a second language becomes bilingual is either arbitrary or impossible to determine. Secondly, not all native speakers are equally perceptive and not all have the same richness of vocabulary or versatility of structure. Thirdly, absolute mastery of two languages is very rare (1956, p. 4).

Furthermore, Mackey feels that bilingual language use must first be studied in an attempt to stabilize the theoretical basis defining bilingualism. From these studies, perhaps the problem of assessment of degree of bilingual proficiency may be approached more realistically and with greater accuracy.

The bilingual classification system that Mackey (1956) favors includes the following divisions:

1. *Number of languages involved:* In specifying the number of languages used, Mackey further extends the study of bilingualism to encompass multilingualism or pluralingualism.
2. *Type of languages used:* This division includes languages used and what the relationship is between them. These may be dialects of the same language, languages of the same family, or generically unrelated languages.
3. *Influence of one language upon another:* This includes phonetic and phonemic influences, lexical influences, and structural influences determined with regard to compatibility, structural function, class size, and frequency.
4. *Vacillation:* Bilingual proficiency is not static and a speaker may change in the proficiency of either language. Speakers sometimes prefer to speak one language rather than the other at certain times in their lives.
5. *Degree of proficiency:* Proficiency may fall anywhere on a continuum from native-like mastery of two languages to incomplete mastery of two languages. Present scales only measure certain types of linguistic skills in specific areas of language. At present, none is complete.

Kachru (1965) conceptualizes bilingualism as existing on a cline, or continuum, with a zero point at one end of the cline representing competence in one language, or monolingualism, and the other extreme representing ambilingualism or native-like control of two languages. The bilingual individual is not seen as occupying a discrete point on the cline but rather as being able to occupy any one of a number of loci depending on his or her skill in handling two languages. It should be noted that while ambilingualism does exist, ambilingual competence usually exists in only one style or register of language due to the allocation of specific styles, domains, and varieties of language to fit contextual situations in each of the bilingual's languages.

The description of bilingualism proposed by Kachru does not attempt to identify the bilingual individual but is better viewed as a schema for future research in the field. Like Mackey, Kachru feels that the theoretical basis of bilingualism needs to be stabilized. Before bilingual proficiency can be assessed, the linguistic exponents that correspond to different areas of the cline must first be determined and analyzed with reference to syntax, lexicon, and phonology. Only after this type of analysis is carried out can the matter of measuring bilingual proficiency be approached realistically.

Bilingualism is defined by Fishman (1966) as "demonstrated ability to engage in communication via more than one language" (p. 122). The definition of bilingualism as the ideal mastery of two languages is regarded by Fishman as unrealistic. He states, "to require that bilingualism be defined in terms of equal and advanced mastery is no more justifiable than to require that intelligence be defined as equivalent to genius or that health be defined as equivalent to the complete absence of any dysfunction" (p. 122). He also adds that such classification would exclude most of the natural bilingual populations of the world, leaving only a few translators and teachers to qualify as bilinguals.

Instead of using the ideal mastery criterion, Fishman (1967) urges that bilingualism be examined in terms of dominance configurations which are derived from the measurement of bilingual performance in terms of the simultaneous interaction of: 1) media—speaking, reading, and writing; 2) role—comprehension, production, and inner speech; 3) formality levels—intimate, casual, and formal levels; and 4) the domains of bilingual interaction—work, home, school, church, government, and other settings. It should be noted that bilingual performance in the aforementioned areas is rarely, if ever, equal, due to a person's personal history and place within the social hierarchy. Dominance configurations do not measure bilingual performance but serve as a schema for the analysis of bilingual language usage.

Halliday's (Halliday and Strevens, 1964) rationale for including monolingual speakers as bilinguals is that their behaviors are very similar. Monolingual speakers use different linguistic varieties of the same language in different situations and for different purposes. An individual varies speech patterns from colloquial to formal speech according to situational context, topic, and listener. Specialized varieties of language that are used in specific social situations are referred to as styles. Stylistic changes not only occur lexically but are also reflected in pronunciation and syntax. The number of varieties that comprise a speaker's verbal repertoire varies with his or her position in the social hierarchy. A person who lives in a homogeneous social environment and has restricted levels of social interaction has little need for a wide range of styles. Typically, laborers, farmers, and housewives fit into a restricted code category while persons in business, politics, and acting have access to wider or more elaborated codes of language.

Studies (Rubin, 1962; Fishman, 1965) have shown that bilinguals alternate between languages for much the same reasons that monolinguals alternate among styles of a single language. The use of one language over another is dependent on topic, listener, and context of situation and serves to mark the speaker in terms of his or her values, attitudes, and position within the social hierarchy (see Walters, Chapter 11, this volume).

In summary, descriptions of bilingualism are varied and extend along a continuum from the strong Bloomfieldian version of ideal mastery of two languages to that of Halliday, who considers monolinguals who use differentiated language varieties of the same language to be bilingual. In between, there are many proposed variations. As one proceeds from the strong to the weak version of a description of bilingualism, there is an ever widening scope of sociolinguistic factors that are seen as crucial to the evolution of an adequate description of bilingualism. Current sociolinguistic thinking is that an adequate description of bilingualism must take into account the sociological context in which bilingualism exists and the speech community's norms for language use in various domains. If such considerations are ignored, attempts at assessing bilingual proficiency must be questioned in terms of their meaning and applicability.

COMPOUND VERSUS COORDINATE VERSUS SUBORDINATE BILINGUALS

Distinctions that are central to the topic of the assessment of bilingualism are the compound/coordinate/subordinate bilingual classifications. While these terms have fallen into disuse in linguistics in recent years, they have been revived in the field of bilingual education in relation to language assessment. For that reason, a brief description of the concepts is presented here, citing the major studies that strived to establish the psychological reality of these concepts.

The abovementioned classifications are used to distinguish among three types of bilingualism that may result from different language-learning contexts (Weinreich, 1953). A *compound* bilingual is thought to have one merged meaning system; there is one meaning and two lexical representations, one for each language. For example, for a compound bilingual in English and Spanish the lexical representations *book* and *libro* would both have the same semantic meaning. This type of bilingualism is thought to be the result of learning two languages simultaneously in the same context.

The *coordinate* bilingual, on the other hand, has two separate semantic meaning systems for representation and meaning in each language. In the case of the bilingual English/Spanish speaker, there are two meanings and two representations in coexisting systems. The linguistic signs have different representations because each language was learned in a different context. For example, language A was acquired at home and language B at school.

Subordinate bilingualism is said to arise when one language is used as a vehicle to learn a second. The semantic system that results from this indirect method of language learning consists of referents of the signs in the language being learned that are not actual "entities," but "equivalent" signs of the native language. For example, the word *libro* is not the actual object, but rather the referent for the English word *book*.

Weinreich's (1953) description of the compound-coordinate bilingual was expanded by Osgood and Sebeok (1954) to distinguish psychological processing patterns in bilingual speakers and listeners. Osgood's explanation is basically the same as that of Weinreich, with the exception that Osgood sees the two concepts as having psychological reality in that they are stored differently in the speaker-listener's nervous system. The concepts are explained by Osgood in terms of sets of mediational responses in the nervous system. In the compound bilingual:

> The messages produced in the two or more languages employ differently constructed and organized units, different grammatical rules, and different and equally arbitrary lexical systems, excepting occasional cognates. To the extent that phonemic systems are different, two sets of differentiations and constancies on the decoding side and two sets of vocalic skill components on the encoding side have to be maintained. Since the entire system of transitional redundancies in two languages are different, alternative anticipational and dispositional integrations have to be established. And since the lexical aspects of messages in two languages are different, alternative sets of semantic decoding and encoding habits have to be maintained—in other words, alternative sets of associations between message events and events in the representations (1954, p. 139).

In the merged meaning system of the compound bilingual, language A and language B are associated with the same set of representational processes or meanings. This is said to be the result of learning two languages within the same context. In the coordinate bilingual, one set of linguistic signs and responses becomes associated with a set of representational processes or meanings in language A, but the set of linguistic signs and responses appropriate to language B carries a different set of meanings.

Osgood states that the coordinate bilingual is a "true" bilingual due to the existence of a fully developed and separate semantic system for each language. The similarities between the two sets of represenational processes is seen as a function of the distance between the cultures that use language A and language B. If two cultures are very similar in the situations and objects dealt with by the respective languages, the processes elicited by translation of equivalent signs in both languages will often be similar.

In decoding, a bilingual has the tendency to interpret a sign in language A as its translation equivalent in language B would be interpreted. In the process of encoding, similarity of meaning and representational processes will lead to delays and blocking of responses in language A when language B would be expected. While these responses are more characteristic of the compound bilingual, they may also appear in the coordinate bilingual speaker in the form of delays or lowered frequencies of response when compared with monolinguals.

It was theorized that Osgood's semantic differential technique would be an index that would have the ability to capture the differences in the semantic systems of bilinguals. By measuring the connotative meanings for translation equivalents, one could place the compound bilingual on a continuum where the translation equivalent signs are identical at one end and different at the other. An important point made by Osgood has been ignored in the flurry of testing that has been carried out among bilingual children. He states, "For any semantic area we would expect speakers of more than one language to distribute themselves along a continuum from a pure compound system to a pure coordinate system" (1954, p. 136).

Evidence supporting the psychological reality of the compound/coordinate classifications was supplied by a study conducted by Lambert, Havelka, and Crosby (1958). They presented empirical evidence that substantiated the theory that compound/coordinate bilinguals differ in the connotative meanings they attribute to translated equivalents in two languages. They found that French/English compound bilinguals were better able to make use of a list of translated equivalents in one language to learn a list of words in the other. The groups did not differ in their translation ability.

Many studies were conducted subsequently that measured bilinguals' speed of response on various tasks in an attempt to test the compound/coordinate distinction. It was postulated that compound bilinguals would perform tasks more quickly as a result of their merged semantic system, that language dominance would show itself in the form of automaticity of response in the stronger or dominant language, and that a balanced bilingual should exhibit equal reaction times for both languages.

Studies that used speed of response in following directions or in task completion, such as word recognition, facility in word deletion, facility in reading, verbal response set, and facility in translating, were conducted by Lambert (1955) and Lambert, Havelka, and Gardner (1959). In both studies, compound bilinguals completed tasks or reacted to directions more quickly than coordinate bilinguals. There was no correlation between subjects' reaction times on tasks and skill in speed of translation.

Another study that was seen as validating the psychological reality of the compound/coordinate distinction was on semantic satiation (Jakobovits and Lambert, 1961). Drawing from the results of a previous study (Lambert and Jacobovits, 1960), which showed that continuous repetition of a word decreases its affective meaning, it was theorized that semantic satiation would occur in both languages of a compound bilingual and would not occur in both languages of the coordinate. The results of the study supported their hypothesis. Other studies that supported the semantic satiation of bilinguals were done by MacLeod (1966) and Lambert (1967).

Subsequent studies, however, have cast shadows upon the initial acceptance of the validity of the compound/coordinate theory. In a study conducted by Olton (1960), bilinguals were given a list of words in French and English to read. Electrical shocks were given to the subjects as they read certain lexical items. Subsequently, they were given a new list of words containing translation equivalents of some of the lexical items that were accompanied by shocks in the first list. It was found that coordinate bilinguals did not differ from compound bilinguals in their responses to translation equivalents as had been expected. Kolers (1968) and Lambert and Moore (1966) conducted word association tests with bilinguals. They found there was a wider range of responses for compound bilinguals than had been expected.

What are the implications of the studies presented thus far which seem to validate the existence of the compound/coordinate distinction and the measurement of language dominance? While the classification of bilinguals as balanced, dominant, compound, and coordinate seem to explain certain behaviors of bilingual individuals, the experimental attempts to prove their existence must be questioned in terms of methodology, applicability, and usefulness outside the experimental situation.

The basic premise of all the dominance studies was that automaticity and speed of response is a function of language dominance. The validity of this assumption is questionable and could be invalidated by speakers from cultures that are not closely related to ours, where speed of response would not imply proficiency but perhaps negative traits such as lack of thought or hastiness. Second, all the dominance studies were conducted with single word stimulus cues in isolation from langage context clues. The last, and perhaps the greatest, fault with these studies is that they assumed equal performance skills in syntax and lexicon for all of their subjects and ignored the functional allocation of language into different domains in the bilingual's repertoire.

DIGLOSSIA AND ITS RELATIONSHIP TO BILINGUALISM

Fishman (1967) states that bilingualism also must be described with regard to the community where it exists. The existence or absence of diglossia will determine which type of bilingualism is present and is crucial for subsequent measurement of degree of bilingualism. The term *diglossia* was first used by Ferguson (1959) to describe

> a relative stable language situation in which, in addition to the primary dialects of the langauge (which may include a standard or regional standards), there is a very divergent, highly codified (often grammatically more complex) superimposed variety, the vehicle of a large and respected body of written literature, either of an earlier period or of another speech community, which is learned largely by formal education and is used for most written, and formal spoken purposes but is not used by any sector of the community for ordinary conversation (p. 233).

Since its introduction, the term *diglossia* has been broadened and is now applied to situations where one variety of language is used for formal purposes, such as religion, politics, and education, and another is used for personal communication in the home and in intimate contexts. The variety that is used for personal communication is standardized to varying degrees and is acquired in the home while the formalized variety is strictly standardized and is learned in school. Each variety is supported by different attitudes and values. The use of one variety over the other is determined by topic, interlocutor, and context of situation, and serves to establish the speaker's position within the social hierarchy.

According to Fishman (1967), the study of bilingualism must be approached from the viewpoint of its relationships to diglossia. Within this framework, bilingualism is defined as being a characteristic of individual linguistic behavior whereas diglossia is characteristic of linguistic behavior at the sociocultural level. The four possible contexts that arise through the interaction of bilingualism and diglossia are: bilingualism with diglossia, bilingualism without diglossia, diglossia without bilingualism, and the absence of both diglossia and bilingualism. Fishman further states that diglossia and bilingualism may be said to coexist

> whereever speech communities exist whose speakers engage in a considerable range of roles; wherever access to several roles is encouraged or facilitated by powerful social institutions and processes; and finally, wherever the roles are clearly differentiated (in terms of when, where, and with whom they are felt to be appropriate (p. 32).

As Macnamara (1967) further points out, "In such situations the vocabulary, phraseology, and literary skills in one language generally have no exact counterpart in the other" (p. 60).

In order for this type of bilingualism to establish itself, a large and complex speech community that has access to a large range of roles must exist. An example of this situation is Paraguay where almost the whole population speaks Spanish and Guarani. Guarani is used in the home and to show intimacy among group members. Spanish, on the other hand, signals distancing and seriousness and is used to communicate in the domains of education, religion, and politics. One language does not replace the other for each serves differing functions.

Bilingualism without diglossia is usually the result of immigration, rapid industrialization, and social change. Here, one social group is under the economic or political control of another. Immigrants for example, learn the dominant language in order to enter the work force. Their children attend school, learn the dominant language, and begin to use it in the home. There is no longer a clear differentiation of which language is seen as appropriate in special social situations. Since both languages are viewed as being equally appropriate and as serving the same functions, the native language is usually replaced by that of the dominant group. For that reason bilingualism in this context is usually transitional in nature (Macnamara, 1967).

In the context where diglossia exists without bilingualism, two highly divergent groups are united functionally via political, economic, or religious ties. Group membership is generally ascribed by birth and is guarded by impassable boundaries. Likewise, linguistic usage is not a matter of choice. Within each speech community, there is restricted access to a wide range of language varieties since the speaker is limited to a narrow range of possible roles. Fishman (1967) points out that "the linguistic states of Eastern Europe and India, and the language problems of Wales, Canada and Belgium stem from origins such as these" (p. 34).

A context with an absence of both diglossia and bilingualism may only be a hypothetical case today but would be characterized by a group living in virtual isolation from other speech communities. Within the group, there would be little or no role differentiation separating members into subunits. Lacking differentiated roles, all members of the speech community would use a single language variety across all social situations. Examples of such groups might be clans or tribes living in isolation from modern society and with little or no contact with other speech communities like themselves.

One of the advantages of analyzing bilingualism within this framework is that it describes bilingual behavior at the level of the individual and also at the sociocultural level. Its relevance to language assessment is that it stresses the importance of studying bilingual language usage in differing varieties and domains of language. Ignoring such usage leads to constructing tests that assess bilinguals for proficiency in varieties and domains of language that are not utilized in their speech communities. Not only do such tests lack content validity, but the results derived from them serve no pedagogical purpose.

By analyzing a speech community's pattern of language use in different varieties and domains, a more accurate description of bilingual behavior should be able to be constructed. This information will not only contribute to the construction of more equitable testing measures but will also help teachers in formulating relevant educational programs for their students.

ASSESSING THE DEGREE OF BILINGUALISM AND LANGUAGE DOMINANCE

Before dealing with the measurement of bilingualism, two preliminary dimensions of bilingualism must be considered. The first is the traditional idea of the balanced bilingual who is seen as having equal skill in all levels of language listening, speaking, reading, and writing. If the bilingual is an educated person, it is assumed that he or she is equally skilled in all these levels. Furthermore, within speaking and listening the balanced bilingual has equal control of semantics, syntax, lexicon, and phonemes; and within writing and reading he or she has equal control of semantics, syntax, lexicon, and graphemes (Macnamara, 1967).

As one can see, the concept of the balanced bilingual reflects the extreme Bloomfieldian definition of bilingualism and, for many of the same reasons, is unacceptable. In addition, the traditional conceptualization of the balanced bilingual must be adjusted for young children who do not yet know how to read or write, as well as for adults who lack literacy skills. A further problem with the traditional definition of the balanced bilingual is that it makes no judgments on the seriousness of weaknesses in one area of language over another. If the purpose of speaking is to make oneself understood, for instance, are syntactic interferences more serious than phonological ones? Conversely, how seriously does non-native-like phonology affect intelligibility, and at what point does it affect comprehension? In reality the traditional definition of the balanced bilingual is something that probably only exists as an idealized state. It is proscriptive and does not allow the inclusion of instances of actual bilingual behavior within its framework.

When a bilingual shows an imbalance and is more proficient in the phonology, syntax, or lexicon, or in reading, listening, speaking, or writing of one language, he or she is said to be dominant in that language in a particular skill, level of language, or in general performance in one of the languages. Macnamara (1967) states,

> The term dominance implies competition between two languages and therefore might be employed to describe two tendencies: (1) the tendency for one of the two languages to be used where from the point of view of both speaker and listener the two langauges are equally appropriate (2) the tendency for the phonological, syntactic, lexical or semantic systems of one language to intrude on those of the other one (p. 59).

What should be noted is that the term *dominance* does not imply proficiency as is generally assumed. Dominance results from measuring language proficiency in two languages in which the language receiving the highest score is said to be the dominant one. It might be the case that a bilingual scores higher in one language in a particular area, but if both of the scores are at the lower end of the proficiency scale the use of the term dominant could be misleading without further qualification. Furthermore, if a bilingual's scores are very close but low, the speaker might be said to be approaching balanced bilingualism, but nothing is said about proficiency in either language. Milan (1978) states that, "A parity of scores can signal either comparable linguistic competence or incompetence" (p. 38). It should be kept in mind that the terms *dominant* and *balanced bilingual* are relative and may indicate scores falling along a continuum from low to high proficiency.

According to Burt, Dulay, and Hernandez (1976), the parameters that comprise language dominance are as follows: lexicon, structural proficiency, phonological control, fluency, and communicative skills. They stress that dominance in one of the parameters does not imply dominance in the others. A bilingual child may be balanced with respect to syntactic proficiency, but dominant in the lexicon of the other language. A child might also be dominant in one aspect of the first language and be dominant in a different aspect of the second language. A complete measure of dominance, it it were possible, would take all of these factors into account, as well as determining the bilingual's use of language according to domains in each language.

Shuy (1977) points out that the Aspira Consent Decree "requires that the placement of children in educational programs using English or Spanish as the medium of instruction be determined by their ability to 'effectively' participate in instruction." Current dominance tests only address themselves to a speaker's competence in specific language areas—syntax, phonology, or lexicon—and say nothing of one's ability to communicate effectively. Furthermore, current dominance tests only attempt to measure degree of bilingualism in terms of the standard varieties of both the first and second language. In many cases, the bilingual child does not have access to either variety outside the school.

Perhaps a more realistic alternative to dominance testing in the classroom situation would be to measure functional language use.

> Functional language competence is the underlying knowledge that allows people to use their language to make utterances to others in terms of their goals. It includes a knowledge of what kinds of goals language can accomplish (the functions of language) and of what are permissible utterances to accomplish each function (language strategies) (Shuy, 1977, p. 81).

Examples of language functions would be giving an order, making promises or apologies, and so on (see Walters, Sridhar, or Omark, Chapters 11, 10, or 12, respectively, this volume). In the case of giving an order, adult speakers of English possess the knowledge that when they wish to give an order they may use one of several strategies to accomplish this goal. For example, they might use one of the following strategies and corresponding utterances.

1. Performative   *I hereby order you to buy me a newspaper.*
2. Direct imperative *Buy me a newspaper.*
3. Wh-imperative   *Won't you please buy me a newspaper?*
4. Statement   *Mary, I need a newspaper.*

An examination of the possible utterances shows that while each conveys the same information, the selection of one utterance over another would depend on the context of situation. Before choosing the utterance that is most likely to result in obtaining a newspaper, the speaker must assess his or her status relative to that of the listener's, be aware of the formality of the situational context, and select an utterance that reflects appropriateness relative to both.

Competence in functional language use, unlike grammatical and phonological competence, is not restricted to certain developmental period. Some strategies, such as attention-getting and interrupting, are learned early by children who are successful in school. Condoling, on the other hand is acquired relatively late and may never be fully mastered by some adults.

At present there are no commercial tests that measure first language functional language proficiency or bilingual functional language proficiency. "To develop the necessary assessment instruments requires an inventory of the functional language competence demanded in the educational setting at various age/grade levels" (Shuy, 1977,p. 83). Such tests are only in the developmental stage but promise to be of more value than traditional dominance tests in giving teachers an estimation of a child's language development level and how effectively the child communicates and accomplishes goals in a second language.

CONCLUSION

Before an adequate theory of bilingualism can evolve, an ever widening scope of sociological factors must be included to explain bilingual speech and languages behavior. Assessment measures that strive to determine a bilingual speaker's proficiency should also include such considerations. Early measures that focused on the initial learning context of the first and second languages and predicted dominance in terms of speed of response and interference between the L_1 and the L_2 are now questioned in terms of their initial conceptualizations, methodology, usefulness, and applicability outside the experimental situation.

The labeling of speakers as dominant, balanced, compound, and coordinate has little pedagogical value and does not help teachers to plan educational programs. A more promising approach is the study of functional language development. Such analysis is being carried out by examining language samples for categories, their occurrences within and across groups, and their generalizability to other populations.

It is hoped that functional language analysis will yield results that are based on the characteristics of actual speaker behavior and provide a more realistic basis for approaching the subject of measurement of bilingual proficiency. After the characteristics of functional language use are identified, second language teachers will have not only a diagnostic measure to describe behavior but also a tool to aid them in formulating a realistic course of study for the child.

Until such measures are developed, teachers should bear in mind the following points when using language assessment measures:

1. The concept of bilingualism as native-like control of languages is unrealistic.
2. Bilingualism must be viewed within its sociological framework.
3. Children should be tested for competence in using the shared rules of their speech community.
4. Bilingual language use must be analyzed in terms of which language varieties are used in various domains of language.
5. The term *dominance* must be qualified by indicating which area of language is being referred to: lexicon, phonology, or syntax.
6. A bilingual speaker may be dominant in a particular aspect of the first language and be dominant in a different aspect of the second language.
7. Use of the terms *balanced* and *dominant* may be misleading unless they are qualified by indicating a speaker's level of proficiency.
8. No single test should serve as the sole indicator of a child's language proficiency.
9. The results of language proficiency testing should be tempered by teachers' judgments when making decisions regarding the child's educational future.

Succeeding chapters provide specific information on a sample of available tests and assessment approaches. In-depth information on functional language and suggestions on how to assess it are also provided.

REFERENCES

Arsenian, S. 1937. Bilingualism and Mental Development: A Study of the Intelligence and the Social Background of Bilingual Children in New York City. Teachers College, Columbia University, New York.

Bloomfield, L. 1933. Language, Holt, New York.

Burt, M., Dulay, H., and Hernandez, E. 1976. Bilingual Syntax Measure Technical Booklet, Harcourt Brace Jovanovich, New York.

Darcy, N. T. A. 1953. A review of the literature on the effects of bilingualism upon the measurement of intelligence. J. Gen. Psychol. 82:21–57.

Diebold, A. R. Jr. 1961. Incipient bilingualism. Language 37:97–112.

Ferguson, C. Diglossia. 1964. In: D. Hymes (ed.), Language in Culture and Society: A Reader in Linguistics and Anthropology. Harper & Row, New York.

Fishman, J. A. 1965. Who speaks what language to whom and when? Linguistique 2:67–88.

Fishman, J. A. 1966. The implications of bilingualism for language teaching and

language learning. In: A. Valdman (ed.), Trends in Language Teaching. McGraw-Hill Book Co., New York.
Fishman, J. A. 1967. Bilingualism with and without diglossia; diglossia with and without bilingualism. In: J. Macnamara (ed.), Problems in bilingualism. Special issue of J. Soc. Iss. 23:210–225.
Halliday, M. A. K. and Strevens, P. 1964. The Linguistic Sciences and Language Teaching. Longmans, London.
Haugen, E. 1969. The Norwegian Language in America: A Study in Bilingual Behavior. 2nd ed. Indiana University Press, Bloomington.
Jakobovits, L. A., and Lambert, W. E. 1961. Semantic satiation among bilinguals. J. Exp. Psychol. 62:576–582.
Kachru, B. B. 1965. The Indianness of Indian English. Word 21:391–410.
Kolers, P. A. 1968. Bilingualism and information processing. Sci. Am. 218:78–86.
Lambert, W. E. 1955. Measurement of the linguistic dominance in bilinguals. J. Abnormal Soc. Psychol. 50:197–200.
Lambert, W. E. 1967. Psychological studies of the interdependencies of the bilingual's two languages. Mimeo.
Lambert, W. E., Havelka, J., and Crosby, C. 1958. The influence of language acquisition contexts on bilingualism. J. Abnorm. Soc. Psychol. 56:239–244.
Lambert, W., Havelka, J., and Gardner, R. C. 1957. Linguistic manifestations of bilingualism. Am. J. Psychol. 72:77–82.
Lambert, W. E., and Jakobovits, L. A. 1960. Verbal satiation and changes in the intensity of meaning. J. Exp. Psychol. 60:376–383.
Lambert, W. E., and Moore, N. 1966. Word association responses: Comparisons of American and French monolinguals with Canadian monolinguals and bilinguals. J. Personal. Soc. Psychol. 3:313–320.
Leopold, W. F. 1939–1949. Speech development of a bilingual child; a linguist's record. Northwestern University Press, Evanston, Ill.
Mackey, W. F. 1956. Towards a redefinition of bilingualism. J. Can. Linguist. Assoc. 3:2–11.
MacKey, W. F. 1962. The description of bilingualism. Can. J. Linguist. 7:51–85.
MacLeod, F. 1966. A study of Gaelic-English bilingualism: The effects of semantic satiation. Unpublished thesis, Aberdeen University.
Macnamara, J. 1967. The bilingual's performance: A psychological overview. J. Soc. Iss. 23:58–77.
Milan, W. G. 1978. End of the "first decade" a time for reflection. NABE, 2:33–41.
Olton, R. M. 1960. Semantic generalization between languages. Unpublished masters thesis, McGill University, Montreal.
Osgood, C. E., and Sebeok, T. (eds.). 1954. Psycholinguistics: A survey of theory and research problems. J. Abnorm. Soc. Psychol. 49:139–146(suppl.).
Rubin, J. 1962. Bilingualism in Paraguay. Anthropolog. Linguist. 4:52–58.
Shuy, R. W. 1977. Quantitative language data: A case for and some warnings against. Anthropol. Educ. Q. 7:73–82.
Weinreich, U. 1953. Languages in Contact: Findings and Problems. Linguistic Circle of New York, New York.

chapter three
Issuses and Procedures in the Analysis of Syntax and Semantics
Linda Locke

In the last decade or two, a great interest in second language research and theory has developed. As is the case in any young field, there is disagreement among investigators and teachers over the conclusions drawn from this research. There has been a controversy between the proponents of contrastive analysis (CA) and the advocates of error analysis (EA) over issues involving the analysis, prediction, and explanation of errors in second language acquisition. Many researchers have taken sides in the debate and endorse either CA or EA as the better method for assessment of syntax and semantics. In this chapter, the methodology, claims, and supporting evidence pertaining to CA and EA are examined first. Next, various combinations of and new additions to CA and EA methods are described. Another section of the chapter discusses conclusions and theories pertaining to L_2 acquisition which were derived from error analysis-acquisition studies. Finally, learners' strategies are examined in an attempt to determine the role they play in L_2 acquisition and in the analysis of syntax and semantics. Throughout these discussions, the reader must bear in mind that CA and EA are not tests, but rather methods or frameworks for language analysis.

CONTRASTIVE ANALYSIS

Strong and Weak Versions of CA

The traditional strong view of the CA hypothesis has as its foundation the belief of Fries (1945) that the best teaching materials should be based on a description of the target language compared with a description of the learner's native language. Lado (1957), an influential writer in the field, held that the differences between the first language L_1 and the second language L_2, which can be ascertained through CA, are the chief sources of difficulty in learning a second language. According to CA logic, one can expect the greatest interference from L_1 in those areas of L_2 that are most different from L_1. Carroll (1968) maintains that learning can be facilitated where there are similarities between languages, and learning can be interfered with or retarded where there are differences. It has been said by Banathy, Trager, and Waddle (1966) that "what the student has to learn equals the sum of the differences established by the contrastive analysis" (p. 37). The extent to which these claims are supported by evidence is examined later in this chapter.

The hierarchy of difficulty devised by Stockwell, Bowen, and Martin (1965) in their contrastive study, *The Grammatical Structures of English and Spanish*, is an example of strong version CA study. The hierarchy is based on the assumption that as the correspondences between the native language and the target language weaken, learning difficulties increase. There are five major classes of correspondence in the hierarchy. Beginning with category I as most difficult, classes I through V of correspondence are in order of decreasing magnitude of difficulty. Some selected examples pertaining to Stockwell, Bowen, and Martin's (1965) 14 sublevels from the five major classes (I through V) of correspondence are:

I. Negative Correspondence in Native Language (Sublevel 1)   Spanish: *Teresa visita a los señores Navarro*. English: *Teresa is visiting Mr. and Mrs. Navarro*. In Spanish a personal *a* obligatorily precedes a direct object that refers to a person or persons, whereas in English there is a no corresponding category. There is a negative structural correspondence because the same structural categories are not represented in both languages.

II. Functonal/Semantic Correspondence (Sublevel 4)   English nominalizations of indefinites: *a young girl*. In Spanish an adjective is used with an article to form a noun: *una jovena*. There is a negative structural correspondence here, but there is a close functional/semantic correspondence.

III. Negative Correspondence in Target Language (Sublevel 7)   English: the auxilliary *do*. Spanish: no such auxilliary. Again there is a negative structural correspondence.

IV. Structural Correspondence but Functional/Semantic Noncorrespondence (Sublevel 11)   English: third person singular *-s* on verb forms: *lives*. Spanish second person singular *-s*: *vives*. Although there is a structural correspondence between these forms, there is a failure in functional/semantic correspondence.

V. Structural and Functional/Semantic Correspondence (Sublevel 14) English subjects obligatory: *I come.* Spanish subjects optional: *(Yo) vengo.* In this instance there is both a structural correspondence and functional/semantic correspondence.

In the spirit of the strong view of the CA hypothesis, the hierarchy was devised as a set of predictions that Stockwell, Bowen, and Martin (1965) admit must be tested against the errors students actually make. More recently, a grammar test was devised to test the predictions of the Stockwell hierarchy and is reviewed in the section on methodological hybrids. Stockwell et al.'s work, as opposed to earlier structural, purely taxonomic approaches to CA, included not only the surface structures of sentences but also deep structures and transformations. Correspondences between the rules of Spanish and English were noted and judged to be semantically and/or structurally equivalent.

Some writers support a more moderate view of CA, considering it to be more of a guide rather than programmatic. For the most part, though, there are two main positions: *CA apriori*, which is also called the strong or predictive version; and *CA aposteriori*, which is sometimes called the explanatory or weak version. CA *apriori* involves four steps: description of two languages, selection of form for contrast, making the contrast, and the prediction of difficulty on the basis of contrast (Whitman, 1970). CA *aposteriori* does not require the prediction of difficulties. It starts with error data and works backward to the language systems involved. Attempts are made to describe the separate systems at those places where the errors were observed to occur.

Criticisms

It has been said that CA *apriori* pays too much attention to predicting what errors the learner will make and not enough attention to the study of which errors the learner actually does make. Three objections to CA apriori occur repeatedly: 1) CA *apriori* sometimes predicts difficulties that do not occur, 2) it does not predict some errors that do occur, and 3) apriori is a long and difficult process to which CA *aposteriori* can provide a shortcut (Oller, 1972; Schachter, 1974). Wardhaugh's (1970) objection to CA *apriori* is that the strong version of CA makes demands of linguistic theory that it cannot meet, because it requires that there be a set of linguistic universals formulated within a compehensive linguistic theory.

The works of Stockwell, Bowen, and Martin (1965) and by Stockwell and Bowen (1965), both part of the Contrastive Structure Series, have been criticized by Wardhaugh (1970). He contends that these authors make too much use of their experience and intuitions in dealing with Spanish and English structures in order to explain the difficulties English speakers have when learning Spanish. They espouse an eclectic theory which contains insights from transformational and structural grammars, but there is no evidence that they use a contrastive theory of any power to predict errors. Nickel and Wagner (1968) also feel that the hierarchy of Stockwell and his colleagues does not take psychological and motivational factors into account. They mention instances where students have worked harder when difficulties are encountered, whereas partial equivalences and similarities cause the students to become inattentive.

Equivalence of Languages

Next, there is the problem of equivalence or compatibility of languages to consider. Catford (1965) said that texts of items from two languages "are translational equivalents when they are interchangeable in a given situation" (p. 49). Krzeszowski (1971) has performed contrastive analyses in which he attempts to establish that "equivalent constructions have identical deep structures even if on the surface they are markedly different" (p. 38). The failure of this hypothesis—that textual equivalents will be derived from a common deep structure—has been demonstrated by Bouton (1967). He points out that there are equivalents in which one member contained more information than the other. Sentences such as *Seymour sliced the salami* and *Seymour used a knife to slice the salami* have been said to have identical deep structures because the same selectional restrictions and other co-occurrence relations are in effect for both sentences. Krzeszowski states that, because the Polish equivalents of these sentences *Seymour pokrajał salami nożem* and *Seymour użuł noża aby pokrajać salami* are subject to the same set of selectional and co-occurrence restrictions, the members of each pair and the pairs themselves can be said to have a common deep structure. Yet it has been shown by Zgusta (reported in Bouton, 1976) that the Polish translations of the English sentences are not fully equivalent to the English ones, since Polish must specify the completion aspect in its verb. The Polish versions convey the additional information that Seymour had cut all the salami he planned to cut. If Seymour had not finished, or if he was involved in a habitual action, the sentences would be slightly different.

Bouton considers these English and Polish sentences to be textual equivalents in Krzeszowski's sense because the sets of sentences can be interchanged in most instances. The English sentences only fail as textual equivalents if the additional information carried in the Polish sentences is a relevant part of the speaker's message. The problem as Bouton sees it is that Krzeszowki makes no provision for differentiating at the deep structure level between those elements of a sentence that are contextually relevant and those that are not. Bouton claims that transformational theory can not now account for structurally distinct textual equivalents, i.e., "those constructions that bilinguals regard as mutual translations of each other but which are structurally disparate" (p. 161).

Other authors point to the equivalence problem in connection with CA. Nickel (1971) feels that formal equivalence can be established fairly easily, whereas functional-semantic differences are very difficult to determine. Individual languages possess unique subsystems and every construction must be regarded as part of the whole. Probably the best one can do is to establish a notion of 'quasi-equivalence' with approximate values. Related to the issue of equivalence are considerations of register and style. CA must involve more than a mere comparison of rule systems. It must also take into account register and style in the determination of equivalence.

It has also been shown that semantic facts are relevant for establishing equivalence between languages. Considering the semantic notions of control and volition in the causative constructions of English and South Asian languages, Kachru (1975) concludes that no clear picture of a simple equivalence emerges between the two languages. In order to establish cross-linguistic equivalences, she suggests that research must be done in the areas of rules of conversation and pragmatics, which will in turn produce a definition and understanding of what is meant by functional equivalence. Kachru further states that "to the extent that no linguistic theory has yet been successful in characterizing a *universal base* for human languages, CA cannot refer to this *base* to characterize equivalence between language" (p. 83). She criticizes CA for not facing up to the fact that congruent structures, i.e., one-to-one correspondences between languages, are rare. Due to this asymmetric equivalence between languages, CA should be based not on structures but on meanings.

Pedagogical Implications for CA

There are those who believe that CA is important as a research tool or method of language analysis, and indispensable as an aid in the construction and evaluation of tests, but not as a pedagogical basis for an ESL or bilingual program. Stockwell, Bowen, and Martin (1965) state that their hierarchy of difficulty is only the raw material for the author of a textbook. The hierarchy is only one of a number of components that goes into the construction of valid pedagogical sequences. They suggest the adoption of the criterion of 'functional load' in establishing a pedagogical sequence that gives priority to "patterns which carry a proportionately larger share of the burden of communication" (p. 293). In sympathy with this view is Rivers (1968), who thinks that the degree of difficulty, pedagogically speaking, should be determined according to a set of criteria which is different from that of theoretical analyses. Some structures that are predicted to be difficult for a student to learn may turn out to be not so difficult in practice. Rivers gives the example of the subjunctive in French, *il faut que je parte*, which is not taught in beginning French because of a high degree of contrast with English, yet students often have learned it with ease much earlier because it is communcatively useful.

The CA hypothesis has implied for some that separate materials are needed for students of diverse linguistic backgrounds. Often, this would be impractical and totally unnecessary in the opinion of many who feel that interference from the native language accounts for only a small number (or at least not all) of the learning difficulties encountered. There are those who think that CA has no place whatsoever in language teaching and is entirely inappropriate as its theoretical basis. Oller (1972) has said that, even as an aid to language instruction, CA offers only a sketchy framework. It does not provide the teacher with necessary information about the psycholinguistic bases of language learning, nor does it suggest teaching techniques that would help the student learn, for example, the distinction between *ser* and *estar* in Spanish.

A Conceptual Approach to CA

Dirven (1976) suggests that CA be redefined. A grammatical approach must be combined with an analysis of the conceptual strategies which shape and are shaped by the grammar of a language. All cultures organize their experiences and impressions into different concepts. The differences in conceptual strategies, according to Dirven, have a number of lexical and semantic consequences. Even two related languages like Dutch and English have enormous differences in the lexicon. For example, *groot* in Dutch is rendered by six separate items in English: *large, tall, big, grown-up, great,* and *major*. In this case the English-speaking child must acquire perceptual strategies not needed by his Dutch-speaking counterpart.

In the domain of semantics, Dirven points out that, in a comparison of English, Dutch, and German, the English word *go* has not retained its specific meaning of 'movement on foot' and now indicates a more general type of movement. Dutch *gaan* can mean both general movement and movement on foot, whereas German *gehen* can only mean movement on foot. It has been noted that the *going to* form or *gaan* + infinitive, which is historically derived from the finite form, is possible only in languages where the verb *go* (or its equivalents) has lost its exclusive meaning, movement on foot. German, accordingly, excludes the use of *gehen* in a "going to" form expressing intention or expectation. Because the English word *go* and the Dutch *gaan* + infinitive can both have the meaning of neutral movement, there can be a greater flexibility in their usage. The examples Dirven gives to demonstrate these differences in flexibility for these forms in English versus Dutch are:

1. I'm *going to* work very hard next week.
   Ik *ga* volgend week hard werken.
2. It's *going* to rain.
   Het *gaat* regenen.
3. I'm *going to* be tired / happy / rich / ill.
   *Ik *ga* moe zijn / rijk zijn / gelukkig zijn / ziek zijn (p. 9).[1]

In conclusion, Dirven suggests that the most important task of CA is to provide refined semantic analyses of particular constructions, taking into account the conceptual strategies involved in their development and use.

In Defense of CA

Counter arguments are provided by James (1971) for some of the criticisms leveled against CA. The major criticism that he rebuts states that interference from one's native language is not the only source of error in the target language and that CA fails to predict any other sources of error. In answer to this, James points out that CA has claimed that interference is the chief or most important source of error, but never the sole source.[2] As long as there are errors that can be explained in terms of interference from L_1, then CA is a valid process. Dušková (1969), in accordance with the predictions that Stockwell, Bowen, and Martin (1965) make from their hierarchy, has found that categories that exist in both languages but display differences in their functions and dis-

---

[1] The asterisk means that this is an ungrammatical sentence.

[2] Researchers in various studies with adults have found varying percentages of errors due to interference. Some have found very little interference, while others found that 30% to 50% of the errors were due to interference. Interference specifically with regard to children's acquisition of L_2 is discussed in later sections of this chapter.

tribution do not cause the greatest difficulties. She concludes, like Stockwell et al., that what is most difficult for learners is a category that does not exist in the mother tongue.

It has been argued that ignorance, not interference, is the real cause of error (Newmark and Reibel, 1968). Since CA intimately involves interference theory, this concomitantly becomes a criticism of CA. James (1971) answers this criticism in several ways. First, he distinguishes between analytic knowledge and manipulative knowledge, or knowledge of skills. It is widely known that having analytic knowledge alone will not produce the required skillful behavior. James uses the example of the Spanish word *teléfono* which English students learn immediately, but English stress interference often causes many instances of *telefóno*, with incorrect penultimate stress. Another fact is that teachers have discovered that students with *equal* amounts of exposure vary as to the ease with which they acquire knowledge of some items. Ignorance in some areas more than in others could not cause such a learning differential, but greater or lesser amounts of native language interference could logically account for the differences. Finally, James says that if ignorance theory were valid, it would be true, for example, that an Italian who has not learned Spanish or Chinese would be equally "ignorant" in both languages. But ignorance theory has no explanatory value because it does not explain why most Italians find it easier to perform better in Spanish than in Chinese.

Schachter (1974) argues rather convincingly in favor of CA *apriori* over CA *aposteriori*. She compared the major restrictive relative clause formation strategies of Persian, Arabic, Chinese, and Japanese and made predictions of probable areas of difficulty in producing English relative clauses for speakers of each of the languages. She made her predictions along three dimensions:

1. *Position of relative clause with respect to head noun.* Schachter predicted that the Japanese and Chinese would have difficulty with English relative clauses because their relative clauses appear to the left of the head noun phrase (NP), whereas Persians and Arabs would have no trouble because their relative clauses are to the right of the head NP as in English.
2. *Subordinate markers in relative clauses.* The prediction was that only the Japanese would have difficulty with the subordination marker *that* because they were the only language group involved that just had subordinate affixes and no subordinate marker similar to English *that*.

3. *The occurrence of a pronominal reflex.* English does not have resumptive pronouns,[3] as do the other four languages, although not all possible syntactic positions. Persian allows more resumptive pronouns in the various possible syntactic positions than does Arabic, while Arabic allows more resumptive pronouns than does Chinese, which allows more than Japanese. It was predicted that Persians would have the most difficulty and that Japanese would have the least difficulty. This was because Japanese, with respect to resumptive pronouns, is the most similar of the four languages to English.

After her *apriori* predictions were made, Schachter compared these with the errors analyzed from 50 English compositions of adult speakers of the four language groups. An examination of only the percentages of errors made revealed that the Persian and Arabs made more errors in the production of English relative clauses. However, when Schachter looked at the productions of just the Chinese and Japanese, she discovered that these two groups produced significantly fewer relative clauses than did the Persians and Arabs (who produced an amount similar to American students). Persian and Arab students find relative clause formation so similar to that of their native language that they assume they can transfer directly their native language forms to English. This accounts for the larger number of English relative clauses that the Persians and Arabs produced. Schachter points out that the Chinese and Japanese, however, must learn to switch relative clauses to a postnominal position when they learn English, and in most cases they need to change the internal order of the main constituents within the relative clause. This is a much harder task than what is required of the Persians and Arabs (i.e., Persians and Arabs mainly must learn that English has no resumptive pronouns). According to Schacter, the Japanese and the Chinese produced fewer relative clauses in English because they were trying to avoid them, and they only used relative clauses in English when they were relatively sure they were correct. This avoidance strategy is in keeping with the predictions of the *apriori* approach, while CA *aposteriori* alone cannot make sense of the observed error pattern.

Since Schacter's study only looked at errors from students' compositions, it is necessary to examine findings from other kinds of tests to see

---

[3] If English did have resumptive pronouns two examples would be: *The man that he ran* (subject resumptive pronoun); and *The man that John likes him* (direct object resumptive pronoun).

if they support her conclusions. Kleinmann (1978) administered a comprehension test, which also involved confidence ratings, an indirect preference elicitation task, an anxiety test, and a success-failure inventory, to three groups of university students: Arabs, Spanish and Portuguese, and native English (as a control). Four English structures were investigated: 1) passive voice, 2) infinitive complements, 3) direct object pronouns followed by infinitive complements, and 4) the present progressive. A CA between English and each of the other three languages predicts that the Spanish and Portuguese would have more difficulty with infinitive complements and direct object pronouns (relative to the Arabs' difficulty), and that the Arabs would experience difficulty with passive and present progressive structures (relative to the Spanish and Portuguese difficulty). These CA *apriori* predictions were confirmed, and Kleinmann says that a group level avoidance strategy was operating in accordance with the CA predictions. Kleinmann concludes that the second language learners in his study made use of an avoidance strategy that could not be attributed to a lack of comprehension or knowledge of the avoidance structure. His study shows that CA is a good predictor of structures that students are likely to avoid, although as Kleinmann admits, CA cannot predict when a structure will be avoided as opposed to when it will be produced correctly.

ERROR ANALYSIS

Support for EA

Error analysis has been around as long as language teaching has, but it was not until the advent of CA, with its seemingly rigorous methodology and strong claims, that EA became revitalized. For many, EA was the "favorite child" of the 1970s. EA traditionally had a taxonomic orientation and consisted of the following steps: 1) error identification, 2) error classification, 3) error frequency report, and 4) delineation of troublesome areas for which remediation was planned. According to Sridhar (1980), a few of the traditional error analyses involved two points which are now usually included in current error analyses: 1) analysis of the underlying source of errors, such as interference and overgeneralization, and 2) determination of the seriousness or degree of disturbances caused by the error. In contrast to earlier error analyses, recent studies are more sophisticated in techniques of language analysis, statistical methods, and categorization of errors.

Traditional EA has considered errors to be deviations that should be avoided. However, with a shift in emphasis away from the teacher and toward a study of learning, a more positive attitude toward errors developed. They came to be viewed as an inevitable part of the learning process and significant to the teacher, learner, and researcher alike. Corder (1967) suggests that it will be useful "to refer to errors of performance as mistakes, reserving the term error to refer to the systematic errors of the learner from which we are able to reconstruct his knowledge of the language to date, i.e., his transitional competence" (p. 167).

Many adherents to the EA approach do not feel that a full-scale analysis of two languages as suggested by CA is necessary or advisable. The main assumption is that EA will reveal learners' actual difficulties and will therefore provide a more reliable basis for constructing remedial materials. CA has been heavily criticized for only being able to predict interlingual errors, those which are caused by mother tongue inteference. As Richards (1971) points out, however, interference from one's native language is not a major factor in the way in which bilinguals construct sentences and use language. In his influential article, Richards distinguishes between interlingual errors (within L_2 itself), and developmental errors. Since CA has not concerned itself with errors other than those caused by interference, it has not specifically addressed itself to analyses of error types noted by Richards, such as ignorance of rule restrictions, incomplete applications of rules, false concepts hypothesized, and overgeneralizations.

Selinker's concept of 'interlanguage' (1972), Nemser's notion of 'approximate systems' (1971), and Corder's 'indiosyncratic dialect' (1971) have brought new dimensions to EA. These terms all refer to the separate, systematic, and yet 'permeable' linguistic systems that a learner constructs in an attempt to master a target language. The theory behind these concepts reflects the attitude that views errors as constructive features of language learning and looks below reported surface phenomena into the psychology of error. Permanent characteristics of such systems are called 'fossilizable items.' Selinker (1972) has identified fossilizable linguistic phenomena as linguistic items, rules, and subsystems that speakers retain in their interlanguage. Explanation or instruction does not influence these structures.

Some researchers who support EA insist that it should entirely replace CA in determining the main areas of potential difficulty in the learning of L_2 (e.g., Wilkins, 1968). Other researchers who advocate a more moderate view indicate that error analyses are both fruitful and necessary and are just as effective as contrastive analyses, if not more so (e.g., Buteau, 1970; Bhatia, 1974). Findings such as those of Buteau (1970) weigh heavily in favor of EA. Her findings indicated that the French sentences she tested that had English equivalents were not necessarily easier for non-native speakers to learn. This, of course, is not what the CA hypothesis predicts. She also noted that a comparison of errors made by students ages 16–20 with various linguistic backgrounds revealed no significant difference in the number of errors made. Last, on the continuum of positive attitudes toward EA, there are those scholars who favor CA *and* EA, suggesting that CA can be profitably supplemented by error-based analyses (e.g. Dušková, 1969), or that CA should not supplant EA in that more than one view of the learning process is required to account for the diverse phenomena involved (Schachter and Celce-Murcia, 1977).

Weaknesses and Problems with EA

Some specific areas of weakness in EA research have been identified. One of the weaknesses recognized is in the first stage of the EA—identification and isolation of errors from the data. Strevens (1969) regards this process as essentially subjective. The problem is that educated native speakers often disagree over the acceptability of an utterance. Hammarberg (1974) notes another problem at this stage. He says that analyzing only the errors and neglecting the careful description of the non-errors is arbitrary and inadequate. Schachter and Celce-Murcia (1977) agree that the correct forms must be noted, too. They report the work of Andersen (1977), whose study of article usage errors by Spanish speakers learning English showed that the Spanish speakers made many errors with *a (an)* and few errors with *the*. When Andersen (1977) examined the instances where the articles were used correctly, it turned out that many of the learners were using the strategy of providing the English equivalent of the Spanish article that was required in that context. This strategy resulted in many *a (an)* errors but few *the* errors. What was mandatory to the discovery of that strategy was a careful consideration of correct forms as well as errors.

Even if one could patch up the first weakness pertaining to the identification and isolation of errors, there would still be the problem of properly classifying identified errors. Classification involves the problem of determining whether or not an item should be considered an error. Strevens (1969) notes that some errors are obvious, but many are either multiple errors or are difficult to categorize. Schachter and Celce-Murcia (1977) provide an example produced by a Japanese student; *Americans are easy to get guns.* It is possible to analyze this as a case of the misapplication of the rule of raising, which raised *Americans* as subject of the lower clause to subject of the higher clause. They identify the possibility that the learner has categorized *easy* as an adjective which allows all types of infinitive complements. This second interpretation is supported by Carol Chomsky (1969), who says that native English-speaking children also interpret the subject of *easy* as the subject of the infinitive.

Schacter and Celce-Murcia (1977) are concerned with other weaknesses that they see in EA studies. They state that studies which must supply numerical error totals are less useful and less informative than those that consider the number of times it was possible for a learner to make an error. They recommend the usage of Agnello's relative frequency ratio which involves "using as numerator the number of times an error was committed and as denominator the number of times the error type could have occurred" (p. 446). Furthermore, even the most comprehensive EA only provides evidence as to what the learner would not do and why, as in the case of avoidance.

Another problem mentioned by Schachter and Celce-Murcia is that certain errors in second language acquisition have been categorized as ambiguous, i.e., as developmentally related or due to interference. Dulay and Burt (1974a) provide examples of such errors in their study, e.g., *Terina not can go.* This sentence produced by a Spanish child reflects Spanish structure but it is also typical of the kind of developmental errors made by children learning English as a native language. If examined carefully, the classification "ambiguous" is no classification at all. Researchers who use this category are guilty of taxonomic default; there is no linguistic reality to "ambiguous." Schachter and Celce-Murcia also say that investigators must be very cautious when categorizing an error type as intralingual or interlingual. Researchers must also be careful not to draw conclusions when working with very limited or biased samples in the areas of background languages of the subjects and data samples provided by the subjects.

Finally, EA has been criticized for its lack of explanatory power. Many error analyses are simply lists of errors and frequency counts. This criticism addresses the lack of understanding that some researchers have as to what constitutes an explanation. Classification is not explanation. It is not up to the reader or to future research to determine the significance of an analysis. Rather, the analyst should present the categories of errors that have been determined as support for a particular hypothesis about language acquisition, or as the answer to a theoretical question being asked about learners' strategies, for example.

METHODOLOGICAL HYBRIDS

This section deals with the various combinations of EA and CA that have been proposed, students' perception of difficulty (SPD) or error explanation, and communicative error analysis. An important study motivated by controversial views concerning both CA and EA was undertaken by Chau (1975). He investigated learners' perception of difficulty and related it to the outputs of CA and EA in an attempt to evaluate the merits and shortcomings of each method, and to find an adequate approach to the problem of difficulty in the learning of L_2. Chau designed a Spanish grammar test and a combination questionnaire and rating scale. The grammar test reflected both Stockwell, Bowen, and Martin's (1965) hierarchy of difficulty (excluding several sublevels) and the expected Spanish proficiency of second year high school students. The test was administered and then perception of difficulty scores were obtained from the same students, who rated the degree of difficulty of the structures on the test. Students were also requested to choose three structures they had rated as the most difficult and three they rated as the easiest. They were then asked to explain why they judged these structures as such. Attempts were made to determine the underlying sources of error. Two empirical hierarchies of difficulty were derived, one from error quotients that were calculated (the EA scale), and the other from the mean scores of students' ratings (the SPD scale). Last, Chau determined the degree of relationship between the difficulty scales—EA and CA (Stockwell's hierarchy), EA and SPD, and CA and SPD—by computing their rank order correlation coefficients.

Basically, Chau found that the greatest single source of errors was first language interference (51 of the total errors were due to interference and 29 were intralingual errors). The predictive value of CA was found to be negligible, as was evidenced by the low correlation coefficient between CA and EA scales. It has usually been assumed by contrastive analysts that a nonexistent category in the native language causes the greatest difficulty. In the hierarchy of Stockwell, Bowen, and Martin (1965), it was further assumed that structural dissimilarity presents more problems than does semantic dissimilarity. None of these assumptions was confirmed by Chau's study. Stockwell et al.'s classes I, II, and IV all had very close to the same error quotients (error quotients being the ratio between the number of wrong occurrences and the total number of occurrences). Chau stated that the variance in error quotients was too small to justify the differentiation between these three levels of difficulty.

The results of Chau's study suggest that unless EA makes use of CA logic, it will be unable to explain the cause of interlingual errors, i.e., interference. Second, it was found that intralingual errors are so diversified that their causes cannot be uncovered by EA in its present state of development. Finally, Chau found that the students' explanations of difficulty provided insights into their learning difficulties. The students' explanations often referred to what Chau calls "extralinguistic factors" such as pedagogical techniques, sequencing of materials, and type of learner. Chau concludes that because of the high correlation between the students' ratings of difficulty and frequency of errors, SPD considered by itself provides the best advice for determining problem areas. He recommends that SPD be used by the teacher as a quick diagnosis of problems. However, he thinks that

> in studies of greater scope, SPD and EA can supplement each other to provide a more accurate diagnosis of areas of difficulty.... Once the problem areas are detected, the resources of EA, CA, and students' perception should be combined in order to adequately explain the cause of difficulty (p. 137).

Elicitation of error explanations (or SPD) has not always been viewed so favorably. Some researchers have found that learners may not have the metalanguage necessary to descibe their errors adequately, and students' intuitions can turn out to be rationalizations instead of true explanations. In their 1976 study, Cohen and Robbins found that informants, for the most part, had a satisfactory metalanguage for explaining a number of their errors. Their informants were usually able to indicate when they thought they were merely speculating about the reason they gave for an error. The informants in Cohen and Robbins' studies were adults, while in Chau's study the informants were about 15 years old. It would be interesting to see if grade school children could provide researchers with their perceptions of difficulty. Since judgments of L_1 grammaticality have been obtained from children as young as 3 (de Villiers and de Villiers, 1972), there is reason to be optimistic that children younger than 15 could give experimenters insights into the difficulties they are having in the acquisition of L_2.

A new approach to EA, called "communicative error analysis" has been proposed by Burt (1975). In order to determine the relative importance of error types, Burt asked native speakers of English to make judgments about the relative comprehensibility of 33 sentences containing two or more errors per sentence. The informants were asked to make judgments about the sentences as each error was corrected one at a time or several at a time. As a result, Burt was able to identify two basic types or errors: *local errors* and *global errors*. Local errors are those that affect constituents in a sentence but do not tend to greatly impair communication. Errors such as these usually involve noun and verb inflections, auxiliaries, articles, and quantifiers. Global errors, on the other hand, are those that significantly hinder communication by affecting overall sentence organization. This type of error causes the listener or reader to misinterpret the spoken or written message. Examples of such errors are: wrong word order (e.g., *The French language use many people*), and misplaced sentence connectors (e.g., *He ate his dinner since he could have the dessert*, where *since* should have been at the beginning of the sentence). Burt engages in a very useful discussion of two instances that often cause global errors: 1) Selectional restrictions on certain types of verbs in sentential complements, e.g., *Sue told the man to have six children*, instead of *Sue told the man she had six children*, and 2) psychological predicate constructions, e.g., *She doesn't interest that company*, instead of *That company doesn't interest her*. In these cases reverse psychological verbs are misused with animate nouns.

Burt's communication approach may become an important method of language analysis because it deals with language communication as few other procedures do. Burt's method can be adopted by a teacher who could record the errors that pupils make in conversation. The teacher would then decide which errors cause the greatest communication problems in a particular group of students. Relevant teaching or remediation would follow according to the results of the teacher's analysis.

CONCLUSIONS AND THEORIES ABOUT L₂ ACQUISITION BASED ON EA

The CA hypothesis, as previously explained, predicts that a person learning a second language will tend to use native-language structures in the production of L_2 and that many of the errors made will be traceable to interference from L_1 regardless of the learner's age. The CA hypothesis reflects the habit formation theory of language learning, which holds that old habits (the use of L_1) hinder or facilitate new language learning (and therefore new habit formation) to the extent that L_1 and L_2 are similar to or different from one another. Dulay and Burt (1973), however, propose that the creative construction theory best describes how children learn L_2. According to this theory, children reconstruct L_2 independent of their knowledge of L_1. The creative construction theory predicts that the errors a child will make will be developmental, that is, not due to the transfer of

L_1 structures onto L_2. Developmental errors are the kinds of errors native children make learning their first language, e.g., irregular plurals are overgeneralized and treated as regular.

Child Errors

In order to test the predictions of the creative construction theory, Dulay and Burt (1974a) administered the Bilingual Syntax Measure (BSM) in three school districts, two in California and one in New York, to 179 5- to 8-year-old Spanish-speaking children who were learning English as a second language. From the speech samples obtained, Dulay and Burt then extracted 513 errors that could be unambiguously categorized as developmental, interference, or unique. They found that only 5% of the errors reflected native Spanish interference and that 87% were developmental errors. This finding lends some support to the creative construction theory, at least with regard to children.

Child Sequences of Acquisition

Encouraged by their findings, Dulay and Burt (1974b) compared the order of acquisition of 11 English functors, such as articles (*a*, *the*), progressives (*-ing*), and plurals (*-s*), by 6-, 7-, and 8-year-old Spanish- and Chinese-speaking children learning English in New York schools. The children, who had English-speaking peers, were receiving some English as a second language instruction and some subject matter instruction in English. Dulay and Burt decided on a cross-sectional design using small corpora of natural speech collected from large numbers of children by means of the BSM. The results showed that the order of acquisition of the 11 functors was virtually the same for Chinese- and Spanish-speaking children. Burt and Dulay concluded from their findings that the creative construction process figures significantly in child L_2 acquisition. For Burt and Dulay, L_2 learning is "a process in which children gradually reconstruct rules for speech they hear, guided by universal innate mechanisms which cause them to formulate certain types of hypotheses about the language system being acquired . . ." (p. 37).

Shortly after their second study, Dulay and Burt (1974c) reanalyzed the data reported in the second study in order to test the "ordering-theoretic" or "tree" method, which was devised as an alternative to rank orders. The advantage to this approach is that it looks for groups of functors that are acquired together and that are ordered. The "tree" they constructed points to the acquisition of certain groups of functors before other groups: Level I, the acquisition of pronoun case precedes the acquisition of all other functors; Level II, copula precedes plural (*-s*) and auxiliary (*is*); and these three, together with *-ing* and articles (*a, the*), precede Level III, which contains past regular, past irregular, possessive, third person, and long plural (*-es*). These ordering relationships were obtained for all three samples—English, Chinese, and Spanish.

The picture is by no means complete. More naturalistic studies should be done in order to compare the results of spontaneous speech versus elicited samples. There are linguistically significant differences, for example, between Dulay and Burt's elicited samples and Hakuta's (1974a) morpheme acquisition order, which was based on spontaneous speech samples from his longitudinal study of a Japanese girl's acquisition of English as a second language. It is also necessary, as Dulay and Burt suggest, to obtain child acquisition hierarchies of English syntactic structures other than functors, since morpheme acquisition orders cannot by themselves be taken as a measure of general language ability. Child acquisition hierarchies for L_2s other than English should be obtained. Hierarchies or natural sequences in acquisition should be determined for children in immersion programs who are only exposed to native adult speech, compared to children in bilingual programs who are also exposed to native English peer speech. Studies that address the last issue would shed light on the question of what effects various types of language learning environments have on children's language.

Adult and Adolescent Errors

It has been hypothesized that children below the age of puberty will make mainly developmental errors and that adults acquiring L_2 will make mostly interlingual errors based on their native language. One might assume, therefore, that child L_2 acquisition is very different from adult L_2 acquisition. Dommergues and Lane (1976) have demonstrated, however, that the syntactic errors adults make in learning are often like those made by children in their first language acquisition. The results of their study of French students learning English were that intralingual errors increase as learning progresses, whereas interference errors steadily decrease as students acquire more proficiency in English. These findings are corroborated by LoCoco (1975) and Taylor (1975). LoCoco reports that, because Dulay and Burt found little L_1 interference in the children they tested and because research on older learners provides evidence for mother tongue interference, it has been hypothesized that interlingual errors increase for older learners. LoCoco's study does not support this assumption, however. It was found that during the initial stages of learning, teenage students rely heavily on their native language structures, but as they learn more of L_2, they rely proportionately less on their native languages. She also notes that even though learners acquiring L_2 make more interlingual errors in early stages of learning than they do at later stages, still, at all levels of learning, the number of interlingual errors produced never exceeds the number of intralingual errors. Hence, at all times reliance on the target language exceeds reliance on native or previously learned language.

Taylor's results fit nicely with LoCoco's. Taylor (1975) did an EA of a test requiring the written English translation of 80 Spanish sentences by 20 adult native Spanish-speaking students of English as a second language at elementary and intermediate levels. His results confirmed that elementary students relied on the transfer strategy to a significantly greater degree than did the intermediate students. His findings for adult acquisition are consistent with a creative construction theory of language in that adults engage in "an actively creative process dependent upon a student's ability to assimilate and subsume new information into already existing cognitive structures" (p. 73). One might conclude from the studies just reviewed that in the initial stages of L_2 acquisition adults may be more affected by interference from L_1 than children are, but that after the initial stages both groups make more intralingual errors than interlingual errors.

Adult and Adolescent Sequences of Acquisition

Continuing with a comparison of adult (and adolescent) versus child L_2 acquisition, this section examines studies that provide evidence for adult natural sequences of acquisition. Bailey, Madden, and Krashen (1974) administered the BSM to 73 adult learners of English as a second language in order to assess their accuracy of usage of eight English functors.[4] They found that there was a highly consistent order or relative difficulty in the use of the functors for both groups tested—Spanish and non-Spanish (representing 11 different mother tongues). The results agreed with those of Dulay and Burt and could be taken to mean that adults (irrespective of language background) and children process language data in similar ways.

Fathman (1975a) devised and tested 120 Spanish and Korean children learning English as a second langauge, ages 6 to 14, with the SLOPE (Second Language Oral Production English) test, a test that covers 20 different structures of English, including present participles, imperatives, and yes/no questions. She found Spanish and Korean profiles to be highly correlated; the difficulty orders for the 20 subtests

---

[4] These were the same functors Dulay and Burt used in their 1973 study.

were similar. For those items common to her study and to Dulay and Burt's studies (1973, 1974b), the order she found did not significantly differ from the order they obtained for children through 8 years old. Fathman (1975b) also administered the SLOPE test to 200 children from diverse language backgrounds who were learning English as a second language in public schools. She found no significant difference in difficulty order between learners who had had extra English as a Second Language (ESL) classes and those who had not. She also found that order of acquisition in second language learning does not change with age.

Krashen, Sferlazza, and Feldman (1976), in an attempt to extend the results obtained by Bailey, Madden, and Krashen (1974), also administered the SLOPE to four different groups of speakers: Spanish, Greek, other Indo-European languages, and Far Eastern non-Indo-European languages. Their results were consistent with Bailey et al.'s findings for Spanish- and non-Spanish-speaking adults, and Dulay and Burt's (1974b) Chinese- and Spanish-speaking children. These studies indirectly lend support to the view that no radical change in learning strategy or ability to process a new language takes place at puberty, as is predicted by the critical period hypothesis.[5] The finding that difficulty order or natural sequence is basically the same regardless of environment gives credence to Corder's (1967) idea that all learners have a "built-in syllabus," a learner-generated sequence of preferred learning.

Although the results of the recent morpheme acquisition studies are very compelling, Larsen (1975) and Rosansky (1976) suggest caution in interpreting their results. Until the rank orderings obtained by the BSM can be tested with sequences obtained through the use of other instruments, we cannot be sure that a general acquisition order is being identified (Larsen, 1975).[6] Rosansky (1976) feels that the validity of some of the conclusions of the morpheme acquisition studies should be questioned. As part of a 10-month longitudinal study of morpheme sequences in the second language acquisition of six Spanish speakers, Rosansky attempted to answer two questions: 1) does the morpheme order obtained using the BSM, an elicitation instrument, resemble the order of morphemes obtained from spontaneous second language samples, and 2) are cross-sectional and longitudinal research findings for second language

---

[5] This is not surprising in that language lateralization is complete well before adolescence. On these grounds, a revision of the critical period hypothesis as formulated by Penfield and by Lenneberg is necessary.

[6] See also Chapter 8 (McCollum and Day) and Chapter 10 (Sridhar) in this volume for critiques of the BSM.

acquisition comparable? Despite the fact that she found significant correlations between BSM-generated and spontaneous speech-based rank orders, these correlations could not be meaningfully interpreted because of large variability for subjects rank orders and for group means (i.e., many of the means exhibited a large variance, with standard deviations occasionally approaching the value of the mean). For two of her adolescent subjects, she also found that the order of morphemes based on the BSM when compared with spontaneous speech-based orders did not correlate for the same individual at the same point in time. In a cross-sectional analysis, Rosansky found that the cross-sectionally based and longitudinally derived rank orders for one of the adolescents that she tested did not correlate. She determined that no cross-sectional point resembled the longitudinal developmental order. In light of these criticisms, the morpheme acquisition studies should be viewed with some skepticism. As Rosansky cautions, we should not hastily conclude that "we have discovered an invariant acquisition sequence for all second language learners based on the rank ordering of the relative frequency of a few morphemes" (p. 413). (See also Porter, 1977, who suggests on the basis of a first language acquisition study using the BSM that the BSM be more rigorously validated with the morpheme acquisition sequence observed in spontaneous production of first and second language learners).

Rates of Learning and Achievement

So far this chapter has discussed types of errors and acquisition sequences. It is time now to examine for a moment the claim upheld by many that young children are capable of learning languages faster or better than adults and adolescents. McLaughlin (1977) points out that there is little evidence in support of this proposition. In addition to the research that has been discussed above in this chapter, many of the controlled studies to date which have compared L_2 acquisition in young children to that of adolescents or adults have found that older children and adults typically do better, learn faster, or learn at least as well as younger children except in the area of phonology[7] (Asher, 1969; Cook, 1973; Ervin-Tripp, 1974; Fathman, 1975b; Snow and Hoefnagel-Höhle, 1978b). Some studies have concluded, however, that teenagers do better than adults

---

[7] Recent research (Oyama, 1976) points very strongly to the idea that there is a critical or "sensitive" period for the acquisition of a non-native phonological system. Evidence does not point to this conclusion, however, for the acquisition of non-native syntax or semantics. See Anderson (Chapter 4, this volume) for an in-depth discussion of phonology.

(Ramírez and Politzer, 1978; Snow and Hoefnagel-Höhle, 1978a). When we observe, as often is the case, that adults fail to acquire native proficiency in a second language, there is no evidence to support that adults have radically different learning strategies or suffer from a cognitive deficiency in their ability to learn another language. Taylor (1974) suggests that a much more plausible explanation will come from an examination of psychological variables like attitude, motivation, lack of permeability of "ego boundaries," and exposure to L_2.

Acquisition Stages for Various Structures

This section discusses the results of a few error analysis–acquisition studies that examine stages through which learners progress in the acquisition of negation and interrogatives. There is disagreement among researchers over whether the stages of acquisition recorded for L_1 are the same as those reported for the acquisition of L_2.

In the literature on first language acquisition, Klima and Bellugi (1966) determined that there were three stages in the acquisition of the negative for Adam, Eve, and Sarah, the three children they were studying. In Stage 1, the negative was sentence external—either before the sentence nucleus or after it, e.g., *No sit there.* In Stage 2, the negative was within the sentence and *don't* and *can't* appeared, e.g., *I no want envelope.* Stage 3 involved the full development of the auxiliary, as modal auxiliaries now appeared in declarative sentences and questions as well as in negative sentences, e.g., *I didn't see something.* Milon (1974) studied the acquisition of English negation by a 7-year-old Japanese child, Ken. He found that there was a striking similarity between the developmental stages of negation described by Klima and Bellugi and the stages that Ken went through in the development of negation in English as a second language.

The results of several other L_2 acquisition studies, however, do not agree with Klima and Bellugi's stages for L_1 negation. Gillis and Weber (1975) studied the acquisition of English by two Japanese children, ages 7 and 8, and found that, for the most part, only Klima and Bellugi's Stages 2 and 3 were present. Cancino, Rosansky, and Schumann (1978) report that, in their study of the acquisition of English negation by native Spanish speakers, they did not find convincing evidence for the stages described by Klima and Bellugi. Cancino et al. (p. 229) found the following developmental sequence of negation:

1. *no* V (*I no understand*)
2. *don't* V (*He don't like it*)

3. aux-neg (*You can't tell her*)
4. analyzed *don't*; disappearance of *no* V (*He doesn't spin*)

L_2 acquisition of negation studies that have defined stages that were similar to those recorded for L_1 can be taken as support for what has been called the identity hypothesis (held, for example, by Burt and Dulay). It claims that L_2 acquisition proceeds in basically the same manner as L_1 acquisition. Wode (1978) takes the opposite position. In a comparative study of German and English that was part of the Kiel Project on language acquisition, Wode documented that L_2 English stages of negation did not have exactly the same surface forms as the respective L_1 English sequences. Wode concluded that L_1 and L_2 are governed by the same set of principles but that these principles will lead to different surface forms for L_2 depending on the structure of L_1. (See also Felix, 1978, for more evidence from the Kiel Project on differences between the early stages of L_1 acquisition and L_2 acquisition).

It appears that, in many instances, children act in accordance with the creative construction hypothesis but that at times their stages in the acquisition of L_2 are more affected by interference from L_1. An interesting study by Milgrom (reported in Ervin-Tripp, 1974) shows that, contrary to what one has been led to expect, the children's performance was affected by interference but the adults' was not. Milgrom found in studying Israeli acquisition of English that children, not adults, went through a stage in the development of *yes/no* interrogation that was influenced by Hebrew. She reports that there is a *yes/no* interrogative morpheme that is sentence-initial in Hebrew and children created a syntactic class of prepositive auxiliaries on the model of tag questions, e.g., *Is I am going to be a rich man?* or *Do you can tell me what is the time?*

Ravem (1968) reports another acquisition study that can be considered to be evidence for a child's productions being "creative" and similar to native English learners' in some ways, and also being influenced by interference from L_1 in other ways. Ravem did an analysis of the auxiliary system of his 6½-year-old Norwegian son, Rune, who was acquiring English in Scotland. In a discussion of Ravem's work, Ervin-Tripp (1970) states that, in English-speaking children's development of negation, before *do* or copulas are systematically present, negators appear between the subject and main verb. In his development of negation, Rune often produced sentences with this pattern. In the acquisition of negatives Rune followed a developmental sequence similar to native English-speaking children. In the case of interrogatives, however, in the stage where *do* was omitted, Rune typically inverted the main verb and subject following Norwegian language rules, e.g., *Like you ice-cream*? American English-speaking children do not usually do this. But as Ervin-Tripp notes, Rune inverted less often in Wh-questions, like American children, *What you did in Rothbury*? When *do* appeared, Rune acquired adult-like English negation patterns, whereas prior to that he had used a negative pattern unlike Norwegian and similar to the developing English of American children. With the interrogative, however, even after *do* appeared, Ervin-Tripp states that the Norwegian pattern dominated and was not similar to the pattern used by Rune's English-speaking counterparts, who relied solely on intonation with inversion.

Ervin-Tripp (1974) observes that in the formulation of simple order rules children sometimes draw on their knowledge of L_1 if there is "some strong second language support," for a particular rule or "if L_1 is much simpler." In the case of Rune, Ervin-Tripp suggests that the boy used the English order rule for negation because it was simpler. She speculates that Rune retained the Norwegian question-inversion rule for main verbs at first because verb-first sentences are highly marked and the salience of placing the verb first in Norwegian interrogative formation was transferred into English.

In a first language acquisition study of interrogatives, Klima and Bellugi (1966) report that in the third stage of acquisition there is a class of verbal forms that inverts with the subject in certain *yes/no* questions, e.g., *Does lions walk*? However, they found that in the same stage the auxiliary verbs in *wh*-questions do not invert with the subject, e.g., *Why kitty can't stand up*? In the second language acquisition literature, Cancino, Rosansky, and Schumann (1978) found little evidence for Klima and Bellugi's claim that there is a stage in which children invert in *yes/no* questions but not in *wh*-questions. Ingram (1973) also found no evidence for such a stage in first language acquisition. In addition, Cancino et al. report that examination of the data from their six Spanish-speaking subjects reveals that *wh*- and *yes/no* questions appear in the uninverted form for all subjects and uninverted *yes/no* questions consistently appear before inverted *yes/no* questions. Cancino, Rosansky, and Schumann (1978) discovered a developmental sequence in the acquisition of *wh*-questions and *yes/no* questions. The following sequence is for *wh*-questions:

Stage I—*Undifferentiation*: learner does not distinguish between simple and embedded *wh*-questions
    a. uninverted—both simple and embedded *wh*-questions are *uninverted*
    b. variable inversion—simple *wh*-questions are sometimes inverted, sometimes not

c. generalization—increasing inversion in *wh*-questions with inversion (incorrectly) being extended to embedded questions. (Note: The author has added "(incorrectly)" to the quotation to clarify that embedded questions should not be inverted, e.g., *I know what is your address*.)

Stage II—*Differentiation*: learner distinguishes between simple and embedded *wh*-questions ... (p. 230).

The acquisition sequence that was observed in yes/no questions after early *do*-inversion (that Cancino, Rosansky, and Schumann (1978) call an "inversion-look") is: first, a "sentence with rising intonation," then "some inversion, gradually increasing, but with variability from session to session" (p. 230).

More L_1 versus L_2 comparative research on the stages of acquisition for all types of syntactic structures is necessary before we can make broad claims about the nature of or the extent to which L_1 differs from L_2 acquisition.

LEARNERS' STRATEGIES DERIVED FROM ERROR ANALYSIS RESEARCH AND CONTRASTIVE ANALYSIS

Descriptions and investigations into the nature of perceptual, learning, and communication strategies are another essential part of the process of understanding L_2 acquisition. In order to perform a meaningful syntactic/semantic analysis, one must ask not only *what* kinds of errors do we predict a learner will make, or what stages does a child go through in the development of a structure, or what is the comparative performance of other learners of different ages, but also *why* does a learner do what he does? A learner uses certain strategies to help him assimilate knowledge of L_2 and to be able to communicate, read, and write in L_2. These strategies often take the form of shortcuts or simplified procedures. By understanding what a learner's strategies are we can often gain greater insight into why particular kinds of syntactic or semantic errors are made.

Perceptual Strategies

Several perceptual strategies of learners of English as a second language are identified by Cowan (1975). Within the context of reading research, Cowan talks about these perceptual strategies as "cognitive routines which shape behavioral responses (expectations) to linguistic events (textual cues)" (p. 32). The following are two examples of Japanese perceptual strategies provided by Cowan. In Japanese the negative marker always occurs in clause final position since Japanese is an SOV (subject-object-verb) language. The native speaker sets up an expectation while reading Japanese that negation, when present, will be indicated at the end of the clause. However, when Japanese learners of English apply this strategy to sentences like *I do not think he will go to the U.S.A.*, Cowan says they will often fail to register the negative in the auxiliary. Another example is in English complex sentences with subordinate clauses introduced by a conjunction, such as *unless*, which has two possible patterns. One is *unless Sentence 1, Sentence 2*, and the other one is: *Sentence 2, unless Sentence 1*. Japanese, on the other hand, only has the second pattern for complex compound sentences. Hence, the Japanese perceptual strategy—expect conjunctions between clauses—combined with the perceptual strategy already mentioned for negation, causes difficulty for the Japanese in the interpretation of sentences like *Unless we all agree, I'm not interested in the plan.*

Cook (1973) also observes the perceptual strategies of learners of English as L$_2$ with seven different mother tongues with respect to sentences like *The wolf is willing to bite* and *The wolf is hard to bite*. She notes the similarities between the way native children and foreign adults perceive this type of structure. Both groups begin with the strategy that the surface structure subject is the same as the deep structure subject. Then both groups go through a stage in which they interpret deep and surface structure inconsistently. Finally, in the last stage, both groups develop a proper awareness of deep and surface structure which enables them to correctly interpret sentences like those given above.

Communication and Learning Strategies

The term *learning strategy* refers to a process of rule formation and is a "tentative hypothesis which the learner forms about the nature of the L$_2$, which is tested and subsequently modified" (Tarone, Frauenfelder, Selinker, 1975, p. 100). The rules produced by learning strategies are unstable, i.e., changing over time. The use of these strategies can result in the correct or incorrect formulation of an element in the target language system. A communication strategy, on the other hand, is defined by Tarone, Cohen, and Dumas (1976) as "a systematic attempt by the learner to express or decode meaning in the target language, in situations where the appropriate systematic target language rules have not been formed" (p. 78). This type of strategy does not necessarily result in a rule since it may involve, for example, avoidance. Taylor (1974) also talks about strategies of communication as those strategies that tell the learner that he or she knows enough of a language to attempt to communicate in it and the strategy encourages the learner to rely on what is already known. It is not always possible to know whether we are dealing with a learning strategy or a communication strategy, since we cannot observe strategies directly but rather must infer their existence. Some authors also have said that learning strategy is involved in a learner's approach to what must be learned in L_2 and a strategy of communication is involved when the learner attempts to communicate in L_2.

The following are examples given in the literature on communication strategies. Most of them have also been used as examples of learning strategies with the exception of overlaboration and avoidance.

Native Language Transfer According to Tarone et al. (1976), in native language transfer learners use a form from their mother tongue where a target language rule is required, which results in an incorrect utterance. In syntax, for example, learners transfer their knowledge of English indirect object pronouns in English to Spanish, e.g., *Dió a ellos* instead of *Les dió a ellos*. It must also be remembered that it has been shown that as proficiency in L_2 increases, reliance on transfer decreases, and reliance on overgeneralization increases.

Overgeneralization In overgeneralization a target language rule is applied to contexts or forms in the target language where it should not have been applied (Tarone et al., 1976). An example of syntactic overgeneralization in English L_2 acquisition they give is: *I don't know what is it*. In this case, subject-verb inversion for question formation has been overgeneralized to declarative sentences.

Prefabricated Routines A prefabricated routine is defined by Hakuta (1974b, 1975) as a segment of speech that is regular and patterned. A child uses a prefabricated routine "without knowledge of its underlying structure" but with an understanding of the appropriate contexts for its use. Some examples he gives are *Do you* and *how to* patterns: *What do you doing, this boy?* and *I know how to read it this*.

Overelaboration Overelaboration is an attempt by the learner to produce careful target language utterances, which turn out to sound very formal or stilted to the native speaker (Tarone et al., 1976). The overuse of the subject pronoun in Spanish is an example: *Yo quiero ir* instead of *Quiero ir*.

Types of Avoidance The following types of avoidance have been identified by Tarone et al. (1976): topic avoidance, semantic avoidance, appeal to authority, message abandonment, paraphrase, and language switch (code mixing, code switching). Under the category paraphrase, word coinage is given. The following are some interesting examples of word coinages from speakers of various African languages: *The girls are* *facing a lot of hardcap* (portmanteau, a combinaton of *handicap* and *hardship*); *The ladies of the town conferred them* (titles) *on me after a very ripe deservation* (Kirk-Greene, 1971); and *The people described the enstoolment of X as illegal* (this means enthronement; West Africans sat on a stool to indicate authority) (Sey, 1973). Although word coinage definitely seems to be an example of a communication strategy, it is not clear why this is classified as a type of avoidance.

Economy Principle Anderson (1978) observes that in a task involving a choice between two complement types, Spanish-speaking adults would respond with an infinitive in an English sentence to a Spanish sentence containing an infinitive (79% of the time). However, when the Spanish stimulus sentence contained a *que* complement, 46% of her subjects responded with a *that* complement because *that* complements are longer than infinitive complements and involve choice of tense. Anderson concluded that the "economy principle" accounts for an apparent preference for shorter forms and can also explain early acquisition of shorter forms.

Reliance on Word Order The strategy of reliance on word order to express semantic relations in the language being learned has been described for speakers of many diverse language families (Dulay and Burt, 1973). For example, *wolf eat chicken* expresses an agent-action-object relationship without the learner having to use English functors.

It can be said that for most of the communication strategies discussed above some type of simplification is involved, perhaps easing learner/speaker's burden of communication. Simplification, therefore, was not treated separately but can be regarded as a principle underlying most of the strategies. Evidence has shown that both children and adults made use of these communication strategies, with possibly the exception of certain types of avoidance for children.

CONCLUDING REMARKS

This chapter has attempted to objectively examine the methods of CA and EA in the prediction and/or analysis of the errors that learners make in the acquisition of L_2. In deciding whether to use CA, EA, or students' perception of difficulty (SPD) in assessment situations, the teacher or tester must determine what kinds of information he or she wants to obtain, what the purpose of the information is, and what time constraints are involved. Furthermore, the development of hybrid approaches, as labeled in this chapter, should also be encouraged because no one method can answer all contemporary questions. Both form and function need to be examined in an evaluation of a learner's acquisition of a target language (Wagner-Gough, 1975). It is a challenging task to be able to determine underlying sources of learners' error and what type of errors will be made. Useful constructs include Stockwell, Bowen, and Martin's (1965) hierarchy of difficulty and Wode's (1978) crucial similarity measure (which predicts that only if L_2 structures have a "crucial" similarity to L_1 will there be interference). These constructs, however, and others like them need to be refined and rigorously tested.

This chapter has also attempted to uncover some of the issues involved in comparing adult and adolescent L_2 acquisition to child L_2 acquisition. Similarities have been noted and it may turn out that what consistent differences there are can be attributed to psychological and motivational factors, factors pertaining to "social distance" (Schumann, 1978), and the effect of teaching versus natural environment on L_2 acquisition. Commonalities and differences have also been noted in the developmental sequences recorded for L_1 learners in their acquisition of various syntactic structures. These developmental sequences for L_1 compared to L_2 must be studied across many languages. Since developmental sequences will vary in certain ways depending on the structure of the language, we should look for general principles according to which L_2 acquisition develops. A theory of L_2 acquisition must be able to *predict* in which ways the acquiring of L_2 can be expected to be similar to L_1 and in which ways it will be different. Such a theory will also call for explanations of acquisition sequences, such as the conclusions derived by Larsen-Freeman (1978) that frequency of occurrence in native speech is the main determinant of oral production morpheme accuracy order. The theory should, finally, be global enough to incorporate the role of social, attitudinal, and cognitive factors in order for it to have important implications for assessment procedures and educational methods.

REFERENCES

Andersen, R. 1977. The improved state of cross-sectional morpheme acquisition/accuracy methodology. Paper presented at the Los Angeles Second Language Research Forum, UCLA, February, 1977. Cited by Schachter, J. and Celce-Murcia, M. 1977. Some reservations concerning error analysis. TESOL Q. 11:441–451.

Anderson, J. 1978. Order of difficulty in adult second language acquisition. In: W. C. Ritchie (ed.), Second Language Acquisition Research. pp. 91–108. Academic Press, New York.

Asher, J. J. 1969. The total physical response approach to second language learning. Modern Lang. J. 53:334–341.

Bailey, N., Madden, C., and Krashen, S. D. 1974. Is there a "natural sequence" in adult second language learning? Lang. Learn. 24:235-243.
Banathy, B., Trager, E., and Waddle, D. 1966. The use of contrastive data in foreign language course development. In: A. Valdman (ed.), Trends in Language Teaching. pp. 35-56. McGraw-Hill Book Co. New York.
Bhatia, A. T. 1974. An error analysis of students' compositions. IRAL 12:337-350.
Bouton, L. 1976. The problem of equivalence in contrastive analysis. IRAL 14:143-163.
Burt, M. K. 1975. Error analysis in the adult EFL classroom. TESOL Q. 9:53-63.
Buteau, M. F. 1970. Students' errors and the learning of French as a second language: A pilot study. IRAL 8:133-145.
Cancino, H., Rosansky, E. J., and Schumann, J. 1978. The acquisition of English negatives and interrogatives by native Spanish speakers. In: E. M. Hatch (ed.), Second Language Acquisition. pp. 207-230. Newbury House Publishing, Rowley, Mass.
Carroll, J. B. 1968. Contrastive linguistics and interference theory. In: J. E. Alatis (ed.), Report of the Nineteenth Annual Round Table Meeting on Linguistics and Language Studies. pp. 113-122. Georgetown University Press, Washington D.C.
Catford, J. C. 1965. A Linguistic Theory of Translation. Oxford University Press, London.
Chau, T.-T. 1975. Error analysis, contrastive analysis, and students' perception: A study of difficulty in second-language learning. IRAL 13:119-143.
Chomsky, C. 1969. The Acquisition of Syntax in Children from 5 to 10. Newbury House Publishers, Rowley, Mass.
Cohen, A. D., and Robbins, M. 1976. Toward assessing interlanguage performance: The relationship between selected errors, learners' characteristics, and learners' explanations. Lang. Learn. 26:45-66.
Cook, V. 1973. The comparison of language development in native children and foreign adults. IRAL 11:13-28.
Corder, S. P. 1967. The significance of learners' errors. IRAL 5:161-170.
Corder, S. P. 1971. Idiosyncratic dialects and error analysis. IRAL 9:147-159.
Cowan, J. R. 1975. Reading, perceptual strategies, and contrastive analysis. TESL Stud. 1:24-37.
de Villiers, P. A., and de Villiers, J. G. 1972. Early judgments of semantic and syntactic acceptability by children. J. Psycholing. Res. 1:299-310.
Dirven, R. 1976. A redefinition of contrastive linguistics. IRAL 14:1-14.
Dommergues, J.-Y., and Lane, H. 1976. On two independent sources of error in learning the syntax of a second language. Lang. Learn. 26:111-123.
Dulay, H. C., and Burt, M. K. 1973. Should we teach children syntax. Lang. Learn. 23:245-258.
Dulay, H. C., and Burt, M. K. 1974. Errors and strategies in child second language acquisition. TESOL Q. 8:129-136.
Dulay, H. C., and Burt, M. K. 1974. Natural sequences in child second language acquisition. Lang. Learn. 24:37-53.
Dulay, H. C., and Burt, M. K. 1974. A new perspective on the creative construction process in child second language acquisition. Lang. Learn. 24:253-278.

Dušková, L. 1969. On sources of errors in foreign language learning. IRAL 7:11-31.
Ervin-Tripp, S. 1970. Structure and process in language acquisition. In: J. E. Alatis (ed.), Bilingualism and Language Contact. Georgetown University Round Table on Languages and Linguistics 1970, Georgetown University Press, Washington, D.C.
Ervin-Tripp, S. 1974. Is second language learning like the first? TESOL Q. 8:111-127.
Fathman, A. 1975a. Language background, age, and the order of acquisition of English structures. In: M. Burt and H. Dulay (eds.), New Directions in Second Language Learning, Teaching and Bilingual Education. pp. 33-43. TESOL Washington, D.C.
Fathman, A. 1975b. The relationship between age and second language productive ability. Lang. Learn. 25:245-253.
Felix, S. W. 1978. Some differences between first and second language acquisition. In: N. Waterson and C. Snow (eds.), The Development of Communication. pp. 469-479. John Wiley & Sons, New York.
Fries, C. C. 1945. Teaching and Learning English as a Foreign Language. University of Michigan Press, Ann Arbor.
Gillis, M., and Weber, R. 1975. The emergence of sentence modalities in the English of Japanese-speaking children. Mimeo paper, McGill University, 1975. Cited by Cancino, H., Rosansky, E. J., and Schumann, J. 1978. The acquisition of English negatives and interrogatives by native Spanish speakers. In: E. M. Hatch (ed.), Second Language Acquisition. Newbury House Publishers, Rowley, Mass.
Hakuta, K. 1974a. A report on the development of the grammatical morphemes in a Japanese girl learning English as a second language. Working Paper on Bilingualism 3:18-44.
Hakuta, K. 1974b. Prefabricated patterns and the emergence of structure in second language acquisition. Lang. Learn. 24:287-297.
Hakuta, K. 1975. Becoming bilingual at age five. Unpublished honors thesis, Harvard University, Cambridge.
Hammarberg, B. 1974. The insufficiency of error analysis. IRAL 12:185-192.
Ingram, D. 1973. The inversion of subject NP and AUX in children's questions. Paper presented at the meeting of the Linguistic Society of America, December 30, 1973. Cited by Cancino, H., Rosansky, E. J., and Schumann, J. 1978. The acquisition of English negatives and interrogatives by native Spanish speakers. In: E. M. Hatch (ed.), Second Language Acquisition. Newbury House Publishers, Rowley, Mass.
James, C. 1971. The exculpation of contrastive linguistics. In: G. Nickel (ed.), Papers in Contrastive Linguistics. pp. 53-68. Cambridge University Press, Cambridge, England.
Kachru, Y. 1975. Toward defining the notion equivalence in contrastive analysis. TESOL Stud. 1:82-98.
Kirk-Greene, A. 1971. The influence of West African languages on English. In: J. Spencer (ed.), The English Language in West Africa. Longman, London.
Kleinmann, H. 1978. The strategy of avoidance in adult second language acquisition. In: W. C. Ritchie (ed.), Second Language Acquisition Research. pp. 157-174. Academic Press, New York.

Klima, E. S., and Bellugi, U. 1966. Syntactic regularities in the speech of children. In: J. Lyons, and R. Wales (eds.), Psycholinguistic Papers. pp. 183–239. Edinburgh University Press, Edinburgh.
Krashen, S. D., Sferlazza, V., and Feldman, L. 1976. Adult performance on the SLOPE test: More evidence for a natural sequence in adult second language acquisition. Lang. Learn. 26:145–151.
Krzeszowski, T. 1971. Equivalence, congruence, and deep structure. In: G. Nickel (ed.), Papers in Contrastive Linguistics. pp. 37–48. Cambridge University Press, Cambridge, England.
Lado, R. 1957. Linguistics across Cultures. University of Michigan Press. Ann Arbor.
Larsen, D. E. 1975. The acquisition of grammatical morphemes by adult learners of English as a second language. Unpublished doctoral dissertation, University of Michigan, Ann Arbor.
Larsen-Freeman, D. E. 1978. An explanation for the morpheme accuracy order of learners of English as a second language. In: E. M. Hatch (ed.), Second Language Acquisition. pp. 371–379. Newbury House, Rowley, Mass.
LoCoco, V. G-M. 1976. A cross-sectional study on L_3 acquisition. Working Papers on Bilingualism 9:44–75.
McLaughlin, B. 1977. Second-language learning in children. Psycholog. Bull. 84:438–459.
Milon, J. 1974. The development of negation in English by a second language learner. TESOL Q. 8:137–143.
Nemser, W. 1971. Approximative systems of foreign language learners. IRAL 9:115–124.
Newmark, L., and Reibel, D. 1968. Necessity and insufficiency in language learning. IRAL 6:145–164.
Nickel, G. 1971. Contrastive linguistics and foreign-language teaching. In: G. Nickel (ed.), Papers in Contrastive Linguistics. Cambridge University Press, Cambridge, England.
Nickel, G., and Wagner, K. H. 1968. Contrastive linguistics and language learning. IRAL 6:233–256.
Oller, J. W. 1972. Contrastive analysis, difficulty, and predictability. Foreign Lang. Ann. 6:95–106.
Oyama, S. 1976. A sensitive period for the acquisition of a nonnative phonological system. J. Psycholing. Res. 5:261–284.
Porter, J. 1977. A cross-sectional study of morpheme acquisition in first language learners. Lang. Learn. 27:47–62.
Ramirez, A. G., and Politzer, R. L. 1978. Comprehension and production in English as a second language by elementary school children and adolescents. In: E. M. Hatch (ed.), Second Language Acquisition. pp. 313–332. Newbury House Publishers, Rowley, Mass.
Raven, R. 1968. Language acquisition in a second language environment. IRAL 6:175–185.
Richards, J. 1971. A non-contrastive approach to error analysis. Engl. Lang. Teach. 25:204–219.
Rivers, W. M. 1968. Contrastive linguistics in textbook and classroom. In: J. E. Alatis (ed.), Report of the Nineteenth Annual Round Table Meeting on Lin-

guistics and Language Studies. pp. 151–158. Georgetown University Press, Washington, D.C.
Rosansky, E. J. 1976. Methods and morphemes in second language acquisition research. Lang. Learn. 26:409–425.
Schachter, J. 1974. An error in error analysis. Lang. Learn. 24:205–214.
Schachter, J., and Celce-Murcia, M. 1977. Some reservations concerning error analysis. TESOL Q. 11:441–451.
Schumann, J. 1976. Second language acquisition: The pidginization hypothesis. Lang. Learn. 26:391–408.
Selinker, L. F. 1972. Interlanguage: IRAL 10:209–231.
Sey, K. 1973. Ghanaian English. MacMillan, London.
Snow, C. E., and Hoefnagel-Höhle, M. 1978a. Age differences in second language acquisition. In: E. M. Hatch (ed.), Second Language Acquisition. pp. 333–344. Newbury House Publishers, Rowley, Mass.
Snow, C. E., and Hoefnagel-Höhle, M. 1978b. The critical period for language acquisition: Evidence from second language learning. Child Dev. 49:1263–1279.
Sridhar, S. N. 1980. Contrastive analysis, error analysis, and interlanguage: Three phases of one goal? In: K. Croft (ed.), Readings in English as a Second Language. Winthrop, New York.
Stockwell, R. P., and Bowen, J. D. 1965. The Sounds of English and Spanish. University of Chicago Press, Chicago.
Stockwell, R., Bowen, J., and Martin, J. 1965. The Grammatical Structures of English and Spanish. University of Chicago Press, Chicago.
Strevens, P. 1969. Two ways of looking at error analysis. ERIC Document Reproduction Service No. ED 037 714.
Tarone, E., Cohen, A. D., and Dumas, G. 1976. A closer look at some interlanguage terminology: A framework for communication strategies. Working Papers on Bilingualism 9:77–89.
Tarone, E., Frauenfelder, U., and Selinker, L. 1975. Systematicity/variability and stability/instability in interlanguage systems. In: H. D. Brown (ed.), Papers in Second Language Acquisition, Proceedings of the Sixth Annual Conference on Applied Linguistics. pp. 112–127.
Taylor, B. P. 1974. Toward a theory of language acquisition. Lang. Learn. 24:23–35.
Taylor, B. P. 1975. The use of overgeneralization and transfer learning strategies by elementary and intermediate students of ESL. Lang. Learn. 25:73–107.
Wagner-Gough, J. 1975. Comparative studies in second language learning. CAL-ERIC/CU Series on Languages and Linguistics. 26.
Wardhaugh, R. 1970. The contrastive analysis hypothesis. TESOL Q. 4:123–129.
Whitman, R. L. 1970. Contrastive analysis: Problems and procedures. Lang. Learn. 20:191–197.
Wilkins, D. A. 1968. Review of A. Valdman (ed.), Trends in Language Teaching. IRAL 6:99–107.
Wode, H. 1978. Developmental sequences in naturalistic L_2 acquisition. In: E. M. Hatch (ed.), Second Language Acquisition. pp. 101–117. Newbury House Publishers, Rowley, Mass.

chapter four

Considerations in Phonological Assessment

Janet I. Anderson

The language specialist in the field of speech-language pathology, bilingual education, or English as a Second Language (ESL), may be called upon to assess the bilingual child's phonological production. In order to do so effectively, one must have an understanding of relevant phonological research from the fields of first language acquisition and second language acquisition. When testing for articulation disorders in the child's dominant language it is necessary to know the normal developmental sequences of the sounds being tested and the ages at which they are likely to appear. It is also necessary to understand the variety of substitution and deletion errors children normally make before they finally achieve mastery of the phonological system. Testing for phonological proficiency in the second language, on the other hand, requires knowledge about second language acquisition, and the extent to which phonological interference from the first language can occur.

Therefore, the purpose of this chapter is to review research on phonological development from the fields of first and second language acquisition, and to demonstrate its relevance to phonological assessment of the bilingual child. Since this chapter requires a knowledge of phonology, the first part of the chapter gives the reader a brief introduction to the study of sound systems of languages and a definition of some terms.

While it is accepted that bilingual education in the United States is conducted in a variety of languages, it is not within the scope of this chapter to review phonological systems of all these languages and potential problems of all the second language learners concerned. Rather, this chapter discusses the issues in a more general sense, using examples from several languages to demonstrate the problems involved. Examples in this chapter are drawn mainly from English, Spanish, French, German, Dutch, and Japanese.

THE STUDY OF SOUND SYSTEMS OF LANGUAGES

Phonetics

Phonetics involves the description of sounds in either *acoustic* terms, which indicate the nature of sound waves, or in *articulatory* terms, which indicate how sounds are produced by the vocal apparatus. A notation system based on articulatory phonetics is used when transcribing the sounds of a language. In this system consonants are described in a single framework according to the *place* and *manner* of articulation, and *voicing*. The notation system used in this chapter is an adaptation of The International Phonetic Alphabet (International Phonetic Association, 1949).

The *place* of articulation is the point at which maximum obstruction occurs during production. Two articulators are involved, such as the lips in *bilabial* consonants (e.g., [p], [b], [m]), or the back of the tongue and soft palate in *velar* consonants (e.g., [k], [g]). At most places of articulation there are several possible *manners* of articulation, or ways in which the articulators operate. For example, if the articulators momentarily cut off the stream of air the manner is referred to as *stop* (e.g., [p], [b], [t], [d], [k], [g]). If the articulators closely approximate each other without cutting off the flow of turbulent air, the manner is known as *fricative* (e.g., [f], [v], [s], [z]).

Voicing refers to the activity of the vocal cords during articulation. If they are vibrating the sound is said to be *voiced* (e.g., [b], [d], [g], [v], [z]); if the vocal cords are stationary the sound is said to be *voiceless* (e.g., [p], [t], [k], [f], [s]). Using the parameters of place, manner, and voicing one can describe the consonants of any language in articulatory terms. For example, the English consonant [b] is described phonetically as a voiced bilabial stop, and [f] is described as a voiceless labio-dental fricative. See Table 1 for a chart of English consonants based on articulatory phonetics.

Vowels, sounds that involve much less obstruction than consonants, are specified in terms of the position of the tongue and lips. The position of the tongue is described along vertical and horizontal axes, and the lips are described according to whether or not they are rounded. The English vowel [u], for example, is high, back, and round. Figure 1 illustrates the English vowels according to their tongue position during articulation.

In addition to these frameworks of description for consonants and vowels, diacritical marks are used to further specify a sound. For example, the diacritic [~] indicates nasalization (Ladefoged, 1975).

Table 1. Chart of English consonants[a]

Manner of articulation	Place of articulation							
	Bilabial	Labio-dental	Dental	Alveolar	Palato-alveolar	Palatal	Velar	Glottal
Stop	p b			t d			k g	
Affricate							tʃ dʒ	
Fricative		f v	θ ð	s z	ʃ ʒ			h
Nasal	m			n				
Liquid				l		r		
Semiconsonant glide						j	w	

[a] Whenever there are two sounds in a cell, the sound on the left represents a voiceless sound and the one on the right a voiced sound. (Examples: [θ] as in think; [ð] as in that; [ʃ] as in show; [ʒ] as in pleasure; [tʃ] as in cheap; [dʒ] as in jewel; [ŋ] as in sing.) All other sounds are voiced except /h/ which is voiceless.

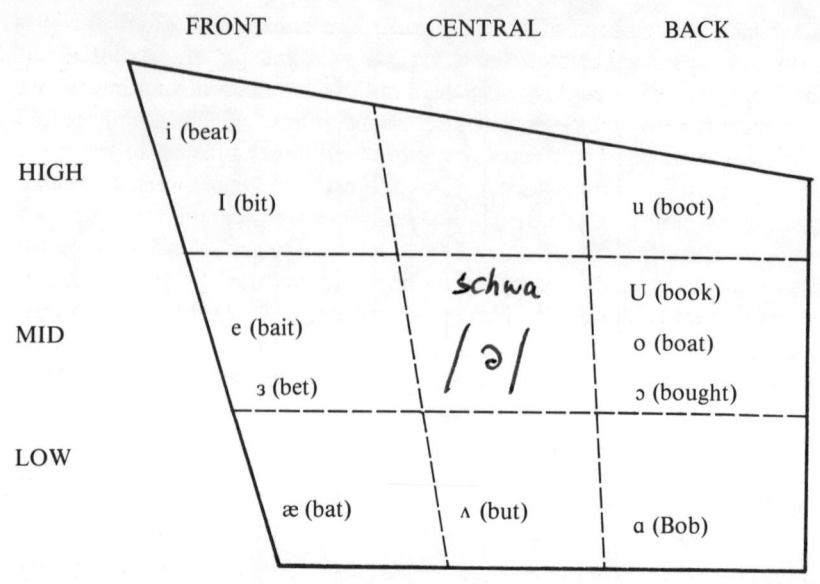

```
                    FRONT           CENTRAL          BACK

         i (beat)
HIGH
            I (bit)                              u (boot)
         ─────────────              schwa        ─────────
                                                 U (book)
MID         e (bait)                 /ə/         o (boat)
            ɜ (bet)                              ɔ (bought)
         ─────────────                           ─────────
LOW
            æ (bat)          ʌ (but)             ɑ (Bob)
```

Figure 1. Charts of English vowels. Examples in conventional orthography are presented in parentheses. The chart does not take into account dialectal variants.

Phonological Analysis

While phonetics is concerned primarily with the description of sounds, phonology is concerned with their distribution and function. One of the first steps in a phonological analysis is to identify the *phonemes*, which are the minimal functional units of sound that signal meaning. The next step is to identify the *allophones*, or variants of the phonemes. (Phonemes are always indicated by slashes, / /, and allophones by brackets, [ ].) To determine whether sounds have phonemic or allophonic status their distribution is studied. If two sounds occur in the same phonetic environment and signal different meanings, they are said to be distinct phonemes. This is illustrated in the following pairs of words:

/pɪn : bɪn/   /fæt : væt/   /kɔl : gɔl/
(pin : bin)   (fat : vat)   (call : gall)

When two sounds are differentiated on the basis of their occurrence in these minimal pairs they are in *contrastive distribution*.

Allophones, on the other hand, are characterized by *complementary distribution*, which means that they never occur in the same phonetic environments. The English phoneme /p/, for example, has two allophones, an aspirated [pʰ], pronounced with a puff of air, and an unaspirated [p⁼] pronounced without the puff. The unaspirated allophone [p⁼] occurs in consonant clusters following /s/ as in *spit* [sp⁼ɪt], in medial and final clusters before another stop as in *opt* [ɑp⁼t], and when not initial and preceding a weak stressed vowel as in chapel [tʃæp⁼əl] The allophone [pʰ] occurs in most other environments, but never in any of those in which the allophone [p⁼] occurs (Gleason, 1961). The difference between these allophones can best be illustrated by holding a piece of paper up to the mouth while pronouncing *pit*, [pʰɪt], and *spit*, [sp⁼ɪt]. The puff of air in the [pʰ] in *pit* will cause the paper to move, while the unaspirated [p⁼] in *spit* causes no movement of the paper. The native speaker of English does not differentiate between these two allophones; they are perceived as the same sound. Phonemes, on the other hand, are considered distinct sounds.

In a phonological description of a language, the phonologist attempts to identify the factors that account for phonetic variation. When these factors are determined, the phonologist writes rules that state the phonetic changes and the environments in which they occur.

Phonological changes are categorized into major processes such as *assimilation*, in which a segment takes on features of a neighboring segment. A consonant may pick up a feature of another consonant or vowel, or vowels might influence surrounding sounds. Another category is *syllable structure*, in which there is an alteration of the distribution of consonants and vowels within the word (Schane, 1973).

Distinctive Features

Sound segments in distinctive feature notation are analyzed by using sets of properties known as features. The same set of features is used to describe all of the segments of a language, and the value for each feature is expressed in binary (±) terms. Thus, segments can be easily examined for differences and similarities. For example, the stop /t/ and the affricate /tʃ/ in English are distinguished from each other by the features of [strident] and [delayed release]. This is illustrated in the distinctive feature matrix in Table 2. In the matrix, an entry where a column and row intersect illustrates whether the phoneme indicated by the column possesses the features indicated by the row (Schane, 1973).

Suprasegmental Phonology

As well as analyzing the segmental phonemes discussed above, one can also analyze the suprasegmental features of stress, intonation, and juncture. *Stress* refers to the relative prominence of syllables, while *intonation*, or pitch, refers to the highness or lowness of tone. *Juncture* refers to certain features that signal phrasing. In addition, every language has its

Table 2. A distinctive feacture matrix of the English consonant phonemes /t/ and /tʃ/

Features	/t/	/tʃ/
Sonorant	−	−
Consonantal	+	+
Continuant	−	−
Delayed release	−	+
Strident	−	+

Adapted from Schane, 1973, p. 29.

own *rhythm*, which is the relationship that stress, intonation, and juncture have with vowels and consonants. Units of rhythm may differ from one language to another. For example, in English, the unit of rhythm is the stress group while in Spanish it is the syllable (Stockwell and Bowen, 1965).

FIRST LANGUAGE ACQUISITION

This section reviews research that is relevant to phonological assessment in the child's first or dominant language. Developmental trends and dialect variation in English are discussed, followed by a brief review of some English articulation tests. Then language development and articulation testing in the Spanish dominant bilingual child are considered.

Developmental Sequences in English

Sander (1972) discusses some of the problems of identifying developmental sequences of consonants and determining the ages at which they are learned. When using group data from articulation tests to determine consonant sequences, an acquisition criterion must be chosen for consonants along with a group percentage criterion. In Sander's analysis, he used data from several different sources that varied in the acquisition criteria and test items.

There are several possible criteria for determining when a sound is acquired. A sound is usually considered to be acquired when a child produces it correctly in three different positions in a word: initial, medial, and final. However, there are other ways of determining acquisition, some which are more stringent, and some which are less stringent. A more stringent criterion would be one that required the child to produce the consonant in various phonetic contexts, including consonant blends. Less stringent criteria would be 1) the age at which a sound first appears, 2) the earliest age at which the child uses the sound correctly in words, or

3) the age of customary production, which is the age when a child produces a sound correctly more often that he or she misarticulates it (e.g., the child can produce the sound in two out of three word positions correctly).

In addition, a decision must be made about the group percentage criterion used, because developmental sequences and ages at which the sounds appear will vary according to the criterion used. For example, if a 50% group criterion is used, the acquisition age assigned to the consonant /s/ is age 3, but if a 90% group criterion is used, the age of acquisition moves up to age 8. This illustrates the high degree of variation in the reported ages at which children acquire consonants, with the variance related to criteria and test items used as well as individual differences.

Sander attempts to deal with these problems by using customary production as the performance criterion and by assigning an age range instead of one acquisition age to each consonant. Sander feels that a more stringent performance criterion would push acquisition ages up considerably higher and would not reflect average performance. In addition, he feels that the age range captures the fact that there is a great deal of variation in acquisition ages among children. Table 3 summarizes the

Table 3. Average age estimates and upper age boundaries of customary consonant productions

English consonant phonemes	Age range (years; months)[a]
/p/ /m/ /h/ /n/ /w/	1;6–3;0
/b/	1;6–4;0
/k/ /g/ /d/	2;0–4;0
/t/ /ŋ/	2;0–6;0
/f/ /j/	2;6–4;0
/r/ /l/	3;0–6;0
/s/	3;0–8;0
/tʃ/ /ʃ/	3;6–7;0
/z/	3;6–8;0
/dʒ/	4;0–7;0
/v/	4;0–8;0
/θ/	4;6–7;0
/ð/	5;0–8;0
/ʒ/	6;0–8;0

Adapted from Sander, 1972, p. 62.

[a] The first figure in the age range column represents the median age of customary articulation; the second figure represents the age when 90% of all children are customarily producing the sound.

average age and the upper age limit of customary production of the English consonants. Some consonants show wider age ranges than others. For example, the age range for the /f/ and /j/ is only 1½ years, while the /s/ shows a range of 5 years.

These age limits provide the language specialist with expectations of normal performance that are helpful in determining 1) whether or not the child's phonological development is delayed, and 2) whether or not therapy is indicated. In addition to having expectations about developmental sequences, the language specialist also needs to have an understanding of the kinds of errors a child is likely to make and the phonological processes underlying them.

Phonological Processes

Oller (1974) argues that phonological processes found in early child language development result in simplifying the task of speaking. The processes he discusses, which have been found in both normal and abnormal child language, are broken down into four categories: 1) consonant cluster simplification, 2) final consonant deletion, 3) assimilation, and 4) substitution.

Cluster simplification means the deletion of at least one consonant in a cluster, whether at the beginning or at the end of a word. For example, the word *stepped* /stɛpt/, might be pronounced [tɛp] as a result of /s/ deletion in the initial cluster and /t/ deletion in the final cluster. Final consonant deletion means dropping a final single consonant. An example of this is the deletion of the final /t/ in *bat* /bæt/, which would be pronounced [bæ]. Assimilation occurs when one sound takes on the characteristics of another sound. In the word *duck* /dʌk/, the initial /d/ may take on the velar feature of the final consonant to be pronounced [gʌk].Substitution includes such processes as the substitution of glides for liquids. An example of this is the replacement of /r/ by /w/ in *rabbit* /ræbɪt/,producing [wæbɪt], which is a frequently heard error in child speech.

An understanding of phonological processes in child language should help the language specialist recognize that articulation errors are often evidence of underlying phonological patterns, rather than indications of articulation difficulty with isolated phonemes. For example, the misarticulation of /d/ in *duck* in the example cited above is not evidence that the child has difficulty with the /d/ sound so much as it is evidence of velar assimilation. In other phonetic contexts the child may articulate the /d/ correctly (Hodson, personal communication, 1979).

A more complete discussion of the processes in normal phonological development can be found in studies that describe the child's acquisition of distinctive features and the development of phonological rules (Hodson, 1975; Menn, 1976; Blache, 1978).

Dialectal Considerations

Certain varieties of English differ to a greater extent from Standard American English than do other varieties. One such variety is Black English. Labov (1972) argues that Black English should not be viewed as a deviant form of Standard English, but rather as a complete linguistic system of its own, with its own set of phonological and syntactic rules.

Some of the major phonological differences that Labov has identified follow:

1. There is a tendency to delete /r/ when it occurs postvocalically. For example, *guard* /gɑrd/ is pronounced [gɑd]. In some regional dialects of Black English there is an additional tendency to affricate /tr/ so that it is pronounced /tʃ/.
2. There is a tendency to delete postvocalic /l/. Thus, *toll* /tol/ would be pronounced [to].
3. There is simplification of consonant clusters at the ends of words, especially those ending in /t/, /d/, /s/, or /z/. Thus, *past*/pæst/, would be pronounced [pæs], *rift* /rɪft/ as [rɪf], and *hold* /hold/ as [hol].
4. There is weakening of final consonants. Thus /d/ is pronounced as [t], and in some cases the consonant may be deleted.
5. Final /θ/ and /f/ merge. Thus, *with* /wɪθ/ is pronounced [wɪf].

The language specialist conducting a phonological assessment must realize that, although these forms are not an acceptable pattern for Standard English, they are normal with reference to Black English. Later in this chapter similar points are made regarding dialect differences of other languages and second language learners. Specialists must be careful not to confuse articulation disorders with dialectal variation, for to prescribe speech therapy for dialectal variation is to deny the child his or her own language.

English Articulation Tests

Speech-language clinicians use screening tests to identify efficiently communication impairments in large groups of children. In-depth testing, on the other hand, is done for the purpose of 1) confirming a phonological delay or disorder and 2) planning an appropriate intervention program. English articulation tests may either determine articulation accuracy of phonemes or test for phonological processes. Phoneme articulation tests are usually discrete point tests that test for articulation accuracy of consonants in initial, medial, and/or final position in words. There are various methods of elicitation: imitation, picture naming, sentence reading, or techniques that elicit spontaneous production. In most tests there are subtests that use different elicitation devices. A quantitative score is given for the test based on correct responses. The score is then compared to test norms to determine whether the child's performance is normal for his or her age. Test results may also be examined for the kinds of misarticulations the child demonstrates.

Examples of frequently used tests are the Arizona Articulation Proficiency Scale (Barker-Fudala, 1970), the Fisher-Logemann Test of Articulation (1971), the Goldman-Fristoe Test of Articulation (1972), and the Templin-Darley Test of Articulation (1960). All of these tests use picture naming as a method of eliciting a speech sample. The Arizona, Fisher-Logemann, and Templin-Darley tests also contain a sentence-reading subtest. The Goldman-Fristoe differs in that it has a test that elicits spontaneous connected speech. In this test the child is required to retell a story that the examiner has told using pictures as stimuli, so that there is some control over the words the child will use. This kind of test is preferable to the sentence-reading test for young children because it avoids the difficulties some children might have in reading. In addition, the child's articulation in spontaneous speech may not be as careful as it is in reading; therefore, a higher percentage of errors are more likely to appear spontaneously.

All of the test manuals include age norms so that there is some basis for comparison of the child being tested with the norms provided for that particular test. In addition, the Templin-Darley provides data for groups classified according to upper and lower socioeconomic status. The Fisher-Logemann booklet contains a section with descriptive information on the various dialects of American English. Separate sets of age norms, however, are not available in any of the test manuals for Black English–speaking children or English-dominant Puerto Rican and Mexican-American children. Such norms are necessary in order to avoid confusion between articulation disorders and dialectal variation.

Recently, articulation tests have been developed that attempt to identify phonological processes rather than simply identifying misarticulations of discrete phonemes. Phonological Process Analysis (Weiner, 1979) is not a test so much as it is a means of eliciting speech patterns of children with communication disorders. It is especially useful in assessing the speech of the unintelligible child between the ages of 2 and 5. There are three basic categories of phonological processes the instrument is designed to elicit: 1) syllable structure processes (e.g., weak syllable deletion), 2) harmony processes (e.g., labial assimilation), and 3) feature contrast processes (e.g., stopping of fricatives). Pictures are used as stimuli for eliciting responses which are then phonetically transcribed by the examiner. The results are analyzed to determine whether any of the three categories of phonological processes is present in a child's speech. The test provides valuable diagnostic and prognostic information which can aid the clinician in planning a remediation program. Hodson (personal communication, 1979) has also developed a screening and in-depth test of phonological processes which is currently being validated.

Developmental Sequences in Spanish

While information on phonological development in languages other than English is not readily available, longitudinal case studies on children acquiring other languages offer a source from which the language specialist can gain information about phonological development. One such study offering insights into the development of Spanish phonology was conducted by Fantini (1974). He reports on a longitudinal study of his own child, Mario, learning Spanish and English. Mario's mother was a native speaker of Bolivian Spanish and the father a native speaker of American English who was also fluent in Spanish. Mario's Spanish preceded his English by 1 year because in the early stages of his linguistic development he was exposed almost exclusively to Spanish. His Spanish development is summarized below, while his English development is reported later in the discussion on second language acquisition.

By 2 years of age, Mario had acquired all of the Spanish vowel phonemes and most of the Spanish consonant phonemes. He had also learned the allophones of all the stop consonants: /b/—[b], [β]; /d/—[d], [ð];and /g/—[g], [ɣ]. The first allophones in these pairs are the stops that have the widest distribution. The second allophones are the voiced fricatives that only appear intervocalically, and sometimes at the ends of words. Their place of articulation is identical to that of their corresponding stops; they differ only in their manner of articulation, which is fricative.

Later in acquisition were the consonants /x/, as in the first consonant of *jugar* (to play), /n/ as in the medial consonant in *baño* (bath), the flap /r/ as in the middle consonant of *caro* (expensive), the trilled /rr/ as in *carro* (cart), and the /f/ as in *flor* (flower). The trill appeared suddenly at 4 years 11 months and for 2 months Mario used it wherever either a flap or a trill was needed. By 5 years 1 month he mastered the distinction between the flap and the trill, but it was found that occasionally he would lose control of the trilled /rr/ and would substitute [x] for it initially and medially. For example, the words *rojo* (red) and *carro* were pronounced [xoxo] and [kaxo], respectively, thus resembling certain dialects of Spanish.

Although the Fantini study throws light on one child's acquisition of Bolivian Spanish, it should not be used as a standard for measuring the phonological development of Spanish-speaking children in general. Developmental norms on phoneme sequences, such as the English consonant norms presented by Sander (1972) above, have yet to be developed in Spanish. Without them it is difficult to determine accurately whether or not the development of a particular sound is delayed.

The dialect of the child must also be taken into consideration. In certain dialects of Puerto Rican Spanish, for example, postvocalic /s/ is often pronounced as [h] and syllable-final /ɚ/ is pronounced as [l]. Also, the trilled /rr/ is sometimes replaced by the velar or uvular [R]. In addition, there is a tendency to delete /s/ at the end of a word (Dalbor, 1969).

Testing for Articulation Disorders in the Spanish Dominant Child

While there are a variety of tests in English that determine articulation disorders, such tests are not readily available in other languages. The only easily available test in Spanish is the Austin Spanish Articulation Test (1976) which determines the articulatory accuracy of Spanish consonants, which are tested in initial, medial, and final positions. It also tests for accuracy of the Spanish vowels, diphthongs, and the major consonant clusters. After the examiner reads a stimulus sentence with a word omitted at the end, the child names the picture/completes the sentence.

The test has content validity in that it surveys the phonemic system of Spanish. However, the interpretation of test scores is difficult because normative age values are not available. Hence, the examiner has no basis upon which to compare the performance of the children being tested. Furthermore, the problem of dialect variation is not adequately treated. Ideally, the assessment of a Spanish-speaking child's phonology should not be conducted without reference to developmental norms in the dialect of the child. For example, norms on Spanish-speaking children from the southwestern United States would not be appropriate for a Puerto Rican or Cuban Spanish dominant child, and vice-versa. In addition, the reliability information reported in the test manual is not based on articulation performance but only on the ability of the subject to name the pictures. Without information on normative age values and dialect variation, the language specialist must use other resources, such as a native speaker of the child's dialect, to help identify any deviance in phonological performance. The dearth of readily available resources for testing the first language of Spanish-speaking children in this country is obvious.

SECOND LANGUAGE ACQUISITION

There are two assumptions rather widely held by language specialists concerned with the bilingual child's phonological development that need to be examined in the light of recent research in second language acquisition. The first assumption is that errors in the second language (target language) can be predicted on the basis of comparison with the native language. This assumption has led some language specialists to believe that the errors on an articulation test of a child who is learning English as a second language can be understood in light of the child's dominant or first language phonology. For example, in the Fisher-Logemann Test of Articulation Competence Manual (1972) information on foreign language phonemes is presented so that they can be used by the examiner to interpret articulation test results.

The second widely held assumption is that children have relatively little difficulty learning the phonology of a second language compared to the much greater difficulty that adolescents or adults have. This assumption is related to the "critical period" hypothesis (Lenneberg, 1967), which is discussed later in this chapter and has important implications for the education of the bilingual child. If phonological development is not considered a problem, then it will probably not play an important role in the curriculum. On the other hand, if it is considered a problem, part of the curriculum may focus on "correcting" a child's phonological usage.

The problems of acquiring the phonology of a second language and their relevance to these assumptions are discussed below. First, a review of theories of second language acquisition is presented. This is followed by a discussion of phonological research conducted in the areas of bilingualism and second language acquisition.

Theories

Scholars in the field of second language acquisition have concerned themselves with such issues as the role of the native language in second language learning, the similarities between first and second language acquisition, and the optimum age for acquiring a second language. (For an in-depth discussion on contrastive and error analysis as it relates to syntax and semantics see Locke, Chapter 3, this volume). The contrastive analysis (CA) hypothesis (Lado, 1957) holds that the learner's first language serves as a filter through which the second language is learned. This hypothesis predicts that sounds in the second language that have equivalents in the native language will be learned first. On the other hand, sounds that do not have correspondences in the native language will be more difficult and hence acquired later. In addition, it is held that a systematic point-by-point comparison of the two languages in question can predict the kinds of errors that the second language learner will make. Errors that reflect the native language are called *transfer* errors.

Stockwell and Bowen (1965) have written a contrastive analysis of the phonological systems of Spanish and English that includes a comparison of the consonants, vowels, and suprasegmental systems of the two languages. Assuming that certain kinds of contrasts would be more difficult than others, they developed a hierarchy of difficulty that predicts the phonological problems a native speaker of American English would have in learning Spanish. In their hierarchy of difficulty, they considered whether the sounds in the two languages were obligatory, optional, or zero. The term *obligatory* refers to allophones; *optional* refers to phonemes; *zero* to the absence of a sound. They identified eight categories of difficulty based on the various kinds of sound correspondences in the two languages using these labels.

The easiest category is a sound that has phoneme status in both languages (*optional:optional* category). An example of this would be the /m/, which occurs in both languages as a phoneme. The most difficult category was a sound that does not occur in the native language but that occurs in the target language as an allophone (*zero:obligatory* category). An example of this for the native speaker of English learning Spanish would be the fricative [β] allophone of the /b/ phoneme. Although the Stockwell and Bowen work represents one of the best contrastive analyses written to date, their hierarchy of difficulty has not yet been rigorously tested.

Wardhaugh (1970) rejects a strong version of the Contrastive Analysis hypothesis because he feels that it is not as good a predictor as previously thought, for it has been found that many errors cannot be attributed to the native language of the learner. He does feel, however, that contrastive analysis is a useful resource in trying to determine the source of some of the errors. This a posteriori approach to second language learning has served as the basis for the use of *error analysis* (EA), which involves the classification of errors and an investigation of their sources. Second language learner errors in English have been found that are similar to the kinds of errors children make in learning English as a first language. These errors have been termed *developmental* or *overgeneralization* errors (Dušková, 1969; Richards, 1971).

The findings from error analysis gave rise to other views of second language acquisition: the first language acquisition/second language ($L_1 = L_2$) hypothesis and the interlanguage hypothesis. The $L_1 = L_2$ hypothesis holds that the native language of the learner has very little influence on the way in which the second language is learned. It is assumed instead that the second language learner encounters many of the same problems that a native speaker does during first language acquisition. Thus, errors for first and second language acquisition will be similar (Corder, 1967; Dulay and Burt, 1974). The interlanguage hypothesis (Selinker, 1972), on the other hand, allows for influences from both languages. This view holds that the learner's second language development consists of a progression of developmental states which are systematic and which demonstrate influence from the learner's native language. In addition, there are difficulties due to the target language itself which give rise to overgeneralization errors. The theory implies that speakers of different languages will have different interlanguage systems when learning English; for example, a Spanish-English interlanguage system will differ from a Japanese-English system. Yet, an interlanguage system cannot be predicted from contrastive analysis alone.

Researchers have also been concerned with the optimum age for learning a foreign language. There are various views on this question. Lenneberg (1967) argues that there is a critical period of language acquisition which occurs around puberty (age 12+). At this critical time, Lenneberg theorizes that language function becomes restricted to the left hemisphere. This specialization of the brain for language function is called *lateralization*. After lateralization occurs, language learning ability drastically declines, which accounts for the apparent difficulty adults have in learning the phonology of a second language. However, this "critical age" view has been disputed. Krashen (1973) has shown that lateralization occurs much earlier, so that if there is a critical period for language learning at puberty it would have to be attributed to other factors. In addition, the view that adults are not as successful as children at second language learning has also been questioned. Macnamara (1973) suggests that adults might prove superior if given the same naturalistic learning environment in which children usually acquire second languages.

Research on Phonological Development in a Second Language

The research reported here is addressed to some of the questions posed above. For the purposes of this chapter only research findings related to phonological development are reported, although some of the studies included findings on syntax and morphology. First, a study by Snow and Hoefnagel-Höhle (1978) on age differences is reviewed. This is followed by a review of three case studies on phonological development of bilingual children (Leopold, 1954; Fantini, 1974; Celce-Murcia, 1978). Finally, a longitudinal study on adult second language learners' acquisition of English phonology is discussed (Dickerson, 1974).

Snow and Hoefnagel-Höhle (1978) studied age differences in second language learning. Their subjects, 69 native speakers of English, were learning Dutch while in Holland. There were both a beginner and an advanced group of subjects, each consisting of five age-divided subgroups. The complete age range tested was from 3 years to adult. The subjects were tested three times at 4½-month intervals to measure progress in the acquisition of Dutch. The results on phonology revealed only marginal age differences. The adults in the beginning group scored significantly higher on phonological production than the younger subjects, but these differences disappeared at the second testing. There was no significant difference on phonological production for any of the age subgroups in the advanced learners. It was also found that none of the advanced learners had achieved perfect, native-like pronunciation. The findings on age differences clearly do not support the critical age hypothesis.

Case studies on bilingual development have been conducted by various researchers who have kept diaries of language development on their own children. These studies are of interest because they investigate the question of how bilingualism develops and whether the phonological systems of the two languages interfere with each other.

Leopold (1954) conducted a study of his daughter Hilda's simultaneous acquisition of German and English. He found that during the first 2 years of life Hilda combined the two languages models into one speech form. For example, the child used the same allophones of the phoneme /l/ for both languages. However, during her third year, she began to become conscious of her bilingualism and soon began to separate the phonemes of English from the phonemes of German.

Celce-Murcia (1978) reports on the language development of her child, Caroline, who acquired English and French concurrently. The data in her study were collected during a 2-month period, from the time the child was 2 years, 2 months until she was 2 years, 4 months. In summarizing phonological difficulties, Celce-Murcia notes a tendency for Caroline to confuse French/English cognates such as *bus*, alternating between her French pronunciation [bys] and her incorrect English pronunciation of /bʌs/ as [bɑs]. She also observed a tendency for Caroline to avoid phonologically difficult words in both languages. If Caroline knew the French and English equivalents for a word that was more difficult phonologically in one language, she would use the easier form no matter which language she was speaking. For example, she avoided *butterfly* in favor of the French equivalent *papillon*, although she had been exposed to the word in both languages. Whether this tendency continued is not known, since the study was terminated when the child was 2 years, 4 months.

Fantini's study (1974) on his bilingual child, Mario, is representative of the case in which development of one language precedes the other. Instead of learning both languages simultaneously, Mario did not begin to learn English until 1 year after his Spanish began to develop (see above). It was observed that his early stages of English development demonstrated considerable phonological interference. Mario would substitute English vowels with the nearest Spanish equivalent. For, example, /ɛ/ was pronounced [e] or [i], /ɪ/ was pronounced as [i], /æ/ was pronounced as [ɑ], and /ʊ/ as [u]. He also substituted consonants with the nearest Spanish equivalent: /dʒ/ was pronounced as [tʃ], /ð/ as [t] or [d], /h/ as [x], /v/ as [f], and /ʃ/ as [s]. However, it should be noted that the /æ/, /dʒ/, /ð/, /v/, and /ʃ/ are also difficult for the monolingual English-speaking child (Leopold, 1954; Sander, 1972) so that their misarticulation cannot be unambiguously attributed to interference from Spanish.

Within a year after Mario began to speak English, he had mastered the entire phonemic inventory of English except the interdental fricatives, /ð/ and /θ/. At 5 years, 8 months, he was still substituting /ð/ with [t] and [d], and /θ/ with [f] and [s]. The substitutions varied according to phonetic environment. In spite of Mario's mastery of English phonemes, he continued to have some difficulty with allophones, which gave his speech a foreign quality.

The only longitudinal study to date on the acquisition of the phonology of a second language by adults has been conducted by Dickerson (1974). Her study, which was an application of Labov's (1972) model of sound change to second language acquisition, investigated the variability of the production of five English phonemes by 10 native speakers of Japanese over a 9-month period. She found that the subjects in her study made a variety of substitution errors (*variants*) for each

English phoneme that she investigated, only some of which were predicted by a contrastive analysis of Japanese and English. For example, the variants her subjects used for the phoneme /ð/ were [z], [dz], [d], and [dð]. The variants [z] and [dz] could be traced to Japanese, but the [d] and [dð] more closely resembled the target phoneme /ð/. She found a higher percentage of the Japanese-like variants at the beginning or the 9-month period than she did at the end of the study when learners were using the English-like variants more often.

In addition to finding variation across time, she also found that there was variation according to phonetic environment and social situation. An examination of phonetic environments revealed that there was a higher proportion of the [d] and [dð] in intervocalic position than in other environments. Social situation defined in terms of the formality of the task was also correlated with the proportion of native-like variants. The most formal task, that of reading word lists, produced the highest proportion of native-like variants.

Although contrastive analysis was rejected as a hypothesis that could account for all of the errors, the notion of native language transfer was not completely rejected. She concluded that the learner's output "consists of a variable system—a language which is both systematic and inherently heterogeneous. Furthermore, the system is neither the native language nor the target language; it is something different . . . a fully regular internally unified system" (Dickerson, 1974, p. 6.08). The findings of Dickerson's study support the interlanguage hypothesis, which views second language learning as a progression of evolving systems influenced by both the native language of the learner and the target language.

Although all of the studies reported above indicated some degree of interference from one language to another, Dickerson's (1974) study of adults, which rigorously tested the contrastive analysis hypothesis, concluded that contrastive analysis is not an accurate predictor of learner errors. Even though she found some evidence for native language interference, there were other errors that could not be traced to the native language.

In view of this research, the assumption that the native language of the learner is an accurate predictor of second language errors is no longer tenable. The acquisition of the phonology of a second language is far more complex than previously thought; there is no simple formula for predicting the second language learner's errors. Furthermore, research in the area of second language phonology has hardly begun, so information on the kinds of errors second language learners from various linguistic backgrounds will produce in their interlanguage phonologies is not available.

The assumption regarding the superior learning ability that children have over adults in acquiring the phonology of a second language should also be seriously questioned. The findings of the Snow and Hoefnagel-Höhle study (1978) demonstrated that there is no significant difference between age groups in learning phonology. Furthermore the Fantini (1974) study indicated that at 5 years, 8 months, even after several years of intensive exposure to English, his child's English still had a foreign quality to it. This research indicates that children as well as adults will have difficulties in acquiring the phonology of a second language.

Testing for Phonological Proficiency in a Second Language

Language tests used in bilingual education are used to determine language dominance, to assess individual achievement, and to assess bilingual program effectiveness. Very often these assessments have not included tests for oral proficiency, and of those that have, phonological proficiency is rarely included.

In a report on tests used in bilingual education projects, the National Consortia for Bilingual Education (1973) listed tests used by Title VII Bilingual Projects across the country. Of the 77 projects reported, only 57% reported using oral tests of any kind, and most of these tests did not contain a phonological subtest.

In a concern for the need to disseminate information on oral proficiency testing, Silverman, Noa, and Russell (1976) evaluated 24 tests that are used to assess the oral proficiency of children in bilingual programs. They found that only five of the tests listed had subtests on phonological proficiency.

An examination of tests that contain a phonology subtest reveal relatively few items that test for phonological proficiency. An example is the Short Test of Linguistic Skills developed by the Chicago Board of Education (1976). The test, designed to evaluate listening, speaking, reading, and writing, has parallel forms in English and 10 other languages. These include Arabic, Chinese, Greek, Italian, Japanese, Korean, Pilipino, Polish, Spanish, and Vietnamese. Of a total of 80 test points, only 10 were assigned to test for phonological problems; of these, five items were designed to test phoneme discrimination in listening and five items tested for phoneme production. Although the test is very good in other respects, too little importance is given to phonology.

The fact that phonological proficiency receives so little attention in testing is an indication that it may not receive adequate attention in school curricula. There is a need to investigate whether or not this is the case, because phonological proficiency, an essential part of verbal communication, should not be ignored.

CONCLUSIONS

In evaluating the phonological production of the bilingual child, the distinction must be made between testing to identify speech disorders and testing to determine second language proficiency to ensure appropriate classroom instruction and placement. In the former case the child's phonological performance is examined from the viewpoint of speech-language pathology, while in the latter case it is examined from the viewpoint of bilingual education.

Assessment for the purpose of identifying speech disorders should always be done in the first, or dominant, language of the child. At present, there are no reliable means to determine whether a child's articulation errors in the second language reflect the child's interlanguage phonology or whether they are evidence of a speech disorder. Consequently, testing for articulation disorders in the second language could result in labeling a normal child as handicapped. In addition, a program of speech therapy might interfere with the child's normal interlanguage development. Therefore, if the clinician suspects that a bilingual child has a speech impairment, the assessment should be conducted in the child's first language so that aberrations in development can be determined more accurately.

Testing in the child's first language, however, often presents problems. First, articulation tests in the various languages spoken by children in the United States often are not available. Second, there is a dearth of information on phonological development in languages other than English, making interpretation of test results difficult. To ensure that bilingual children receive the same quality of evaluation procedures as monolingual English-speaking children receive, articulation tests must be constructed and developmental norms must be determined for the native languages spoken by these children. Until that time the clinician may have to resort to using a native speaker of the child's language to help determine whether there is any disorder present.

There is also a need to develop phonological tests for educational purposes. The brief survey reported above on second language proficiency testing demonstrates that phonology is not evaluated as often as grammar and vocabulary. This apparent lack of concern for phonological proficiency may be a reflection of the widely held assumption that children have little difficulty in learning the phonology of a second language. Since recent research indicates that children do, in fact, encounter phonological difficulties when learning a second language, there should be an effort on the part of educators to develop more tests to explore these difficulties.

Phonological proficiency is the most basic level of communication and may have both social and educational consequences. Therefore, it would be helpful if all professionals involved in assessing the communication of bilingual children assumed the responsibility of improving testing procedures and adding to the needed developmental information for phonologies of languages other than English.

REFERENCES

Austin Spanish Articulation Test. 1976. Learning Concepts. Austin, Tex.
Barker-Fudala, J. 1970. Arizona Articulation Proficiency Scale: Revised. Western Psychological Services, Los Angeles.
Blache, S. E. 1978. The Acquisition of Distinctive Features. University Park Press, Baltimore.
Celce-Murcia, M. 1978. The simultaneous acquisition of English and French in a two year old child. In: E. M. Hatch (ed.), Second Language Acquisition: A Book of Readings. pp. 38–53. Newbury House Publishers, Rowley, Mass.
Corder, S. P. 1967. The significance of learners' errors. IRAL 5:161–169.
Dalbor, J. B. 1969. Spanish Pronunciation: Theory and Practice. Holt, Rinehart, & Winston, New York.
Dickerson, L. J. 1974. Internal and external patterning of phonological variability in the speech of Japanese learners of English: Toward a theory of second language acquisition. Unpublished doctoral dissertation, University of Illinois, Urbana.
Dulay, H. and Burt, M. 1974. A new perspective on the creative construction process in child second language acquisition. Lang. Learn. 24:253–278.
Dušková, L. 1969. On sources of errors in foreign language learning. IRAL 7:11–33.
Fantini, A. E. 1974. Language acquisition of a bilingual child: A sociolinguistic perspective. Unpublished doctoral dissertation, University of Texas, Austin.
Fisher, H. B., and Logemann, J. A. 1971. Fisher-Logemann Test of Articulation Competence. Houghton Mifflin Co., Boston.
Gleason, H. A. 1961. An Introduction to Descriptive Linguistics. Holt, Rinehart & Winston, New York.
Goldman, R., and Fristoe, M. 1972. Goldman-Fristoe Test of Articulation. American Guidance Service, Circle Pines, Minn.
Hodson, B. W. 1975. Aspects of phonological performance in four year olds. Unpublished doctoral dissertation, University of Illinois, Urbana.
International Phonetic Association. 1949. The Principles of the International Phonetic Association. London.

Krashen, S. 1973. Lateralization, language learning and the critical period: Some new evidence. Lang. Learn. 23:63–74.
Labov, W. 1972. Language in the Inner City. University of Pennsylvania Press, Philadelphia.
Ladefoged, P. 1975. A Course in Phonetics. Harcourt Brace Jovanovich, New York.
Lado, R. 1957. Linguistics across Cultures. The University of Michigan Press, Ann Arbor.
Lenneberg, E. 1967. The Biological Foundations of Language. John Wiley & Sons, New York.
Leopold, W. F. 1954. A child's learning of two languages. Georgetown University Round Table on Languages and Linguistics. Georgetown University Press, Washington, D.C.
Macnamara, J. 1973. Nurseries, streets, and classrooms: Some comparisons and deductions. Modern Lang. J. 57:254–258.
Menn, L. 1976. Pattern, control, and contrast in beginning speech: A case study in the development of word form and word function. Unpublished doctoral dissertation, University of Illinois, Urbana.
National Consortia for Bilingual Education. 1973. Tests Used in Bilingual Education Projects. National Consortia for Bilingual Education in Cooperation with Title VII ESEA Bilingual Programs. Fort Worth, Tex.
Oller, D. K. 1974. Simplification as the goal of phonological processes in child speech. Lang. Learn. 24:299–303.
Richards, J. C. 1971. A non-contrastive approach to error analysis. English Lang. Teach. 25:204–219.
Sander, E. K. 1972. When are speech sounds learned? J. Speech Hear. Disord. 37:55–63.
Schane, S. A. 1973. Generative Phonology. Prentice-Hall. Englewood Cliffs, N.J.
Selinker, L. 1972. Interlanguage. IRAL 10:201–231.
Short Test of Linguistic Skills. 1976. Board of Education of the City of Chicago, Chicago.
Silverman, R. J., Noa, J. K., and Russell, R. H. 1976. Oral Language Tests for Bilingual Students: An Evaluation of Language Dominance and Proficiency Tests. Northwest Regional Educational Laboratory, Portland, Ore.
Snow, C. E., and Hoefnagel-Höhle, M. 1978. Age differences in second language acquisition. In: E. M. Hatch (ed.) Second Language Acquisition: A Book of Readings. pp. 333–344. Newbury House Publishers, Rowley, Mass.
Stockwell, R. P., and Bowen, J. D. 1965. The Sounds of English and Spanish. University of Chicago Press, Chicago.
Templin, M. C., and Darley, F. L. 1960. The Templin-Darley Tests of Articulation. State University of Iowa, Iowa City.
Wardhaugh, R. 1970. The contrastive analysis hypothesis. TESOL Q. 4:123–130.
Weiner, F. F. 1979. Phonological Process Analysis. University Park Press, Baltimore.

chapter five

Conceptualizations of Bilingual Children
Testing the Norm
Donald R. Omark

The field of linguistics has diversified rapidly over the last few decades, including the development of specialities such as psycholinguistics and sociolinguistics. Testing of language capabilities, whether in children or adults, perforce lags behind theoretical and research innovations; the newest test instrument always depends upon "yesterday's findings" and, hence, is almost immediately obsolete. The first part of this volume reviews samples of various types of tests and assessment approaches. The latter part of this volume overviews current research findings and attempts to illustrate some testing procedures that can be used with those children who do not respond to standardized testing situations.

If one wants to nitpick, fault can be found with any test, whether it assesses language capabilities, IQ, or school achievement. The purpose of this volume is neither to condemn particular tests nor to suggest there is only one way to approach assessment. Rather, we prefer that readers use the critiques of these tests and the suggestions for more contemporary approaches as guides for examining or developing any language assessment instrument they intend to use.

This chapter raises some questions about the way in which tests are currently being developed. The construction of communicative assessment tests depends not only on current linguistic and psychological theory, but also upon statistical manipulations, sampling from appropriate populations, and matching of the questions to children's actual capabilities. Ultimately, the way in which tests are constructed and used depends upon the way in which children's capabilities are conceptualized. This chapter, as well as the remainder of this volume, explains how these conceptualizations are changing.

CONCEPTUALIZING CHILDREN'S CAPABILITIES

The prevailing tendency within western educational systems has been to establish a series of standards against which children are tested as they grow older. In many European countries, and countries that derive their educational systems from them, there are dividing points which determine the particular scholastic tracks that students will subsequently follow.[1] Those students who pass the tests administered at the dividing points may then proceed along an "academic" career path, while those who fail follow "vocational" paths, assume apprenticeships, or simply leave school to seek work. The schools (or the state testing boards) are then in the position of deciding the ultimate career paths of most children (DeBlassie and Franco, 1981).

Various testing programs in American schools effectively accomplish the same purpose of dividing students into different career orientations. A basic premise behind such testing procedures appears to be that everyone is given a chance, but some students are not capable of maintaining academic excellence. A second premise *must* be that a relatively homogeneous population of children is being tested (e.g., middle class Anglos).

A homogeneous population permits the tester to use test results to differentiate the various capabilities within that population. For a population that is heterogeneous the second premise cannot be met, and problems follow if that factor is ignored, as is illustrated later in this chapter. When a population is heterogeneous to the extent that some part of the population is readily "identifiable" by other than test measures, and that part almost always fails the tests, it is a sham to continue to test them with the old "standard" tests. If such children can be *a priori* identified as potential failures then the ways in which tests are constructed and administered must be questioned.

The dilemma then arises within democratic societies about how to establish criteria (of excellence) without making *a priori* assumptions about individuals. The United States is currently facing this dilemma with regard to bilingual, limited English speaking (LES), and non-English-speaking (NES) children. This problem also is confronting many of the European countries that have invited in *Gastarbeiters* (guest-workers)[2] and now find that they have foreign speaking children to educate. The most *a priori* identifiable groups, the ones who will fail standardized tests, are those who speak some other language or a nonstandard version of the national language. Yet, countries from which the parents of

---

[1] The recent Public Law 94-142 (Education for All Handicapped Children Act) should effectively eliminate most tracking systems, which were once quite common in the United States. While the elimination of such systems may not benefit all of the children, at least it reduces harmful effects of "standardized" testing, as this chapter demonstrates.

[2] Euphemism for migrant workers.

bilingual children emigrate have doctors, lawyers, engineers, educators, and whatever else their society requires. As a group, immigrants should obviously not be expected to be stupid, but then, why do they fail the standardized tests?[3]

Educators are faced with the task of preparing students for the tests that will determine their career paths. Most of the tests illustrated in this volume derive from a learning theory or behavioristic approach. Under these theories, language testing and second language teaching methods treat language as a series of discrete units. For example, the use of plural endings might form one daily lesson plan. Test items could then be developed to see if the children had acquired knowledge on when and how to use plural endings. Such tests would be labeled "discrete point" tests—from the theoretical perspective that language is made up of discrete items.

Such an approach is based on learning theory that is applicable to any learning situation, including language learning. Furthermore, it conceptualizes all children as being approximately equivalent in their abilities to learn. Therefore, if the child does not learn, it appears that there is some problem with the child (i.e., he or she was not paying attention, has a bad family situation, or is retarded). Since up to half of the children in bilingual populations are now failing school or dropping out (Stewart, 1981), it is time to question this approach to both teaching and testing, rather than continually blaming the children and their environment (Willig, in preparation). The learning theory approach to language testing and teaching is obviously not working.

All children do not respond similarly to educational or testing situations. Each sex behaves differently, beginning, at least, in the early school years (see Maccoby and Jacklin, 1974; Omark, Strayer, and Freedman, 1980). Furthermore, various ethnic groups respond differently to educational and testing programs (Lesser, Fifer, and Clark, 1965; Omark, 1981a).

If a holistic perspective is taken when conceptualizing children's capabilities, learning paradigms will be revealed as not equally applicable to all children. The holistic approach recognizes each child as being

---

[3] One might argue that it is those who cannot succeed in their own society who emigrate. If so, then the United States is composed almost entirely of such people. Since this country has not done too badly among the society of nations, this argument can be rejected. The author simply does not accept any argument that early immigrants were better than are those of more recent years. Most Americans are immigrants or descendants of immigrants. All that is important is that each new group be dealt with in a way that will maximize the subsequent contributions it can make to our society.

genetically unique (Hirsch, 1963, 1970). This uniqueness, interacting with the environmental experiences that each child has had, produces unique individuals (Freedman and Omark, 1973; Omark, 1979, 1981b; Watson et al., 1980). The aforementioned sexual and ethnic differences are just statistical manipulations that abstractly reflect these individual differences.[4] In general, statistical manipulations compress individual differences into a hypothetical "mean" individual who simply does not exist. With a holistic perspective one returns to a consideration of the individual in relationship to that individual's environment.

Educational programs purport to recognize individual differences, but the goal has always been to develop educational models that are "generalizable" to large populations, if not to all students. Similarly, testing procedures consider the variance within groups as measures of capabilities, but the tests are presumed to be applicable (or are erroneously applied) to large populations. Neither approach really attempts to deal with individuals as individuals, and the rest of this chapter elaborates upon this point (for an individualized assessment approach see Omark, Chapter 12, this volume). It is time to consider the individual and not rely upon panaceas that claim to cure all of our problems.

If we are to educate students, then the old maxim of starting where they are and moving onward from there is appropriate. Where the bilingual students generally "are" is within another language/culture framework. It is not easy to learn a new language, but that does not mean that all learning must cease until the new language is learned. As Kachru (personal communication) suggested, a native English-speaker arrives in school in first grade with something approaching 15,000 hours of experience in English. It will be a long time before the bilingual child accumulates even part of that experience (by which time the English speaker has even more experience). Some skills appear to be transferable from one language to another: math certainly is (using Arabic numerals and Greek letters),[5] reading abilities are, and all of the fine arts and science skills are (all of them are readily taught in other cultural settings). In these fields it is the concepts that are important rather than the language in which they happen to be stored in the brain. Hence, education can continue while a new language is being learned.

---

[4] See also Hersen and Barlow (1976) for the effect of such differences in clinical populations.

[5] What is meant by this statement is that more abstract mathematical formulae (i.e., Algebra and beyond) are expressed as mentioned and understood by technicians and scientists anywhere. The actual words used while computing (e.g., *uno, dos, tres*) may be said or thought in the L_1 of the individual.

To maximize learning, it seems less essential to place a child immediately into an English langauge setting than it is to make an accurate assessment of an individual's capabilities. The rest of this volume discusses test evaluation, limitations of available test materials, and new approaches to communicative assessment that currently are being considered by linguists and others. This brief chapter presents an introduction to how tests are normed and the conceptualizations behind such test procedures.

TEST CONSTRUCTION

Linguists attempt to define the rules that operate within a speech community by sampling the speech of individuals within that community. Test constructors attempt to design instruments that reflect these rules so that characteristics such as *language dominance* and *competence* can be determined in school-age populations. In essence, the linguist draws a sample of individuals, listens to what they say, and compiles this into a set of rules. The tester then takes these rules and changes them into the question "Does the child know—rule?" An independent sample of subjects is drawn, and the tester then sees how well the children know the rules. This latter sample provides a distribution of scores (i.e., some individuals "know" the rules better than others) against which future student populations can be compared.

If the process just described were a scientific process rather than a commercial process, it would reflect back upon itself. How well the tested population did on the test would be compared with the original language-producing population (i.e., are the rules really "true"). If the tested population deviated significantly from the original population, then the rules would be seriously questioned. This is apparently rarely done. Linguists are left to argue among themselves, but once rules are formulated no further testing occurs. Instead, these theoretical rules are taken as given and applied to new populations. As one can begin to see, when the test constructors step in, any theoretical developments that may be underway within a field can become codified and solidified at that time. This is true of virtually all commerical tests ranging from measures of academic achievement to IQ testing.

As Leemann (Chapter 6, this volume) discusses, all that is questioned is whether the test will give repeatable results on the same or different populations (reliability) and whether the test items adequately reflect the assumed-to-be-true rules (validity). The results of the test constructors' initial test administration may indicate that some items are of no value because they do not differentiate the children (i.e., everyone passes them or everyone fails them). In some instances the results from part of the test may also predict (i.e., by high correlation with) results on other parts of the test, and consequently appear to be redundant (see Leonard et al., 1978). Some of these items probably would be discarded. From the remaining set (after possible additions and retesting) the test developer produces a mean score for each age or grade tested, and standard deviations, range, or percentiles to show the spread of scores.

The assumption behind this reporting of scores is that the population tested is a *random* sample from the total population that will eventually receive the test once it is marketed. Thus, when assessing the potential usefulness of a test the first thing to examine is whether or not its sample population included or resembled the population to be tested. For example, Chicanos in San Diego or Los Angeles might be considered similar, but tests developed on Hispanic populations in Texas, Chicago, or New York might not represent a similar population. Since language is the factor being assessed, and since some aspects of language such as lexicon and phonology will vary in groups that are isolated from each other, aspects being tested in one area may be relatively unknown in another.

The conceptualizations behind reporting the mean and standard deviations of a test are that these figures represent a "typical" child. Furthermore, these figures may be used as potential cutoff points for assignment to particular programs (e.g., Spanish transitional classes versus mainstreaming into English-only classes). The "typical child" is, however, a hypothetical child. Comparisons of this "child" with children in a particular geographical region may provide bases for determination of the skills of the children in that region. Once the geographical region and the selected test instrument are matched, further normative information, such as socioeconomic status (SES), cultural backgrounds, and other variables of the sample population and of the children from the particular region to be tested, also should be examined. This information is important in order to decide whether these two populations can be compared. A test is a valid test (i.e., the rules being tested are appropriate for the children being tested) only to the extent that the hypothetical "typical child" resembles children from any particular region.

All tests, whether linguistic, psychological, or achievement, have to be examined for their relevancy. For example, Hare (1977) has demonstrated for two measures of self-esteem that general measures (the combined scores of school, home, and peer measures of self-esteem) were directly related to school measures of self-esteem for white-collar Anglo children. However, the general measures were related to home and peer measures for Blacks and for Anglos of other SES levels. This suggests that tests normed on Anglo middle-class children have to be carefully examined as to their relevancy for other groups. School-related factors and/or linguistic factors have to be probed in order to see whether a test is appropriate for the population that is to be tested. An elaboration of this point for Black, Chinese, Jewish, and Puerto Rican populations appears in Omark (1981a).

NATIONALLY NORMED TESTS

Most language tests used for NES, LES, or bilingual children are normed on relatively localized homogeneous populations, as later chapters clearly show. At the other extreme are tests such as achievement tests that are normed on "national" samples. Language assessment tests apparently have not yet been so normed, but because this is a standard procedure for many of the so-called IQ tests, one can expect that some of the larger test development corporations will soon produce those also.

In developing such national tests, a variety of approaches might be taken. For example, developers could devise a test instrument containing items that academics agreed reflected a "standard" version of English, or they could collect a variety of speech and language samples from around the country. The former would be the expected approach. While academics across the country may agree, more or less, on a standard English test, what should be the standard for, say, Spanish?[6] Would it be the way it is spoken in Spain (from which little of our immigrant population comes), in Mexico, in Puerto Rico, in Cuba, or in other parts of Latin America; or perhaps, would indigenous Spanish become the standard, but, again, from where—Los Angeles, Houston, Miami, Chicago, New York? In terms of the items used in the test, it is obvious that problems appear immediately.

The test developers may decide to choose a variety of sample groups to test. If they have decided upon some "standard" version (e.g., as developed by Spanish teachers), a variety of groups can be tested and compared with this standard. One or more groups may excel on this

---

[6] The problems with nationally normed tests in English (e.g., IQ or achievement) are already apparent. Adjustments in scores are typically made for different areas of the country (e.g., the South), or typically not made for particular groups (e.g., Blacks). Labov and others have shown how different the language patterns of different groups can be, and these obviously can interfere with test results.

standard form and their scores would then provide the standard for comparison of all subsequently tested groups.[7] A marked complication in such a procedure for most of the linguistic populations of interest is that there is limited or no developmental research available on these populations. Therefore, it would be difficult to develop expected "standard" versions of what should be appropriate criteria for such populations.

The more typical approach for test norming would be to take some stratified sample of children from the national population. The number of children selected to be tested from each stratum would be in relation to each stratum's representation in the total population. For a test of English, the strata might be the representative percentages of upper-, middle-, and lower-class Anglos, and similar class groups of Blacks. For a test of Spanish, similar strata might be developed for Chicanos, Mexican-Americans (recent immigrants), Puerto Ricans, and Cubans.

Harrington (1975), however, demonstrated that for tests standardized on populations containing majority and minority populations, the minority populations will always be weighted *against* in measures of their rate of success. To illustrate this point, suppose that a stratified sample (based upon size of population) is selected. Also, suppose that Chicanos accounted for 70% of the population that contributed to the setting of this score, Puerto Ricans were 25% of the population, and Cubans were 5%. If the Chicanos on the average scored X, Puerto Ricans Y, and Cubans Z, then the total average score (T), would be determined by T = .70X + .25Y + .05Z. One can then see that most of the determination of T depends upon X, some upon Y. but little upon Z.

In the above example one might find that Cubans on the average scored higher than the other groups (Z > Y, X). In that case, why worry about them since they will appear to do better anyway? The process of test construction involves selecting and discarding test items until some reasonable variance in difficulty has been built into the test. The larger groups will more directly affect this process and, consequently, items initially favorable to the Cubans may easily be discarded with little apparent effect on the instrument. At the same time, however, discarding those items can have a significant effect on the Cubans who take the final form of the test.

The consideration of percentage representation for different population segments is a common means of constructing test populations for

---

[7] Test developers obviously do not use the scores of groups that do not match the "standard" because 1) this would lead to questions about the choice of the "standard," and 2) such scores would not provide enough spread or range for making future comparisons.

norming national tests. The minority groups will always be weighted against by such procedures, as is evident by the typically lower scores for Blacks on so-called IQ, achievement, and entrance tests. It should be noted that IQ tests from the very beginning made adjustments for the differences in responses made between white boys and girls. In essence, the boys have one set of items which permit them to get average scores of 100, and the girls similarly have a set of items so that they can average 100. Comparable adjustments have not been made for other groups so that they, too, can average 100 on the selected items (see Omark, 1981a). This adjustment should certainly be looked for when, and if, nationally normed language tests become available.

SAMPLE SIZE

The field of linguistics has in the past been primarily concerned with the development of the appropriate rules to explain linguistic phenomena. This was primarily a procedure of deciding when phonology, lexicon, and syntax were or were not correct. In their simplest, and earliest, forms, these decisions were made by a single judge—the linguist—who sometimes simply examined what he himself said. The sample size therefore needed to be no larger than one. The earlier studies of language development (Bloom, 1970; Brown, 1973) similarly focused upon one or very few children.

More recent approaches have shifted from studies of language (as produced by linguists) to studies of speech (as produced by "civilians" or the populus in general—see McCollum, Chapter 2, this volume). This shift meant that more than one individual was being studied. The rules were then found to be less rigid than originally supposed, since this variety of individuals obviously thought that what they were saying was correct. Any language can supposedly generate a large finite variety of ways of communicating,[8] but, on the other hand, what is communicated has to be understandable by others. The latter constraint places bounds upon what is communicated, and these bounds permit the delineation of the rules that any particular speech community may be using. This shift to the study of broader populations is quite recent (e.g., Labov, 1972).

It should be noted that what is being communicated on a day-to-day

---

[8] Linguists recognize this variety of communication possibilities. A limited region will be described as having a *dialect* distinct from other regions, and individuals will have their own *idiolects*. One of the reasons why idiolects occur is discussed by Omark (1979, 1981a).

basis is not dependent upon what linguists, academicians, school teachers, the media, tests, or any others say should be the way things are communicated. Language, and the ability to communicate, are part of our capabilities as a species (cf. Brown, 1958). Each of us decides, ultimately, what we will say and how we will say it. If what we say is not understood, then we try again. The linguists and others can only attempt to figure out what rules are being followed, but they cannot decide what rules must be followed because language is a continuously evolving dynamic process. This fact will become obvious in the chapters that follow.

Part of the mystique developing out of the educational and psychological testing movements is that a large number of subjects is "better" than a small number. The reason for this feeling appears to stem from the use of the test of significance procedures frequently employed in educational and psychological studies. As Bakan (1969) pointed out, the statistical procedures used to test for significance have the rather strange quirk built into them that the larger the N the greater will be the chance that a difference between populations will be significant. In reality, if two groups of a large size are tested, absolutely trivial differences between the groups will be significant. One of the author's students (Swain, 1978) illustrates this point in Table 1 for two different tests. She observed the behaviors of children with working or nonworking mothers in nursery school. Different numbers (n) of the children produced different amounts of the observed behaviors. The Mann Whitney U and the Student's t tests were used to determine the significance levels for the original population. She then increased the group size mathematically but left the ratio of original responses by each group the same. For example, if the 8 children of working mothers had produced 20 "aggression" behaviors, and the 8 children of nonworking mothers had produced 10 of such behaviors (the N column), then the $2N$ column has 40 aggressive behaviors by 16 children versus 20 aggressive behaviors by the other 16 children. As can be seen, nonsignificant ratios can become significant simply by increasing group size.

Such a fact holds for virtually all statistical tests. Where procedures have been developed upon a small pilot population, one assumes population size should be increased so that the results will be significant or generalizable. The important point to note is that real differences between populations (subjected to different treatments) are more probably real (i.e., significant) the *smaller* the populations are that are tested (Bakan, 1969; Carver, 1978). If we now return to what linguists have done and are doing, then one can begin to examine available tests

Table 1. How sample size changes the chance for results to be considered "statistically significant"

Child's behavior	Working mothers (n)	Nonworking mothers (n)	N	Mann Whitney U Test Significance levels at different population sizes[a]		
				2N	3N	4N
Aggression	8	8	0.07	0.02–0.05*[b]	0.008*	0.001–0.002*
Social—boys	4	3	0.20	0.07	0.05*	0.20–05*
—girls	4	5	0.17	>0.10	0.07	0.02*
Watch	8	8	0.07	0.02–0.05	0.005*	0.001–0.002*
Cry and pucker	6	3	0.04*	0.002–0.02*	0.007*	<0.001*
Play alone—boys	4	3	0.20	0.07	0.05*	0.02–0.05*
—girls	4	5	0.37	>0.10	>0.10	>0.10
			Student's t test			
Aggression			0.07	0.001–0.01*		0.001*
Social—boys			0.25	0.10–0.20		0.05*–0.10
—girls			0.25	0.05*–0.10		0.02–0.05*
Watch			0.25	0.05*–0.10		0.01–0.02*
Cry and pucker			0.15	0.05*–0.10		0.02–0.05*
Play alone—boys			0.45	0.20–0.30		0.10–0.20
—girls			0.25	0.10–0.20		0.02–0.05*

[a] The original population's characteristics (N) are simply multiplied by 2, 3, and 4.
[b] Those results on a particular test that equal or exceed the 0.05 level are marked with an asterisk (*). For further details about the behaviors examined see Swain (1978).

critically, or to consider alternate procedures. If a given linguistic rule is *truly general* within a population, then almost every individual should possess that rule; an N of 1 is not too small provided that individual is not retarded or delayed linguistically. Test constructors need not then impress us with 1,400 subjects, or lead us to consider that test over one which involves only 20 or 100 subjects.

For most middle-class white American populations upon which a test might be normed, there is a wide variety of linguistic features in common. Which particular population for norming purposes is chosen or how large the norming sample is probably is not very important. The population upon which the test will be used *is* important, as well as the way in which the test will be used. Labov (1972) and others have demonstrated how populations other than white middle-class will deviate linguistically from the verbal productions of that class. Basically, few general rules have been discovered. Language is a living entity that develops as individuals use it, and each individual and every group of individuals will use language differently. Therefore, no test should be taken as the "correct" criterion against which new populations should be compared.

The rest of this volume considers how to examine tests as they currently exist. After examining the available tests to see which one(s) most closely approximate the cultural and linguistic characteristics of one's local population, one additional step is necessary. Any test should then be re-normed on the local population. At a minimum, this procedure will then bring the selected test in line with the characteristics of the local population. It should not be *a priori* expected that any nationally normed test, or regionally normed test upon a different group, will be adequate to reveal the linguistic characteristics of the local group. Toronto (1981) and Watson et al. (1980) discuss how tests may be locally normed and/or developed for local populations. After this norming or re-norming has been done, the test can be used for initial selection/decision purposes. Following this procedure will lead to a test that will provide information about a limited set of linguistic features.

These scores from locally normed tests will differentiate between different segments of the tested population. They will not, however, tell much more than that one part of the population "passed" on this set of linguistic features while another segment failed. The first round of decisions will be made on this set of scores; some children will be mainstreamed, some sent to bilingual classrooms, and some sent for further linguistic testing by a language specialist. As Leonard et al., (1978) point out, because of the way language tests are constructed the information provided is not specific enough to provide clues for remediation. They suggest "nonstandardized approaches to the assessment of language behaviors," and a few such approaches are explained in more detail later in this volume.

CONCLUSION

Children are individuals and the speech and language patterns they produce reflect their personal endowments because these capabilities have interacted developmentally with each individual's particular experiences. While each individual's speech patterns can be expected to be more-or-less different, these various speech patterns have to be understood by others, for communication to occur. This understanding is the basis for any linguistic rules that may be developed. However, because language is a dynamic process, occurring at different rates and in different ways within various groups, rules must be relatively flexible.

If the above principles are accepted, a test selected for use with a particular population should reflect the linguistic characteristics of that population. When children are to be tested in a second language the test should, again, reflect the possible linguistic models to which the children may have been exposed. Because language is a developmental phenomenon, initial testing should reflect the language of comparable second language peers. As the child grows older the tests might be changed to reflect broader linguistic characteristics (e.g., the media), but these tests should still be examined, and re-normed if necessary, when sex, SES, or cultural influences are indicated.

The purpose of testing is, or should be, a first step in the development of an appropriate educational program for children. When tests do not adequately or correctly differentiate among children, wrong diagnoses and misplacements will result. The purpose of this book is to provide examples of how to examine tests, how to conceptualize communicative abilities in more contemporary terms, and how to develop alternative strategies when the tests do not provide adequate information about children. In the long run, children will have to be examined as individuals and we hope to demonstrate that this is not as difficult and onerous a task as it may seem at first.

REFERENCES

Bakan, D. 1969. On Method: Toward a Reconstruction of Psychological Investigation. Jossey-Bass, San Francisco.

Bloom, L. 1970. Language Development: Form and Function in Emerging Grammars. The MIT Press, Cambridge, Mass.
Brown, R. 1958. The comparative psychology of linguistic reference. In: R. Brown (ed.), Words and Things: An Introduction to Language. Free Press, New York.
Brown, R. 1973. A First Language: The Early Stages. Harvard University Press, Cambridge, Mass.
Carver, R. P. 1978. The case against statistical significance testing. Harv. Educ. Rev. 48:378-399.
DeBlassie, R. R., and Franco, J N. 1981. Psychological and educational assessment of bilingual children. In: D. R. Omark and J. G. Erickson (eds.), The Bilingual Exceptional Child. Charles C Thomas, Springfield, Ill.
Freedman, D. G., and Omark, D. R. 1973. Ethology, behavior genetics and education. In: F. A. J. Ianni and E. Storey (eds.), Cultural Relevance and Educational Issues. Little, Brown & Company, Boston.
Hare, B. R. 1977. Racial and socioeconomic variations in pre-adolescent area-specific and general self-esteem. Int. J. Intercultural Relations. 1:31-51.
Harrington, G. M. 1975. Intelligence tests may favor the majority groups in a population. Nature 258:708-709.
Hersen, M., and Barlow, D. H. 1976. Single Case Experimental Studies. Pergamon Press, New York.
Hirsch, J. 1963. Behavior genetics and individuality understood. Science 142:1436-1442.
Hirsch, J. 1970. Behavior-genetic analysis and its biosocial consequences. Semin. Psychiatry 2:89-105.
Labov, W. 1972. Language in the Inner City: Studies in the Black English Vernacular. University of Pennsylvania Press, Philadelphia.
Leonard, L. B., Prutting, C. A., Perozzi, J. A., and Berkley, R. K. 1978. Nonstandardized approaches to the assessment of language behaviors. Asha 20:371-379.
Lesser, G. S., Fifer, G., and Clark, D. H. 1965. Mental abilities of children from different social-class and cultural groups. Monographs of the Society for Research in Child Development. Vol. 30.
Maccoby, E. E., and Jacklin, C. N. 1974. The Psychology of Sex Differences. Stanford University Press, Stanford, Cal.
Omark, D. R. 1980. Human ethology: A holistic perspective. In: D. R. Omark, F. F. Strayer, and D. G. Freedman (eds.), Dominance Relations: An Ethological View of Human Conflict and Social Interaction. Garland, New York.
Omark, D. R. 1981a. Genetically inferior or just different: Conceptualizations of the bilingual child. In: D. R. Omark and J. G. Erickson (eds.), The Bilingual Exceptional Child. Charles C Thomas, Springfield Ill.
Omark, D. R. 1981b. Assessment procedures and bilingual education: The need for reconceptualization. In: D. R. Omark and J. G. Erickson (eds.), The Bilingual Exceptional Child. Charles C Thomas, Springfield, Ill.
Omark, D. R., Strayer, F. F., and Freedman, D. G. (eds.), 1980. Dominance Relations: An Ethological View of Human Conflict and Social Interaction. Garland, New York.

Stewart, J. L. 1981. Communication disorders in the American Indian population. In: D. R. Omark and J. G. Erickson (eds.), The Bilingual Exceptional Child. Charles C Thomas, Springfield, Ill.

Swain, R. E. 1978. An examination of the relationship between maternal employment and the behavior of preschool childen. Unpublished master's thesis, University of Illinois. Urbana.

Toronto, A. S. 1981. Developing local normed assessment instruments. In: D. R. Omark and J. G. Erickson (eds.), The Bilingual Exceptional Child. Charles C Thomas, Springfield, Ill.

Watson, D. L., Omark, D. R., Grouell, S. L., and Heller, B. 1980. Nondiscriminatory Assessment: Practitioner's Handbook, Vol. 1. California State Department of Education, Sacramento.

Willig, A. In preparation. Differences or deficits? A look at the assumptions underlying two approaches to the education of minority groups. In: H. T. Trueba, M. P. Phillips, and S. Arvizu (eds.), Bilingual Education and the Classroom Practitioner. Newbury House Publishers, Rowley, Mass.

chapter six

Evaluating Language Assessment Tests
Some Practical Considerations
Elizabeth M. Leemann

Until fairly recently, foreign language testing in the United States was almost exclusively a matter of mastery testing, that is, of evaluating students' language performance in terms of the curriculum they were expected to have covered at some given point. Within the past decade, however, there has been a significant shift in the emphasis of language testing. There is now a greater concern with predicting the individual's ability to function effectively in a given language context. This has occurred, in part, as a result of the current emphasis on communicative competence as a major goal of foreign language education, as well as in response to the urgent needs in bilingual education. Both of these areas of education are in search of tests that accurately predict a child's ability to use a given language effectively in day-to-day classroom situations.

The pressing demand for bilingual language assessment instruments has resulted in the development of a number of new tests, and translations of tests originally used for assessing English abilities. Crucial decisions have to be made about which test(s) to use, because the choice will determine the course of education offered to children from non-English language backgrounds. The rest of this book discusses a variety of testing approaches ranging from discrete point to competence measures. Once the type of test has been chosen, the variety of tests of that type should be examined in terms of the statistical data available for each instrument.

The teacher, administrator, or professional in charge of selecting language assessment measures should be informed of basic statistical information that should be used in test selection. This chapter summarizes the statistical criteria by which language tests may be evaluated. The following discussion outlines some of the basic concepts of educational evaluation, discusses the application of these concepts to the specific context of language testing, and reviews some of the language testing procedures currently in use.

VALIDITY

The first essential notion in test evaluation is the concept of *validity*. Validity can be defined as the extent to which a test measures what it purports to measure. Simplistic as this notion may seem, the principle is so frequently violated in actual testing practice that it indicates a considerable amount of misunderstanding of what validity entails. A test must be valid *for some specific purpose* (e.g., a valid test of spelling ability, of mastery of the first-semester Spanish curriculum, of speaking proficiency in German, of aural comprehension of English). For this reason, it is absolutely essential for test users to define precisely what information they want to obtain from a test before they can decide whether or not it is valid.

The concept of test performance as a *sample of behavior* is closely related to the question of validity in language testing, as in any other field. Even at a very elementary level of language learning, it would be impossible for learners to demonstrate everything they know about a language in one testing situation: their entire vocabulary, every original sentence they can form, their sense of the appropriateness of various utterances, their range of comprehension, and so forth. Even by dint of wearing a microphone so that everything one might say in a period of 24 hours could be recorded for evaluation, the individual would still be providing only a sample of what he or she knows about the language. This brings into focus the importance of knowing exactly what is to be sampled. If, on the one hand, language competence is thought of as the ability to manipulate grammatical structures, one sort of behavior sample will be required. On the other hand, if language competence is seen as the ability to carry on a conversation, a different sort of sample is necessary.

This is not to imply that test validity can be readily determined just by an examination of the tasks involved. The term *face validity* refers to the mere appearance of validity without the support of empirical data. Unfortunately, although face validity can be grossly misleading, tests are all too often chosen on this basis alone. No matter how valid a test looks, it should not be adopted without empirical evidence of its suitability for the purpose it is to serve. In the case of a standardized test, the test manual should state clearly what the test is designed to measure and what research has been conducted to support its validity for that purpose. Any literature on new testing techniques should also describe in detail what means have been used to ascertain that the test is indeed valid for the purpose described.

The empirical method most frequently used to determine the validity of a language test is to administer it to a group of subjects and then compare their scores with another set of scores, obtained by the same group on some other measure of proficiency. Validity established by this procedure is called *criterion-referenced validity*, also referred to as *concurrent* or *correlational validity*. If there is a high degree of correlation between the two sets of scores, it is likely that the new test is measuring the same skills as the one used as a criterion or that the skills measured by the two tests are closely related.

As in the case with any statistical information, however, these data must be interpreted with caution. It is clearly essential that the criterion itself be a valid measure of whatever the new instrument is supposed to test. This presents an obvious problem: if a valid measure already existed, there would generally be no need to design a new one. Therefore, there is seldom, if ever, a perfect criterion available against which to validate a new test. For this reason, a new measure is generally studied in relation to several other measures, chosen for their appropriateness in terms of the information that the new test is designed to obtain. In considering the literature on any criterion-related validity study, it is essential to look not only at the statistics themselves, but also at the nature of the criterion used. For example, you may be more interested in knowing how well the results of a new measure correlate with results obtained on a test of listening comprehension than in finding out how they compare to results obtained on a spelling test. If the criterion itself is not a valid measure for your purposes, then the correlation statistics do not give you useful information about the validity of the measure under consideration.

Another factor to be considered in interpreting the results of this kind of validation approach is the sample on which the study has been conducted. If a test is to reflect children's typical abilities with regard to some measure, then generally a larger sample will better reflect these abilities. Small samples are more subject to the effects of chance and bias (see Omark, Chapter 5, this volume). Equally important is to consider what subjects constituted the sample. The results obtained on studies using a sample of foreign students at an American university may be misleading in determining the ultimate value of an English proficiency test to be used for evaluating the English language skills of, for example, Navajo-speaking adolescents from a rural area.

A test may also be considered in terms of its *content validity*. This term indicates that the test measures a representative sample of behavior within the framework of the area of the competence to be assessed. A test that focuses narrowly on certain aspects of language behavior and neglects others lacks this kind of validity. To use a simplistic example, say that a given test purports to measure a child's English vocabulary by asking him or her to identify words related to the school context: blackboard, desk, book, pencil sharpener, and so on. It is conceivable that a child might have a fairly wide range of vocabulary, yet be unfamiliar with the vocabulary of the classroom. Conversely, the child might know many words relating to the schoolroom but not many relating to other contexts. In this case, the test is not a valid measure of the child's vocabulary because its range is too narrow; in other words, the test is biased. Another example of poor content validity is apparent when a test purports to measure language proficiency and then tests only for vocabulary or certain morphological markers. In order to avoid content bias, it is essential for the test user to define the objectives carefully and to determine the range of behavior that needs to be sampled in order for these objectives to be met.

Another type of validity is referred to as *construct validity*. A "construct" is a theoretical concept developed with reference to some psychological quality which may help explain certain aspects of behavior. In the field of foreign language learning, examples of relevant constructs might be language aptitude, motivation to learn a language, or even ethnocentrism. Testing a psychological construct is a somewhat different matter from testing a specified field of learned behavior such as addition or driving a car, in that a psychological construct is basically theoretical. Its existence is assumed but, to evaluate it, hypotheses about how it can be demonstrated must be developed. These hypotheses must, in turn, be verified through research.

Since this chapter is primarily concerned with the evaluation of language proficiency, one need not be overly concerned with constructs such as motivation and aptitude. However, it can be argued that language performance is simply an indication of some fundamental mechanism in the human brain which enables us to use a language, and that there is no direct way to test this mechanism that we assume to exist. In this context, construct validity in tests of language proficiency can be thought of as the extent to which a test may be interpreted in terms of an underlying competence in a given language.

RELIABILITY

For a test to be valid by any of the standards described above, it must also be reliable. The term *reliability* refers to the consistency of test results from one measurement to another. A test is unreliable if it provides very different results when administered to the same group at different times or when administered to two different groups of equal ability. Of course, no individual's performance on a given task can be expected to remain absolutely stable over a number of trials; a certain amount of fluctuation because of factors such as mood, fatigue, motivation, and learning is inevitable. But inconsistency stemming from the test itself, for example, in the test content or in the way the test is administered or scored, must be minimized if the test is to provide meaningful results.

The most useful single indication of reliability for the test user is the *standard error of measurement*. This statistic provides an estimate of the amount of fluctuation that could be expected in any one individual's performance if he or she were to take the test repeatedly. The greater the standard error, the greater the amount of fluctuation that can be expected. Not only is this a good indication of the stability of the measurement, but it is also essential to interpretation of test scores. The standard error of measurement is especially useful because of its high degree of stability across populations. In other words, even when the test is administered to a group quite unlike the one whose scores were used in determining the standard error measurement, the standard error itself is likely to remain stable. For these reasons, it is an essential statistic to understand and to consider in evaluating a test.

A test manual will generally give not only the standard error of measurement but also one or more reliability coefficients. These figures may have been obtained in a number of ways. The most obvious way is to administer the test twice to the same group of subjects and to establish the correlation between the two sets of scores. One limitation of this method is that subjects may remember their responses from one testing session to another. Another limitation is that if the intervening time lapse is increased to exclude the effects of memory, the subjects may actually have learned enough in the meantime to change their scores significantly. Therefore, one can never be sure how much of the variance between the two sets of scores can actually be attributed to the test itself.

Some tests have two or more forms that are equivalent in all significant aspects such as length, difficulty, and format. In this case, a reliability coefficient may be established by administering both forms of the test to one group of subjects and comparing the results. When this procedure is used with a time interval between the administration of the two forms, all of the major sources of possible variance are accounted for in the scores: the effects of time, the equivalence of the two forms, the stability of the measurement, the sampling of tasks, and the constancy of what is being measured. For this reason, the equivalent-forms method is generally considered to be the soundest procedure for estimating reliability. The problem, of course, is that this procedure can only be used when two equivalent forms exist.

Two other common methods of estimating reliability require just one administration of a single test form. In the first of these methods, the test is administered and then divided into equivalent halves, usually by separating the even-numbered items from the odd-numbered items. The halves are scored separately, so that two scores are obtained for each test subject, and the resulting sets of scores are compared. A reliability coefficient for the full test can then be established, based on the correlation between the two sets of scores. (The most commonly used procedure for establishing this correlation is the one developed by Spearman and Brown.) This coefficient provides a good estimate of the internal consistency of the test, that is, of the extent to which the test items provide a representative and consistent sampling of what is being measured.

Another procedure, known as *rational equivalence* is based on an analysis of the proportion of test subjects who pass and fail each item. This is usually done by means of a formula developed by Kuder and Richardson. Like the split-half method, this procedure indicates the internal consistency of the test. Neither of these methods, however, indicates the amount of fluctuation that is likely to occur in one subject's performance over a period of time.

Tests that require the scorer to judge responses according to some criteria, rather than simply marking right or wrong answers, are a special case. For example, on an oral interview or a written composition, a number of different scorers, each using their own criteria for evaluation might give widely disparate ratings for the same response. In this case, the scorers are asked to rate the same set of test responses using given criteria. The ratings are then compared to provide an estimate of inter-rater reliability. The applicability of this estimate to any other testing situation, of course, implies that the people who score the test use the same criteria as those whose ratings were used in the reliability study.

When evaluating a test on the basis of information provided in the manual, or in other literature, it is important to look not only at the reliability coefficients themselves, but also at the procedures that have been used to establish them, since each of the procedures yields a different kind of evidence on the estimated reliability of the test results. The particular kind of evidence and the degree of reliability that one should look for will depend on the specific objectives of the test user. This brief overview of methods for establishing a reliability coefficient should not be seen as a substitute for the more detailed information that can be found in any standard textbook on educational measurement. The point here is to stress the importance of reliable measurement and emphasize the need for critical examination of the evidence pertaining to the reliability of any test under consideration.

It should be clear from the preceding discussion of validity and reliability that the specific objectives of the test user are absolutely critical to an intelligent evaluation of any test. The statistics that result from studies of test reliability and validity are not meaningful in themselves. A test user must look critically at how the statistics have been obtained and must determine what these studies indicate about the value of the test in terms of the kinds of decisions that will be based on it. It cannot be overemphasized that even the most reliable test will yield misleading results if it does not measure data pertinent to its planned use.

CURRENT ISSUES IN LANGUAGE TESTING

At present, the process of defining a valid test of language proficiency has attracted considerable research and discussion in the field of foreign language teaching and bilingual education. Traditionally, it had been generally assumed for testing purposes that if a student had "learned" a language, his or her competence would be reflected in an ability to manipulate it in certain ways (e.g., by conjugating verbs, transforming sentences from affirmative to negative, recognizing sound-spelling correspondences, and so on). The structuralist approach to the study of language, which has had enormous influence on the methodology of teaching and testing foreign language, supported this assumption. In the structuralist view, language is analyzed as a series of progressively larger units: phonemes combine to form words, which fall into classes (nouns, verbs, adjectives, etc.), and these in turn are organized into sentences according to given patterns. It follows from this account that language proficiency would be reflected by mastery of discrete points, such as units of phonology, morphology, vocabulary, and syntax. In this view there was little need for tests designed to evaluate language use in a meaningful context (see Omark, Sridhar, and Walters, Chapters 12, 10, and 11, respectively, this volume).

Within the past decade, however, the assumptions underlying discrete point testing have been seriously challenged by linguists and educators alike, and the interest in measuring something that may be called "global language proficiency" has increased dramatically. This interest is, at least in part, an outgrowth of Chomskian linguistic theory, which stresses the creative aspect of human language and posits the existence of unique capacities in the human brain that enable a speaker of a language to create an infinite number of novel and meaningful sentences. In this context, the competence of the second language learner becomes less a question of how many grammatical structures he or she can duplicate than of the extent to which he or she can use the language in a meaningful context.

The need for pragmatic language tests is particularly urgent in view of recent legislation pertaining to bilingual education, as Shuy (1977) points out:

> The Aspira Consent Decree requires that the placement of children in educational programs using English or Spanish as the medium of instruction be determined by their ability to *effectively participate* in the instruction. This legislation precedes by a wide mark the technology upon which it can be based. No assessment instruments are available which purport to test this ability. There is a growing consensus among second language specialists that tests of grammar and phonology are not accurate predictors of effective participation and that functional language competence is far more crucial. That is, a child's ability to seek clarification or get a turn seems much more critical than his ability to use past tense markers properly (p. 79).

Shuy also notes that grammar, vocabulary, and syntax, being readily observable aspects of language use, are more easily evaluated than are the underlying functional and semantic meanings. This is certainly one of the reasons why available standardized tests still maintain an almost exclusively discrete point approach to language assessment, despite widespread recognition of the need for tests of functional language proficiency. At first blush, one might expect that a functional test would necessarily involve subjective evaluation of a speech or writing sample such as an oral interview or a composition, and that the individual judgments of various scorers would seriously interfere with reliable scoring. Recent research, however, suggests that such evaluations can be highly reliable and that they are, in addition, more valid as tests of global proficiency than are discrete point tests. Furthermore, some "indirect" testing procedures have been developed that can be scored quickly and reliably and that provide valid information about global language proficiency.

It should be made clear at this point that tests of linguistic accuracy and tests of global proficiency are not always clearly distinguishable from one another by their form alone. Oller (1973b) notes that one might speak in terms of a continuum ranging from discrete point items (testing a single item of language use at a time) at one end, to full-scale language use at the other. The most obvious way to test functional language ability is, in fact, to obtain a sample of real language use, as through a face-to-face interview. However, it is misleading to assume that every evaluation based on a speech sample is a priori an evaluation of global proficiency. If the speaking test is scored solely on the basis of discrete points of linguistic accuracy, it is in effect a test of linguistic accuracy, no matter how true-to-life the testing procedure may be (cf. Oller's review of the Bilingual Syntax Measure, 1976).

Perhaps the greatest problem in oral proficiency testing at present is the lack of clear-cut guidelines, other than grammatical accuracy, to define *proficiency*. Recent studies in the area of oral proficiency testing have generally relied on rating scales as a means of scoring, but there is considerable variation in the criteria used. The Foreign Service Institute of the Department of State (Wilds, 1975) uses a checklist that rates five areas: accent, grammar, vocabulary, fluency, and comprehension. Savignon (1972) uses criteria such as: effort to communicate, amount of communication, comprehensibility, naturalness, poise, and fluency (see Day, Chapter 9, this volume, and Cazden et al., 1977). Bartz (1974) uses three scales: fluency, quality of communication, and amount of communication.

Despite the diversity and the apparent vagueness of these categories, interrater reliability coefficients between 0.95 and 0.99 have been reported (Clark, 1972; Upshur, 1973; Bartz, 1974; Schulz, 1974). These results are particularly striking in view of the widespread assumption that any scoring procedure involving judgment on the part of the scorer is doomed to unreliability. It is crucial that the criteria used in scoring a direct speech sample reflect the kind of language proficiency that the test purports to measure and that these criteria are clearly understood and shared by all participating examiners.

Oller (1973b) points out that both dictation and composition can yield a wealth of diagnostic information about language proficiency. Here, as in oral proficiency tests, the scoring procedures are crucial in ensuring that the test measures overall proficiency rather than linguistic accuracy alone.

These three procedures—oral interviews, dictation, and composition—might be classified as *direct* tests. That is, the subject is asked to engage in a language activity that approximates "real-life" behavior: speaking, writing down one's ideas, or writing down what someone else says.

Another approach to proficiency testing is to design a test procedure that reflects, in an indirect manner, the same skills that are required for real-life use of language. One such technique, which has been the subject of some very interesting research, is the *cloze procedure*. A cloze test consists of a passage from which words have been deleted at regular intervals (usually every 5th to 7th word) and the examinee is asked to read the passage and to fill in the missing words. Extensive studies of the cloze procedure have yielded impressive results in terms of the internal consistency and reliability of the procedure (Oller, 1972, 1973a). The studies have also yielded high correlations with standardized tests of English as a Second Language, and particularly with tasks involving listening comprehension. The fact that a cloze test can be constructed, administered, and scored very easily, even by people with no specialized training in test construction, is a great advantage. Finally, the cloze test can be standardized simply by administering it to a group of native speakers, whose scores provide a criterion to which the scores of non-native speakers can be compared.

The rationale of the cloze procedure is based on what Oller (1973a) has called a "grammar of expectancy," which enables a native speaker of a language to make sense of incomplete or distorted utterances on the basis of the native's intuitive knowledge of how the utterance could reasonably have been completed. This is done by forming a hypothesis about the utterance, checking this hypothesis against the available information, and accepting or rejecting it accordingly. All of this, of course, takes place in much less time than is required to explain it, and it is probable that we are constantly carrying out this sort of analysis in all of our language activity—not only in listening but also in reading, writing, and speaking. Oller (1973a) maintains that language competence is best characterized by a grammar of expectancy and that this sort of competence is measured by cloze tests.

The same notion that Oller calls a "grammar of expectancy" is referred to by Spolsky (1968) as "redundancy utilization." Spolsky (1973) also argues that this kind of competence is crucial to the creative use of language and that the principle of redundancy in language activity can be used effectively to measure underlying language competence. He has developed a testing procedure in which test subjects reproduce sentences they hear on a tape, to which varying amounts of noise have been added, thus masking a portion of the original signal. Spolsky (1973) points out the clear distinction between the performance of native and nonnative speakers on this test:

> This is to be explained by the nonnative's inability to function with reduced redundancy, evidence that he cannot supply from his knowledge of the language the experience on which to base his guesses as to what is missing. In other words, the key thing missing is the richness of knowledge of probabilities—on all levels, phonological, grammatical, lexical, and semantic—in the language. It is possible to factor out each of these elements and explore the exact nature of the language learner's mastery of each item, but in the broad matter of functioning in a language, all combine to form an integrated whole, the exact contribution of each part being indefinable (p. 170).

The above discussion was intended primarily to emphasize the need for tests of integrative skills and to give some examples of various procedures for measuring global proficiency. Further discussion of integrative tests is found in succeeding chapters. It should be noted that there is no established catalogue of language functions or skills to be measured by tests of global proficiency, like the catalogues of phonemic, morphological, lexical, and syntactic features that serve as a basis for discrete point tests. This is a fact with which testing specialists may be uncomfortable, given that testing theory in general still relies heavily on the principle of sampling behavior from a list of narrowly defined "behavioral objectives." Still the need for tests of global proficiency is indisputable, and the evidence in their favor is summed up by Oller (1973b):

> In spite of the fact that some of the integrative skills tests seem to have little in common, and regardless of the fact that they may seem to be unreliable as far as scoring is concerned, repeated studies show that scores on tests of integrative skills tend to correlate better with teacher judgments, better among themselves, and better with other measures of language skills than do any of the discrete-point types because they more nearly reflect what people do when they use language (p. 198).

AGE AND CULTURAL BIAS

Within the context of bilingual education, the testing of children is a particularly crucial issue. Devising a valid test of language ability for children involves some rather obvious problems such as short-term memory constraints and understanding of the tasks involved. In other words, a test that is reputable and widely used for adults may be inappropriate for children simply because the tasks are too complex and too demanding.

In the absence of a standardized instrument for measuring functional language ability in children, it is crucial for educators involved in testing for bilingual programs to be aware of the limitations of the tests currently available and to take these into account, both in choosing the instrument and in interpreting the test results. It is certainly reasonable to expect that the literature about any given test should make clear how and to what extent the instrument can be expected to predict a child's ability to participate effectively in instruction in an English-speaking classroom.

Another factor that can seriously affect the validity of test results is cultural bias (Cazden, 1973). Briere (1971) argues that linguistic and cultural factors in testing are frequently inseparable, and that most standardized tests are culturally biased for any group whose sociocultural background differs from that of the group on whom the norms were established (the modal group). Cultural bias is not easily detectable by a person better acquainted with the culture of the modal group than with that of the group being tested. Briere cites numerous examples (drawn from widely used tests) of test items that depend on experience common to white middle-class children but not necessarily common to children of other cultures within the United States. These may be questions relating to some experience that is not universal for all cultures within the United States, to a vocabulary item that is common in one culture but irrelevant in another, or to a judgment that directly reflects cultural conditioning. In each case, the answers accepted as "correct" are those that reflect the values and experience of white middle-class culture, while answers that are accurate within the context of another culture are rejected.

Cultural bias exists not only in test items, but also in testing procedures, such as the practice of asking a child to speak up and look at the examiner while answering a series of direct questions—whereas children in many cultures are taught to lower their eyes as a sign of respect and not to do much talking in the presence of an authority figure. Such procedures, Briere points out, result in tragic mislabeling and misplacement of children.

The ideal solution to the problem of cultural bias would be to use tests geared specifically to the cultural context within which they are to be used. Such tests, however, are seldom available. At the very least, the test user should look for instruments that provide set norms established on children from the same cultural background as those who are to be tested.

Briere specifically warns against the tempting but highly questionable expedient of translating a test directly from one language into another, because this practice merely translates all the cultural biases of one test into another language. Differences in the ways experience is conceptualized and expressed in different languages make direct translation a delicate task in any context; and in testing, the use of a paraphrase or near-equivalent expression can destroy the validity of an item. Moreover, all currently available standardized language tests are based on some sort of a structural analysis of the language being tested or on a study of the differences between that language and the language of the intended test subjects. Thus, translating the test items into any other language completely destroys the underlying rationale of the test.

CONCLUSION

There is an urgent need for tests of functional language ability, free of cultural bias, and appropriate for use in large-scale testing in public schools. It is essential for test users to be aware of these current issues in language testing so they can choose the best available measurement instruments and interpret test results wisely. The importance of carefully defining the test user's specific goals can not be overemphasized. Before considering any instrument for future use, the test user should determine exactly what decisions will be based on the test results and what information is necessary to make these decisions. Then the various instruments must be studied in terms of their appropriateness to the test user's goals, the age and background of the group to be tested, and the time, space, and personnel available for the administration and scoring of the test. Finally, the test user must be aware of the limitations of the chosen instrument and must bear these limitations in mind when interpreting the test results.

REFERENCES

American Psychological Association. 1974. Standards for Educational and Psychological Tests. American Psychological Association, Washington, D.C.

Bartz, W. H. 1974. A study of the relationship of certain learner factors with the ability to communicate in a second language (German) for the development of measures of communicative competence. Unpublished doctoral dissertation, Ohio State University, Columbus.

Briere, E. 1971. Are we really measuring proficiency with our foreign language tests? For. Lang. Ann. 4:385–391.

Cazden, C. 1973. Cross-cultural biases in language tests. In: J. W. Oller, Jr., and J. C. Richards (eds.), Focus on the Learner. Newbury House Publishers, Rowley, Mass.

Cazden, C., Bond, J. T., Epstein, A. S., Matz, R. D., and Savignon, S. J. 1977. Language assessment: Where, what, and how. Anthropol. Educ. Q. 8:83–90.

Clark, J. D. 1972. Foreign Language Testing: Theory and Practice. Center for Curriculum Development, Philadelphia.

Oller, J. W., Jr. 1972. Scoring methods and difficulty levels for Cloze tests of proficiency in English as a Second Language. Modern Lang. J. 56:151–158.

Oller, J. W., Jr. 1973a. Cloze tests of second language proficiency and what they measure. Lang. Learn. 23:105–118.

Oller, J. W., Jr. 1973b. Discrete point tests versus tests of integrative skills. In: J. W. Oller, Jr., and J. C. Richards (eds.), Focus on the Learner. pp. 189–199. Newbury House Publishers, Rowley, Mass.

Oller, J. 1976. The measurement of bilingualism: A review of the Bilingual Syntax Measure. Modern Lang. J. 60:399–400.

Savignon, S. J. 1972. Communicative Competence: An Experiment in Foreign Language Teaching. Center for Curriculum Development, Philadelphia.

Schulz, R. A. W. 1974. Discrete point versus simulated communication testing: A study of the effect of two methods of testing on the development of communicative proficiency in beginning college French classes. Unpublished doctoral dissertation, Ohio State University, Columbus.

Shuy, R. W. 1977. Quantitative language data: A case for and some warnings against. Anthropol. Educ. Q. 8:73–82.

Spolsky, B. 1968. Language Testing—the Problem of Validation. TESOL Quarterly 2:88:94.

Spolsky B. 1973. What does it mean to know a language; or how do you get someone to perform his competence? In: J. W. Oller, Jr., and J. C. Richards (eds.), Focus on the Learner. pp. 164–176. Newbury House Publishers, Rowley, Mass.

Upshur, J. A. 1973. Context for language testing. In: J. W. Oller, Jr., and J. C. Richards (eds.), Focus on the Learner. pp. 177–183. Newbury House Publishers, Rowley, Mass.

Wilds, C. P. 1975. The oral interview test. In: R. L. Jones and B. Spolsky (eds.), Testing Language Proficiency. Center for Applied Linguistics, Arlington, Va.

chapter seven

Discrete Point Language Tests of Bilinguals
A Review of Selected Tests
E. Catherine Day, Pamela A. McCollum, Valerie A. Cieslak, and Joan Good Erickson

This chapter defines and describes discrete point tests used in assessing first and second language proficiency and dominance. In addition, descriptions and criticisms relevant to the more commonly used discrete point tests are reported. The information in the preceding chapters regarding bilingualism and test factors is salient to the understanding of the following information.

Discrete point language tests are currently used in most academic second language and bilingual instructional settings. Although they originally arose out of the thinking of structural linguistics prominent in the 1950s, this type of test still dominates the commercial market. The structural view of language reflected the behaviorist school of psychology in that both first and second language acquisition were seen as a result of habit formation. Language was seen as a series of distinct structural units (e.g., phonemes, morphemes), and mastery of each of these separate units was judged to be equivalent to mastery of the language. Adequate instruments to test each of these individual structural units were desired; therefore, discrete point tests were developed. Discrete point tests are the natural result of a structural approach to language learning.

In addition to its underlying structural linguistic theory, a paper-and-pencil discrete point testing approach suggests that responses to a written exam will generalize to verbal skills. For example, many English admissions tests for foreign students are based upon the assumption that knowledge of the third person singular regular verb form in English (which takes an *s*), as shown through a written response to a reading task, indicates habitual use of that morpheme marker given the same or similar context when orally communicating. However, an excellent score on a discrete point test in and of itself is not a valid predictor of a speaker's communicative competence. Frequently, the contrary is true.

Second language teachers are often frustrated and dismayed by the discrepancy between their students' scores on written tests and their subsequent use of language as an effective and functional means of communication. Similarly, second language students have been perplexed and frustrated by receiving high scores on discrete point tests, yet simultaneously lacking the ability to order a meal in the country where their second language is spoken.

There are those, however, who would argue that discrete point tests are purposeful in that they tap the individual's metalinguistic knowledge about the language. Indeed, the proliferation of discrete point tests on the market seems to testify to the strength of this argument. Discrete point tests might adequately measure an individual's abstract knowledge of the second language system and indicate the necessity for remediation of reading and writing skills. This type of test might also sample verbal comprehension and production of discrete points such as lexical items, morphological markers, or various syntactic forms. They do not necessarily adequately assess an individual's oral proficiency or ability to communicate in the second language. As the sample reviews indicate, discrete point tests may not give an evaluator adequate information even from a structural point of view.

Discrete point tests, however, are entrenched in the testing system and therefore, should be examined. Despite recent calls for more integrative testing instruments, and despite federal legislation that has prompted the need for instruments that determine a child's ability to function in a second language, many of the instruments currently employed in bilingual programs are essentially discrete point in nature. There is broad use of these instruments albeit little evaluation of their merits and, for the most part, they are not evaluated in the second language testing literature. This chapter provides descriptive and evaluative information concerning some of the typical assessment instruments currently used with bilingual bicultural children. The instruments described are only a representative sample of current practices. Other discrete point instruments currently on the market can be evaluated by the reader in a similar manner by using the information in the chapter by Leemann along with the prototype evaluation approach that this chapter provides.

JAMES LANGUAGE DOMINANCE TEST (*James, 1975*)

General Description

The James Language Dominance Test was designed by Peter James to assess production and comprehension of the Spanish and English lexicon used by Mexican-American kindergarten and first grade children in the Austin, Texas, area. Test results are used to determine the child's present bilingual proficiency and to permit subsequent classification into one of the following five categories: 1) Spanish dominant, 2) bilingual with Spanish as the home language, 3) bilingual with English as the home language, 4) English as the dominant language, but bilingual in comprehension, and 5) English dominant in both comprehension and production. Educational programs are then implemented with respect to the child's categorical classification.

Procedure

The author suggests that the simplicity and relative ease of administration are positive features of this test. It is recommended that the test examiner be a bilingual paraprofessional. Test administration requires no more than 10 minutues. Production and comprehension responses are elicited from individual children through the presentation of 40 picture cards in conjunction with the questions "What is this?" and "Where is the _____?" respectively in both Spanish and English. Of the 40 test items, only numbers 19 and 20 call for a two-word (noun and verb) response in correct grammatical sequence, while other items require only a one-word (noun) response. In addition, the child's language dominance in the home environment is determined solely on the basis of the responses to three test items that delineate the lexicon: *hose/manguera*, *stove/estufa*, and *tie/corbata*. Inadequate sample size and lack of supportive data substantiating these lexical items as representative of the home language environment severely undermine the applicability of using these responses to predict the child's language dominance in that setting. Furthermore, inaccurate judgements about the urban child's language dominance in the home may be rendered as a result of the use of the possibly unfamiliar and, therefore, inappropriate test item *hose/manguera*.

Each correct response is awarded one point. Total production and separate home item scores are then recorded and used to classify children into one of the five previously cited categories. However, the limited corpus of vocabulary items tested and the arbitrary classification cutoff points in relation to each adjacent category invalidate the strength of this instrument as a precise measure of the child's bilingual proficiency. An example of the total scores that can result in a student's classification into the second or third categories, respectively, exemplifies and lends support to this contention:

Student 1		Student 2	
Spanish comprehension	20	Spanish comprehension	20
Spanish production	19	Spanish production	16
Total Spanish score	39	Total Spanish score	36
Total Spanish House Items	2	Total Spanish House Items	1
English comprehension	20	English comprehension	20
English production	14	English production	14
Total English score	34	Total English score	34
Total English house items	0	Total English house items	0

Category 2

Bilingual with Spanish as
the home language

Category 3

Bilingual with Spanish and
English at home

Thus, students were designated into their respective categories simply because of a 1-point difference on Spanish home items. In an effort to quantify language behavior, the question of dominance has been reduced to mere hair splitting and can result in the implementation of inappropriate educational programs. Those programs, in turn, can have far-reaching and detrimental effects on the children who are enrolled in them.

Reliability and Validity

The statistical data presented in the technical manual are sketchy. The test was initially normed on one kindergarten and three first grade classes. The test was then revised and readministered to these same children 6 months later. Final revisions were made, and the resultant test form was administered to 464 Mexican-American children in Del Valle, Texas, in 1974. Data are not provided concerning the selection and distribution of this extremely small regional sample in terms of sex, socioeconomic status, education, home environment, and overall language development.

Reliability studies are also not reported, although the author does assert that the test has content, criterion-related, and concurrent validity. However, since validity is a function of reliability (which, due to lack of information, is assumed to be nonexistent for this test), it is considered invalid. Therefore, the actual value of this test as a true measure of any child's bilingual proficiency is seriously in question. To uphold the assertions of content, criterion-related, and concurrent validity, the author cites that items were developed in conjunction with intensive language observations, scrutiny of classroom workbooks and of the home environment, teacher agreement with the classroom placement of children, and correlation of open-ended questionnaires to the perspective category classification of children.

Substantiating data and analysis to support any of the above contentions are not given. Furthermore, it is not stated whether responses to the open-ended questionnaires were generated by parents or the children themselves. In addition, correlations between categorical classification and classroom placement do not look at the dominant language spoken in the home environment, the factor that distinguishes group 2 from 3, and subsequently do not indicate the validity of the categorical classifications themselves.

Reviewers' Comments

Positive characteristics of the James Language Dominance Test include ease of administration and scoring and its attempt to compensate for phonological and dialectal variations. Referring to these compensations, the author states that phonological variants produced by 10% of the sample were disregarded, while any comprehension item missed by 50% of the sample was considered a dialectal variation rather than an error. Scorers are, therefore, warned to accept immature versions of /rr/ and /br/ in Spanish as in the case of *calo/carro, pelo/perro,* and *lumble/lumbre.*

The test examiners must bear in mind that the instrument was developed for and normed upon Mexican-American children. Thus, application of its norms and compensations do not account for language deviations made by other Spanish-speaking groups. For example, Puerto Rican dialectal substitutions apparent in *cajo/carro, perjo/perro, jojo/rojo, puetta/puerta,* and *colbata/corbata* are not cited. Different varieties of Spanish representations are also available for some of the test items although they are not provided. For instance, *serpiente* could replace *víbora, avión/aeroplano,* and *fuego/lumbre* in other areas of the United States. While this is not a fault of the test, an examiner may not be aware of these variations. Such oversights could result in incorrect categorical classification of a child because three additional errors would alter the child's status.

In sum, the negative features of this test include its limited size and sampling of language items, particularly those concerned with the home environment; poor sample size used for standardization; lack of reported selection criterion in regards to this sample; and lack of information supporting its theoretical base, categorical classification cutoff points, reliability, and validity.

DOS AMIGOS VERBAL LANGUAGE SCALES (*Critchlow, 1974*)

General Description

Dos Amigos Verbal Language Scales, developed by Donald Critchlow, are designed to provide a measure of language dominance as well as to define developmental levels in Spanish and English for individual children within the age range of 5 years, 0 months to 13 years, 5 months. Although, in essence, the scales are a vocabulary test, the author goes to great lengths in the manual to prove that this vocabulary task involves the processes of association, integration, decoding, and encoding as it elicits meaningful responses at the "... comprehension or conceptual level in both languages" (p. 11). In addition, the author states that inferences drawn from test results could be used by other professionals to assist in identifying learning disabilities as well as indicating the level of the child's functional communication ability in both languages. The test can also serve as a screening tool.

Procedure

The test should be administered to individual children by a bilingual examiner in a relatively brief period of time. Test administration and subsequent scoring for each scale requires approximately 10 minutes.

The test itself consists of two scales that possess 85 stimulus words per language, arranged in order of increasing difficulty. Before presenting the actual test items, the examiner should review the concept of opposite and call for the child to demonstrate his or her comprehension of, or ability to produce, opposites. This may be accomplished by delivering an open-ended statement such as, "If a child is not a boy, the child is a _____," to the child.

Administration and scoring are straightforward and clearly reported in the manual. The examiner reads the stimulus item to the child and records a plus (+) or a zero (0) to discriminate between correct and incorrect responses. Alternatives are supplied in both language scales for some responses and, if given, should be accepted and credited as correct; for example, in English, item 34 presents *absent* as the stimulus word and provides for either *present* or *here* as the correct response.

Test administration continues until the child misses five consecutive items or completes the entire examination. Correct responses are summed for each scale and constitute the child's raw score. Corresponding percentile values are then obtained from the appropriate age tables in the manual and are used to determine language dominance. The language possessing the higher percentile for the child's age level is the dominant language.

Since these percentiles indicate the individual child's language development as compared to a sample of other bilingual bicultural children of the same age, the author cautions the examiner against using the test with monolingual monocultural children. Furthermore, Critchlow states that a child who is below the 50th percentile in both languages should be further evaluated for possible auditory deficits, visual perception deficits, and/or psychological problems.

Reliability and Validity

Test items were selected after 2 years of observing oral language activities in kindergarten through sixth grade classooms and subsequently compiling a list of the most commonly used words for each grade level. From this group, a random sample of 100 pairs of words in both English and Spanish was generated. These word pairs were given preliminary testing, reviewed by a panel of consultants, and reduced to the present 85.

During preliminary testing, a number of unexpected Spanish responses were noted. These were recorded and referred to a panel of Mexican-American individuals for acceptance or rejection. Responses deemed representative of a sample being tested and, therefore, acceptable were added to the test manual as possible and appropriate responses. Final order of difficulty was based on frequency analysis of preliminary testing responses, rather than on developmental levels in either language. Developmental levels with respect to each pair of words do not necessarily correspond in both languages.

Preliminary field testing was done on more than 300 children of Mexican-American ancestry and rearing, whose first language was Spanish. They were selected from three sites (a university reading-learning clinic, a public school reading laboratory, and a special education diagnostic center for a public school district) to serve as subjects and were tested by bilingual examiners.

The standardization sample consisted of 1,224 kindergarten through sixth grade children from southern Texas who met the aforementioned criteria. Test administration was once again conducted by bilingual examiners. Information on the distribution of sex, socioeconomic status, type of education, home environment, parent interaction, growth and development, and overall language ability is not given. No reliability or validity studies are reported.

The manual does infer a correlation between Dos Amigos and the Wechsler Intelligence Scale for Children (WISC). Specifically, the manual states that "Clinical studies reveal that those children who score at or below the mean in both English and Spanish reveal conceptual weaknesses when further tested with the Wechsler Intelligence Scale for Children" (p. 16).[1] Although Table 4 in the manual gives a conceptualization score in both English and Spanish based on the average of the WISC subtests of Comprehension, Similarities, and Vocabulary, the inferred correlation is not substantiated because of a lack of supporting information on the language employed in administration, sample size and representationality, and reliability and validity correlations.

Reviewers' Comments

Evaluation of Dos Amigos by Silverman, Noa, and Russell (1976) resulted in the following overall ratings: fair in measurement validity, good in examinee appropriateness, poor in technical excellence, and fair in administrative ability.

Teschner (1977) questioned how the original word count was obtained from the 2 years of observations. Specifically, he inquired about the use of recordings and/or transcriptions, and subsequent arrangement of these data. Teschner was also concerned over the lack of more possible alternative responses as well as the strict scoring system which could result in the misclassification of an individual child. Three and seven alternative responses are permitted for each of the 85 selections in English and Spanish, respectively, although many of the stimulus words in both languages allow for multiple opposite responses not listed. "... thus *costly* can be 'inexpensive,' ... as well as '*cheap*,' (listed) ... and for Spanish ... *enfermo/sano* can also stimulate '*curado, mejorado, aliviado*,' even '*bien*' ..." (p. 202).

Teschner continues, "I am surprised that the various Chicano educators assisting in the autochthonization of Critchlow's materials did not spot the possibility that stimulus words such as *pesado* and *crudo* would draw responses other than, respectively, '*ligero-liviano*' and '*cocido*'; the antonym of *pesado* as in 'Me cae pesado' is hardly going to be 'Me cae *ligero/liviano*' just as *crudo's* spontaneous antonym might well be 'uno que no se emborrachó' rather than *cocido*" (p. 202).

His insistence that this is a point to be considered is based on the fact that the purpose of the test is not only to determine dominance but also to determine functional levels for the child's language in general and that "... the consequences of an overly rigid, lock-step grading system

---

[1] *Editors' note:* This finding, of course, could simply mean that the WISC should not be given when communication has not been established.

may well be more far-reaching than first meets the eye" (p. 203). A child may be judged below normal through use of regionally accepted antonyms that are not classified as acceptable alternatives. He adds that Spanish dominance could be underestimated here, because the majority of cases where multiple antonyms for responses are readily discerned are present in the initial portion of the Spanish test form. He concludes by suggesting that this test should be carefully used by alert bilingual examiners who are willing to exercise greater latitude in the choice and acceptance of antonyms in response to test items than Critchlow presently permits. However, if Teschner's suggestion to consider alternative responses that could be considered correct is used, the examiner can no longer use the normative data supplied in the test manual.

Additional factors must also be considered. While it is assumed that the manual would directly state that this test was specifically designed for use in southern Texas, it does not. If other cultural heritages and regions were taken into account, even more acceptable alternatives could be generated. For example, Puerto Rican children who are sports fans could readily respond with *ganar* when presented with the stimulus item *perder*.

The test is easy to administer, although the time factor of 20 minutes per exam in the classroom setting would detract from its usefulness and the reliability of its results. If, as Teschner suspects, the test underestimates Spanish dominance, children may be misclassified and, therefore, misplaced because of their test scores. In addition, while test scores may assist classroom teachers in designing individual programs, extreme care must be exercised when these scores are used in reference to a child's placement in an entirely monolingual or bilingual program.

SHORT TESTS OF LINGUISTIC SKILLS (*Fredrickson and Wick, 1976*)

General Description

Short Tests of Linguistic Skills (STLS) were designed to assess general language achievement and dominance of 7- through 15-year-old bilingual students enrolled in grades three through eight. Parallel tests exist in English, Arabic, Chinese, Greek, Italian, Japanese, Korean, Pilipino, Polish, Spanish, and Vietnamese. The tests measure the four linguistic areas of listening, reading, writing, and speaking.

Separate individual testing of skills is discrete point in nature. However, the scoring for the oral and written responses, which consists of three classifications, tends to be more integrative.

Procedure

English and a parallel test form can be administered in approximately 1½ hours; however, it is recommended that only one language be assessed per day, beginning with the child's suspected dominant language. Time allotments per group section are as follows: 10 minutes for introduction, 15 minutes for listening, 10 minutes for reading, and 10 minutes for writing. An optional 10-minute break may be taken between the reading and writing sections. Individually administered speaking tests require approximately 5 minutes per student per language.

At the onset of the examination each student receives a test booklet and fills in the appropriate information. Responses for the first three tests of each form are either written in by the student or selected from the given choices by blackening the correct circle.

The listening test consists of four parts, each of which presents an example and five stimulus items. Items cannot be repeated by the examiner. The test divisions are as follows: sound discrimination, written representations of auditory cues, yes/no questions, and following commands at the sentence level.

The reading test similarly consists of four parts with five stimuli items apiece. Parts A and B measure the student's ability to complete open-ended statements by selecting the correct word from among four given choices; for example, *He is writing with a* _____, followed by the choices *den, hen, pen,* and *ten*. Students are instructed to raise their hands for assistance should a question arise. The latter two parts, C and D, assess reading comprehension at the sentence level through questions and sentence completions.

The third test, writing, is also divided into four parts, each containing five items. In Part A, the students must be able to identify correct and incorrect spelling. Before beginning actual test items, students are informed that there is one correct response per item. Students are then to blacken in the circle in front of any misspelled word, or if there are none, in front of "No Mistakes." Part B requires students to finish an incomplete sentence appropriately based upon a pictorial cue. An example, showing a drawing of a fountain pen and an accompanying incomplete response, is provided. Statements, such as "Where did the children go? They _____ to school," are listed and the students are to fill in the blanks. Part D requires the student to respond to a picture and a direct question with a complete sentence. Upon completion of this part, the test booklets are collected.

Before administration of the speaking test, the students then complete a self-rating instrument. The text examiner delivers questions that explore the student's view of his or her language comprehension in the dominant language, and a one- to four-point rating scale is used to code the student's response:

Do you understand everything they say? (4 points)
Do you understand almost everything, except for a word or two? (3 points)
Do you understand only some of what they say? (2 points)
Do you understand only a word or two? (1 point)

This same rating system applies to questions dealing with reading, writing, and speaking skills. There are no directions on how the examiner is to determine language dominance prior to administration of the test batteries.

The speaking test, in four parts, is then completed on an individual basis. Scoring is done simultaneously with testing. The test examiner should be a native speaker. Therefore, the classroom teacher may not be qualified to administer the test. In Part A, the student is instructed to answer five questions in complete sentences. The example is: "What is the name of your school? The examiner is instructed to avoid making cues or gestures when eliciting the student's response. In Part B, complete sentence responses are obtained through the presentation of questions in conjunction with visual and motor activities, and other aids. Five questions about Chicago are used to obtain complete sentence responses in Part C, and a picture is used to elicit five descriptive sentences in Part D. At the conclusion of this part, the examiner is instructed to thank the student for his or her time and tell the student that he or she did very well.

Specific and detailed scoring procedures are given in the examiner's manual in addition to examples. (The tests, however, can be scored by a combination of machine- and hand-scoring, or by hand-scoring alone.) For example, in Part B of the writing test, the student is asked to use correct and appropriate word forms in the respective language being tested. In scoring, one point is awarded if the word recorded by the student creates a grammatically correct sentence, without regard to spelling accuracy. No credit is awarded if the written response is illogical, given in another language, or is an inappropriate description of the stimulus picture. The example from page 47 of the manual is as follows:

> Rabbit, rabet, raddit, etc.
> Bunny, buny
> Hare (must be a singular noun)   one point (1)
>
> Rabbits, rabits (incorrect because of plural)
> Bird (inappropriate to picture)
> Conejo (not in language being tested)   no points (0)

In Part C, one point is given if the response is a grammatically correct sentence completion and meets the aforementioned criteria.

Part D is scored in three categories: one point is given if the student's response is a complete sentence, answers the question, is grammatically correct, is composed of appropriate vocabulary, and has no spelling errors that would interfere with communication. One-half point is awarded if the student's response is short of a full point answer but does not show the faults that would call for no credit. The sentence must be a complete sentence and show understanding of the question, but it may have minor errors in grammar, some inappropriate vocabulary words, and spelling errors that do not prevent communication. The example given is as follows:

> How many persons are there in the picture?
> There are four persons.
> Their are fore pelpo in the picture. (Correct grammar,
> misspellings only.)   One point (1)
>
> There are foure.
> There four persons in picture. (Minor grammar or
> vocabulary errors.)   One-half point (½)
>
> Four.
> Four person. (Incomplete sentence.)
> I don't know. (Little or no evidence that the question
> was understood.)   No points (0)

The scoring for the English speaking test is similar; however, it emphasizes functional language abilities. To receive one point the student's response must be a complete sentence, answer the question (although the information may be inaccurate), possess appropriate vocabulary and correct grammar, and be free from pronunciation errors that interfere with communication. The one-half point response, although a complete sentence, falls short of the above but indicates some understanding of the question.

A zero point response is an incomplete sentence or a complete sentence that is deficient in content. If the latter is given, then the sentence does not answer the question, vocabulary is unrelated to the test item, major errors in grammar are present, or pronunciation errors exist that interfere with communication. For example:

What is the most popular beverage served in your country?
Coffee is the most popular beverage.
I don't understand the meaning of the word "beverage." One point (1)
Wine are good with meals One-half point (½)
Football, or no response. No points (0)

Reliability and Validity

There were no reported studies for reliability or validity in the manual. Furthermore, no studies that were reported dealt with the actual equivalence of the different language forms.

A revised version of the STLS (from the original pilot of 1974–1975) was administered in March, 1976, to a sample of 120 students. There were 10 students in each of 12 groups which were divided by dominant languages (monolingual English, English dominant, Spanish dominant, and monolingual Spanish) and by age groups (third through fourth grades, fifth through sixth grades, and seventh through eighth grades). These groups were chosen to determine the degree of discrimination of the test. Minimally, the test needs to allow monolingual English students to do well on the English half and poorly on the non-native half. If the English-speaking students do well on the non-native half, then the test is measuring something other than language fluency. As was expected, the monolingual groups performed at the chance level on the non-native language half of the test. Test scores increased with age, except for the scores of the English dominant group on the Spanish half of the test. The listening test tended to be the easiest, while the writing test was the most difficult. Item statistics and inconsistencies in scoring were then discovered, and revisions in each were made in the test manual.

The STLS is in the process of being normed in Chicago. The procedure developed will enable teachers to place children in different categories of language dominance based upon each child's absolute score on the English half of the test, and also by comparing that score to scores on other portions of the language test.

Reviewers' Comments

Oller (1976) in reviewing the Bilingual Syntax Measure made a comparison to the STLS. He stated, "As far as I know, few published tests (and none in the field of bilingual education) have been so thoroughly planned and researched, nor have the bases of the tests, been so clearly and explicitly stated in readily accessible published format. The *BSM* in this respect is far superior for instance, to the series of Short Tests for

Linguistic Skills produced by the Board of Education, City of Chicago" (p. 399).

There are a few things, nonetheless, that must be considered in regard to the Short Tests for Linguistic Skills. First, although the manual states that a total of 90 minutes for the administration of the test in two languages is adequate, it must be remembered that the two 5-minute individual interviews are included in that total 90-minute span. If this interview time is multiplied by 25 students in a classroom, the total testing time per class would certainly exceed 90 minutes—the chances of having equal numbers of interviewers and interviewees are rather slim. Other factors that need to be considered in the individual oral interviews include testing space, organization, and training of interviewers. This does not mean the test should not be used. Rather it shows that administration must be carefully planned and that the manual is somewhat misleading in its time assumptions.

Second, although it is stated that the different language tests are parallel and not translations, there is neither explanation nor proof that the tests are indeed parallel. The program guide only reports that

> A parallel format is used throughout all the tests using the same linguistic areas, the same subtests, and a parallel selection of items. Items are chosen so that they are culturally specific in terms of names, places, pictures, and terms that should be familiar to the student of a particular culture. The items are also language specific in that they test for particular sounds and words that are characteristic of the language being tested (p. 6).

However, evidence that the tests are in fact parallel is lacking. All that is known is that "... more than eighty test writers, technical advisors, and language experts" (p. 6) worked on the different language tests. The guide also states that the test items have been chosen so that they increase in difficulty as the test progresses; in each subtest the first two items are easier than the last two, and the middle is about average in difficulty.

There is a dearth of research on order of acquisition in non-English languages, and controversy and gaps exist in knowledge of English acquisition order for native speakers as well as for second language learners. Thus, the order of difficulty may or may not be actually parallel. For instance, in Spanish/English oral test questions, there seems to be some uneven difficulty equivalence: "¿Como se llama tu maestro bilingüe?" (What is your bilingual teacher's name?) is paired with "Do you prefer big cities or small towns?" (examiner's manual, pp. 25, 43).

The authors are careful to include a section on the uses and limitations of the tests. Factors they specifically mention are the brevity of the tests, which accordingly only provide approximate indications of a student's level of skills, and omission of descriptions on very advanced or very retarded levels. The necessity of teacher observation and other essential information about each child is needed prior to making decisions about placement in a bilingual program. Caution and discretion should be exercised before placing a child on the basis of the STLS alone. It is also advisable to review placement decisions periodically to determine if individuals have been appropriately placed. This is true, however, of any system, particularly if placement is based solely on a test score.

One particularly troublesome scoring area is the insistence upon complete sentences in the speaking portion of the exam; people do not always speak in complete sentences. Forcing such an unnatural condition may inhibit a child and result in an unrealistic measure of any true functional communication ability in the language. This same insistence for complete sentences in the writing test is not such a contradiction to real-life use of language since writing is a more formal use of language, which is usually congruent with complete sentences.

The authors state that the STLS will do a number of things (program guide, p. 6). Yet nowhere is there any information on how to interpret scores or on how to adapt, change, modify, or develop curricula on the basis of individual's scores. According to Anastasi (1976), the crucial item to be included in any test manual is how to interpret test scores. This information is totally overlooked in the STLS Manual. Despite the fact that norms had not been established in 1976, minimal help for the teacher in interpreting test scores could have been provided. Furthermore, there is no information on how the students in the normative sample were assigned to the subgroups. Students who had been rated by their teachers as truly bilingual were the only ones being included in the normative sample, yet how this rating was accomplished is not stated, nor are the criteria for comparing non-bilinguals with these data. Division of students into different degrees of dominance is also not explained.

For anyone interested in language assessment, it is extremely frustrating to see so much effort and time put into a test and so many "experts who served as technical reviewers" listed without knowing what questions, problems, and concerns they may have had. This is particularly bothersome in terms of an apparent dichotomy in this test: it does not attempt to isolate four skills in purist terms (program guide, p. 9), yet it provides scores that could readily be interpreted in that way.

The problem of an assessment instrument for use in large urban multilingual multicultural settings is a very real one, and the STLS is an attempt to solve that problem. However, there is a great deal of work still needed to have an effective, easy-to-administer, interpretative instrument for such settings.

THE BOEHM TEST OF BASIC CONCEPTS (*Boehm, 1971*)

General Description

The Boehm Test of Basic Concepts was designed to assess kindergarten, first, and second grade children's picture recognition vocabulary in English. A Spanish version was added later. The test uses a multiple-choice format of 50 verbally presented basic concepts that the author calls essential for academic achievement in these primary school years. Items were chosen in a multistage process from what is called a comprehensive selection of preschool and primary reading, science, and arithmetic curriculum materials. Supportive data and references are not given.

The test can be administered individually or to an entire class. Concepts are presented approximately according to level of difficulty in two test booklets of 25 concepts each. While subtests are not delineated, arbitrary classification of the concepts into the categories of Space (location, direction, orientation, dimensions), Quantity (number), Time, and the collective Miscellaneous provides for categorical analysis of results. Boldface type is used to distinguish the context category of the concept tested by the Boehm, as opposed to the other contexts in which it may be employed. However, this presentation of type renders an impossible visual discrimination task for the reader.

Analysis of errors, the author suggests, may be performed on individual and/or classroom responses. This information can then be used to assist the teacher in developing an appropriate remediation program.

Procedure

The simplicity of administration is a strong feature of the Boehm. The format permits division of test administration into two separate sessions pending the examiner's determination of the child's fatigue and attention span. However, both booklets should be given in their entirety, and once begun, should be completed. The test takes approximately 20 minutes, although it is not a timed test. A booklet and utensil for marking responses to the items are required. Each response is indicated by placing an X on the picture that corresponds to concepts being presented. If the child wishes to change a response, the error must be circled or erased and another X made. Indicating responses in this manner presents a paradox: the test, designed to ascertain the child's knowledge of 50 possibly unfamiliar school-oriented concepts, requires the child to have mastered the similarly oriented concepts of placing an X or drawing a circle around a pictured item.

Bold print is used for ready recognition of the verbal directions to be given by the administrator, and detailed directions and procedures are also supplied. Nonetheless, these directions do not address responses that could be indicated in other ways, such as by pointing. While variation in mode of response is a violation of standard procedure, and therefore prevents the application of normative data, it would not interfere with the results. The author herself suggests use of this pointing response format when adapting the test to pre-kindergarten children.

Each page is coded with a picture of a common object in a shaded box in the corner. This approach facilitates group administration because it assures the classroom teacher that children are on the page that parallels the stimulus being presented and, therefore, compensates for their difficulty in turning and locating pages.

Reliability and Validity

The percentage of children from the normative group passing each item is given according to grade level (kindergarten, first, second), which is further divided into socioeconomic level (low, middle, high). Both beginning-of-the-year and mid-year information is presented. Percentile equivalents of raw scores, means and standard deviations, reliability coefficients, and standard errors of measurement are presented by grade and socioeconomic level for the mid-year norms. This same information is provided for the beginning-of-the-year norms, but without reliability coefficients and standard error of measurement. Percentiles are reported in five percentile units, except for the extremes.

Normative information was developed following a trial testing of a sample of 267 kindergarten, 306 first grade, 264 second grade, and 297 third grade pupils from four schools in New York state, which reportedly represented various socioeconomic levels. Approximately 100 concepts were employed. Analysis of data resulted in selection of the fifty best items that 1) each measured a different concept, 2) had point-biserial correlations exceeding 0.30, 3) showed fairly even rises in percent-passing values across age levels, and 4) together yielded a roughly normal distribution of percent-passing values centered around 0.50 for the kindergarten pupils. These 50 items were then arranged in order of difficulty, although no criteria for this judgment is given. Minor revisions were made and the items reevaluated on a second sample of children which was approximately three times larger than the initial sample. The order was rearranged to improve order of difficulty, and the final revision was used to obtain normative data.

The author states that the test was designed as a "screening and teaching instrument, rather than for predictive or administrative purposes," in an attempt to justify her failure to select "standardization samples representative of children in the kindergarten, first, and second grades in the nation as a whole" (p. 15). However, because the author has noted that lack of conceptual ability may be a possible source of poor scholastic achievement, test administrators may attempt to predict a child's academic achievement on the basis of this score. In so doing, they would conclude that scores at or above the mean corresponded to academic success, while scores below the mean corresponded to poor achievement. In addition, school administrators were given the freedom to establish their own criteria upon which to judge socioeconomic levels of the children employed in the normative sample. A total of 16 schools across the United States were chosen to participate in the study.

No information is given as to sex or preschool experience of the young children involved in the normative sample, both of which are potential variables in language acquisition. Chronological ages were not reported because grade level was the factor considered. This information would be important on a language measure, since school districts can vary as much as 4 months on birthdate cutoffs for entrance. One must also take into consideration that kindergarten is not mandatory in many states.

A total of 9,737 children were used to establish beginning-of-the-year norms, whereas 2,669 were used for mid-year normative data. Through chart analysis of standardization samples, the reviewers find that the same schools were not used for beginning and mid-year testing. The mid-year testing was conducted first (1968–1969), over a 3½-month period (mid-November to late February), whereas the beginning-of-the-year data was collected the following year over a 2-month period (September to October). The author presents misleading conclusions in regard to the normative data: "The groups that score the lowest on the test in the fall (and, therefore, have the most to learn) tend to make the largest gains in mastery of concepts over the course of approximately a half-year" (p. 16). These groups referred to are not only from different areas of the country but are also the younger grades and lower socioeconomic levels. Therefore, one can speculate that these findings only represent different geographical areas or, more important, adjustment to the task required rather than increased concept mastery.

Although the author states several times that the normative group only represents a wide geographical distribution and not a representative sample of the country, the table on standardization samples by city, grade, and socioeconomic level suggests this "wide geographical distribution" statement is misleading for the two following reasons:

1. In the beginning-of-the-year sample, nearly all of the 16 school districts were in large cities, whereas only three of the five school districts used for mid-year testing were in large cities.
2. Although the distribution of cities included an adequate representation of the midwest, west, and east, the number of subjects from each area varied a great deal. For example, four western cities provided a total of 1,577 subjects (three in California at 150, 973, and 64 each and one in Washington at 390) out of the total of 4,659 first graders but only 548 of the 3,517 kindergarten children were from western states.

The Spearman-Brown Prophecy Formula, a correction for test length, was used to obtain split-half correlations for mid-year data. These correlation coefficients ranged from 0.68 to 0.90 for children at each grade and socioeconomic level. Similar reliability coefficients were calculated for each group of pupils, namely, all kindergarten, first, and second grade pupils. These coefficients were 0.90, 0.85, and 0.81 for these three groups, respectively. Standard error of measurement computed for each of these groups resulted in the deviations of 2.7, 2.1, and 1.7, respectively. These measures of error are an indication of the low reliability of this test instrument. Calculating the mean of means for each of the three grade levels results in the new mean scores of 18.5, 50 (51.26 actual score calculated due to the author's omission of one group of children), and 46.15. These measures can then be used to calculate the 95% confidence interval with respect to the standard error of measurements. These intervals would be as follows:

   13–23 Kindergarten
   46–50 First grade
     (estimated as mean of 0.50 was employed)
   43–50 Second grade

These 95% confidence interval levels indicate that if the same test was administered many times to the individual who scored at the new mean on the first administration, 95% of the retest scores would be expected to be in these intervals. In other words, if the true score of an individual were at the mean, for instance that of 18.5 for kindergarten children, successive testing should result in scores no lower than 13 and no higher than 23. This 10-point range is quite large.

The author contends that the test has content validity; however, the frequency of occurrence of each of these verbal concepts in various curriculum materials is not reported. It would be difficult for the reader to determine if indeed the items chosen represent the content of various curricula used in constructing the test. It is also difficult to ascertain if this test measures verbal comprehension of "school language" or verbal comprehension of language in general. In addition, if test items reflect the concepts employed in classroom curricula, the test itself would be of value only in regard to these specific materials. Since new texts and updated materials have come out, perhaps the same conceptual representation would not be found. Thus, the test could be totally out of date.

Reviewers' Comments

In addition to the above criticisms of test format and statistical support, several other problems should be addressed.

Variation in the number and format of test items per page was not controlled; some pages have three items while others have four. Some items present three separate referents, whereas others consist of a total picture with parts to be identified housed in one large box. This is a potential source of confusion for the child. In addition, while the pictures are of adequate size and clarity, their depiction of the author's intent is, at times, somewhat ambiguous. For example, the concept *almost* is depicted by three bottles containing various quantities of liquid; one is almost full, the other almost empty.

Two plans are presented for scoring the test booklets and recording results on the Class Record Form. At times these details are not only unnecessary but also somewhat insulting because they imply that the test administrator lacks common sense. For instance:

> Place together the two booklets for each child (with Booklet two following Booklet one.) Then stack the pairs of booklets in any order desired (for example, alphabetically).

or

> If there are more than thirty children in the class, two Class Record Forms should be fastened together . . . (p. 8).

The Class Record Form facilitates scoring and recording of percentiles both of each child's score and of the class average because it contains miniature pictures of the items with the correct answers indicated. In addition, this form permits easy retrieval of the information on the pattern of these responses. A chart for determining the percent of children passing an item in each class is also provided. No description is given of acceptance or rejection of the children's markings or of what would indicate an acceptable response. Examiner qualifications are not designated; however, since the child's picture recognition is partially contingent upon the examiner's verbal presentation of test items, it is hoped that he or she would have normal speech and adequate knowledge about the behavior of young children. The room should have optimum visual and auditory conditions as well.

Interpretation and use of the test results are explained at great lengths in terms of remediation, the discussion of which alludes to the weaknesses of this instrument. Boehm does not adequately differentiate between concepts and linguistic labels for concepts. In discussing reasons for concept difficulty, she does point out some problems in generalizing a linguistic concept and difficulty in representing some concepts pictorially. Contemporary research findings in semantics would have enhanced this section of the manual.

Concerning the child's inability to respond or inappropriate responses to test items, the author suggests that the examiner determine: 1) whether it is due to ambiguity of the pictorial representation or whether it is out of the child's realm of experience, 2) language difficulty where the specific label is not known or alternative concept labels are unfamiliar, or 3) inherent difficulty with the concept itself. However, how the examiner is to determine the cause of the child's difficulty is not explained. Suggested remediation indicates that the actual test items should be taught. The most common error made by the children interviewed, the author reports, was that the children employed the opposite concept. This seems to indicate that the children are developing the correct concepts, or the concepts that are vital to their environment without remediation, or specific conceptual drills.

Following is a summary of the six reviewers' comments in the *Seventh Mental Measurements Yearbook* (Buros, 1972). Reviews and excerpts were presented by B. R. McCandless, C. D. Smock, F. S. Freeman, G. Lawlor, V. H. Noll, and B. B. Proger (pp. 625-629) and focus on the English form, not the Spanish translation. Many of the same criticisms are mentioned in these reviewers' comments. Each reviewer makes positive comments about the test booklets and ease of instruction; Two reviewers point out that the drawings also attend to racial aspects. Most reviewers criticized the value of using this test with second graders or first graders from middle to high socioeconomic levels since normative scores are so high. Most reviewers also questioned its validity, specifically the claim of content validity.

McCandless was skeptical that the test, although easy to administer, could be used with large groups without proctors. He also recognized the disproportionate number of subjects in specific groups for obtaining normative data, indicating a large number of the low socioeconomic children came from a southeastern school system. Smock reinforces the notion that "disadvantaged children" frequently do not know the school concepts for which the Boehm test probes. (This of course is part of the identification/remediation purpose of the Boehm.)

Noll strongly questions the validity and asks the important question: "Is there any relation between mastery of them [concepts tested] and quality of school achievement?" (p. 627). Since Boehm does not substantiate the supposition stated at the beginning of the manual and, furthermore, denies the use of the test as a predictor (no predictive validity), Noll essentially questions the value of the test. He also points out that "most of the statistical data provided are superfluous" (p. 628). Proger notes there is a high degree of internal consistency for mid-year scores, but that no reliability for beginning year scores is presented. He also suggests that the author present some stronger evidence (e.g., literature review) regarding theories underlying the test's development.

Lawlor makes reasonable criticisms especially when he suggests items should deal with only one basic concept. Actually, the items do deal with one concept, but the inference is that they deal with more than one aspect of that item. For example, the concept *middle* is tested as a spatial concept but categorized as a spatial and temporal concept. Freeman very strongly criticizes Boehm's statement about cognitive development. He points out that many tests have long been used to probe this area. Unfortunately, Freeman did not further point out another part of the same statement that the test has "implications for further achievement" (p. 629). If Boehm considers this test to be related to future achievement, there are no validity measures to support this claim.

From the viewpoint of the authors of this chapter, positive characteristics of the test include a clearly written examiner's manual, ease of administration and scoring, and somewhat satisfactory pictures. There is potential for use in identifying individual children who are having difficulty with the concepts tested and potential for establishing class norms and remediation procedures.

Negative characteristics of the test include an unsupported theoretical base, lack of predictive validity, ambiguity of some items, testing concepts in one context only, questionable content validity, and poor control of population selection (particularly concerning socioeconomic levels). The test has questionable use with second graders because of the high means obtained. In addition, there are incomplete descriptions of subjects regarding early educational experience, a lack of reliability measures on beginning of the year data, and low split-half correlation coefficients for mid-year data.

Other weaknesses are apparent. Norms were established on a population that is admittedly not representative of the nation as a whole (and, in fact, was not as geographically representative as the author claims), yet the normative information is presented for the teacher to use and compare test findings of individuals and classes for planning a remediation program. Furthermore, the author refers to the test as a "screening" device and then presents information on how to teach the concepts tested as if the test were a comprehensive measure. With these serious weaknesses in the English version of the test one can only question the use of a Spanish translation. Not only is the information on the non-English version sparse, but the advisability of measuring a child's home language by studying school vernacular is also highly questionable.

TEST OF AUDITORY COMPREHENSION OF LANGUAGE (*Carrow, 1973*)

General Description

The Test of Auditory Comprehension of Language was originally designed as a diagnostic tool to measure children's comprehension of language structure by having them select a picture in response to a verbal stimulus. This instrument was developed for the 3- to 7-year age range. Carrow (1968) designed the Spanish version of the test to compare the comprehension of English and Spanish in Mexican-American preschool children and to analyze the developmental sequence of both languages in these children in comparison with the performance of a group of monolingual English speakers. Performance determines the child's developmental level of comprehension as well as indicating specific areas of weakness, the need for intervention, educational planning, and remediation in English or Spanish. A screening form of the test is also available.

The test booklet is in a durable three-ring binder. It is well-organized and is self-inclusive with the manual and 101 test plates. There is a brief history and rationale for the development of the test in the foreword, and supportive studies for assessing language comprehension as a predictor of language ability are reported in the introduction. Information concerning the actual test design and construction, special directions on the administration of both the Spanish and English forms, and test validity and reliability information charts are also included.

The subcategories tested are form classes and function words that include vocabulary (nouns, adjectives, verbs, prepositions, and adverbs), morphological markers (*-er* and *-est*), grammatical constructs (involving contrasts of case, gender, number, tense, status, voice, and mood), and syntactic structures (predication, modification, and complimentation).

Although norms for the subcategories are not available, the score sheet design does permit grouping of test items according to various linguistic categories. Baseline data on these categories may aid the examiner in determining the child's specific area(s) of difficulty. Each item may also be examined to obtain the age at which either 75% or 90% of the children passed it. A revised test form that combines the morphological and grammatical items to comprise one subgroup is on the market at present (Blood and Greenberg, 1978). The new test form consists of three subcategories rather than four. Blood and Greenberg caution against the application of the summary mean and standard deviation charts from the four categories to the new test form.

Procedure

The test is easy to administer and has explicit directions that supply the examiner with the stimulus statement. Only a pointing response is required. The examiner is specifically instructed not to elaborate on any item, nor to provide encouragement or discouragement through facial expression or remarks. Stimuli may only be repeated if they were misstated initially. The test requires approximately 20 minutes to complete; however, it is not a timed test.

The test does require that the examiner be thoroughly familiar with the test items and manual. In addition, it is suggested in the manual that he or she should hold a bachelor's degree in either education, psychology, or sociology, and have significant testing experience. Regarding the Spanish version, it is advisable to have a qualified person of the child's same cultural group administer the test, because studies indicate that children respond with their maximum performance when the examiner is of the same cultural group. Interpretation of scores should be done by someone with a firm knowledge of linguistics.

Each of the 101 plates is designed with three line drawings to decrease the possibility of guessing. These realistic line drawings are readily recognizable and thus capture the child's attention. Their size, clarity, and placement are appropriate in that these attributes serve to eliminate confusion and distractibility of detail and space. It is interesting to note, however, that the human pictorial representations do not include any of the minority groups, despite the fact that the test is supposed to include these groups in its basic purpose and design. The line drawings are arranged so that each one represents the referent for the linguistic item being tested, and an alternative picture(s) represent(s) the referent(s) for the contrasting linguistic form(s). If only one such contrast exists, the third picture is then a decoy. Redundancy in signaling has been avoided in testing grammatical forms.

Scoring procedures are easy and quick to complete. The examiner scores one point for each correct item marked on the score sheet. These points are then totaled to obtain the raw score, which may be converted to an age equivalency score through the use of a table in the manual. Age equivalency norms range from ages 3 years, 0 months to 6 years, 11 months. Percentile rank equivalents are also available, using the child's chronological age and raw score as well as tables. The entire test must be used to apply normative data, because items are presented by linguistic category rather than by age level or difficulty. Concerning table 9 (p. 26) in the manual, the percentiles are not equally spaced within each age group. The tables are basically self-explanatory, but rather explicit and detailed instructions for their use are also delineated in the manual.

Since median performance and variability for each age group is also designated, the examiner may compare the child's performance to that of his or her peers by calculating the number of standard deviations above or below the mean score nearest which the child happens to fall. (See sample information on normative data, when deciding whether this is a true sample and indication of peers' performance).

Specific analysis of linguistic categories is possible and may be desired if the child has demonstrated abilities well below his or her chronological age. Norms for the subcategories are not available, although baseline data and the ages at which 75%–90% of the children passed each item are provided. This information may be beneficial in determining a focus for therapy.

Reliability and Validity

The English version of the fifth edition of the Test of Auditory Comprehension of Language was normed on a middle-class sample of 200 Black, Anglo, and Mexican-American children, ages 3 through 6, with 50 children in each age group. The author justifies combining performance of the three ethnic groups by noting a study by Jones in 1972 that resulted in a minimal correlation coefficient for Black and Anglo children of 0.77, and an unpublished study that she conducted (no date or data are reported). Lack of information concerning her study, and the minimal correlation coefficient, tend to raise doubt about the stated conclusion that the performance of middle-class children within these three ethnic groups does not vary significantly.

The major problem with the test lies with the normative data, specifically the sampling distribution upon which the test was standardized. The procedure used in obtaining the sample is not supplied, nor is the region, sex, education, language proficiency, handicaps, and ethnic breakdown per age group reported. If the examiner assumes that the procedures used were the same as those employed in the initial formation of the test (Carrow 1968, 1971), then the test is highly regional and restricting at best. In preceding cases the author has used samples drawn from the Austin, Texas, school districts because they were convenient and available, ignoring the rest of the United States. Furthermore, it is questionable whether this sample will represent the children for whom this test was developed.

The fifth edition of the English version is the only one that provides a normative study with a description of the population upon which the test was standardized. Even if it is assumed that sex and ethnic breakdown are equal, and that all educational levels and regions were represented proportionately, the limited sample size would result in a breakdown which places approximately four children in each cell by sex, age, and ethnicity (Black, Anglo, Mexican-American). The norms indicate that all standard deviations, percentiles, and mean scores are applicable only for a middle-class child within these three ethnic groups, and that these standards are based on a sample size of approximately four children at 6-month intervals, or eight children at yearly intervals, if all characteristics are deemed equal. Thus the inferences the examiner makes from the test results are questionable, particularly since table 6 (p. 21) in the manual does indicate some ethnic variance in the English form of the test.

Preliminary testing resulted in subsequent revision of actual test items and modification of test plates. Initially a total of 123 items were presented to a sample of 159 children within the ages of 2 years, 10 months through 7 years, 9 months (2;10-7;9), "who had I.Q.'s over 80; were free from severe speech and hearing problems, and were monolingual" (Carrow, 1968). These children were considered to have passed a test item when 60% of their respective age group passed that item. In light of the small sample size and the 33% factor of chance per each referent, a cutoff of 80% with a larger sample size would have been more accurate as an indicator of a child's actual comprehension of the linguistic item being tested.

Concerning the Spanish version, the test was initially tested on 40 children, ages 2;6 to 6;6, to standardize the procedure, revise specific items, and establish a reference point where 60% or more of the children passed each item. The test was then administered to 99 children from below poverty levels with Mexican-American surnames, ages 3;10 through 6;9, at four day care centers in Harris County, Texas, and three centers in Houston, Texas (Carrow, 1971). Regional and educational variations were not taken into account nor were variations in language proficiency. However, sex was considered, although the sample size for each age level was quite small. The breakdown is shown in Table 1.

Language fluency and competency were then determined on the basis of a language sample, and depended on subjective judgments of the examiner who did remain the same, for some consistency throughout the testing procedure. Specific information on the age at which the second language was acquired, the extent of bilingual background, and language proficiency were not indicated. However, 30% of the children were reportedly bilingual. This was based on the author's definition as "... exposure of two languages, regardless of the degree of competency" (Carrow, 1971). This sample in turn was compared to the English monolingual control group previously mentioned. Educational background, sex, and age were not matched in subsequently making comparisons and drawing conclusions. These factors must be considered when examining the reliability and validity of the test instrument.

The examiner should also be aware of the fact that although tables 3-7 (pp. 17-22) in the manual appear to be norms for the Spanish and English forms of the test, they are not. Some of the studies concerning

Table 1. Breakdown by age and sex of 99 children with Mexican-American surnames who were given a preliminary version of the Test of Auditory Comprehension of Language in Spanish

Age range (years;months)	Sex Boys	Girls	Total number of children
3;10-4;3	10	7	17
4;4-4;9	8	8	16
4;10-5;3	16	7	23
5;4-5;9	11	13	24
5;10-6;9	10	9	19
	55	44	99

reliability are inapplicable since the test data did not include representations of these populations in the normative sample. Furthermore, the test sample should include the individuals for whom the test was designed, and should represent their individual differences. Because of the composition of the normative sample, the test should be administered to normal middle-class children within the previously stated three ethnic groups and should not be used in reference to children outside of this category. In addition, no statistical procedures are supplied, and in one instance a study is reported that found predictive ability for dysphasic children at a 1-year interval. These data should have been reported under the validity information.

Test-retest reliability correlation coefficients were first obtained in 1971 for the English and Spanish versions. Once again, sample size was small and specific information on the breakdown of children was not indicated. The reported test-retest correlation coefficients were 0.93 and 0.94 for Spanish and English, respectively, which suggests a high correlation. Since reliability is only valid for the ages that were tested and retested, the breakdown on age rather than mean age would have been more appropriate and lent more information. Reliability correlation coefficients were also obtained from the studies performed on kindergarten and first grade students by Leon P. Edmonston of the Division of Research and Evaluation, Data Processing Branch, Southwest Educational Development Laboratory in 1969–1970. These correlations were 0.69 and 0.61 for the English and Spanish versions, respectively. These correlations are quite low and are not considered to be significant. No scorer reliability measures were obtained.

Construct validity was employed because age, an outside factor, was correlated with test performance. That is, the test was asserted to be valid because an increase in age corresponded with an increase in score, children with language disorders or handicaps scored lower than children without handicaps, and handicapped children's performance also increased with time or age (the dysphasic study). However, test validity may not be substantiated by studies on samples that were not represented in the original normative sample. Underlying all developmental tests is the assumption that development does take place. Basing test validity on this one assumption is poor for three reasons: The tight growth curve 1) does not take into consideration the plateaus in development, 2) seriously underestimates the population variance because it accounts only for normals, and 3) establishes a confidence interval that is poorer at the tails. Therefore, the age range for which the test is useful should be smaller than that tested.

In addition, since the population is also so limited, the correlation between age and score would not be a good predictor or indicator of performance. The population is shown in Table 2 (p. 14 in the manual), but breakdown of attributes of the sample are not available, and reasons for the sample size varying at each age level are not provided. The small, unequal sample sizes at the extremes and lack of female/male comparability are two of the sample faults that should be corrected. Carrow (1968) found that language comprehension subscores and total scores were larger for girls than for boys; yet construct validity and test norms do not reveal or account for this. Growth curves could also have been fit to the six t scores obtained from the seven means (p. 14).

The author does not indicate that the translation corresponds to the developmental information on the Spanish language, and she does not give reference to any studies that do provide this information.

Reviewers' Comments

In addition to the serious statistical problems suggested above, specific items in the Spanish version of the Test of Auditory Comprehension of Language (shown in Table 2) have been found to be representative of only the Mexican form of Spanish spoken by those for whom the test was designed. Therefore, several items are not appropriate for other Spanish-speaking populations or regions. In addition, some items clearly indicate that the test is a transliteration, rather than translation. The manual does not explain whether or not reverse translation was employed in developing the Spanish form (i.e., English to Spanish and then an independent translator providing a translation back to English to check for accuracy).

The test examiner should review the test items and their comparability with English presentations as well as their applicability to the Spanish group being tested. If the test items are altered, normative data may not be adhered to, but only used as a reference.

In general, the major strengths of the Test of Auditory Comprehension of Language are that it is a quick and easy to administer screening test of linguistic ability. The pictures are easy to recognize and the test is portable and fairly durable. A total raw score as well as subcategory and individual item analyses are provided along with suggested normative data. The test's weaknesses lie with the lack of information supplied on the procedure used in obtaining the sample, the limited sample size, and poor representation of attributes, poor validity, and unpublished information on the Spanish version. The procedure used in the studies that were conducted to obtain the test questions or their Spanish counterparts and norms should be summarized or referred to at some point so that the

Table 2. Items in the Spanish version of the Test of Auditory Comprehension of Language that represent only the Mexican form of Spanish, rendering them inappropriate for other Spanish-speaking populations

Item number	Words	Other choices or interpretations
5	rancho ranchos	hacienda, granja, cortijo, (South American) estancia The given response item can be the food in the army or a poor house, like a hut. (Rancho es la comida en el army o puede ser una casa muy pobre.)
6	borrego	oveja, carnero Can refer to a stupid person as a borrego. (Borrego se le dice a un tonto o estúpido también.)
9	pintura	cuadro, paisaje
10	par	dos, una pareja
11, 97	colorado/a	rojo/a, encarnado
15	rápido	apurado, velóz
16	chica	pequeña/o, menudo/a, poco, menor
17	blandito	suave, tierno/a, delicado/a
24	Halla el carro de en medio	Encuentra el coche; automóvil, auto, máquina
47, 48, 49, 79	Also employ carro	
27	algunos	pocos, no muchos
34	viene	Participle form for coming as represented in other -*ing* items, viniendo
35	Se va	Going–participle, yendo
36	Pescando	Agarrando Cogiendo not used in Mexico—bad word. (Fishing, or the action to catch in the act, not to catch a ball.)
41	suavemente	Dulcemente, poco a poco, despacio
50	Ranchero	granjero, agricultor, labrador
55	más alta	Feminine ending eliminates one pictured referent.
67, 96, 100	pelotas	bolas
68	sacos	abrigos, levitas, sobretodos, americanas
70	Spanish is not comparable to the English item, omits borrego, oveja, canero-sheep.	
71	Similarly, los peces has been omitted.	
73, 88	La muchacha está brincando.	. . . está saltando.

(continued)

Table 2. (*continued*)

Item number	Words	Other choices or interpretations
78	Spanish not comparable to English as it looks at pronominal comparison also.	
80	The English to given in the passive form, while the Spanish is not.	
	The donkey is carried by the man.	
	Given: Al burrito se le está cargando.	
	Replace: El burro es llevado/transportado/cargado por el hombre.	
81	El niño es perseguido por el perro.	El chico/muchacho es acosado por el perro.
87	Forms are not comparable due to the omission of muchacha.	
39	Vete	Váyase
90	No Crucen	No cruces, no pases.
93	Apunta al carro que va por la calle.	carro, coche, auto . . .
		Encuentra/Halla el ____ que está en la calle por/by or through the street, rather than on the street, can be taken as another referent.
	Apunta can also be mostrar or enseñar.	
101	bebé	Signifies human baby; an animal's baby is a peque.

examiner may determine the specific applicability of the test measure for his or her client. Caution should be exercised when using the Spanish version with non-Mexican-American children. Test administrators may wish to use local norms based on relevant dialects. A tape for standardized delivery in the local dialect of Spanish could also be developed.

SUMMARY

The five discrete point tests that were reviewed in this chapter are representative of the cadre of measures commercially available or distributed through the Title VII bilingual dissemination centers or school districts. They share several characteristics, ranging from ease of administration to poor statistical support. The most obvious shared characteristic is that they reflect language as a series of discrete points that can be measured.

Oller (1973) described the discrete point test situation this way:

> The discrete point test is a reflection of the notion from teaching that if you get across 50,000 (or some other magic number) structural items, you will have taught the language. The trouble with this is that 50,000 structural pat-

terns isolated from the meaningful contexts of communication do not constitute language competence; nor does a sampling of those 50,000 discrete points of grammar constitute an adequate test of language competence. The question of language testing is not so much whether the student knows such-and-such pattern in a manipulative or abstract sense, but rather, whether he can use it effectively in communication (p. 198).

The next two chapters present a discussion of alternative tests and approaches that have been used in bilingual and ESL programs. They are representative of an attempt to provide a more integrative approach to assessment of communicative competence. The final chapters provide theoretical constructs and various innovative approaches to assessing language function in addition to form.

REFERENCES

Anastasi, A. 1976. Psychological Testing. 4th Ed. Macmillan Publishing Co., New York.
Blood, G. W., and Greenberg, B. R. 1978. Normative data for the revised score sheet of the test for auditory comprehension of language. Lang. Speech Hear. Serv. 9:210-212.
Boehm, A. E. 1971. The Boehm Test of Basic Concepts. The Psychological Corporation, New York.
Buros, O. K. (ed.). 1972. The Seventh Mental Measurements Yearbook. The Gryphon Press, Highland Park, N.J.
Carrow, E. 1968. The development of auditory comprehension of language structure in children. J. Speech Hear. Disord. 33:99-111.
Carrow, E. 1971. Comprehension of English and Spanish by pre-school Mexican-American children. Modern Lang. J. 55:299-306.
Carrow, E. 1973. Test of Auditory Comprehension of Language. Learning Concepts, Austin, Tex.
Critchlow, D. E. 1974. Dos Amigos Verbal Language Scales. Academic Therapy Publications, San Rafael, Cal.
Fredrickson, C. K., and Wick, J. W. 1976. Short Test of Linguistic Skills. Department of Research and Evaluation, Board of Education, Chicago.
James, P. 1975. James Language Dominance Test. 2nd Ed. Learning Concepts, Austin, Tex.
Jones, B. J. 1972. A study of oral language comprehension of black and white middle and lower class preschool children using standard English and black dialect in Houston, Texas, 1972. Doctoral dissertation. University of Houston.
Oller, J. W., Jr. 1978. Discrete-point tests versus tests of integrative skills. In: J. W. Oller, Jr., and J. C. Richards (eds.), Focus on the Learner. Newbury House Publishers, Rowley, Mass.
Oller, J. W., Jr. 1976. The Measurement of Bilingualism: A Review of the Bilingual Syntax Measure. (Review Essay.) Modern Lang. J. 60:399-400.

Silverman, R. J., Noa, J. K., and Russell, R. H. 1976. Oral Language Tests for Bilingual Students: An Evaluation of Language Dominance and Proficiency Instruments. Northwest Regional Educational Laboratory, Portland, Ore.

Teschner, R. V. 1977. Review: Dos Amigos Verbal Language Scales (An English-Spanish Aptitude Test). Modern Lang. J. 61:202–203.

chapter eight

Quasi-integrative Approaches Competence
Discrete Point Scoring of Expressive Language Samples

Pamela A. McCollum and
E. Catherine Day

Some interesting mixtures of discrete point and integrative oral language production instruments are currently being used to assess bilingual children. These approaches to assessment are attempts that recognize the importance of spontaneous language sampling as the basis of assessment. Examples of marketed tests are the Oral Language Evaluation (OLE), the Basic Inventory of Natural Language (BINL), and the Bilingual Syntax Measure (BSM). Each of these approaches calls for a sample of natural language, cued by pictures, which is then scored in a discrete point fashion, with the emphasis on syntax, vocabulary, and/or length of utterance. The three commercial tests and two scoring approaches are described and discussed in this chapter as representative of quasi-integrative approaches.

ORAL LANGUAGE EVALUATION (*Silvaroli and Maynes, 1975*)

General Description

The Oral Language Evaluation is designed for use with children in both English and Spanish. The three aims of the test are identification of children who need second language training, assessment of individual oral language production, and diagnosis of the types of oral language structures produced by the children who are identified as needing second language training.

Procedure

Part I, identification, is completed for each child and is done by teacher judgment, observation, and the use of school records. Its primary purpose is to determine if the child should be assessed. Part II, assessment, is conducted to determine if oral language training is needed before reading instruction is begun. This part, administered individually, takes about 1 minute per child. The child is shown a picture and asked to discuss it, in whichever language is of interest to the examiner. The obtained language sample is then compared to a list of five language development steps described in the manual. Definitional characteristics for each step are provided for the examiner's reference. For example, one-word responses (usually nouns) are listed as representative of step one and simple descriptions (limited to subject–verb language structure) indicate step two. If the child's sample indicates that he or she is using the language at step one or step two, he or she is classified as needing oral language training before beginning reading instruction in that language. If the child places into step three or higher, then he or she is classified as reading ready for that language.

Part III, the diagnosis, takes about 5 minutes per child and also is administered individually. In this section the student is shown one of four pictures containing related items and is asked to talk about the picture. Responses are taped and the examiner tries to elicit as much conversation as possible from the child. In scoring, the sample is transcribed, which according to the author takes about 10 minutes per child. The transcription is then compared to the "typical" responses provided in the manual for each of the four pictures.

These Language Usage Examples are provided in both Spanish and English for the four pictured settings of park, zoo, school, and home, and are categorized only in terms of language structures used. Frequency of use of each structure is recorded on the transcription form. Since the emphasis is on syntax, the test is integrative in sampling but discrete point in scoring. By comparing the student's responses from the taped sample with the typical ones listed in the manual, the teacher can determine how the student compares to a "typical" student. The completed transcription form should also indicate areas of concentration for teaching emphasis, which the authors state the teacher "should be able to prescribe" after looking at Part III.

Reliability and Validity

The OLE manual reports no studies of validity or of reliability. Responses were collected from 100 Spanish-surnamed Anglo and Black children to determine the Language Usage Examples. The authors then selected those responses that were "... in our judgment, most illustrative of each language structure used in the OLE Test" (Preface). Thus, a sample of 100 students serves as the basis for typical usage examples for four pictures in two languages. The limited applicability of sample is further compounded by the fact that the authors do not state the criteria used to select the listed examples. The preface contains thanks for the collection of samples in Arizona, Florida, New Jersey, and Texas. However, no other demographic information concerning these 100 students is given. How many students from each category come from which region of the country remains unknown to the reader. The authors beg the issue of any type of norms by saying, "Each teacher is urged to utilize his or her individual criteria in determining the type of language structures elicited by each child" (p. 20).

Reviewers' Comments

Silverman, Noa, and Russell (1976) give the following overall ratings of the Oral Language Evaluation: poor in measurement validity, fair in examinee appropriateness, poor in technical excellence, and poor in administrative usability. Only Parts II and III were rated. The Oral Language Evaluation appears to be a tool for the classroom teacher, but it certainly does not lead to any type of standardized measure for use in classification of students, even within the same classroom.

The authors suggest that a random sample of children be tested in Part III if a large number of students are identified as needing assessment. While this may make sense administratively (5 minutes of teacher time to administer Part III to each child, 10 minutes to transcribe each child's tape, time for transcription analysis), random sampling would not necessarily provide for an individualized program of instruction for each child judged to be needing assessment. Yet individualized instruction as a result of the diagnosis is one of the reasons the authors give for the use of this test. It should be noted that they do not provide the teacher with any help about what to do in the classroom as a result of the diagnosis.

Although the test has a practical format, the reviewers would question whether the teacher actually knows any more about each student after giving the Oral Language Evaluation than before. On the other hand, if a school district were to standardize ratings, scoring, and examples of usage for its own district, then the Oral Language Evaluation might be much more useful for a teacher trying to compare any given student with others in that specific district. Since most tests are normed on populations that can be expected to be different (certainly linguistically) from the local population, this latter suggestion should prove to be valuable for any school district. This procedure requires time and money but should result in a very valuable instrument.

The OLE authors also state that they hope to help the teacher who is not a trained linguist, yet they expect the examiner to be familiar with collecting oral language samples and with transcribing and analyzing taped samples, with no help except for the few lanuage use examples given in the manual. There is nothing noted concerning appropriateness of usage, communicative competence, or pragmatics; strictly structural complexity is analyzed. The manual does list a few examples of nonstandard English, but it does not list any in Spanish—nor are there dialectal or phonological variations listed for either Spanish or English. Considering the number of Spanish subgroups in this country, such a void of possible acceptable vocabulary differences makes it extremely difficult for the nonlinguistically trained evaluator to analyze the extensive samples accurately.

The total omission of reliability data, validity data, and field-testing information makes the OLE highly suspect as a testing instrument for more than an individual classroom with individually developed standards. The only advantage to a teacher-developed instrument lies in its emphasis on collecting samples of oral production as the basis for decision making rather than relying on written test scores or intuition.

BASIC INVENTORY OF NATURAL LANGUAGE (*Herbert, 1977*)

General Description

The Basic Inventory of Natural Language is a criterion-referenced system of language examination that assesses natural oral language in one or more languages, and can be used to determine language dominance, fluency, complexity of language, and language development. It also prescribes for classroom teachers language development activities for children on the basis of individual scores. The BINL is suitable for any language. Sample norms are provided for Spanish and English. There are also data available for Portuguese, Italian, and other languages.

Procedure

The test is administered in small group settings which are similar to regular language activity settings in order to facilitate gathering natural language samples for each child. This means that practice sessions of about 20 minutes a day for 1 to 5 days are necessary before the taped samples for the test are taken. In these sessions children in the small groups use the Talk Tiles, Sequence Stories, and Story Starters to tell a story or talk about an experience suggested by the picture to other children. The Talk Tiles are small drawings mounted on cardboard, and the child chooses a certain number to make up a story that will use all of the selected drawings. The Sequence Stories come from a series of ditto masters, and each child arranges his or her set of pictures in the sequence preferred. Then this story is retold to the others in the group. The Story Starters are large full-color posters that the child chooses and then tells a story about—either factual (describing the picture) or imaginary (suggested by the picture). The adult or teacher does not ask questions to prompt the student, but does encourage other students to ask questions or add comments to the individual stories. All of the practice sessions are taped so that the students become accustomed to the tape recorder and are not intimidated by it in the sampling situation.

When the teacher is certain that the children are ready and familiar with the activity, taped samples are gathered from the children in exactly the same manner as they were in the practice sessions. Time for collecting the samples will vary for each child and for each classroom. An adequate sample, however, must have a minimum of 10 sentences.

Once the sample is recorded, it must be transcribed. The manual contains detailed instructions for transcription for both hand-scoring and machine-scoring. In the 10-sentence sample, each new sentence is placed on a separate line. The number of words in each is counted, giving a fluency score. The directions for hand-scoring are included in the manual, along with examples for both Spanish and English. When the transcription is totally scored, each child has an Index of Language Ability Score, an Average Sentence Length Score, and an Average Level of Complexity Score.

The manual states that the BINL may be used for kindergarten through grade 12, but the norms provided do not extend beyond the eighth grade for English and Spanish samples. The test itself is a mixture of integrative and discrete point approaches in that the language sample is integrative but the scoring of syntax and vocabulary is discrete point.

Reliability and Validity

There are no studies reported for validity or for reliability. No field tests are reported in the manual, but the sample norms were drawn from five school districts in California and Illinois. Both rural and urban classrooms from grades K–8, classified as either ESEA Title I or Bilingual, were included in the sample from which the norms were developed.

Reviewers' Comments

Silverman, Noa, and Russell (1976) give the following overall ratings to the BINL: poor in measurement validity, fair in examinee appropriateness, poor in technical excellence, and poor in administrative usability.

Sanchez (1976) includes the BINL in his review of oral language assessment instruments. In favor of the BINL, he states that the best way to measure child language is by eliciting language in a conversational situation, because this method allows for the use of phrases, structures, and lexical items that could not be elicited through direct questions. However, he questions the kit materials themselves (e.g., the use of an obviously Peruvian picture for a non-Peruvian student). Sanchez suggests that teachers could use their own materials, which would be cheaper and more relevant to their own students. The emphasis on the importance of taping practice sessions before actually administering the test is commended by Sanchez; this should eliminate the problem of not eliciting a fair sample from students who would feel uncomfortable with the machine at first. Sanchez also applauds the fact that the BINL consciously relates testing to teaching and demonstrates awareness of the need to develop language skills and to train students for the test.

In considering the above two reviews, the present authors would have to disagree in terms of examinee appropriateness and administrative usability. For children, the idea seems very valid. While the BINL may not be what administrators would want, it seems very useful for teachers since it is linked directly with ideas for classroom teaching.

As for Sanchez's remarks, the present reviewers would certainly concur with the emphasis given to eliciting natural language in a familiar setting with the use of a tape recorder. The problem of unfamiliar picture content noted by Sanchez can easily be dismissed because the student chooses his or her own pictures. However, the use of the same scoring system continues to emphasize discrete point testing instead of integrative testing. Syntax and vocabulary are the basis for scoring, not communication. Systems of scoring such as the one devised by Savignon (1972) could certainly work in analyzing this type of speech sample (amount of information conveyed, the appropriateness of language used, etc.) in order to make it a more integrative test (see Day, Chapter 9, or Sridhar, Chapter 10 this volume. This type of scoring along with the discrete point recording might give a better and more complete picture of the individual child's oral language ability in any language sampled.

While the test scoring in the manual neither insists upon correct grammatical usage nor detracts for elliptical phrases, the point system is controlled by syntactic considerations. Another point is that the author claims the test can be used to determine dominance, but does not give any guidance on how to do it; if simple comparison of scores in both languages is to be used, the author also does not indicate how this is to be interpreted.

Lack of information concerning how levels were determined and the small number of subjects listed in the norms reported seem to be drawbacks to the general applicability of the test. The amount of time for an individual teacher to learn how to transcribe, score, and analyze the language sample should not be considered a drawback. At first glance it might appear as such, but if one considers the relationship that exists between the testing and the suggested teaching activities, the instrument itself may be very appealing for a teacher who has little or no experience in dealing with this type of student population. Since the materials in the kit are also used for classroom language development activities, the expense is not as great as it would appear at first. The test instrument itself could be a good teaching vehicle.

BILINGUAL SYNTAX MEASURE
(*Burt, Dulay, and Hernandez-Chavez, 1976*)

General Description

The Bilingual Syntax Measure was designed to determine the child's dominant language, level of second language acquisition, and degree of maintenance or loss of the first language. For children in grades K–2, the test instrument assesses the language competency of an individual child by measuring syntactic ability that, according to the authors, is more stable across idiolects and dialects than either pronunciation or vocabulary skill. Upon completion of the test, items passed are summed and used to assign children to one of five levels of competency per language: 1) no English or Spanish, 2) receptive in English or Spanish skills only, 3) survival English or Spanish, 4) intermediate English or Spanish, and 5) proficient English or Spanish.

Procedure

Test administration requires only 20 to 30 minutes for both the Spanish and English versions. Each version consists of 20 questions (not translation equivalents) that are intended to elicit particular grammatical structures about a series of seven pictures. These pictures are brightly colored, of appropriate size, durable, and attractive.

Responses for both versions of the test are recorded in their respective scoring booklets and later analyzed for acceptability and point value. Responses are deemed acceptable if they are grammatically correct, despite their appropriateness to the question that was delivered or their length. Therefore, single word responses are also awarded points. For example, when the child is presented with a picture of small birds in a nest and asked "What are those?" the following responses would be scored as indicated below:

Question A

Grammatically Correct	Incorrect
Babies	Baby
Baby birds	Baby bird
They are babies	They babies
They're ducks	He is a duck

Likewise, when reference is made to a picture of a fat man and the question "Why is he so fat?" is delivered, the following responses would be scored as indicated below:

Question B

Grammatically Correct	Incorrect
Because he drinks beer	Because him drink beer
Because he eats junk	Because he eat junk

(From the BSM technical manual, p. 10.) Scoring is accomplished by awarding one point or no points to grammatically correct or incorrect responses, respectively. The points are summed, and the child is placed in one of the five previously mentioned categories in either Spanish or English.

Concerning the field test edition, structural scoring that relied on the concept of obligatory occasion was employed. Each obligatory context was regarded as a test item that the child passed by supplying the required morpheme or failed by supplying none or one that was incorrect. Every time a child set an obligatory occasion for a structure, two scores were obtained; the expected score, which consisted of two points per occasion, and the actual score, which varied according to the child's performance on a structure. Two separate scores were summed for all occasions of a specific structure with respect to each child, and percent of accuracy in producing that structure was obtained by dividing the total score by the total expected score. Following the precedent of Brown (1973), the criterion of acquisition was 90% correct usage across all obligatory occasions of that structure. Cutoffs for competency levels were established as follows: 95%–100%, proficient; 85%–94%, intermediate; and 45%–84%, survival.

Reliability and Validity

The BSM field test was carried out with Anglo-American, Afro-American, Chicano, Puerto Rican, Cuban, and other Spanish speakers in grades K–2. The sample was judgmental rather than random. The authors state that the nature of the target population did not permit probability sampling. Students were selected from bilingual programs in urban, rural, and suburban schools.

Twenty centers from nine states and one school district on the U.S.–Mexican border participated. A total of 1,603 students were administered tests. Of these, 914 were tested both in Spanish and English, 232 were tested only in Spanish, and 457 were tested with the English version only, giving a total of 2,517 tests administered. Subgroup norms are provided in the technical manual for specific age and ethnic groups.

The authors state that the construct validity of the BSM is supported by:

1. The body of psycholinguistic research supporting the concept of natural sequences of acquisition
    a. Children acquire certain syntactic structures in a systematic manner as they progress through successive stages of language acquisition (Brown, 1973).
    b. The acquisition of these structures in an ordered and systematic manner applies to second language as well as first language learners, although they differ in some respects.
    c. Children of diverse language backgrounds will follow a similar pattern of progression in learning a common second language (Dulay and Burt, 1973, 1974; Fathman, 1975).
2. The statistical procedures and research that have resulted in the production of both the acquisition hierarchy and the scoring system that is based on the hierarchy
3. Evidence that the BSM classifications reflect the relationships expected to be found among bilingual children (Burt, Dulay, and Hernandez-Chavez, 1976, pp. 31–32)

Two reliability studies were conducted on the BSM. In the first, a test/retest study, the stability of proficiency level classifications for each language was computed separately. The traditional product-moment correlation could not be used because the distribution across levels was not symmetric and is defined differently over different parts of the scales. Cohen's Kappa coefficient was used to express reliability (Cohen, 1960). The obtained figures were 66.1 for the BSM English version with a standard error of measurement of 0.064, and 76.2 for the BSM Spanish version with a standard error of measurement of 0.100.

A test/retest study was also done on the dominance classifications from administering the BSM in Spanish and English. The Kappa coefficient obtained was 64.7 with a standard error of Kappa of 0.053.

The second study that measured interrater reliability reported higher figures for the English version of the BSM. The Kappa coefficients were 83.8 and 80.1 for the English and Spanish versions respectively, with a standard error of Kappa of 0.053. The authors attribute this result to the fact that Spanish has a wide range of dialectal variations, so that raters in this country disagree about judgments of grammaticality.

Reviewers' Comments

One of the basic assumptions underlying the BSM is that children learn a first language (L_1) as well as a second language (L_2) by the same process—creative construction. Furthermore, the same universal processing strategies are said to be applicable to both. Implicit in this statement, however, is the assumption that we know what the strategies for L_1 learning are. Porter (1975) comments that "It is probably premature to refer to universal language processing strategies used in L_1 learning as a reference point for L_2 research" (p. 49).

Dulay and Burt drew heavily upon L_1 research in conducting their L_2 studies. The two studies that contributed most heavily were Brown's (1973) longitudinal study and de Villiers and de Villiers (1973) cross-sectional study of morpheme acquisition. Due to the high intercorrelations of the two studies, it was assumed that cross-sectional studies of L_2 performance would yield reliable information about the acquisition process. Rosansky (1975) states that "It has never been shown that L_2 acquisition follows the same kind of developmental curve that L_1 learning does. Nor have L_2 researchers found a valid means of equating the subjects in their samples with L_1 subjects" (p. 410).

Rosansky (1975) posed two important questions related to the BSM. First, she asks if the morpheme order obtained using an elicitation instrument (the BSM) resembles the order of morphemes obtained from spontaneously collected second language acquisition data. Secondly, she asks if cross-sectional and longitudinal research findings in second language research are comparable.

To study the first question, Rosansky taped six Spanish speakers learning English for 1 hour, after 10 months' exposure to English. The transcripts were scored for morphemes following Dulay and Burt's methodology, and both group scores and group means were tabulated. Rosansky hypothesized that the rank order of morphemes derived from spontaneous speech would not correlate with the BSM elicited data. Surprisingly, the Rosansky order correlated with Dulay and Burt as well as with the de Villiers' order.

After reanalyzing the data, Rosansky concluded that the use of the BSM itself might be affecting the outcome, at least in respect to the rank ordering of morphemes. She states that possible explanations might include the following:

1. The preliminary questions administered to ensure vocabulary comprehension may be providing models for some but not all of the morphemes
2. The limited nature of the questions with respect to the content of the pictures may systematically bias opportunities for the subject to create a sufficient number of obligatory contexts for some of the morphemes
3. The sheer limitation of the number of utterances may restrict opportunities for the subject to create a sufficient number of obligatory contexts for some of the morphemes (Rosansky, 1975, p. 419)

To study the question of the comparability of cross-sectional and longitudinal data, Rosansky took the cross-sectional order of one of the children in the previous study and compared it to her order of morpheme acquisition over the entire 10-month study. The cross-sectional scoring procedure remained the same, while the longitudinal data were scored for morphemes and an individual score was computed for each morpheme at each 1-month interval.

Findings showed that the cross-sectionally based and longitudinally derived rank orders of the morphemes for the same individual did not correlate. Furthermore, the rank orders of the morphemes from month to month appeared to fluctuate and did not resemble the longitudinal data.

Porter (1975) conducted a study with 30-month-old children learning English as a first language to compare the results of L_1 learners with those of Dulay and Burt's subjects in L_2 research, in an attempt to compare the learning strategies of the two groups. Natural speech was elicited from the children with the BSM and was analyzed by means of obligatory occasion analysis, the group score method, the group means method, and the SAI method (see the BSM Technical Manual). In addition, the children were asked to perform an imitation task (see Maratsos, 1973).

Results of this study showed that the strong evidence presented for an invariant order of morpheme acquisition for L_1 learners learning English by Brown (1973) and de Villiers and de Villiers (1973) did not correlate with the order of functor acquisition in L_1 learners as determined by the BSM. Porter concluded that the Dulay and Burt sequence of morpheme acquisition could possibly be an artifact of the BSM testing situation.

Further analysis also showed that some of the 11 morphemes that are supposed to be elicited by the BSM were elicited so infrequently that their inclusion in the sequence of morpheme acquisition is questionable. One case in particular is the past regular, which never appeared in the present study. On the other hand, Dulay and Burt cite 90 out of 115 children who supplied the past regular at least once.

Subsequently, Porter (1975) administered the BSM to a colleague and the past regular did not occur once. Furthermore, the only occurrence of the past irregular and the irregular plural required the same word. Porter states that "One wonders how a measure designed to elicit 'natural' speech from both L_1 and L_2 learners failed to elicit even one example of the past regular, a regularly occurring phenomenon, at least in the English language" (p. 59).

The BSM is an instrument that measures standard English syntax and is not appropriate for measuring Black English speakers' oral proficiency. Such typical Black English constructions as do insertion and copula deletion would be scored as ungrammatical and would yield lower proficiency levels for persons who are native speakers of English.

While this has not been tested, the results of Dulay and Burt's (1973) study point to this indirectly. There the acquisition sequence and degree of acquisition of morphemes of three Spanish-speaking groups were studied: Chicanos from Sacramento, California; Mexicans studying in San Ysidro, California; and Puerto Ricans in East Harlem, New York.

While the acquisition sequences were similar, the acquisition level of the East Harlem Puerto Ricans was substantially lower than that of the other two groups. The reasons for this are not discussed, but it is possible that the lower performance of the Puerto Rican group is attributable to the occurrence of Black English constructions in their speech. These were scored as incorrect responses by the BSM, which only accepts standard English constructions as correct. This point challenges the suitability of the BSM as an appropriate measure for all Spanish-speaking groups and suggests that using standard English syntax as the metric for oral language proficiency may be biased in testing certain populations.

In response to criticisms regarding the low reliability figures of the BSM, the authors state that these scores reflect changes that take place in child language. Sometimes structures may be used for awhile and then discarded before they are fully acquired. They feel that extremely high reliability coefficients would indicate insensitivity to such changes. Oller (1976) states, "This, however, is a just defense [of the BSM] only if the low reliabilities, in fact, indicate real changes in the child's speech. This has certainly not been demonstrated" (p. 399). He also believes a more integrative approach would be preferable to its present strictly discrete point approach.

While the BSM is an improvement over previous discrete point tests, both in its approach and in the amount of preliminary research that preceded it, it still needs to be put to more rigorous tests. Both the Rosansky and Porter studies raise serious questions regarding the BSM that must be answered before one can say with confidence that the BSM has construct validity and that the sequences it produces are indeed invariant learning sequences that result from universal processing strategies in L_2 acquisition.

CONCLUSIONS

The three tests discussed in this chapter, the Oral Language Evaluation, the Basic Inventory of Natural Language, and the Bilingual Syntax Measure, may all be considered quasi-integrative approaches to language testing. They have been classified as such because they use natural language samples elicited through the use of pictures but also employ discrete point scoring systems. These scoring systems only accept certain grammatical responses, vocabulary items, and length of utterances as correct responses. While the attempt to collect natural language samples from students is commendable, the discrete point scoring system seems to defeat the purpose of collecting natural language samples. An alternative scoring system, such as the one devised by Savignon (1972), was suggested. Another approach to analysis of expressive language samples in English and Spanish is the scoring of a corpus of utterances according to mean length of utterance (MLU) or similar surface structure analyses (see Erickson, Chapter 1, and Linares, Appendix B, this volume).

Of the three tests discussed, the BSM seems to be superior in the amount of research that preceded it as well as being grounded in current linguistic theory. However, its use of standard English syntax as the metric for measuring language proficiency is questionsed. Many native

English speakers use nonstandard syntax and are still considered to be intelligible speakers of English.

Regarding validity and reliability information, none was stated for the OLE or the BINL. The BSM reports no validity figures and low reliability figures that, according to the authors, reflect characteristic changes in children's acquisition of grammatical structures. Oller (1976) states that the authors' justification for the BSM's low reliability figures has yet to be proved.

Among the positive features of each test are the following:

1. The OLE urges the use of natural language instead of written tests of teacher judgment.
2. The BINL is directly related to ideas for classroom teaching.
3. The scoring of the BSM does not depend upon the child's knowledge prior to the testing situation because answers that are contrary to fact but grammatically correct are scored as correct.

The authors urge persons contemplating using these tests to be aware of their limitations and to realize that they do not necessarily measure what they purport to measure.

REFERENCES

Brown, R. 1973. A First Language. Harvard University Press, Cambridge.
Brown, R. and Bellugi, U. 1964. Three processes in the child's acquisition of syntax. Harvard Educ. Rev. 34:133-151.
Brown, R., Cazden, C., and Bellugi, U. 1969. The child's grammar from I to III. In: J. P. Hill (ed.), 1967 Minnesota Symposium on Child Psychology. 1969. Minneapolis. University of Minnesota Press.
Burt, M. K., Dulay, H. C., and Hernandez-Chavez, E. 1976. The Bilingual Syntax Technical Handbook. Harcourt Brace Jovanovich, New York.
Cohen, J. 1960. A coefficient of agreement of nominal scales. 1960. Educ. Psychol. Measurement. 20:37-46.
de Villiers, J., and de Villiers, P. 1973. A cross-sectional study of the development of grammatical morphemes in child speech. J. Psycholinguist. Res. 2:267-278.
Dulay, H. C. and Burt, M. K. 1972. Goofing: An indicator of children's second language learning strategies. Lang. Learn. 22:235-252.
Dulay, H. C. and Burt, M. K. 1973. Should we teach children syntax? Lang. Learn. 23:245-258.
Dulay, H. C., and Burt, M. K. 1974. A new perspective on the creative construction process in child second language acquisition. Lang. Learn. 24:253-278.
Fathman, A. 1975. Language background, age, and the order of acquisition of English structures. In: M. K. Burt and H. C. Dulay (eds.), New Directions in Second Language Learning, Teaching and Bilingual Education. TESOL, Washington, D.C.

Herbert, C. H. 1977. Basic Inventory of Natural Language. CHEKpoint Systems, San Bernardino, Cal.

Maratsos, M. P. 1973. The effects of stress on the understanding of pronominal coreference in children. J. Psycholinguist. Res. 2:1–8.

Natalicio, D. S. and Natalicio, L. F. S. 1971. A comparative study of English pluralization by native and nonnative English speakers. Child. Dev. 42:1302–1306.

Oller, J. W., Jr. 1976. The measurement of bilingualism: A review of the Bilingual Syntax Measure. The Mod. Lang. J. 60:399–400.

Porter J. H. 1975. A cross-sectional study of morpheme acquisition in first language learning. Lang. Learn. 27:47–61.

Price, E. 1968. Early bilingualism. In: C. J. Dodson, and I. T. Williams (eds.), Towards Bilingualism. University of Wales Press, Cardiff, England.

Rosansky, E. J. 1975. Methods and morphemes in second language acquisition research. Lang. Learn. 26:408–425.

Sanchez, R. 1976. Critique of oral language assessment instruments. NABE: J. Nat. Assoc. Biling. Educ. 1:120–127.

Savignon, S. J. 1972. Communicative Competence: An Experiment in Foreign-Language Teaching. The Center for Curriculum Development, Philadelphia.

Silvaroli, N. J. and Maynes, J. O., Jr. 1975. Oral Language Evaluation. D. A. Lewis Associates, Clinton, MD.

Silverman, R. J., Noa, J. K., and Russell, R. H. 1976. Oral Language Tests for Bilingual Students: An Evaluation of Language Dominance and Proficiency Instruments. Northwest Regional Educational Laboratory, Portland, Ore.

chapter nine

Assessing Communicative Competence
Integrative Testing of Second Language Learners
E. Catherine Day

This chapter discusses selected integrative second language assessment instruments, describes what these instruments attempt to measure, and examines some of the ways in which they are used. In contrast to the previous chapters on quasi-integrative measures that are examples of a movement away from discrete point testing, this chapter more clearly shows the movement toward more functional integrative second language assessment approaches.

Professionals involved in language testing have noted an increasing dissatisfaction with discrete point test scores as valid predictors of an individual's ability to function in a second language. Discrete point tests have been inadequate as an approach to classifying children for placement in bilingual classrooms or a means of identifying communicative capabilities for exiting a bilingual program. Dissatisfaction has come from government officials, international business executives, teachers, speech-language pathologists, bilingual specialists, and administrators who, for a variety of reasons, need to know how well an individual can function in a second language. The new emphasis in linguistics on the creative as well as the functional use of language has aroused an interest in assessing second language oral performance in contrast to testing the discrete points of language structure via an oral or written approach.

An awareness that language is more than just the sum of its discrete parts stimulated the development of integrative tests of language proficiency. It was hoped that integrative tests would reveal more about a person's underlying total competence than the tests that measured awareness of the various units of language. Furthermore, it was thought that such global measures would be more predictive of a person's actual performance in a second language than the previously used discrete point tests. Oller (1973) reported that integrative skills tests, which on the surface seem to have little in common and which often appear to be unreliable in scoring procedures, actually correlate better with teacher judgment about student oral performance in a second language, and better among themselves, than with the discrete point type of language test described elsewhere in this volume.

Integrative tests have been developed mainly for use with adult second language learners. Thus far, they have proved to be better predictors of functional second language performance than earlier discrete point tests. The knowledge gained from an awareness of these type tests needs to be used to develop or adapt oral language assessment instruments for bilingual programs for children who supposedly are assigned to such programs on the basis of their functional language ability. As Shuy (1977) describes this situation, however, "legislative and judicial action ... requires educational technology that is only beginning to be developed" (p. 79).

The following sections include detailed descriptions of four integrative language assessment instruments and the approaches used with second language learners. The four approaches presented are the Foreign Service Institute Oral Interview, the Savignon Communicative Competence tests, the Ilyin Oral Interview, and the High/Scope instruments. Only the latter was designed for use with children. The author's experience in using such measures for placement purposes and achievement testing in both second language teaching programs and in overseas work situations will be used as a basis for indicating how these integrative tests provide more accurate procedures for assessing an individual's ability to function in a second language. Finally, recommendations for further research and development of new language assessment instruments based on ideas described in these approaches are given.

FOREIGN SERVICE INSTITUTE (FSI) ORAL INTERVIEW

The Foreign Service Institute (FSI) Oral Interview ratings (known as S-ratings) have been in existence for about 20 years (Wilds, 1975). This measure of second language oral proficiency, neither readily available nor well-known among people who have not had contact with the federal government, grew out of a need for the United States Government to be able to judge personnel for State Department, military, career diplomat, and overseas positions that required functional use of a second language.

The oral interview is structured by the tester to fit the experience and abilities of the examinee and is judged on the basis of the rating scale, which includes both linguistic and functional elements in its definition of each point. The usual procedure involves both a native speaker of the language that is being tested and a certified tester conversing with the examinee. (The certified tester is either an experienced native-speaking language instructor or a linguist thoroughly familiar with the language being tested.) In each interview, the native speaker usually conducts the test and the linguist or certified tester observes and takes notes. The interview, as much as possible, is structured as a relaxed conversation in which the certified tester does not participate actively but shows interest.

The first part of the interview consists of simple social formula, such as introductions, greetings, and comments on the weather. Depending upon the examinee's response, the tester then continues in one of two ways. If the examinee has a hard time with the openers, then a tentative ceiling is put on the difficulty of the questions to be asked. "He will be asked as simply as possible to talk about himself, his family, and his work; he may be asked to give street directions, to play a role (e.g. renting a house), or act as interpreter for the certified tester on a tourist level" (Wilds, 1975, p. 31). If the examinee handles these kinds of problems well, despite initial difficulty, then the tester will continue with discussions of current events or job details. On the other hand, if the examinee coped adequately with the initial aspects of the interview, then the tester leads the examinee into normal conversation on both personal and professional topics. The experienced interviewer tries to elicit naturally all essential grammatical features and a broad range of vocabulary and comprehension in the first 5–10 minutes. The rest of the interview is spent collecting data to verify the preliminary rating and to confirm the final decision.

At times the examiners use an informal interpreting situation to judge comprehension, fluency, or grammatical features that seem to have been avoided. Another method involves giving the examinee instructions written in English and asking that these instructions be conveyed to the native speaker. Wilds (1975) quotes an example of telling "your landlord that the ceiling in the living room is cracked and leaking and the sofa and rug are ruined" (p. 31). According to the author, this type of situation is useful for testing an examinee who is highly proficient when dealing with formal topics, or the examinee who needs to be challenged in terms of linguistic self-confidence (p. 31). At all times an attempt is made to push the examinee's ability to the limits—both functionally and structurally—to make the examinee personally aware of his or her capacities and limitations.

In many testing situations, once the rating is decided upon, the examinee is given detailed feedback about the strengths and weaknesses demonstrated in the interview situation. The examinee can then concentrate on particular areas to improve his or her own skills. When interviews are taped, and the examinee is interviewed both at the beginning of his or her second language training and at the end, then the progress can easily be heard by the individual second language learner.

There is a highly involved checklist and weighted scoring system that can be used to assign a rating. However, most trained testers do not use this system as much as a "careful interpretation of the amplified definitions of the S-ratings" (Wilds, 1975, p. 32). The checklist does serve as a means for examiners in all languages to keep within the same standard for ratings. Even though the scoring system has never been made compulsory, Wilds comments that the initial mistrust of staff of statistical scoring has been overcome because the accuracy of the scoring has been demonstrated.

The five areas used for judgment of the S-rating are: accent, grammar, vocabulary, fluency, and comprehension. Accent and grammar are easily described for each language being tested. Vocabulary, fluency, and comprehension are much more difficult to delineate, except in functional terms. With only the small sample of speech from the interview, it is suggested that a more refined scale would be difficult to validate. The actual determination of the rating in any individual case depends upon the working relationship between the two testers. At the Foreign Service Institute, the one rule that applies is that if a half-point (plus) discrepancy cannot be resolved by discussion between the interviewers, or by averaging the computed scores from the checklist, then the lower rating is given. This is done to protect both the examinee and the future supervisor, viewing it better to underrate than to overrate in terms of future government assignment. According to Wilds, the CIA (Central Intelligence Agency) tends to be more interested in functional effectiveness than in the examinee's detailed performance. The CIA testers thus use a slightly different formula to compute S-ratings, making marks on a segmented line which are later averaged for the final rating.

The ratings range from 0, which indicates no competence in terms of oral proficiency, to 5, which indicates the equivalence of an educated native speaker. Below are simplified definitions of each rating:

S-1 *Elementary Proficiency* Able to satisfy routine social demands and minimum courtesy requirements.
S-2 *Limited Working Proficiency* Able to satisfy routine social demands and limited work requirements.

S-3 *Minimum Professional Proficiency* Able to speak the language with sufficient structural accuracy and vocabulary to participate effectively in most formal and informal conversations on practical, social, and professional topics.

S-4 *Full Professional Proficiency* Able to use the language fluently and accurately on all levels normally pertinent to professional needs.

S-5 *Native to Bilingual Proficiency* Speaking proficiency equivalent to that of an educated native speaker.

As currently used, any of the ratings except S-5 may be modified by a plus (+), which indicates that the proficiency substantially exceeds the minimum requirements for that level, but does not reach the next level.

When the Peace Corps began operation in the early 1960s the FSI Oral Interview was usually given to all volunteers at the completion of their 2 years of service. After a few years of overseas experience, the agency began to demand certain levels of language proficiency of a trainee before that individual could be sworn in as a volunteer or sent to a specific job. This base level was established for different jobs on the basis of past volunteer experience and recommendations, and on comments from host country co-workers as well. In Latin America, for example, training programs for university teachers aimed at ensuring that individual trainees received at least an S-3 rating before being assigned to a teaching position overseas. A high S-rating is necessary to qualify as an official government interpreter.

Many people, particularly second language teachers, have tried oral interviews as a means of judging proficiency. They have complained that such interviews are highly subjective and that there is no necessary correlation between judgments of a person's proficiency by different interviewers. The FSI Oral Interview, when given by trained interviewers, has an extremely high interrating correlation from different interviewers (Clark, 1975; Wilds, 1975). This same high correlation has been noted in other oral interviews from trained interviewers by Upshur (1973).

However, the problems of administration time and expense in using oral interviews as a measure of oral proficiency are very real. The face validity and the predictability of performance on the basis of the S-ratings certainly seem to make the expense, the time, and the effort worthwhile for both the person examined and the agency of the government involved. The S-rating, according to Wilds (1975), "has become so widely known and well understood that a reference to a point on the scale is immediately and accurately intelligible to most people concerned with personnel assignments in the numerous Government foreign affairs agencies who now use the FSI rating system" (p. 29).

To people unfamiliar with this type of an integrative oral test, as contrasted with set patterns of questioning for an oral test (described by MacKenzie, 1961; Chastain, 1976), numerous problems may seem to be involved. Establishing such a system for any large program does involve confronting a great number of problems. However, it should be reemphasized that reliability is not one of the problems—provided, of course, that the testers are trained, and that they test often.

One of the most recurrent problems in scoring oral interviews concerns the use of different varieties of a language. At FSI this has been resolved by maintaining a strict preference for the standard variety of speech. The problem first arose when numbers of Peace Corps volunteers and foreign aid program personnel were tested and found to be conversationally fluent, but speaking a nonstandard variety of the language. Many of these individuals had worked with illiterate, semiliterate, or second language speakers of the language being tested, and thus had acquired the particular variety of the language spoken by their coworkers. This variety often was not accepted by most educated native speakers of the language, and caused a dilemma for the certified testers. The standard variety was finally maintained as the scale for educated speech at FSI since official diplomats must speak the standard dialect if they are to be respected. This decision also avoided the problem of evolving several different rating scales for other agencies, such as the Peace Corps, within the government (Wilds, 1975).

Two other questions concerning the oral interview raised by Wilds (1975) include the following: "(1) Does the proficiency of the speaker of a foreign language fluctuate measurably from day to day? (2) Does his performance vary with the competence and efficiency of the examiners?" (p. 34) Other problematical issues focus on the possible confusion of linguistic ability and intellectual ability when pushing the examinee to the limit of linguistic competence, and getting the examinee to talk enough for an untrained tester, or a new tester, to make a fair judgment.

This system would seem extremely expensive and unwieldy for use in the normal academic situation where end-of-term testing comes all at once, and where using two teachers to test each student would create problems of scheduling facilities, time, and payment. In some colleges and high schools, the oral interview has been used as a means of discovering the total teaching program effectiveness as well as the individual students' strengths and weaknesses in using the second language (Wilds, 1975). In summing up, Wilds (1975) states:

> The fact of the matter is that this system works. Those who are subject to it and who use the results find that the ratings are valid, dependable, and therefore extremely useful in making decisions about job assignments. It is, however, very much an in-house system which depends heavily on having all interviewers under one roof, able to consult with each other and share training advances in techniques or solutions to problems of testing as they are developed and subject to periodic monitoring (p. 35).

Stolz and Bruck (1976) include the FSI Oral Interview as the best example of a direct integrative test. They add nothing to the excellent description of the test by Wilds, but do add some other comments. They state that there are no data on the predictive validity of the test—a questionable assertion in light of the Peace Corps' training and field experience. They additionally bring up the problem of a situational conversation, noting that when an individual knows he or she is being evaluated, there is no way in which the conversation remains totally natural. The expense, time, sophistication, and scoring of the interview are all mentioned as considerations of which to be aware. They do suggest that there is a possibility that acceptable results in this type of procedure might be obtained with some groups in specific situations with less costly training procedures than those at FSI. Strick (1975) mentions many of the same points in his description of the FSI Oral Interview.

One institution that used an adapted FSI Oral Rating for at least 3 years is the Institute of Communicative English, Catholic University, Ponce, Puerto Rico. English was a required course for all graduates of the university, and the requirement could be fulfilled either in the English Department or in the Institute. Students were initially sent to one or the other on the basis of their College Entrance Examination Board English scores. The courses in the English Department were comparable to courses in any mainland university English Department. The Institute classes were English as a Second Language, with the goal of getting students to communicate in English. Those students who came from the schools in Puerto Rico had been exposed to English for many years in their high school and elementary classes, but many of them had attained only minimal proficiency in speaking the language and did not trust their comprehension.

The oral interviews were used as a means of evaluating the Institute's program goals, establishing more realistic goals, and emphasizing to students that oral communication was a real goal of the

Institute—not just a paper one, as had happened in the past for many students. Once certain ratings were established as realistic expectations for student progress at each semester level of course work, these ratings were then made part of the criteria for passing from one level to the next.

Problems of testing in this normal academic setting, as noted by Wilds, did exist. However, expense for testers was not a problem because all staff members were trained to test and were expected to do so as part of their job descriptions. Problems encountered were: loss of class time for students; difficulties in finding appropriate places to test in a limited period of time; pressures for the teaching staff, who had to schedule and test more students in a day than FSI would recommend; and in almost all instances, having to rely on one tester per student instead of two.

No formal study of interrater reliability was carried out, yet the comparison of scores of students over time, and for interviewers, did lead to what was perceived as high reliability by all concerned. Furthermore, some students were tested more than once, for one reason or another, and were rated exactly the same (within a plus) by different examiners.

The FSI ratings did not differentiate enough for the use of the Institute staff in the middle levels of the six-semester program, due to the difficulty in progressing at that level. Therefore, further distinctions were made specifically for this particular group of students in the program. These differentiations resulted in more accurate descriptions of individual students' performances on the interviews and also gave the staff feedback on direction for the following semesters.

Using this adaptation of the FSI Oral Interview not only gave face validity to the overall goals of the Institute, but it also gave what Oller (1975) described as "psycholinguistic validity" to the student (1975, p. 27). Such validity was doubly important where English was a required university course with a variety of political implications and ramifications for these university students.

For the majority of the Institute students, the adapted FSI Oral Interview worked extremely well. For the small percentage of Institute students who were Vietnam veterans (studying on the G.I. Bill) or who had lived in New York for some time (not an unusual occurrence in Puerto Rico), there were problems of the language variety spoken being judged against standard English. These students could communicate orally with minimal difficulty, but they did not have control over the grammatical structure and vocabulary appropriate for professional or formal occasions. These students would have been downgraded in job interviews conducted in English, for example, because of the variety of English they spoke.

Student reaction to being interviewed often convinced the Institute staff that the time and effort were worth the trouble. Students were unanimously of the opinion that the interview demanded they use this second language in a realistic setting. At first, students were very nervous about being judged in an interview; after two semesters, they began to look forward to the interview as at least one opportunity to speak the second language privately with a teacher (not their own) and to prove to themselves that they could do it. It was this means of demonstrating to the students their capabilities in the second language and how much they had improved from one time to the next that made the effort worthwhile for teachers.

SAVIGNON COMMUNICATIVE COMPETENCE TESTS (*Savignon, 1972*)

Other examples of integrative oral proficiency tests are those developed by Savignon (1971) to "assess a student's ability to use the French s/he had learned in a variety of very practical situations." These tests seem particularly appropriate for early levels of second language acquisition. Students are asked to perform in four different contexts with no particular syntactic or lexical knowledge being tested. The four contexts are: discussion, information getting, reporting, and description. Students are told that the tests are a measure of how well they can communicate and that the evaluation will be based on how effectively they convey their point. Descriptions of each of the Savignon tests and the results for the three groups of students who were given the tests follow.

In the first part, discussion, the student was to talk with a native speaker who would be helpful and see how much information could be exchanged in 4 minutes on an assigned topic (randomly chosen) for which the student was not prepared. The students were encouraged to use gestures, ask for help, or even use a word in English. As much as possible, physical surroundings were that of a home.

Part two, information getting, required the student to interview a native speaker, who this time would not be helpful, in a more formal interaction. The student was to find out as much as possible in 4 minutes. Notes taken by the student were then written in English. Evaluation was to be based on the accuracy and amount of information reported by the student, and how the student conducted the interview.

Part three, reporting, consisted of talking for 3 minutes in French on one of three topics assigned randomly. The student was instructed to speak first in English to get his or her thoughts organized, and then to talk about the same things in French. Both the English and French reports were recorded, but they did not have to be exactly alike. Students were given 1 minute for English, and 3 for French.

Part four, description, consisted of the student watching an ongoing activity and describing it as it happened. The student was told that an actor would come into the room and do a variety of things. The student was first to describe the actor and then what the actor did. For practice, the student could do the same thing in English before attempting it in French for evaluation. The props that the actor used as well as the activities had been chosen from the basic vocabulary used in the textbook (Savignon, 1972). The English warmup lasted 45 seconds and was not the same as the French. The actor reentered with a different variety of objects. He gave the student 1 minute to describe him, and then performed the selected actions for another 1½ minutes. Sequence and nature of the activities of the actor were different for each student. The student's description was tape-recorded for later evaluation.

The native speakers who helped administer parts one and two participated in a training session to gain practice in how to handle the discussions and to establish the criteria for evaluation of the students' communicative ability. Two criteria were identified for the first part: 1) effort in communicating, and 2) amount of communication. A six-point scale was used for rating both criteria. Five criteria were set up for part two: 1) comprehensibility and suitability of the introduction, 2) naturalness and poise, or the ability of the student to keep the interview in hand, 3) comprehension by the native speaker, the degree of hesitation in interpreting the student's questions, and the number of repetitions, 4) the comprehensibility and suitability of the conclusion, and 5) the amount of communication, i.e., how many accurate statements about the native the student was able to make at the conclusion of the interview. Native speakers rated student performance on the first four criteria using a six-point scale. The fifth criterion was rated by an evaluator, who had not been present and did not know the students, by counting the number of correct statements that had been checked by the native speaker for accuracy.

The individual students' tape recordings were used for evaluating the third and fourth parts. Again, a six-point scale was used by a native speaker to rate each performance in terms of fluency and comprehensibility. The native speaker also wrote in French what he understood from the tape; this was not a transcription, but the ideas expressed. Another evaluator then scored these accounts, giving one point for each complete idea in part three. While this conceptualization of a complete idea was arbitrary at first, guidelines quickly became established. Accuracy for the fourth part was controlled by comparing the recorded description of the student with the actor's account, one point being given for each item of correct information.

In addition to the formal evaluation of the students' performance, the students were asked to write their reactions to the experience. They were positive in their reactions despite having experienced difficulty with the tests. They viewed the tests as fair and valid for the skills they were supposedly learning. The ongoing description was the most difficult test according to the majority of the students. In this instance they did not have a choice of expression, nor help from the participant as they did in the two-way tasks.

The three groups of students who were given the series of Savignon tests also took the CEEB Listening and Reading tests in French, and were graded along regular departmental standards. There were no significant differences among the groups on the CEEB tests nor in the final grades. There were, however, significant differences among the groups in terms of the communicative competence tests, with the first experimental group doing much better. The same held true for the instructor's evaluation of oral skills for each of the students involved. Additionally, while all of the students took the MLAT (Modern Language Aptitude Test) and there were no differences among the groups on MLAT scores, the first experimental group correlation between MLAT scores and communicative competence tests was 0.80 (Savignon, 1972, p. 63). The other two groups had correlations of 0.38 and 0.12. The differences seemed directly attributable to the teaching strategy used in the first experimental group. (For detail, see Savignon, 1972).

ILYIN ORAL INTERVIEW (*Ilyin, 1976b*)

The Ilyin Oral Interview (IOI) is a test designed for adult students who are studying English as a Second Language (ESL) in intensive language training programs. The test uses a rating scale that gives credit for understanding the question or task and responding in an appropriate manner, and gives additional credit for using correct structure in the appropriate response. It thus is integrative in nature, and does not rely on syntax for a discrete point scoring system. It is the only commercially available instrument described in this chapter.

The test arose from a need to assess functional oral communication ability of students, without regard to accuracy in syntax, for placement in an ESL program. Ilyin states that the use of tests that were inappropriate for the specific population led to student disillusionment, poor attitudes, and subsequent dropout from a program that had been specifically designed to meet the needs of such students (1976a). Tests designed for the foreign-born university student in the United States are heavily oriented toward students with a great deal of academic training, both in their own language and in English. Students in intensive adult programs often do not have that background, and need to learn English for other reasons than the foreign-born university student. The adult-program student most often needs English to communicate in the workday world, not to study university subjects.

Adult ESL programs have often avoided using tests of speaking ability due to the problems connected with administering such a test, the time such a test consumes, and suspicion about its objectivity. Student placement is usually based on a quick oral interview and a lot of intuitive guesswork. If the student thinks that the ensuing placement level is wrong, problems can arise if there is no objective score to justify the decision. The IOI was designed to overcome the problems of oral interviewing in adult ESL intensive programs.

The IOI has a set pattern of scoring, requires only one examiner per individual tested, and has a short form (30 items) that correlates highly with the longer (50 item) form. Furthermore, very little training is required to administer the test effectively. The strong point of the test, according to the author, is that the test is not too hard for students who have some English, and that it is designed to avoid student feelings of failure and frustration.

There are two versions of the IOI, Bill and Tom, for use depending upon the actual day of the week. Each test is an individually administered oral interview that is terminated when the student reaches the frustration level. If the examiner judges that the student has reached that level (by totally misunderstanding three or four test items in a row, two or three easy questions are asked so that the student has a feeling of success before the interview is ended by the examiner. Although the test was originally developed for English as a Second Language, it could easily be adapted for other languages.

Each version of the test consists of a series of pictures about the same individual; each picture contains a clock showing the time. The examiner describes the series, tells the story by pointing out each of the pictures as described, and checks to make sure that student understands. The test begins with asking questions about the pictures, such as *What is Bill doing in this picture?* and *What time is it in the picture?* Different time expressions or verb tenses can be elicited by use of the picture series.

Since the test is designed to be stopped at the individual student's level of frustration, the administration time for each student varies, but usually ranges from 5 to 30 minutes. If the short (30) item option of the test is selected for the more intermediate and advanced students, the time allotment can be kept fairly short, according to the manual.

The scoring of the test calls for a three-point system as follows:

0—Information given is inappropriate or unintelligible. (Grammar and structure may or may not be correct.)
1—Information given is appropriate and intelligible. (One or more mistakes in grammar or structure.)
2—Information given is appropriate and intelligible. (No grammar or structure mistakes.)

Sample tests, scoring examples, and suggestions for the tester are included in the manual, as are placement levels for the program for which the IOI was initially designed. Diagnostic information is described, and the possibility of using the two forms of the test for measurement of achievement across a semester is suggested. One point worth consideration for other integrative instruments is also mentioned—the author instructs a new examiner to "give the tests to about five educated native speakers of English" (Ilyin, 1976b, p. M3). This brings up the very real situation of alternative answers that would need to be judged. The author continues, "Remember that any structure which a native speaker would use in the situation is acceptable" (Ilyin, 1976b, p. M3). Again, note the emphasis on an integrative as opposed to a discrete point approach to assessing proficiency.

Although the IOI was originally designed for adults, it has been used for junior high, secondary, and upper elementary students. It seems appropriate for all of these groups. A close look at individual tests would give diagnostic information for the teacher concerning each student.

The manual reports the field testing and first edition studies for the IOI. In those groups, the reliability coefficients ranged from 0.86 to 0.98. The populations tested were from varied backgrounds and many different levels of English. In total, over 1,000 persons, ranging in age from 18 to 86, were tested. Some small studies are reported for the correlations of student scores on the IOI with other means of evaluation, but the number of students who took each test was relatively small (15 to 78). It is hard to be fair in giving an overall judgment because of this fact, yet all of the tests seem to correspond to some extent with the more advanced ESL tests, correlating better with the higher placement level groups, as would be expected.

It would be interesting to see correlations of the IOI with the FSI Oral Interview in English, although the relatively lower level of the IOI might not reveal exactly the functional competence levels of the higher FSI scores. However, the FSI may be most amenable to correlation as another integrative measure of oral proficiency.

In summary, the IOI gives credit for comprehension and communication as well as for structural correctness, which is in marked contrast to most other commercially available oral language tests. It yields a measure of the individual's capabilities within the language, and is fairly straightforward to administer and score. The one problem noted is that of insisting upon complete sentence responses. While the test makes comparisons among students more generalizable by insisting upon complete statements, native speakers do not always respond that way. This appears to be the one false note in the integrative approach.

Use of the IOI would readily lend itself to the establishment of local norms, and of a measure of student pre- and post-class achievement, if the two versions of the test were used. With a different interest level, this type of test, aimed at younger children, would seem to be a much more valid and reliable measure of oral language assessment than published instruments that rely only on syntax or vocabulary.

The IOI is an instrument that is integrative in concept, fairly easy to administer and score, and certainly worth considering as a measure of English oral proficiency for non-native English speakers. The scoring procedure described could also prove helpful to all teachers bothered by not being able to give credit to student responses that are contextually and culturally appropriate, even if those responses contain errors in syntax or pronunciation. The emphasis on being aware of the feelings of frustration of the student is certainly one that needs to be considered in bilingual placement testing, as well as in adult second language testing.

HIGH/SCOPE INSTRUMENTS (*Bond, Epstein, and Matz, 1977*)

The High/Scope Educational Research Foundation has developed some language assessment procedures that fall within the integrative category. These were originally developed as tools for program evaluation and not for evaluation of individual children. However, they offer a new perspective for ways of measuring children's communicative language ability. The tests, described by Bond, Epstein, and Matz (1977), are the Productive Language Assessment Tasks (PLAT) and Mutual Problem-Solving Task (MPST).

The PLAT consists of two tasks: reporting and narrating. Children work with real objects among themselves. They are given material and tools and told to make anything they wish. After about half an hour they are asked to write how they made the finished product. While writing, the children are again allowed to interact with each other.

The task of narration is similar. Children are given sets of unstructured materials and are encouraged to make up a story. Typically they engage in "intensive dramatic play" (Bond, Epstein, and Matz, 1977, p. 85). After being involved in this task for about 15 minutes, they are given time to write a story.

Linguistic and communicative competence are the two dimensions examined by the PLAT. The variables for the former include the length of the story—a measure of fluency; the average length of T-unit, or single independent predication together with any subordinate clauses or phrases that may be grammatically related to it; and vocabulary diversity. The variables for communicative competence currently include numbers of descriptive words and phrases, quantity of statements that are explanatory, and ratings of the quality of the reporting and organization. These variables measure how successfully meaning was communicated and with what degree of sophistication.

In both areas of assessing language ability, the emphasis is on deriving communication from real discourse where divergent behavior is encouraged, unlike the normal situation in a discrete point test. The tasks for the PLAT have been used and proved appropriate for second through fourth graders, according to the authors, and the children were overwhelmingly positive about the experience.

The MPST is an attempt to look at a situation analogous to that of the home. It is used for both verbal and nonverbal measurement. In this situation mothers and children are observed baking cookies together. The families are instructed that there is no right way to do this, that the examiners are interested only in how children and mothers work together. A choice of recipes, ingredients, and utensils is given so that mothers and children have to make decisions, and their respective involvement in that process can be analyzed. Audio recordings are made, and a trained observer codes behavior.

This task takes about 20 minutes and has been administered to about 50 first and second grade children and their mothers. The authors state that the task seems applicable to not only a broader range of ages but to other problem-solving groups as well; they also suggest the possibility of utilizing other problem-solving tasks.

The audio recordings are analyzed using a modified version of the PLAT procedures for analysis. The observations are analyzed using the Interaction Category System, which codes behavior sequentially. Conversational reciprocity, reliance upon verbal communication, and effectiveness in requesting information are coded.

The experience using the PLAT and MPST has brought about efforts to develop other assessment instruments. For example, one is a version of the PLAT in which oral presentations are sought from the children. Additionally, procedures for analyzing and eliciting oral language production from preschool children are being developed. The third effort reported includes an adaptation of the MPST for elementary-age children. Observations include both verbal and nonverbal interactions that occur while the children are working on the assigned task (Bond, Epstein, and Matz, 1977).

While these instruments have been used with first language speakers, the theoretical construct underlying the approach is certainly applicable to second language speakers. Indeed, eliciting natural samples of oral production from younger children would be an ideal way to begin to assess each child's functional ability in the second language. Furthermore, problem-solving tasks are often used as teaching vehicles in adult second language classes, and would easily serve as a means of assessing second language functional abilities, given a uniform scoring procedure.

SUMMARY AND NEEDS FOR RESEARCH

The majority of the oral language assessment instruments that can truly be categorized as integrative have been developed for use with adult second language learners (FSI, IOI, Savignon). The lessons learned through examining these instruments are useful in designing instruments or ways of assessing child first and second language proficiency in a bilingual situation. It is important to keep in mind why new methods of assessing child first and second language proficiency are being designed. If the reason is only to meet the federal funding guidelines for bilingual programs in terms of language dominance, then perhaps the discrete point type of test will suffice, despite the fact that linguists and psychologists are not in agreement about dominance, its definition, or its meaning. If, however, the rationale for assessing child first and second language proficiency is to best place and help each individual child learn, more sophisticated measuring instruments are desperately needed—instruments derived from data-based knowledge of what a child actually knows and needs to know for the multiple contexts of his or her daily life. Knowledge gained from the High/Scope type of assessment procedure will help define what monolingual English speaking children use, know, and need to know. This type of information is sadly lacking in many contexts and in other languages.

There is a need for in-depth longitudinal studies of child language acquisition in a bilingual setting throughout the United States. Also needed is an accurate determination of what language a bilingual child uses in which situation, and what is needed for effective communication within the situations that child encounters in daily life. Such studies could serve as the basis for more appropriate and realistic assessment instruments resulting, to take one example, in a rating along a continuum, instead of a number on a discrete point test. The score from a discrete point test does not tell the classroom teacher anything useful about the child's functional language ability in either language.

A rating as suggested above could be interpreted, as can the S-ratings of the FSI Oral Interview, to predict a child's ability to function in certain situations with a certain amount of communicative and linguistic competence. An instrument such as this would be a vast improvement over what is currently available. Language variety would need to be recognized (as the FSI does not) and emphasis should be on what a child can do with the language(s). Credit should be given for functional use and appropriate response (as in the IOI), rather than being tied to strict linguistic standards of correct usage. The Savignon type of tests seem directly applicable to lower FSI levels and also to younger children. Other factors to keep in mind would include nonverbal communication, pragmatics, kinesics, and prosody (see Omark, Chapter 12, this volume).

Within a given community and school, teachers, aides, parents, and children themselves should be able to define what a child needs to be able to do, in which language variety. With this commonly determined description, tasks could be designed (keeping in mind the ideas of Savignon and High/Scope) that would be appropriate for the age level and cultural background of the local school/community. The suggested rating would lend itself to this type of situation easily.

Teachers, aides, volunteers, and specialists could then be trained to score this type of oral proficiency assessment rating. Procedures for scoring such as those described by Ilyin and Savignon might lend themselves well to such a continuum. Experience using such a rating scale over time would lead to the establishment of local norms. Thus, teachers, second language specialists, and other professionals could be involved not only in assessing children but also in more accurately diagnosing strengths, abilities, and each child's need for improvement. Most likely, a range of instruments (or ratings) relevant to children of different ages and more reflective of functional abilities within contextual parameters would evolve.

It is important to remember student reaction to the integrative type of assessment instruments described earlier. The positive reaction noted by Savignon and this author even when class grades were being assigned is also emphasized by Ilyin and the High/Scope personnel. The testing experience itself is not the usual one. For children in a bilingual setting, where the school situation itself may be strange, making the assessment experience realistic, enjoyable, and definitely related to the purpose for which the test results are going to be used is sound educational practice. Results can be expected to reflect the individual student's abilities more accurately.

The experience of researchers and language professionals with adult integrative oral proficiency assessment instruments that give credit for communication without penalizing for linguistic syntactic error (as in the IOI), or that differentiate levels of functional abilities linked with linguistic abilities (as in the FSI Oral Interview), can and should be of value to professionals who work with bilingual bicultural children. This combination of experience from theories of sociolinguistics, psycholinguistics, second language pedagogy, and assessment, linked with the elementary education bilingual bicultural experts' knowledge and experience, could result in much more accurate assessment of oral language proficiency for the students involved in bilingual bicultural education programs.

REFERENCES

Bond, J. T., Epstein, A. S., and Matz, R. D. (with C. B. Cazden). 1977. Methods for assessing the language production of the young child. In: Language assessment: Where, what and how. Anthropol. Educ. Q. 8:84–86.

Chastain, K. 1976. Developing Second-Language Skills: Theory to Practice. Rand McNally, Chicago.

Clark, J. L. D. 1975. Theoretical and technical considerations in oral proficiency testing. In: R. L. Jones and B. Spolsky (eds.), Testing Language Proficiency. pp. 10–28. Center for Applied Linguistics, Arlington, Va.

Ilyin, D. 1976. Assessing oral communication in adult program English second language classes. (ED 119 463, FL 607 286).

Ilyin, D. 1976. Ilyin Oral Interview, Newbury House Publishers, Rowley, Mass.

MacKenzie, N. 1961. English proficiency testing in the British Commonwealth. In: J. B. Carroll (ed.), Testing the English Proficiency of Foreign Students. pp. 54–72. Center for Applied Linguistics, Washington, D.C.

Oller, J. W., Jr. 1973. Discrete-point tests versus tests of integrative skills. In: J.

W. Oller, Jr., and J. C. Richards (eds.), Focus on the Learner. pp. 184–199. Newbury House Publishers, Rowley, Mass.

Oller, J. W. Jr. 1975. Discussion following presentation by J. L. D. Clark. Theoretical and technical considerations in oral proficiency testing. In: R. L. Jones and B. Spolsky (eds.), Testing Language Proficiency. pp. 10–28. Center for Applied Linguistics, Arlington, Va.

Savignon, S. J. 1971. A study of the effect of training in communicative skills as part of a beginning college French course on student attitude and achievement in linguistic and communicative competence. Unpublished doctoral dissertation, University of Illinois, Urbana.

Savignon, S. J. 1972. Communicative Competence: An Experiment in Foreign-Language Teaching. The Center for Curriculum Development, Philadelphia.

Shuy, R. W. 1977. Qualitative language data: A case for and some warnings against. Anthropol. Educ. Q. 8:73–82.

Stolz, W., and Bruck, M. 1976. A project to develop a measure of English language proficiency. Final Report to the National Center for Education Statistics under Contract #300-75-0253. Center for Applied Linguistics, Arlington, Va.

Strick, G. 1975. State-of-the-art paper on testing language proficiency (mimeo). Center for Applied Linguistics, Arlington, Va.

Upshur, J. A. 1973. Context for language testing. In: J. W. Oller, Jr., and J. C. Richards (eds.), Focus on the Learner. pp. 200–213. Newbury House Publishers, Rowley, Mass.

Wilds, C. P. 1975. The oral interview test. In: R. L. Jones and B. Spolsky (eds.), Testing Language Proficiency. pp. 29–34. Center for Applied Linguistics, Arlington, Va.

chapter ten

Pragmatics and Language Assessment
Kamal K. Sridhar

This chapter relates recent linguistic and psycholinguistic research in pragmatics to the assessment of the language of bilingual children. First, the chapter describes pragmatics and the role it plays in the communication process involving language. This introduction to pragmatics includes some new directions in psycholinguistics and sociolinguistics that have arisen from the recognition of the need to consider the role of pragmatics in linguistic interaction. (For further discussion, see Walters, Chapter 11, this volume.) In the second part, a few widely used tests in bilingual programs are discussed in light of pragmatics and some tentative and largely programmatic suggestions are offered for incorporating pragmatic skills in such instruments.

PRAGMATICS AND LANGUAGE

The term *pragmatics*, as applied to the study of language, derives from the philosopher Morris (1938), who vaguely characterized it as an independent component of language in contradistinction with syntax (the study of the form of sentences) and semantics (the study of the literal meaning of sentences). In this use, pragmatics is a "level" of linguistic organization and is different from other levels insofar as it makes reference to the use of language in context. A more restricted definition of pragmatics was offered by Bar-Hillel (1954). He defined pragmatics as the study of indexical expressions such as *I*, *you*, *here*, and *now* whose meaning depends on the speaker, the addressee, the locale, and other contextual factors. In recent years, linguists and philosophers have used the term rather loosely to include a wide range of phenomena. Thus, speech acts, conversational implicature, presuppositions, speaker beliefs and expectations, perceptual context, and participant relationships have all been counted among "pragmatic" factors crucial for the transmission of meaning. As Morgan (1977) rightly points out, "What unites all these apparently disparate areas under the same term is the crucial role in each of inference, in context, about the intentions of the speaker" (p. 57).

The impetus for recent work in pragmatics comes from the Oxford philosopher Austin (1962). Austin observed that sentences do not exist in a vacuum but, rather, they perform various kinds of functions. People use sentences "to get things done," i.e., to inform, to request information, to thank, to apologize, to warn, to order someone to do something, and so on. The functions they serve are critical to communication. Speakers expect listeners to recognize those functions and act accordingly. For example, whenever they ask a question, they expect their listeners to realize that their utterance is a request for information. Each of the thousands of sentences we utter every day is an instantiation of one of several kinds of speech acts (Searle, 1969).

For linguistics, the notion of speech acts has proved to be almost as revolutionary as that of transformational grammar itself. Up until the late 1960s, American linguists had been primarily interested in analyzing sentences as formal objects.

In transformational generative grammar (Chomsky, 1965), sentences are generated by a set of rewrite rules that expand abstract symbols, like sentences, into constituents such as noun phrases and verb phrases which, in turn, are expanded into categories such as nouns, verbs, adjectives, and articles. The structures generated in this fashion (called "phrase markers") constitute what is referred to as the "deep structure" of sentences. Semantic interpretation is based on deep structure. In the case of most sentences, however, a further set of syntactic rules (called transformations) apply, adding, deleting, or permuting elements. The structures that result from the application of transformational rules (called the "surface structure" of sentences) are given phonological interpretation to yield sentences as they are actually pronounced by speakers. Notice that in this model it is the syntax that is generative; the semantic and phonological components merely "interpret" the structures generated by the syntactic component.

Despite the avowed claim that the task of the linguist is to characterize the systematic relationships between sound and meaning, *meaning*, until the 1960s, was interpreted as essentially the literal meaning of a sentence. The pragmatic or contextual meaning of a sentence—which is quite often very different from its literal meaning—was not considered at all, probably not because its importance was unrecognized but because the mechanism involved in deriving a sentence's contextual meaning was assumed to be incredibly complex and not readily susceptible to formalization. Whatever the reason, the way sentences are put to various kinds of use by speakers was not considered part of linguistic description. All this began to change, however, as linguists came to realize the relevance of the theory of speech acts put forward in the works of Austin and Searle. Pragmatics—the general appellation for work on questions of meaning dependent on contextual factors—is now a flourishing component of linguistics and certainly one of the most controversial.

Direct and Indirect Speech Acts

To return to speech acts, sentences often explicitly indicate the type of speech act intended by the speaker. For example, consider sentences 1 through 5:

1. I warn you to stay out of this.
2. I promise you I will be there tomorrow.
3. I sentence you to 30 years in jail.
4. I appoint you my watchdog.
5. I thank you for not calling me names.

The main verbs in these sentences make it clear that the speaker intends to warn, promise, or otherwise affect the listener. Another interesting feature of these sentences is that the very act of uttering them constitutes the actions of warning, promising, and so on. Austin calls verbs of this type "performative verbs" and the sentence type "performative sentences" because these utterances themselves "perform" the speech acts.

However, one can perform speech acts without using performative verbs or the full performative construction. In fact, this is generally the case. Notice how tedious it would be to introduce every statement with the expression "I tell you . . . ," or every question with "I ask you . . . ," or every order with "I order you . . . ." Speakers instead simply use the declarative, interrogative, and imperative constructions (as in 1–3) and expect the listener to figure out the speech act intended by them.

1. Daddy's not home yet.
2. Where'd you been?
3. Get out!

The expectations are most often fulfilled because there is normally a reliable correspondence between these speech acts and sentence types; i.e., declaratives are normally employed to make an assertion, interrogatives to request information, imperatives to give a command, and so on.

The problem is that there is not always a neat match between a given construction and a speech act. In other words, speech acts may be expressed indirectly, using a construction other than that specifically meant for it. The most common, straightforward way to get someone to do something is by using an imperative, but that is not the only way. The same speech act (or speech function) may be performed by, among other things, a statement of personal preference, or just a simple, remotely related statement. This can be seen by comparing a, the imperative, with b–h, variations:

- a. Put on your shirt.
- b. Won't you put on your shirt?
- c. Why not put on your shirt?
- d. Where's your shirt?
- e. Haven't you forgotten to do something?
- f. I'd rather you put on your shirt.
- g. It's always good to protect your skin from the elements.
- h. It's cold out there.

Utterances such as a where a speech act is directly expressed by a construction specifically designed for that function are known as "direct speech acts." Utterances such as b through h where the communicative function is expressed by a construction other than that specifically designed for it are known as "indirect speech acts."

The task of characterizing the indirect correspondence between speech acts and sentence types has attracted the attention of a number of contemporary linguists and philosophers of language. It is obvious that a purely structural description of sentences—an account of the correspondence between the sounds and the literal meaning—is inadequate to capture the intended meaning. The situational context of the speech act must play a crucial role. It is here that pragmatics comes into the picture.

From the above examples, it seems that a basic model of verbal communication must involve several factors that speakers and hearers should share. According to Smith and Wilson (1979), these are:

1. A body of linguistic knowledge (a grammar)
2. A body of nonlinguistic knowledge and beliefs (an encyclopedia)
3. A set of inference rules (a logic)

Given these, an utterance would be analyzed as conveying two different types of information: 1) a set of propositions deducible from the sentence uttered by purely linguistic (semantic) rules, and 2) a further set of propositions deducible from the sentence uttered, together with some item(s) of nonlinguistic knowledge shared by speaker and hearer, and a set of shared inference rules.

While a given speech act may be expressed by the use of a variety of indirect means, the choice of sentences cannot vary indefinitely. If the latter were the case, every sentence would be open to infinite interpretations, making reasonable communication impossible. As in many other areas, language seems to operate within certain limits of variability, permitting an extensive range of alternations but in a rule-governed fashion, eliminating many more possible but impractical alternatives.

Maxims of Conversation

The most insightful and influential work toward explaining the rule-governed nature of indirect speech acts has been that of Grice (1967). According to Grice, both the potentials and the limitations of pragmatically determined meaning follow from the fact that participants in a linguistic interaction subscribe to an implicit code of conventions that he refers to as the *cooperative principle*. Adherence to the cooperative principle involves satisfying four "maxims" of conversation. These maxims are to "be informative," "be truthful," "be relevant," and "be clear." Simple as these precepts may seem to the layman, they have been shown to convey much more than what is actually said. Assuming that the speaker adheres to these maxims prompts the listener to look for and find meanings not actually expressed.

Consider the following exchange:

A: John doesn't seem to have a girl friend these days.
B: He has been visiting New York pretty often, though.

Although B did not actually say it in so many words, he has managed to convey that John may have a girlfriend in New York. Speaker A would never have been able to comprehend this implied meaning if he did not assume that B's response was relevant to his question (an example of the maxim of *relevance*).

Similarly, the importance of being informative is illustrated by the following dialogue.

A: John is meeting a woman for dinner tonight.
B: Does his wife know about it?
A: Of course she does. The woman he is meeting is his wife.

In this conversation, A, by withholding information, misled B into thinking that John might be up to some hanky-panky. Other maxims also have similar pragmatic consequences. The maxim of "be truthful" is equally important. Consider this reaction from a wife, "Honey, you look handsome!" especially when the husband walks in soaking wet from the rains outside. Even if the statement is made with sincerity, it appears to be untrue. Similarly, clarity is important when exchange of ideas takes place. By not being clear, the speaker appears to dodge the issue. This is the frequent complaint lodged against diplomats for using expressions such as, "We have had very fruitful discussions with the leaders from Egypt and Israel...."

Grice (1975) uses the term *conversational implicature* to explain the way speakers manage to convey meanings without actually expressing them. It is because listeners expect the speakers to conform to the maxims of conversation that they are able to comprehend such implied meanings. Notice that this is very different from *logical implicature* in that there is no necessary logical relationship between the propositions expressed that would lead to such an implication. The maxims referred to above are more than a code of conversational etiquette. They are critical to the very meaning of what the speaker said. Consider this exchange:

A: I am out of gas.
B: There is a gas station around the corner.

On the surface, speaker B has merely expressed the presence of a gas station nearby. But by implication, much more can be derived from the above utterance. If speaker A considers speaker B's utterance as relevant, A would assume the following: 1) the gas station is probably open, and 2) it sells gas. This is an instance of conversational implicature. Speaker B has not expressed it directly, but has implied that the gas station is open and sells gas.

Beyond its literal semantic interpretation provided by the grammar, an utterance has three main types of pragmatic implications: first, those implications that follow from the utterance itself, together with a preceding remark and any item of shared knowledge needed to establish a connection between the two; second, those additional premises, not already part of shared knowledge, needed to establish connection; and third, those implications that follow from these additional premises, together with the utterance itself, the preceding remark, and any necessary item of background knowledge. All of these types of pragmatic implications may contribute to establishing the relevance of the utterance as intended by the speaker; none will follow unless the utterance is treated by the hearer as relevant.

The maxims of conversation account for a wide range of linguistic phenomena, the potential of which has only begun to be discovered. For example, much of irony, sarcasm, understatement, and metaphor involve comprehending the conversational implicature by the application of the maxims. The maxims are of crucial relevance in explaining the organization of given and new information in discourse, in the interpretation of conjoined sentences involving implicit temporal and causal relationships, and so on (Schmerling, 1975; Clark and Haviland, 1977). It is not possible to go into these matters in this chapter.

Grice points out that the maxims of conversation are only a special instance of the general means by which we understand any form of behavior as rational—a point (often overlooked) that underlies the important and intimate interaction between linguistic and nonlinguistic behavior. A number of psycholinguists and sociolinguists have discussed this aspect of language behavior. For example, Osgood (1971) has argued that linguistic and nonlinguistic (perceptual) cognizing share a common level of organization, as is apparent in instances of sentences involving pronominal usage with perceptual but not linguistic antecedents. To cite Osgood's example, watching a mini-skirted coed pass by on the quad, a speaker might tell his friend, "She also dyes her hair," where the antecedent of *she* is perceptual and not linguistic. Similarly, a number of studies in *Interactional Sociolinguistics* have pointed out that many aspects of language are influenced by the speaker's and hearer's awareness of the situational context. An excellent, although oft-cited, example is the choice of pronominal address forms (e.g., *tu* versus *vous* in French, *tu* versus *usted* in Spanish, *du* versus *Sie* in German, *tum* versus *aap* in Hindi, and so on), which is determined by the relationship between the speaker and the hearer in terms of "power" and "solidarity" (Brown and Gilman, 1960). The same awareness of participant relationships in a social interaction that makes an Indian student get up when his teacher walks into the classroom and also makes him address his teacher with *aap* rather than *tum*. Some scholars have extended the term presupposition to include phenomena of these sorts and label them psychological and pragmatic presuppositions (Bates, 1976).

Frameworks for Discourse Analyis

There have been many attempts in linguistic literature to deal with such situationally determined phenomena, but a satisfactory model is still a desideratum. As early as 1957, the British linguist Firth observed that "the technical language necessary for the description of contexts of situation is not developed, nor is there any agreed method of classification ..." (Palmer, 1968, p. 177). Firth maintained that linguistic analysis must state "the interrelationship of elements of structure" and the "context of situation." He put forward a tentative framework consisting of the following parameters:

(i) The participants: persons, personalities, and relevant features of these.
(ii) The relevant objects and nonverbal and nonpersonal events.
(iii) The effect of the verbal action (Palmer, 1968, p. 117).

Halliday, McIntosh, and Strevens (1964) and other students of Firth have employed this framework in their work on discourse analysis, especially in the analysis of "registers" of specialized uses of language appropriate to various speech situations. However, the notion of context of situation has yet to be fully articulated.

Working along the same lines, Hymes (1967) has proposed a slightly more elaborate framework for the analysis of discourse. Hymes sets up the following parameters to explain the intimate relationship between language and the social context: setting (including time and place); participants; intentions; the characteristics or the rules relating a form to a topic; the tone or manner in which the speech act is made (e.g., mocking); the code itself and the channel in which it is transmitted; norms of interaction and interpretation (including loudness, when to interrupt); and types of speech acts and events (such as, conversations, curses, etc.).

Context and Language Acquisition

Psycholinguistic studies of the past decade show an increasing recognition of the role of the context and the speaker's intentions in interpreting the meaning and function of utterances. This approach constitutes a departure from earlier approaches to the study of language acquisition in which acquisition of language was equated with the acquisition of structure, the acquisition of sentences. The *rich interpretation* approach employed by Bloom (1970), Brown (1973), and the others departed from the structure-oriented approach, making reference to the child's "semantic intentions" (the meaning of the child's utterance) as inferred from the context of the utterance. For example, several instances of the utterance "Mommy sock" were found to have different meanings for the child depending on the context in which they were uttered. Thus, "Mommy sock" could indicate possession ("Mommy's sock") as well as an agent-object relationship ("Mommy is putting on Kathy's sock"). This richness of meaning intended by the child would be underrepresented by a purely structurally based theory of child language, which would assign the same cultural description to both instances of the utterance.

Recent studies of child language acquisition have explored the development of the child's knowledge of the functions of language and pragmatic conventions. For example, Halliday (1975) analyzed prelinguistic intonational patterns in terms of social functions such as naming and requesting. Analysis of the data in Leopold's diary by Ingram (1971) indicated that the child differentially employed even one-word utterances to signal speech functions such as interrogative, imperative, and declarative. Gruber (1973) also analyzed one-word utterances in terms of speech acts, especially those of ordering, naming, and so on. Dore (1973, 1974) observed that even before the child acquired sentential structures, he or she possessed systematic knowledge about the pragmatics of language that is best described in terms of primitive speech acts expressed either as a single word or a single prosodic pattern.

Peters (1977) observed that some children use two kinds of speech, the *analytic* (clear, one-word-at-a-time speech) and the *gestalt* (holistic speech), and that the two were often correlated with social settings. Thus, analytic speech may be used in referential contexts, such as naming pictures in a book (*horsie, doggie*), labeling a quality (*hot, cool*), and naming a desired object or action (*Cookie! Milk! Up!*). Gestalt speech, on the other hand, may be used in more "conversationally defined contexts": opening conversations/summonses (*What's that? Mommy*), playing with other children (*Airplane go up*), requesting something, as different from demanding, (*I want milk*), and discussing objects socially (*Silly, isn't it?*). Peters goes on to suggest that "there is probably a continuum of children who are very analytic right from the beginning through those who use mixes of Analytic and Gestalt speech in varying proportions, to those who may start out with a completely holistic approach and have to convert slowly and painfully to a more analytic approach to language" (p. 571). Peters criticizes the linguistic descriptions of language acquisition for taking an almost entirely analytic approach—looking at vocabulary counts and acquisition of analytic syntax and vocabulary and ignoring the holistic attempts at communication.

Other recent language acquisition studies have discussed the acquisition of indirect speech acts and conversational implicature. Bates (1971) and Shatz (1974) point out that even 2-year-olds understand and appropriately respond to direct as well as indirect requests (for example, "Can you shut the door?"). On the other hand, the *production* of indirect speech acts follows that of direct speech acts. For instance, Garvey (1975) observes that older children (7-year-olds) use indirect forms for permission and prohibition, such as "I don't mind your swinging" and "I would rather you didn't swing," while 5-year-olds would use the more down-to-earth "You can swing" and "You mustn't swing."

APPLICATION OF PRAGMATICS TO LANGUAGE INSTRUMENTS USED IN ASSESSING BILINGUAL CHILDREN

It is clear from the preceding sections that an approach to language concerned only with an analysis of vocabulary or sentences as formal, quasi-mathematical objects suspended in space fails to account for the full range of communicative functions of language. The native speaker not only uses generalizations based on the structure of language, but goes beyond this to exploit clues from the context of an utterance. Furthermore, conventions of conversations that suggest and infer communicative intent are another important component in communicative interactions and pragmatics analysis. Studies in pragmatics attempt to describe the kind of competence involved in getting at the full meaning of utterances in context starting from the literal meaning conveyed by a knowledge of the grammar and moving to a broader framework.

Considering the important role played by pragmatic conventions in linguistic interaction, it is worth asking to what extent the existing instruments on language assessment in general, and bilingual bicultural education in particular, reflect this knowledge. Previous chapters in this volume describe and evaluate various discrete point, quasi-discrete point, and integrative measures. This section discusses some of these tests and others with the suggestion they be extended into a pragmatic framework.

In the field of bilingual bicultural education, language tests are used primarily for diagnostic and placement purposes. Specifically, they are used to determine the dominant language of the child and to assess the child's competence in a given language or languages. Recent studies in pragmatics have a general and important implication for such tests at the very outset, namely, in defining linguistic competence itself. For a long time now, linguistic competence has been equated with the knowledge of the structure of the language, or grammatical competence. This thrust has led to a neglect of what is termed *communicative competence*, or the ability to use language effectively and appropriately in a variety of real-life situations.

If pragmatics offers any lessons for a better understanding of language, they are: 1) that there is an explicit recognition that language is used for communication, 2) that each utterance is intended to perform a specific function, and 3) that a good deal of meaning is conveyed indirectly, exploiting conversational conventions and contextual clues. As this volume illustrates, most existing instruments of bilingual language assessment have been concerned primarily, if not exclusively, with assessment of structures and vocabulary, almost always without regard to context. Only a few tests have been developed to elicit natural language responses. These tests are discussed below in relationship to the previous discussion on pragmatics.

A review of the literature on oral proficiency tests reveals that some effort has been made to measure the speaking skills of bilingual children by the elicitation of natural speech. Carrow (1957) reported that in her test children were required to retell a story that they had just heard (rather than have them make one up) as a measure of fluency. This approach to testing was also used by Lambert and Macnamara (1969) in Montreal.

Stemmler (1967) designed a test that explored spontaneous language and methods of thinking, called the Language Cognition Test. Spontaneous language elicitation was made possible by giving children two types of tasks. In the first task, objects such as a cap, a ball, and a pen are presented and the child is asked to name the object. For the second task, the child is given a picture in which some action is occuring, for example, a child hugging a new pair of shoes. The examinee is then asked to make up a story that goes with the pictures. The child's responses are analyzed according to basic types of sentence patterns with their transformations, verb constructions, adjectival usage, and the relationships of time sequence and cause and effect. The Language Cognition Test was normed on 78 randomly selected, disadvantaged, Spanish-speaking first graders in San Antonio, Texas. According to the authors, the LCT "... is showing promise as an instrument for assessing the language and cognitive status of one kind of disadvantaged children ..." (Stemmler, 1975, p. iii).

In an effort to elicit and analyze natural speech samples, Ott (1967) devised a test of oral fluency that consisted of prerecorded questions. These questions were intended to elicit three levels of speech: literal, inferential, and imaginative. In another experiment, Taylor (1969) used a tape cassette-film strip device developed in Austin to elicit stories. (Due to the expense, few bilingual programs can afford to use it.) Brisk (1972) reports using a concealed microphone for the elicitation of natural speech in response to picture books, toys, puppets, and other objects. All of the above test instruments and research approaches have attempted to collect speech samples using pictures and other types of stimuli that are subsequently analyzed in various ways.

A test that has been used to some extent is the Language Facility Test (Dailey, 1968), which, because of its applicability to pragmatic reinterpretation, is discussed in some detail. In this test a photograph, a painting, and a drawing are used to elicit original stories from children. The photograph is of a school scene (teacher and students outside the school); the painting depicts a home scene (father holding baby, mother and dog watching); and the sketch is of a neighborhood scene (boy sitting on the ground, pointing at a cat in a tree).

Mycue (1968) reports using Dailey's Language Facility Test (LFT) for the purpose of developing norms for minority children. Her sample consisted of 48 Mexican-American bilingual preschool children from Ft.

Worth, Texas, who the examiners tested for English language performance using the LFT. The purpose of the study was to determine if the spontaneous production of English would be better after the bilingual children were first allowed to perform in Spanish. The study also aimed to find if the English language performance of Mexican-American bilingual children would be better when tested by a Mexican-American examiner rather than an Anglo-American examiner. The results of the study indicate that the ethnic membership of the examiner and previous experience in Spanish of the child improved the production of the subjects' spontaneous speech in English. Bilingual children tested by a Mexican-American examiner performed better in English than children tested by an Anglo-American examiner. The bilingual children performed best in English when the examiner was Mexican-American and when a similar task in Spanish was completed first.

Cohen (1975) found several weaknesses in the LFT during pilot testing and decided to modify it before using it. Summarized below are the weaknesses discussed by Cohen:

1. The pictures represent three different media—a snapshot, a painting, and a sketch. There is no way one can measure if the differences in scores are due to the fact that children respond to these media differently. Experience tells us that children find sketches more confusing than, say, pictures or paintings.
2. The test asks children to tell a story, and some children really did not know what was expected of them. It appears that the children needed to have an example of a story.
3. The Dailey scoring scale confounds three very different dimensions. For the sake of simplicity, the examiner is told to rate each of the three stories on a single 0–9 rating scale. For a child to get high scores he or she not only needs linguistic proficiency in the language(s), but also needs the capability of describing situations, and the ability to draw inferences.

Thus, argues Cohen, language appraisal here is combined with the assessment of cognitive development. The evaluation is not valid unless the language elicitation could be measured separately from cognitive development. Cohen attempted to do just this in his Storytelling Task.

In the Storytelling Task (Cohen, 1975), the child was first required to view a snapshot and hear a story about it. Then the child was asked to tell his or her own story. Dailey's pictures were used, but the scoring system was replaced by one based on the measurement of storytelling by Lambert and Tucker (1972). The latter system rates storytelling according to general fluency, grammar, pronunciation, rhythm, and intonation. Cohen used roughly the same categories with the addition of two more: *language alternation* and *descriptive ability*. Language alternation refers to the entire range of language switching, from switching out of one language into another in the middle of a sentence, to the mixing of single words from one language into sentences in another language (these two phenomena are known as *code-switching* and *code-mixing*). Language alternation was included as a measure of language independence. This scoring system was intended to give an indication not only of how much a bilingual alternates between his two languages, but also of whether words and phrases from one language are more likely to be inserted into the other language.

Descriptive ability was added to provide a separate scale for cognitive development, rather than combining it with linguistic ability, as was done in the Dailey test. Cohen recommends more refinement of the above two categories for future tests. There is virtually no interpretation or discussion concerning the data in the areas of language alternation and descriptive ability. As the author himself points out, a cartoon or a picture sequence would be more useful because single pictures prompt children to describe the objects in it, and spontaneous speech elicitation becomes virtually impossible. However, information gained from the above test "... is not only a source of feedback concerning language learning at school, but can also provide some indication of maintenance and shift of language patterns of bilinguals in a variety of other social domains..." (Palmer and Spolsky, 1975, p. 183). This latter kind of information is needed for pragmatically oriented tests, and insights from such studies will be extremely valuable in the development of future tests.

Most of the tests used to assess language dominance and development rely on pictures, puppets, toys, and other kinds of visual stimuli. One weakness of the method of eliciting descriptions from pictorial stimuli—a method commonly employed in bilingual tests—is that it does not test the child's versatility in using different kinds of speech acts. As is clear from some of the developmental psycholinguistic studies discussed earlier and many others not mentioned in this chapter, children perform and respond to a wide range of different kinds of speech acts from the earliest stage. In this respect, the method of eliciting language in a conversational situation adopted in a test such as the Basic Inventory of Natural Language (BINL) by Herbert (1974) seems to be more effective (see McCollum and Day, Chapter 8, this volume).

Several tests use illustrations as a means of eliciting speech from children. In the case of the Bilingual Syntax Measure (Burt, Dulay, and

Hernandez, 1975), specific syntactic structures are elicited. This practice of using illustrations to elicit a response restricts the child's capacity to talk about issues that excite or interest them. Studies such as those of Peters (1977) and Nelson (1973) indicate that children employ different learning strategies, analytic or gestalt, referential or expressive, and that these may vary depending on the kind of speech act and the context. If this indeed is generally correct, then an undifferentiated elicitation of structures such as that employed in the Bilingual Syntax Measure might lead to underrepresenting the competence of the child.

Another test that deserves some attention is the Oral Language Evaluation[1] (OLE) by Silvaroli, Skinner and Maynes (1977). The OLE is an oral language measure of both English and Spanish. It is purportedly designed to: 1) *identify* those children who need training in oral language, 2) quickly *assess* individual oral language production, 3) *diagnose* the level of oral language production, and 4) *prescribe* activities in order to develop the child's oral language. Language samples in response to pictures are obtained and scored according to the levels listed below:

1. *Labeling:* single-word responses
2. *Basic Sentences:* structures in which no words are omitted
3. *Language Expansion:* information is added to indicate where, how and when
4. *Connecting, Relating, and Modifying:* basic and expanded sentences have connectives, such as *and, but, if, until, because,* and *since,* and usually relate and modify ideas by indicating why and how
5. *Concrete/Simple Storytelling:* the student perceives the picture as merely one part of a larger story; responses include time, place, and cause-effect ideas
6. *Abstract/Complex Storytelling:* responses combine all previous levels and add responses that indicate mood, emotion, etc.

The OLE with its elaborate system of *Levels* and *Parts* is based on the observations and experiences of the authors, and thus prevents their view of "general language development." It seems that a very crucial level is missing, one that needs to be incorporated between Levels 1 and 2. Developmental studies of language acquisition indicate that most children go through two-, three- and four-word sentences using telegraphic speech, omitting function words such as modifiers, prepositions,

---

[1] An earlier version of this test, written by Silvaroli and Maynes, was published by D. A. Lewis Associates in 1975 with a second edition in 1977. For a review of that similar version, see McCollom and Day, Chapter 8, this volume.

conjunctions, and determiners. This stage of language acquisition is completely missing from the OLE. The above phenomenon is not only evidenced in children's speech samples, but also in adults learning a second or third language. It is a natural level for all ages of learners and an important one, too; hence, it needs to be incorporated.

Levels 5 and 6 are more indicative of a child's cognitive development rather than his linguistic competence. Responses that incorporate notions of time, place, cause-effect, coupled with those of mood and emotion can certainly not be expected from young children. Cognitive skills have been confused with linguistic skills, and the two need to be separated before any assessment can be made regarding the children's linguistic capabilities.

The pictorial stimuli of scenes from a park, zoo, school, and home carry familiar themes but limit speech production to what is in the picture. A better method would be to collect natural speech samples in playgrounds and other unstructured situations, where children talk to one another with no constraints imposed on them (see Omark, Chapter 12, this volume).

Another pragmatically oriented test that deserves attention is the Functional Language Survey (FLS) (Walberg, Valdes, and Rasher, 1978). The FLS was developed by the Chicago School Board to assess five areas that could be used as the basis for identifying children in need of bilingual instruction. These five areas are listed below:

1. *Production/Repetition:* the ability to reproduce or repeat an utterance
2. *Direct Action:* the ability to follow spoken directions
3. *Discrimination/Identification:* the ability to provide verbal descriptions or labels to visual or tactile stimuli
4. *Verbal Dialogue:* the ability to give extended or elaborated verbal response to questions requiring more than one-word answers
5. *Directed Dialogue:* the ability to follow verbal directions requiring the use of spoken language

Notice that numbers 2 and 3, and 4 and 5 are parallel in the sense that they are sets, where one requires comprehension followed by production. While the above is true of 2 and 3, the same is not true of 4 and 5. Receptive and productive skills are measured through a series of questions that require the children to identify themselves. If a child answers with one word, he is prompted through further questioning on the subject to ensure increased verbal output. However, one-word answers or the common phenomenon of ellipsis is characteristic of adult discourse, an acceptable form of an answer. Rarely do people respond with complete sentences in these situations. For example:

> Question: What time is it?
> Answer: 4:30.

If the above answer is an acceptable one from adults, why not from children? Also, why are one-word answers considered to be indicators of undeveloped speech patterns? Since this instrument, by its very title, claims to test the functional language skills of children, one needs to examine this test in the light of the above claims. However, the FLS is one of the few tests that includes a census component, which records data such as the student's country of birth, the language spoken at home, an evaluation of language proficiency (Level *1*–Level *6*), and, if the student is a bilingual program participant, the program model and the number of years the student has been enrolled in the program. The student's prior experience and home background are both taken into account as equally important indicators of functional language usage. Another positive aspect of the test is that the questions asked are short and simple. Yet the test cannot be claimed to be pragmatically oriented, because pictures of automobiles, animals, or children in a park are used to collect free speech samples, and the children are prompted to describe what they see. Once again the cognitive and linguistic aspects of development have been confused and are treated as one and the same.

FURTHER IMPLICATIONS FOR LANGUAGE ASSESSMENT

Pragmatic considerations play an important role in the assessment of language dominance. As a large number of studies dealing with code-switching and code-mixing (e.g., the works of Blom and Gumperz, 1972; Kachru, 1978; Sridhar, 1978) have noted, the choice of language by a bilingual is determined by contextual and pragmatic factors (such as participant relationship, topic of discourse, formality, or speech setting). It is obvious that these factors are critical in the assessment of language dominance.

An insight from another area of research that needs to incorporated in pragmatically oriented tests is that of *revision behaviors*. Gallagher (1977) designed a study to investigate the relationships between the development of language structure and the development of conversational strategies for a specific type of communicative interaction—communicative failure (when the speaker says something and the listener indicates he does not understand). She investigated the linguistic behaviors associated with recoding and with similar types of communicative events. The data indicate that revision behaviors are systematic and that they change as the child's knowledge of language structure changes. Gallagher (1977) concludes:

> A pragmatic orientation, therefore, allowed a more sensitive description of one aspect of communicative competence than would be possible from either a grammatical analysis of structure or a frequency count of conversational categories. A generative grammatical analysis of the language structures the children used would have dealt with each child's entire corpus and would have led to purely descriptive statements ... (p. 316).

Gallagher recommends the use of probing questions such as *who*, *when*, *what*, and *where* for gaining more information from the child. More information is needed on the role played by probing questions.

Studies in pragmatics also call for a reconsideration of the criteria of evaluation adopted in language assessment. For example, it is well known that adult discourse involves a heavy use of ellipsis, as in the following example from Holzman (1971):

Question: When are going?
Answer: Tonight.

As Lakoff (1973) points out, the single-word response is perfectly natural and appropriate here, precisely because the response is informative to the right degree. Applying Grice's maxim, Lakoff shows that the response presupposes part of the question and expresses only the new information. Exactly the same process is observed in child language as well. A purely structurally oriented approach to language might consider such elliptical responses as symptomatic of a "nonverbal" child, while a pragmatically oriented approach would give the child credit for following the rules of discourse. This aspect of test bias has been discussed in some detail by Trueba and Sridhar (1978).

In the absence of a pragmatically oriented test, the best method for collecting natural speech samples is through observing and recording children's conversation with their peers in the playground, in the classroom, at birthday parties, and during all sorts of unstructured activities. Presence of adults (whether they are parents, teachers, or testers) somehow affects the naturalness of children's speech. Children become self-conscious and aware of adult presence. If the adult asks questions (as in the testing situation), some children respond because they feel it is expected, rather than because they want to respond. Then the answers of those children who are shy, quiet, not very sociable, or not easily excitable are not indicators of either their language "competence" or "performance." Language "competence" simply refers to what one knows and is capable of saying, and language "performance" means what one actually does or says. Thus, the speech samples collected in most test situations are not authentic samples of children's comprehension and speech abilities.

An alternative suggestion is to use one of the tests or techniques discussed in this chapter or elsewhere in this volume and compare the results of the tests to the child's performance outside the classroom. The two scores could then be combined to arrive at a more realistic score. The context in which sentences are uttered, the uniqueness of the answers, and the logical explanations that children offer are all important indicators of language development. Yet, these aspects are ignored in most of the existing language assessment instruments. The employment of different strategies in responding, such as one-word answers or complete answers is another area that needs to be further explored.

These are only some of the many possible implications of recent developments in pragmatics as a basis for language assessment. The nature of pragmatic conventions to be incorporated in a bilingual test will, of course, depend on the level for which a given test is designed (for example, the more subtle forms of conversational implicature are obviously not appropriate in the early stages), and the purpose of the test. Nevertheless, it will not be denied that all kinds of bilingual language assessment instruments stand to gain by recognizing the communicative function of language and the interdependence of context and utterances.

REFERENCES

Austin, J. L. 1962. How to Do Things with Words. Oxford University Press, Oxford.

Bar-Hillel, Y. 1954. Indexical expressions. Mind 63:359–379.

Bates, E. 1971. The Development of Conversational Skill in 2, 3 and 4 Year Olds. Unpublished master's thesis, University of Chicago, Chicago.

Bates, E. 1976. Pragmatics and sociolinguistics in child language. In: D. Morehead and A. Morehead (eds.), Normal and Deficient Child Language, pp. 411–463. University Park Press, Baltimore.

Blom, J. P., and Gumperz, J. 1972. Social meaning in linguistic structures: Code-switching in Norway. In: J. Gumperz and D. Hymes (eds.), Directions in Sociolinguistics: The Ethnography of Communication. Holt, Rinehart & Winston, New York.

Bloom, L. M. 1970. Language Development: Form and Function in Emerging Grammars. The MIT Press, Cambridge, Mass.

Brisk, M. E. 1972. The Spanish syntax of the pre-school Spanish American: The case of New-Mexican five-year-old children. Unpublished doctoral dissertation, University of New Mexico, Albuquerque.

Brown, R. 1973. A First Language: The Early Stages. Harvard University Press, Cambridge, Mass.
Brown, R., and Gilman, A. 1960. The pronouns of power and solidarity. In: T. Sebeok (ed.), Style in Language. The MIT Press, Cambridge, Mass.
Burt, M. K., Dulay, H. C., and Hernandez, C. H. 1975. Bilingual Syntax Measure. Harcourt Brace Jovanovich, New York.
Carrow, M. A. 1957. Linguistic functioning of bilingual and monolingual children. J. Speech Hear. Disord. 22:371–380.
Chomsky, N. 1965. Aspects of the Theory of Syntax. The MIT Press, Cambridge, Mass.
Clark, H. H., and Haviland, S. E. 1977. Comprehension and the given-new contract. In: R. O. Freedle (ed.), Discourse Production and Comprehension, pp. 1–40. Ablex Publishing, Norwood, N.J.
Cohen, A. D. 1975. The sociolinguistic assessment of speaking skills in a bilingual education program. In: L. Palmer and B. Spolsky (eds.), Papers on Language Testing, 1967–1974. Ch. 18, pp. 173–186. TESOL, Georgetown University, Washington, D.C.
Dailey, J. T. 1968. Language Facility Test. The Allington Corporation, Alexandria, Va.
Dore, J. 1973. The development of speech acts. Unpublished doctoral dissertation, City University of New York, New York.
Dore, J. 1974. A pragmatic description of early language development. J. Psycholinguist. Res. 3:343–350.
Gallagher, T. M. 1977. Revision behaviors in the speech of normal children developing language. J. Speech Hear. Res. 20:303–317.
Garvey, C. 1975. Requests and responses in children's speech. J. Child Lang. 2:41–60.
Grice, H. P. 1967. Logic and conversation. Unpublished manuscript, University of California at Berkeley, Berkeley.
Grice, H. P. 1975. Logic and conversation. In: P. Cole and J. L. Morgan (eds.), Syntax and Semantics, pp. 41–58. Vol. 3. Academic Press, New York.
Gruber, J. 1973. Correlations between the syntactic construction of the child and adult. In: C. Ferguson and D. Slobin (eds.), Studies in Child Language Development, pp. 440–445. Holt, Rinehart & Winston, New York.
Halliday, M. A. K. 1975. Learning How to Mean. Edward Arnold, London.
Halliday, M. A. K., McIntosh, A., and Strevens, P. 1964. The Linguistic Sciences and Language Teaching. Longmans, London.
Herbert, C. H. 1974. Basic Inventory of Natural Language. Checkpoint Systems. San Bernardino, Calif.
Holzman, M. S. 1971. Ellipsis in discourse: Implications for linguistic analysis by computer, the child's acquisition of language, and semantic theory. Lang. Speech. 14:86–98.
Hymes, D. 1967. Problems of bilingualism. In: J. McNamara (ed.), J. Soc. Iss. 23:8–28.
Ingram, D. 1971. Transitivity in child language. Language 47:888–910.
Kachru, B. B. 1978. Toward structuring code-mixing: An Indian perspective. In: B. B. Kachru and S. N. Sridhar (eds.), Aspects of Sociolinguistics in South Asia. pp. 27–46. (Special issue of Int. J. Sociol. Lang. 16.) Mouton, The Hague.
Lakoff, R. 1973. Questionable answers and answerable questions. In: B. B. Kachru, R. B. Lees, Y. Malkiel, and S. Saporta (eds.), Papers in Linguistics in

Honor of Henry and Renée Kahane. University of Illinois Press, Champaign-Urbana, Ill.

Lambert, W. E., and Macnamara, J. 1969. Some cognitive consequences of following a first-grade curriculum in a second language. J. Educ. Psychol. 60:86–96.

Lambert, W. E., and Tucker, G. R. 1972. Bilingual Education of Children: The St. Lambert Experiment. Newbury House, Rowley, Mass.

Morgan, J. L. 1977. Linguistics: The relation of pragmatics to semantics and syntax. Ann. Rev. Anthropol. 6:57–67.

Morris, C. 1938. Foundations of the theories of science. Int. Encyclopedia Unified Sci. 1:77–138.

Mycue, E. I. 1968. Testing in Spanish and the subsequent measurement of English fluency. Unpublished master's thesis, Texas Women's University, Denton. (ERIC Document Reproduction Service No. ED 026 192).

Nelson, K. 1973. Structure and strategy in learning to talk. Monog. Soc. Res. Child Dev. 38. (Serial No. 149).

Osgood, C. E. 1971. Where do sentences come from? In: D. A. Steinberg and L. A. Jakobovits (eds.), Semantics: An Interdisciplinary Reader in Philosophy, Linguistics, and Psychology. Cambridge University Press, Cambridge.

Ott, E. H. 1967. A study of levels of fluency and proficiency in oral English of Spanish-speaking school beginners. Unpublished doctoral dissertation, The University of Texas at Austin, Austin.

Palmer, F. R. (ed.). 1968. Selected Papers of J. R. Firth, 1952–1959. Indiana University Press, Bloomington.

Palmer, L., and Spolsky, B. (eds.). 1975. Papers on Language Testing. TESOL, Washington, D.C.

Peters, A. M. 1977. Language learning strategies: Does the whole equal the sum of all parts. Language 53:560–573.

Schmerling, S. F. 1975. Asymmetric conjunction and rules of conversation. In: P. Cole and J. L. Morgan (eds.), Syntax and Semantics, Vol. 3: Speech Acts. Academic Press, New York.

Searle, J. R. 1969. Speech Acts: An Essay in the Philosophy of Language. Cambridge University Press, London.

Shatz, M. 1974. The comprehension of indirect directives: Can 2 year olds shut the door? Paper presented to the Linguistic Society of America. (December). New York.

Silvaroli, N. J., Skinner, J. T., and Maynes, J. O. 1977. Oral Language Evaluation. EMC Corporation, St. Paul, Minn.

Smith, N. V., and Wilson, D. 1979. Modern Linguistics: The Results of Chomsky's Revolution. Penguin, Harmondsworth, U. K.

Sridhar, S. N. 1978. On the functions of code-mixing in Kannada. In: B. B. Kachru and S. N. Sridhar (eds.), Aspects of Sociolinguistics in South Asia. pp. 109–117. (Special issue of Int. J. Sociol. Lang. 16.) Mouton, The Hague.

Stemmler, A. O. 1967. The LCT, Language Cognition Test. *TESOL Q.* 1:35–43.

Stemmler, A. O. 1975. The LCT, Language Cognition Test (Research edition) A test for educationally disadvantaged school beginners. In: L. Palmer and B. Spolsky (eds.), Papers on Language Testing. Ch. 10, pp. 102–111. TESOL, Washington, D.C.

Taylor, T. H. 1969. A comparative study of the effects of oral-aural language training on gains in English language for fourth and fifth grade disadvantaged

Mexican-American children. Unpublished doctoral dissertation, The University of Texas at Austin, Austin.

Trueba, H. T., and Sridhar, K. K. 1978. Language assessment and evaluation. In: L. A. Valverde (ed.), Bilingual Education for Latinos. Ch. 3, pp. 35–50. Association for Supervision and Curriculum Development, Washington, D.C.

Walberg, H. J., Valdes, M. E., and Rasher, S. P. 1978. Report on bilingual test research. (Mimeo.) Bilingual/Bicultural Program, University of Illinois at Chicago Circle, Chicago.

chapter eleven

The Role of Contextual Factors in Language Use and Language Assessment
Joel Walters

The role of context in language use is an area of investigation marked more by variability than by agreement. Among the linguists, sociologists, sociolinguists, and psycholinguists who have studied the context of a conversation, very few have even referred to the definitions of others, let alone concurred with them. In fact, less than a handful of researchers in these fields have systematically treated the concept labeled "context." This review, which attempts to provide a framework for this topic, is one necessarily based on implications and inferences rather than explicit notions.

The focus of this chapter is a review of the literature that defines and discusses the relevance of context in linguistics and language acquisition. This knowledge is applied to the definitions of context and the ways in which it has been measured. Some generally representative works of philosophers and linguists, sociologists, sociolinguists, and cognitive and experimental psychologists are examined first. Then, a review of the contextual factors of greatest relevance to the field of assessment and the experimental work investigating these factors is presented. The contextual factors examined in this section include the language background, age, sex, and ethnic identity of the conversational participants as well as the kinship and familiarity among them and the setting and topic of the conversation. The treatment of context in bilingual research, a much more limited body of knowledge, is examined separately but within the same framework.

DEFINITIONS AND RELEVANCY OF CONTEXT IN THE STUDY OF LANGUAGE

Generative linguists and philosophers of language have restricted the domain of their investigations to the level of the sentence. It has been only recently that the more unorthodox researchers in these fields have ventured beyond this restriction to consider utterances as a unit of analysis. Moreover, even those who have permitted contextual elements in linguistic and logical descriptions have failed to incorporate a formal notion of context into their theories.

Working from a philosophical perspective, Grice (1967) necessitates a notion of context to develop his scheme of conversational implicature.[1] In Grice's scheme, contextual factors are important in deriving the implied meaning from the conventional one. His notion of context includes knowledge of the identity of the topic of conversation, the time of the utterance, and "other items of background knowledge" (p. 50). In other words, in order to understand the implied meaning in the following example, topic and background knowledge must be incorporated into the picture. Without a context, the sentence *It's cold in here* serves only as a comment on the weather. Relevant background information is that a woman says this to her husband, a window is open where the conversation takes place, and the sentence has been used before to request that the window be closed. Thus, the context helps to carry the implied meaning of the sentence. Searle (1975) adopts a similar notion for the purpose of deriving primary illocutions from literal ones. For Searle, the primary illocution is the intended meaning. It corresponds to Grice's implied meaning and is the meaning in the example above that intends that the listener close the window. According to Searle, information outside of the linguistic description is necessary to explain how a speaker communicates more than what is actually said. Gordon and Lakoff (1971) indicate basically the same role for context—as a determinant of "conveyed meaning" (p. 101). Deciding when the speaker is misleading, when to be taken seriously, what the attitude is toward a third party, and what the hearer's response is to the speaker's request are all examples Gordon and Lakoff use to provide a description of the setting and participants.

Contextual information is used by Green (1975) to distinguish among a range of what she calls "impositives" (more recently labeled *directives*) which are speech acts such as orders, demands, requests, pleas, suggestions, hints, and warnings. For Green it is the context of the utterance as well as the grammar that determine for the hearer which speech act is being performed.

Fraser (1975) offers an explanation of the distinction between two

---

[1] Conversational implicature is, in essence, the implications that are made when, where, and how a conversation is occurring that could not be derived from the actual words spoken.

types of performatives and also suggests a taxonomy for illocutionary acts. Following Searle (1969), Fraser sees the intent of the speaker as the "primary factor in differentiating illocutionary acts" (p. 189). Although Fraser, like Green, does not define context explicitly, their work with directives allows one to extrapolate the factors that they consider relevant to the role of context. For both, the power/authority relationship between the speaker and hearer seems to be central to their analyses. While Green uses this construct somewhat unsystematically to describe differences among impositives, Fraser develops his taxonomy of directives on the basis of distinctions in speaker/hearer relationships. In Fraser's classification scheme, the speaker holds three potential positions of power with respect to the hearer. If the speaker is powerless in that relationship, speech acts such as appealing, begging, pleading, and soliciting are performed. Asking, inquiring, requesting, and calling on are acts appropriate to a neutral speaker/hearer relationship. Finally, a speaker who is more powerful than the hearer may successfully command, enjoy, instruct, order, and require. This approach does not account for the factors that may be involved in establishing this relationship.

Grice (1967) and Searle (1975) imply that context can be limited to both the linguistic context of the utterances and "mutually shared factual background information of the speaker and hearer" (Searle, 1975). One can infer from Searle's example (*Can you pass the salt?*), that background information involves the conversational setting and knowledge of the speaker about the hearer. It seems to suffice for Grice and Searle to say that background knowledge plays a role and to indicate the place this knowledge would be used in several examples without specifying the nature of that role.

Rich examples of what context includes are provided by Gordon and Lakoff (1971). At times it is the hearer's knowledge about the speaker, at times the effect of the setting, at times familiarity of the speaker with the hearer, and at times their status relationship. They claim that context can be "characterized by a finite, consistent set of logical structures."

The list of contextual factors proposed by philosophers and linguists is still incomplete. What is more disappointing, however, is that beyond mentioning the existence of contextual factors, no writers in this area have confronted the difficult problem of describing and explaining the relationship of language use to social context.

Sociological Approaches

Descriptive sociology has accomplished a great deal toward the limited goal of formulating the parameters of the social situation in conversation. Erving Goffman's (1967) interest in diverse forms of interactional behavior makes him perhaps the dean of this field. In an early programmatic article, Goffman (1964) sets forth the parameters of context and communication that interact in social situations of varying types. Among the contextual factors he names age, sex, caste, class, country of origin, generation, religion, schooling, bilingualism, and cultural cognitive assumptions. He believes these have a systematic influence on the phonetic, phonemic, syntactic, morphemic, semantic, expressive, paralinguistic, and kinesic elements of speech behavior. These variables operate in what Goffman calls *encounters*, which have rules for initiation, termination, and the entrance of new participants, How these *rules* interact with contextual factors or even what the rules would look like are unanswered questions. Nevertheless, the bias that speech behavior cannot be studied without a consideration of the social situation represents a position that would clearly complement the work of the linguists and philosophers described above.

In a discussion of context similar to Goffman's, Fishman (1972) mentions participants, relationships, roles, topics, locale, and time as factors important in "situational shifting." "A situation is defined by the co-occurrence of two (or more) interlocutors related to each other in a particular way, communicating about a particular topic, in a particular setting" (Fishman, 1972, p. 48). He cites an example of the same group of people in a beer hall and in a university lecture as situationally different because the setting, topic, and time are distinct.

The relevance of context for Fishman goes well beyond its importance for the philosopher and linguist. Factors such as those indicated above are determinants of what he calls *language variety use*. Within this notion of variation, he includes social, occupational, and regional dialects as well as choice and shift between two different languages. Fishman defines the task of descriptive sociology of languages as the determination of domains and domain-appropriate usage. He would define a domain as a class of situations differentiated from another class by a particular language variety.

Berstein, like Fishman, is influential in studying the relationship between language use and social structure. Their view occupies a position at a much broader (societal) level than that described in the experimental work reviewed later in this paper. Nevertheless, empirical evidence offered in support of the systematic interaction of language and social organization is important to present here. Bernstein (1972) cites a British study conducted by Geoffrey Turner in which 5-year-old working class children used "fewer linguistic expressions of uncertainty" in response to picture stimuli than did middle class children. He attributes this evidence to the influence of the experimental context, claiming that *formally framed contexts* restrict the use of alternatives or varieties of meaning. Those restrictive contexts involved telling a story from picture stimuli and describing what is happening in a series of cards. One wonders whether it is the artificially framed nature of the task or the two dimensionality of the stimuli that restricts language use. Certainly the interesting findings of this work lie in the task parameters, if not in the differences between working class and middle class children.

In addition to Bernstein's effective interpretation of experimental evidence, he demonstrates an emphasis that seems to differ from Fishman and Goffman. He sees the kind of research he does as a "study of rules, formal and informal, which regulate the options we take up in various contexts in which we find ourselves" (1972, p. 161).

Representative Work in Sociolinguistics

The work of at least two sociolinguists leads us in the same direction as that developed above. Hymes (1967), in addition to an elaborate taxonomy for investigating language and social settings, speculates about the interaction of sociolinguistic rules with the components of speech and context. In his model of social settings, he lists the speech community, speech situation (e.g., a party), a speech event (e.g., a conversation), and speech act (e.g., joke, request, apology) as the social units of analysis. The speech components Hymes identifies are: setting, including time and place; participants; intentions; art characteristics, or the rules relating a form to a topic; the tone or manner in which the speech act is made (e.g., mocking); the code itself and the channel in which it is transmitted; norms of interaction and interpretation, including loudness, when to interrupt, etc.; and types of speech acts and events (e.g., conversations, curses, and prayers).

The sociolinguistic rules specify a relation among the various components of his taxonomy, usually referring to no more than two or three of the aforementioned components. Hymes lists examples such as relations between code and participants, between code and topic, and among code, participants, and setting. Finally, he discusses hierarchies of importance among the various components, the specification of which he defers until a time when more data have been collected and analyzed. The definition of context here is long and rigorous in comparison with other works reviewed thus far. The importance of context is clear, since without it there would be no beginning and certainly no rules.

Labov's work in sociolinguistics exhibits perhaps the greatest degree of formalism of any in that field. In a characterization of *ing* as a stable sociolinguistic variable (i.e., /ɪŋ/ versus /ɪn/), Labov (1971) claims that socioeconomic class and contextual style are the major determinants of use while age, sex, and ethnicity contribute only secondarily. On the other hand, in discussing mitigation of requests he cites age, socioeconomic class, and the relative status of the speaker and hearer as critical to the degree of mitigation. Labov (1971) indicates that these factors will eventually be written into what he has labeled *variable rules*. Those rules would apply according to probabilities defined by contextual factors. Based on these probabilities a particular form (e.g., *ing*, *be*, nominalization, mitigation of requests) would be chosen for use. Rules of this type would represent an attempt to quantify the role of context.

Although space does not permit a review of the empirical work in sociolinguistic variation, an outline of the major variables investigated can be presented. The great majority of these studies examined the contextual variation within the phonological system of a language. Generally, the contextual categories were grossly defined. Fischer's (1958) study of the alternation of *ing* and *in* categorized context as formal or informal. Ma and Herasimchuk (1968) used the same dichotomy in their investigation of a variety of phonological alterations in Puerto Rican Spanish and English in Jersey City, New Jersey. These particular researchers refined the informal classification into casual speech, careful speech, and list recitation. The formal contexts, limited to reading as opposed to speaking, were divided into list reading and text reading. These contexts were defined by the task parameters and judgments made by the experimenters and were not derived empirically by the results of the research. Other investigations similar to the above approach were Labov, Cohen, and Robin's (1968) and Wolfram's (1969) work in black English speech variation. Some of the work in code-switching follows a sociolinguistic framework, and it will be reviewed below with other bilingual investigations. For the most part, however, sociolinguistic research has focused only on phonological variation.

Earlier Psycholinguistic Investigations

Ervin-Tripp (1968) and Cazden (1970) independently review a range of experimental work that investigates the role of participants, speech act function, topic, setting, and task on the linguistic form produced. After introducing her paper by defining the parameters of setting, participants, topic, function, and form, Ervin-Tripp restricts the review mainly to a report of findings. In the category of participants, she reports on Bernstein's (1962) results of differences between middle-class and working class adolescents in both functional and formal uses of language. Working class adolescents tend to offer information more, use more requests for social responses, and use more personal pronouns than do middle-class boys and girls. She also lists the changes Ferguson (1964) noted in speech to infants. They include lexical changes, grammatical simplification, reduplication, reduced consonant clusters, and labialization.

Focusing on child language studies only, Cazden (1970) lists several pieces of research in which the age of the listener in a conversation correlates with the length of a child's utterances. Smith (1935) found that children ages 18 to 70 months produced longer utterances when talking to adults than they did to peers. Cazden (1967) and her students Yurchak and Bernat found substantially the same phenomenon with speakers ages 3, 6, 9, 11, and 13. There is a lack of agreement in these studies about whether a child's peers or those younger are the recipients of the child's shortest utterances. In addition, both the Yurchak and Bernat studies had uncontrolled, confounding variables. In the former, the participants in the conversations were related to each other; in the latter, the speakers were all male and the addressees female.

Modification in linguistic form as a result of the topic of conversation is referred to only briefly by Ervin-Tripp (1968). In this vein she mentions Fischer's (1958) study of the distribution of /ɪŋ/ and /ɪn/. That work demonstrated that pronunciation of *visiting*, *correcting*, and *reading* are school oriented while *chewin*, *swimmin*, and *hittin* are play oriented. It is difficult to imagine how the element of style (formal versus informal) and the role of participants (adults versus peers) can possibly be separated out of these data.

Cazden (1970) indicates several studies that she claims produce variation as a result of topic and task. From studies by Cowan, Weber, Hoddinott, and Klein (1967), Berlyne and Frommer (1966), and Williams and Naremore (1969), she concludes that a range of language differences results from the variation in pictures or toys shown to the children or the subjects of the conversation in which the experimenter engaged the child.

Recent Psycholinguistic Research

The 1970s brought with them an economic depression and a flurry of activity in the pragmatics of child language acquisition. As is evident from a review of a representative sample of that work, these psycholinguistic researchers have not gone far beyond the previous work cited in terms of defining the parameters and relevance of contextual factors. The strength of their work lies, rather, in the experimental techniques they have employed.

Of all the psycholinguists, Dore (1977) and Garvey (1975) define context very much like Searle (1975), restricting the notion to knowledge shared by the speaker and listener. Garvey's interest in context lies in its relation to sequencing in conversation. That interest means that the level of analysis will be discourse (i.e., the relationship between two or more utterances). Dore's main focus, however, is the communicative intent of a child's speech act. He concludes that "the speaker's utterances that are contingently related to the target utterance being coded" are the most important determinants of intention. By contingently related utterances, Dore means those that precede or follow the speech act. In this approach, which Garvey shares, he adheres to the linguists' and philosophers' restrictive view of context. In so doing, he relegates social context to the status of an indicator that is "often crucial" in determining intent, a conclusion that is contradicted by some of the evidence (see next section).

In analysis of her students' observational, tape-recorded, and experimental data on directives, Ervin-Tripp (1976) reports on the use of certain requesting strategies in specific social contexts. She indicates that a need statement (*I* need *X*) requires the speaker to hold rank over the addressee. She claims that addressees of higher rank and age than the speaker elicit a greater use of *please*. In addition, female speakers exhibited the greatest variation in the use of *please* as a function of addressee. Other contextual factors mentioned by Ervin-Tripp include familiarity, role, physical distance, and territoriality.

Bates' (1976) longitudinal and experimental research with Italian children and Shatz's (1977) investigation of one particular aspect of context are unique from theoretical as well as experimental perspectives. Bates sees the study of pragmatic[2] development as extremely significant because of its position at the juncture of linguistic, cognitive, and social development. The particular aspect of pragmatic competence that Bates investigates is the child's development of politeness. She conceptualizes this function in terms of Piaget's notions of reversibility, indicating that competence in this pragmatic function entails an ability for children to consider simultaneously their own and the listener's perspective. One can infer from her Piagetian perspective and experimental procedures that she limits the notion of context to the speaker/listener relationship, excluding setting and topic from the domain.

Her experimental procedures to study the acquisition of politeness involve the child as a conversational participant with an elderly female puppet by the name of Signora Rossi. Thus the parameters of context included the adult-child and puppet-child relationships as well as descriptions of child and adult activities. She suggests that the longitudinal data

---

[2] For a full explanation of this term and its history, see Sridhar, Chapter 10, this volume.

only allowed uncertain inferences about the child's intention and, hence, no attempt was made in the experimental work to control for other aspects of context such as setting or topic, as well as age, sex, class, or role of participants. Nevertheless, the data do provide evidence about the developmental milestones for the acquisition of polite forms in Italian preschoolers.

In contrast, Shatz (1977) sets forth four categories of contextual factors that come the closest to encompassing critical aspects of the assessment context. She includes: 1) a physical dimension (i.e., time, place, presence of other people, activities); 2) the interpersonal relationship between the speaker and hearer (namely, the history of the participants' interaction and previous utterances in the conversation); 3) cultural rules to account for interaction among unacquainted participants; and 4) prescribed status relationships. The influence of previous utterances in a conversation of children's (age 19–34 months) comprehension of directives produced by adults are then investigated experimentally. Her claim, which finds support in the data, is that context produces an expectancy that limits the interpretation of otherwise ambiguous utterances.

Experiments were used by Shatz to look at the responses (nonverbal or verbal) children made to eight types of directives. The children's responses were mainly of the action type, indicating they had interpreted imperatives and other less explicit types as directives. In a succeeding experiment, two conditions were used to test the influence of context. In one, the experimenter emitted three to four imperatives before the test sentence, which was ambiguous as to interpretation. In the other condition, the experimenter spoke three to four interrogative requests before the same test sentence. The *imperative* context produced more action responses while the *interrogative* context produced more informational responses from the children. Thus *context*, defined as history of the conversation, appears to play a significant role in the understanding 2-year-olds have of directives.

INVESTIGATIONS OF CONTEXTUAL FACTORS

The review here centers on the specific characteristics of context with the greatest relevance to assessment procedures. In so doing, this portion of the review is limited to experimental studies of children's alteration of language as a function of the following contextual factors: 1) age of addressee, 2) sex of speaker and addressee, and 3) setting/topic. The setting and topic of conversation are considered in an undifferentiated way—first, because the two are rarely treated separately in any of the experimental literature, and second, because of the difficulty in experimentally manipulating one without the other.

By limiting this section of the review to children's speech, a large body of literature interested in the "input" language of caregivers is not treated at all. In addition, studies that have produced speech alteration as a result of varying degrees of familiarity (Garvey and Hogan, 1973) and status (Brown and Gilman, 1960; Williams and Naremore, 1969) in the conversational context will not be considered. The focus here is not on the match between adult and child structures in spontaneous interaction but on the range of the child's linguistic variation as a function of social context. Tables 1 and 2 summarize the contextual parameters and language measures used to determine the extent of variation.

Language Variation as a Function of Age of Addressee

A relatively great amount of research has investigated the variation in children's language as a function of the age of the addressee (see Table 1). The familiarity or intimacy between subject and addressee stands out as a confounding variable in much of this work. Only Shatz and Gelman's (1973) study examines an age of listener factor in conversations among unfamiliar children, and in all of the other studies reviewed, this confounding variable might lead one to question the interpretation of the results. Nevertheless, because of the diversity in methodologies, the range of subject's ages (2 to 8 years), the wide range of listeners, settings, topics, and the multiplicity of linguistic measurements taken, certain results ring very clearly. First, and most basically, children as young as 2 years old have the capability of producing a great deal of linguistic variation. Second, that variation seems to be a very systematic one.

Positive results indicating that children vary language as a function of the age of the addressee show a tremendous amount of consistency. These results derive from dependent measures that fall into three groups: utterance length, structural complexity, and miscellaneous (including attentionals, repetitions, and disfluencies). The number of utterances a child produces in a conversation is related positively to the number of utterances his or her partner produces (Garvey and Ben Dabba, 1972). In the same study the researchers found no correlation, however, between the length of children's utterances and those of their age-peer conversational partners. Length as measured by mean length of utterance, mean preverbal length (the number of words preceding the verb), and average length of the longest utterance (from those greater than four words) did show significant differences as a function of listener's age in Cazden (1967), Shatz and Gelman (1973), Anderson and Johnson (1974), and Sachs and Devin (1975). In general, children's utterances were longer to adult addressees than to peers and younger listeners. In fact, Shatz and Gelman (1973) even found significant differences in length in children's speech to older 2-year-olds (more than 28 months) as compared with younger 2s (less than 28 months).

In terms of complexity, more complex structures (e.g., more tenses, subordinates, relatives, and complements) were directed at adult addressees than at peer and younger listeners (Shatz and Gelman, 1973; Sachs and Devin, 1975). Finally, in the miscellaneous category more vocatives (e.g., *Johnny*, *Miss*) and attentional words (e.g., *hey, excuse me*), more repetitions, and more comparatives are used in talking to younger children than to adults, while disfluencies, including hesitations and false starts, occurred more in speech to adults.

Language variation as a function of the age of the listener seems to have at least one constraint. Rather than treating all addressees differently (i.e., with varying utterance lengths and complexities), peers and adults are addressed in much the same manner by children. Younger addressees do elicit shorter and less complex utterances from children. It is noteworthy that children of varying ages and sexes interacting in a variety of settings produced these trends.

Language Variation as a Function of Sex of Speaker and Addressee

The results of studies investigating speaker sex differences in children do not demonstrate the same consistency as those cited above. Table 2 summarizes two studies of most direct relevance to this issue. Other relevant studies are listed in Table 1. Fischer (1958) reports significant differences between male and female children on a linguistic measure (alternate using of /ɪŋ/ and /ɪn/ for the progressive morpheme). Shatz and Gelman (1973) report no significant effects due either to the sex of the speaker or the sex of the listener in their study. Garvey and Ben Debba (1972) in a study of the natural statements of preschool dyads indicate that the sex of their dyads did not account significantly for the variance. Weintraub (1974) found boys and girls made equal numbers of requests and demonstrated no differences in type of requests made in experimental conversations with children their own age.

More complete reviews of the acoustic differences in boys' and girls' speech and the variation of input language to male and female children can be found in Sachs (1975) and Cherry (1975). Although strong evidence favors the ability of adults to perceive sex differences in male and

Table 1. Studies focusing on linguistic variation as a function of age of addressee

	Speaker		Listeners				
N	Age	Sex	Age	Sex	Setting/Topic	Linguistic variation	Researcher
15	3 4–5 6–8	m, f	Babies Younger Peers Peers Parents	m, f	Subject's homes Outdoor Nursery Experimenter's home	Talk/silence Whining Baby talk Peer talk Formal talk	(Gleason, 1973)
3	1;9 3;4 5;2	f m m	Pets Peers Family members Experimenter			Whisper Softness Loudness Clarification Fuzzy speech High pitch Grammatical modification Phonetic modification Exaggerated intonation Mimicry	(Weeks, 1971)
36	3;6–5;7	m, f	Peers	m, f	Laboratory	Number of utterances Words per utterance	(Garvey and Ben Debba, 1972)
4	3;9 3;11 4;0 5;5	f f m f	Baby doll Baby Peer Mother		Role-playing as a baby	Mean length of utterance Mean preverbal length Proportion not present tense Proportion not subordinates Proportion not relatives Proportion not names Proportion not repetitions Proportion not questions Proportion not imperatives	(Sachs and Devin 1975)

16	$\overline{X}$ = 4;4	m, f	Younger $\overline{X}$ = 2;2 Peers Parents Experimenters	m, f	Describe a toy 1) ark 2) dumping station Spontaneous speech	Number of utterances Mean length of utterance Distribution of utterance length Average longest utterance Coordinate conjunctions Subordinate conjunctions "That" complements Attentional words	(Shatz and Gelman, 1973)
2	6	m, f	Peers Experimenter— Male	m, f	Retell a story Free conversation about home Telephone interview Describe hidden candlestick School TAT Arithmetic game	Length of sentence	(Cazden, 1967)
1	8	f	1;6 5 Peer Adult	m m f f	Storytelling Explain block-stringing Free play	Mean length of utterance Hesitations False start Type/token ratio Repetitions 1) partial 2) complete 3) paraphrase Fundamental frequency	(Anderson and Johnson, 1974)

Table 2. Studies focusing on linguistic variation as a function of sex of addressee

	Speaker		Listeners				
N	Age	Sex	Age	Sex	Setting/Topic	Linguistic variation	Researcher
6	3;6	m	Experimenter		Sentence completion	/ɪŋ/ versus /ɪn/	(Fischer, 1958)
6	3;6	f			Formal questionnaire		
6	7;10	m			Informal interview		
6	7;10	f					
1	3;6	m	Peer		Free play	Percentage of requests	(Weintraub, 1974)
2	3;6	f				Percentage of request type	
3	5;0–5;7	m				1) imperative	
4	5;0–5;7	f				2) imbedded imper.	
						3) need statement	
						4) request for info.	
						5) indirect	

female speech (acoustic differences), very little data support any systematic variation in the speech of children as a function of the sex of a conversational addressee (language use).

Variation as a Function of Setting and Topic

Three studies exhibited significant differences as a function of different settings and topics, although the limited sample in each case makes generalization difficult. One of his 10-year-old male subjects, which Fischer (1958) claims to be exemplary, is reported to show a greater use of /ɪŋ/ in the story completion task, /ɪn/ in the formal interview, and no difference in the linguistic forms for the formal questionnaire. Cazden (1967) reports an interaction between sex of speaker and type of task. The male 6-year-old in her study produced his longest utterances in structured tasks (e.g., retelling a story, description of a hidden candlestick, and an arithmetic game). The female 6-year-old exhibited her longest utterances in interviews and spontaneous conversations. Finally, the significant variation as a function of age of addressee in the Anderson and Johnson (1974) study was obtained only in the free play condition (see Table 1).

The above studies suggest that the phenomenon relating contextual factors to linguistic alterations is a real one. In nine investigations, more than 100 children ranging in age from 2 years, 2 months through 10 years were studied. The age of listeners spanned the full spectrum from early childhood through adulthood. Speakers and listeners of both sexes were examined. The settings included children's homes, experimental laboratories, nursery schools, and outdoor play areas. Topics of conversation involved spontaneous speech, directed interaction about the child and his or her home, and specific tasks to describe a toy, explain a game, and complete sentences. This range of contextual factors, coupled with the wide variation in linguistic forms studied (cf. Table 1), make the results described fairly reliable.

CONTEXTUAL VARIATION AMONG BILINGUALS

Since the work in this area is even more meager than in the former sections, the review is rather brief. It is divided into three sections. The first looks at three studies of societal bilingualism. The next section examines two representative studies of code-switching. The final section reviews one study that treats contextual parameters of greatest relevance to the field of language assessment.

Bilingual Usage in Society

Those studies that examine bilingual usage from a societal perspective do so for various reasons. Ferguson (1959) wishes to characterize the features of diglossia. He distinguishes diglossia, or two varieties of the same language in a speech community, from geographically based dialect distinctions and from bilingualism. Thus, he lists a wide range of other contextual factors to support his notion of diglossia. Fishman (1965) views context as a source of explanation for language maintenance and language shift in a society. Rubin (1968), in her research on bilingualism in Paraguay, uses context as a measure of which language is being used more in a society.

Twelve speech functions are listed by Ferguson (1959), which all fit roughly into the categories that have been previously discussed: setting, topic, and participants. Among those functions related to setting are the sermon, the political speech, and the university lecture. Topically relevant functions include newspapers, personal letters, poetry, and news broadcasts. Finally, he lists speech variation to servants, waiters, workers, clerks, family, friends, and colleagues. These can be categorized as part of the participant function for which dialects are differentiated.

Fishman (1965) sets forth three chief subdivisions by which the domains of language use can be studied. Among his participant factors he includes age, sex, race, religion, and subjective identity. In the situational variables subdivision he lists: participants, physical setting, topics, functions, and style. He further elaborates on the stylistic factor by considering dichotomies such as intimate–distant, formal–informal, solidarity–nonsolidarity, and status equality–inequality. His third main subdivision, which he labels *topic*, allows for the notion of appropriateness of a particular language in speaking about a given topic. In an analysis of the maintenance and shift in the use of Yiddish and English in the United States, Fishman considers four sources of variance in language use: 1) media variance over the modalities reading, writing, and speaking; 2) role variance—usage differences for inner speech, production, and comprehension; 3) situational variance along a continuum from formal to informal to intimate; and 4) domain variance, which includes family, friends, acquaintances, mass media, and organizations.

After reviewing the work of Geertz, Hasselmo, and Stewart (see Rubin, 1968) on contextual factors relevant to bilingual usage, Rubin concludes that three factors are most relevant to Guaraní-Spanish usage in Paraguay. She lists speaker/hearer relations in terms of intimacy and status as one, speaker/hearer attributes in terms of class and origin as another, and setting as defined by Stewart (1962) on a formality dimension as the third. Through a questionnaire to 106 speakers in two Paraguayan towns she determines which language (Spanish or Guaraní) is spoken in which setting (rural or nonrural), in which speaker–hearer relationships (doctor–patient, teacher–student, authority–ruled, intimate–nonintimate) for which topics, and for what effect. The result is a hierarchy of the contexts in which each language is used; with Guaraní appearing more in rural settings, and in nonrural settings where the discourse is not serious or the subject of conversation is intimate; Spanish appears in formal, nonintimate, and/or serious situations.

Code-Switching as Variation in Language Use

Since the bulk of the relevant research deals with a phenomenon known variously as code-switching, diglossia, and language mixing, a brief clarification here seems in order. The claim implicit in the studies reviewed is that the alternate use of two (or more) languages/dialects varies systematically as a function of context. Gumperz (1967) states, "the same social pressures which would lead a monolingual to change from colloquial to formal or technical styles may lead a bilingual to shift from one language to another" (p. 48). This shifting can occur from conversation to conversation, from speaking turn to speaking turn, from utterance to utterance, and even within an utterance. It is plausible to assume that social pressures differ according to the domain of application. In fact, there are probably forces that are not even social operating on an individual to bring about code-switching. For example, many bilingual speakers report anecdotally that a principle of least effort is a determinant of code-switching that occurs within an utterance. The concern in this review is not with the linguistic properties of the phenomenon, but rather, the contextual basis for it.

These next two studies consider code-switching or alternate use of two languages at a more individual level of analysis than the previous ones. Blom and Gumperz's (1971) work on Ranamal and Bakamål, two variants of Swedish, examines contextual factors in natural conversation as a methodology for studying the interaction of language and society. They identify contextual factors that are highly consistent with those in this review. These factors include: 1) participants (i.e., speaker, addressee, and audience); 2) ecological surroundings (i.e., physical setting and social situation); and 3) topic(s). Blom and Gumperz take their participant–observer study into a wide range of settings and find the standard language (Bakamål) confined to church services, teachers' lessons, and radio reports. They noted the use of Ranamål in the home, workplace, public meeting hall, and when strangers join a conversation or when a teacher wishes to encourage a discussion. They propose that there are subconscious code-selection rules that "may be independent of overt intentions."

The relevance of code-switching for Gumperz and Hernandez-Chavez (1972) is much more applied than theoretical. Their review of the functions of code-switching within an utterance is directed toward assisting teachers in adapting to children's communicative styles. They bring evidence of code-switching as a function of the topic of conversation, age, and sex of the addressee, and means to express social/ethnic identification. They also mention confidentiality and solidarity as reasons for code-switching. These functions (except topic) represent a highly differentiated way of looking at speaker/hearer attributes and relations.

Code-switching as a Function of Setting and Addressee

The remaining studies exhibit more experimental approaches to the examination of contextual factors involved in language variation. In a brief report on the findings of a 2-year research project McClure and Wentz (1975) indicate all of the same contextual factors that other studies have identified with one relevant addition. That additional factor is the language background of the listener. These researchers noted that children younger than 5 took this factor into account in expressing themselves. If the child was monolingual in Spanish and the listener monolingual in English, the child remained silent or expressed him- or herself nonverbally after a very short period of exposure. This evidence has tremendous importance for bilingual education and assessment. If the child is monolingual in Spanish and thinks that the teacher or language tester is not familiar with his or her language, then the child may choose silence and/or nonverbal expression as the mode of communication. The language tester should be aware of these possible means of communication.

Other contextual factors studied by McClure and Wentz (1975) have included the age and child's relative familiarity with the addressee, setting, and topic of conversation. Older children spoke to preschoolers in Spanish more often than in English, while siblings tended to address each other in English more often than did two unrelated conversants. In terms of setting, Spanish was elicited more often in the home and English more often in monolingual classrooms. The effect of setting on the children's language use was relatively restricted, however. In fact, the effect of both setting and topic reflected what seemed to be impressionistic findings in comparison to the clear importance of age, language background, and familiarity between the speaker and hearer.

It is clear from other studies of code-switching (DiPietro, 1978; Lipski, 1978; Shaffer, 1978) that concern appears to be centered more on linguistic aspects of code-switching than on what code-switching can teach about the interaction of language and context. There are certainly other linguistic phenomena (such as those investigated by first language acquisition researchers) that can contribute to our knowledge of context in the acquisition of two languages. The final section of this chapter turns to these concerns.

CONTEXT AS RELATED TO LANGUAGE ASSESSMENT

Two very direct applications can be derived from the study of contextual factors in language use. Research in this area addresses the field of language assessment in general and the assessment of language ability of bilinguals in particular.

Most language assessment instruments used in bilingual programs can be categorized as measures of central tendency. They look at how a bilingual child measures up to a standard or norm. In terms of the levels of language assessed, these instruments require that the child produce a target sentence, word, or morpheme. Generally, the number of target items on which the child scores correctly is compared to the population norms. The population on which an instrument has been normed rarely conforms to the population being tested (Omark, in preparation). For example, Spanish-speaking children who take the Peabody Picture Vocabulary Test (Dunn, 1959) are compared with a population of white school children from Nashville, Tennessee. Often children are examined at only one linguistic level (e.g., morphological or lexical), and conclusions are drawn on this limited basis with respect to language dominance.

This approach, besides being one that assesses discrete points, obviously does not consider language context. The work of Walters (1978) demonstrates a possible assessment technique that might serve as one indicator of a child's communicative competence. In this study 32 Puerto Rican children ages 7;7 to 11;4 interacted with puppets manipulated by two experimenters. In a similar experiment, Walters (1979) involved 13- to 15-year-old Armenian children learning English as a second language and their monolingual American counterparts in conversations with puppets. The methodology for these studies is described in detail below in order to provide an example of how to assess a child's communicative ability. Protocols for eliciting requesting behaviors are given as a model for developing a repertoire of other speech acts in a controlled situation.

The setting for the experiments contained a table and chairs for the child and two testers (although in a language testing situation the protocol could be modified for use by a single tester). A tape recorder was placed inconspicuously on the table along with the protocols that detailed the scripts to be read by the tester. In order to reduce testing bias and variation in the protocols, copies of the scripts were accessible and the protocol was well practiced and memorized by the evaluators.

The eight puppets, which served as addressees to which the subject made requests, were hidden from the child's view until the time arose for them to participate in a conversation. In the experimental situation, one experimenter manipulated a single puppet matching the age and sex of the child. This puppet functioned as a "friend" of the child. The other experimenter manipulated the eight listener puppets. In a language testing situation it seems that the "friend" puppet might be expendable. A single tester, then, would need to function both as "friend" and as "listener." The tester could either take the role of "friend" or manipulate the "friend" puppet in one hand and the listener puppets in the other. With eight listener puppets a tester might find these acrobatics with puppets and protocols a difficult feat to accomplish. As seen below, however, the number of listeners does not contribute nearly as much to the variation in request types as do the setting and topic of conversation.

Puppets were selected so that their heads represented the most human-like forms available. Furthermore, in order to focus the child's attention on the interaction the experimenter always held the puppet in a direct line between the child's eyes and his or her own. This approach helped avoid the possibility that children were viewing the experimenters as listeners rather than the puppets.

The protocol itself contributed the most to the spontaneous aspects of the interaction. It involved a 2-minute spontaneous conversation with the puppets that revolved around the age, school, and interests of the subject. Following that conversation the "friend" puppet initiated one of the four situations described here in terms of their settings and topics:

1. Supermarket
    a. Requesting to be shown rice
    b. Requesting to get ahead in the checkout line
2. Lunch money
    a. Requesting lunch money in the cafeteria
    b. Requesting lunch money in the school office

3. Outside at play
   a. Requesting to play in the listener's yard
   b. Requesting a ball to play with
4. Outside selling cookies
   a. Requesting that the addressee buy some cookies
   b. Requesting that the addressee sign a form

Although setting and topic were not varied in a completely systematic way (e.g., lunch money is a single topic with two settings), a range of social domains was sampled. These included domains of everyday life most likely to produce language variation; namely, home, school, and the public sector.

In order to provide a complete picture of the nature of the situation, the protocols of all four domains are provided below:

SUPERMARKET/RICE

Friend: What are you gonna do on your vacation?
S(ubject):
Friend: My parents are gonna take us to New York. Do you wanna go?
S:
Friend: Hey, _____. I have to go to the supermarket. I have to buy milk and some rice for my mother. Will you come with me?
S:
Friend: Well, here we are. Hey, look. That _____ over there has some rice. Go ask _____ to show you where the rice is and I'll go get the milk. I'll meet you back here in a minute.
S: (TARGET REQUEST)
(Puppet 1): It's over there . . . on the top shelf.
Friend: Did you get it?
S:
Friend: Wow! The lines are really long. I've got to get home by three or my mother will kill me. Ask this _____ in front of us if we can go first.
S: (TARGET REQUEST)
(Puppet 2): Sure, you only have two items. Go ahead.

CAFETERIA/LUNCH MONEY

Friend: Boy, am I hungry! They have American chop suey for lunch today. Do you like it?
S:
Friend: I'm really starved but I forgot my lunch money. I bet I could borrow some from that _____. _____ is really nice about lending kids money. Only _____ yelled at me in class today. Hey, would you ask _____ if he(she) will lend you 35¢? _____ is not mad at you.
S:
Friend: Come on. Please ask _____ for me. I know _____ let you have it.
S: (TARGET REQUEST)

(Puppet 1):	I'm sorry, I can't give you any money. Go ask them for some money in the office.
Friend:	Come up to the office with me. They're tired of giving me lunch money because I always forget it. There's _____. Ask _____ for 35¢.
S:	(TARGET REQUEST)
(Puppet 2):	Do you promise to bring it back tomorrow?
S:	
(Puppet 2):	Okay, here it is.

STREET/PLAY

Friend:	Hi _____! Let's go outside and play, okay?
S:	
Friend:	What do you like to play outside?
S:	
Friend:	Let's play ball, okay?
S:	
Friend:	The Johnsons have a really big yard but if we play there we'll have to ask one of the Johnsons because it's their house. Let's go knock on the door and ask them if we can play there.
(Puppet 1):	Hello, I'm _____. Who's your friend?
Friend:	Go ahead, tell _____ who you are.
S:	
Friend:	Go ahead, ask _____ if we can play in the yard.
S:	(TARGET REQUEST)
(Puppet 1):	Okay.
Friend:	Oh good. Let's go. Wait. We forgot to borrow a ball. I'll go find some more kids. You ask _____ for a ball.
S:	(TARGET REQUEST)
(Puppet 2):	It's in the back yard.

NEIGHBORHOOD/SELLING COOKIES

Friend:	I'm selling cookies for my sister. If she sells the most then she wins a new 10-speed bicycle. Do you wanna sell some with me?
S:	
Friend:	Here, you take this paper and go to that house and ask if they wanna buy any. They cost 50¢ each, and if you sell any, then you can have a ride on my sister's new 10-speed bike. Go ahead. Knock on the door.
S:	(TARGET REQUEST)
(Puppet 1):	I don't know about this; I'll go check.
(Puppet 2):	We'll take two boxes. How much are they?
S:	
Friend:	Get _____ to write down _____ name and what kind of cookies _____ wants.
S:	(TARGET REQUEST)

There are both advantages and disadvantages to an experimental rather than a naturalistic approach to collecting speech act samples. This experimental technique offers obvious efficiency in terms of the time it takes to gather the relevant language samples and analyze them. It is felt, however, that these elicitation procedures do not allow for the spontaneity of children's requests that could be obtained by using techniques in naturalistic settings (e.g., the home or classroom). On the other hand, while observational procedures may suffice for an assessment of a speaker's ability to perform speech acts, they may be lacking when it comes to measuring sociolinguistic competence.

An observational assessment does capture the spontaneity of the speaker's production. In addition, it avoids the objection to the role-taking procedures that claim the speech act strategies elicited would not be the same as those produced in natural conversation. Observational procedures cannot, however, measure the range of request strategies a speaker may be capable of producing. They can only identify those strategies a speaker does produce. A more experimental technique can isolate both those he or she can use effectively and those he or she cannot use or chooses to avoid.[3]

By having the child produce (or comprehend) requests and other speech acts in a variety of contexts, a number of phenomena emerge. First, and most important, an instrument of the above type would provide a measure of semantic variation in a variety of communicative contexts. A by-product of this approach would be lexical and morphological data to compare with the child's variation ability. In addition, a well-designed social context could target vocabulary items and morphemes appropriate to an assessment of the child's ability in these areas. This more or less comprehensive assessment, if carried out in both of the child's languages, will provide a better measure of dominance than any of the instruments currently on the market. Moreover, by using each child as his or her own control, one will avoid comparing the child to spurious norms on standardized achievement and language devices on which he or she will invariably score lower than monolinguals.

The research reviewed in this chapter also clarifies the importance of the language assessment context. The notions of setting, topic, and participants in natural conversation all have counterparts in clinical and educational contexts. One must ask whether the assessment setting has been stigmatized by any previous association. Sometimes the school

---

[3] Advantages and disadvantages of this approach are elaborated in Walters (1978).

psychologists' office or a resource room will take on this character in a school. Even the principal's office may elicit less than naturalistic language data from the child. Ideally, language assessment should occur within the child's own classroom, assuming noise and other disruptive factors can be controlled. Unfortunately, the task of assessment can never shed completely its test-like quality. It can be minimized, however, by relating to the task as a game-like endeavor. The more game-like the task is and the more naturalistic the interaction is, the more accurate a measure of the child's language ability will be. Finally, the relationship between the child and the tester will clearly have a bearing on the results of the assessment. Among the most critical factors in the assessment of bilingual children are the familiarity between tester and child and the ethnic and linguistic origin of the tester. Since very little can be done to convert an anglophone tester into a latino, emphasis should probably be placed on building rapport between the child and the tester.

SUMMARY

This chapter has reviewed recent research in several disciplines that consider the role of contextual factors in language use. The contributions of linguists, sociologists of language, sociolinguists, and psycholinguists to the study of language in context is examined from a critical perspective. Finally, it is suggested that this body of literature can be applied to issues in language assessment of bilingual children.

REFERENCES

Anderson, E. S., and Johnson, C. E. 1974. Modifications in the speech of an eight-year-old as a reflection of age of listener. Stanford Occasional Papers in Linguistics. 3:149–160. University of California, Berkeley.

Bates, E. 1976. Language and Context. Academic Press, New York.

Berlyne, D. E., and Frommer, F. D. 1966. Some determinants of the incidence and content of children's questions. Child Dev.37:177–189.

Bernstein, B. 1962. Social class, linguistic codes and grammatical elements. Lang. Speech 5:221–240.

Bernstein, B. 1972. Social class, language and socialization. In: P. P. Giglioli (ed.), Language and Social Context. Penguin Books, Great Britain.

Blom, J. P., and Gumperz, J. J. 1971. Social meaning in linguistic structures: Code-switching in Norway. In: J. J. Gumperz and D. Hymes (eds.), Directions in Sociology. Holt, Rinehart, and Winston, New York.

Brown, R., and Gilman, A. 1960. The pronouns of power and solidarity. In: T. A. Sebeok (ed.), Style in Language. The MIT Press, Cambridge, Mass.

Cazden, C. 1967. On individual differences in language competence and performance. J. Spec. Educ. 1:135–150.

Cazden, C. B. 1970. The situation: A neglected source of social class differences in language use. J. Soc. Iss. 26:35–60.
Cherry, L. 1975. Teacher-child verbal interaction: An approach to the study of sex differences. In: B. Thorne and N. Henley (eds.), Language and Sex. Newbury House Publishers, Rowley, Mass.
Cowan, P. A., Weber, J., Hoddinott, B. A., and Klein, J. 1967. Mean length of spoken response as a function of stimulus, experimenter and subject. Child Dev. 38:199–203.
DiPietro, R. 1978. Code-switching as a verbal strategy among bilinguals. In: M. Paradis (ed.), Aspects of Bilingualism. Hornbeam Press, Columbia, S.C.
Dore, J. 1977. Children's illocutionary acts. In: R. O. Freedle (ed.), Discourse Production and Comprehension. Lawrence Erlbaum Associates, Hillsdale, N.J.
Dunn, L. M. 1959. The Peabody Picture Vocabulary Test. American Guidance Services, Circle Pines, Minn.
Ervin-Tripp, S. 1968. An analysis of the interaction of language, topic and listeners. In: J. A. Fishman (ed.), Readings in the Sociology of Language. Mouton Publishers, The Hague.
Ervin-Tripp, S. 1976. Is Sybil there? The structure of some American directives. Lang. Soc. 5:25–66.
Ferguson, C. 1959. Diglossia. Word 15:325–340.
Ferguson, C. 1964. Baby-talk in six languages. Am. Anthropol. 66:103–114.
Fischer, J. L. 1958. Social influences on the choice of linguistic variant. In: D. Hymes (ed.), Language in Culture and Society. Harper & Row, New York.
Fishman, J. A. 1965. Who speaks what language to whom and when? Linguistique 2:57–88.
Fishman, J. A. 1972. The sociology of language. In: P. P. Giglioli (ed.), Language and Social Context. Penguin Books, Great Britain.
Fraser, B. 1975. Hedged performatives. In: P. Cole and J. Morgan (ed.), Syntax and Semantics, Vol. III: Speech Acts. Academic Press, New York.
Garvey, C. 1975 The contingent query: A dependent act in conversation. Unpublished manuscript, Johns Hopkins University, Baltimore.
Garvey, C., and Ben Debba, M. 1972. Effects of age, sex and partners on children's dyadic speech. Unpublished manuscript, Johns Hopkins University, Baltimore.
Garvey, C., and Hogan, R. 1973. Social speech and social interaction: Egocentrism revisited. *Child Dev.* 44:562–568.
Gleason, J. B. 1973. Code-switching in children's language. In: T. E. Moore (ed.), Cognitive Development and the Acquisition of Language. Academic Press, New York.
Goffman, E. 1964. The neglected situation. Am. Anthropol. 66:133–136.
Goffman, E. 1967. Interaction Ritual. Doubleday & Co., Garden City, N.Y.
Gordon, D., and Lakoff, G. 1971. Conversational postulates. In: Papers from the Seventh Regional Meeting. Chicago Linguistic Society, Chicago.
Green, G. 1975. How to get people to do things. In: P. Cole and J. Morgan (eds.), Syntax and Semantics, Vol. III: Speech Acts. Academic Press, New York.
Grice, H. P. 1967. Logic and conversation. Unpublished manuscript, University of California, Berkeley.

Gumperz, J. 1967. On the linguistic markers of bilingual communication. J. Soc. Iss. 23:48–57.

Gumperz, J., and Hernandez-Chavez, E. 1972. Bilingualism, bidialectalism and classroom interaction. In: C. Cazden, D. Hymes, and V. John (eds.), The Functions of Language in the Classroom. Teachers College Press, New York.

Hymes, D. 1967. Models of interaction of language and social setting. J. Soc. Iss. 23:8–28.

Labov, W. 1971. The study of language in its social context. In: J. A. Fishman (ed.), Advances in the Sociology of Language. Mouton Publishers, The Hague.

Labov, W., Cohen, P., and Robins, C. 1968. A Study of the Non-standard English of Negro and Puerto Rican Speakers in New York City. Cooperative Research Project 3288. Office of Education, Washington, D.C.

Lipski, J. L. 1978. Code-switching and the problem of bilingual competence. In: M. Paradis (ed.), Aspects of Bilingualism. Hornbeam Press, Columbia, S.C.

Ma, R., and Herasimchuk, E. 1968. The linguistic dimensions of a bilingual neighborhood. In: J. A. Fishman, R. L. Cooper, and R. Ma (eds.), Bilingualism in the Barrio. Indiana University Press, Bloomington.

McClure, E., and Wentz, J. 1975. Functions of code-switching among Mexican-American children. In: Papers from the Eleventh Regional Meeting. Chicago Linguistic Society, Chicago.

Omark, D. R. 1981. Genetically inferior or just different: Conceptualizations of the bilingual child. In: D. R. Omark and J. G. Erickson (eds.), The Bilingual Exceptional Child. Charles C Thomas, Springfield, Ill.

Rubin, J. 1968. Bilingual usage in Paraguay. In: J. A. Fishman (ed.), Readings in the Sociology of Language. Mouton Publishers, The Hague.

Sachs, J. 1975. Cues to the identification of sex in children's speech. In: B. Thorne and N. Henley (eds.), Language and Sex. Newbury House Publishers, Rowley, Mass.

Sachs, J., and Devin, J. 1975. Young children's use of age-appropriate speech styles in social interaction and role-playing. J. Child Lang. 3:81–98.

Searle, J. 1969. Speech Acts: An Essay in the Philosophy of Language. Cambridge University Press, Cambridge, England.

Searle, J. 1975. Indirect speech acts. In: P. Cole and J. Morgan (eds.), Syntax and Semantics, Vol. III: Speech Acts. Academic Press, New York.

Shaffer, D. 1978. The place of code-switching in linguistic contacts. In: M. Paradis (ed.), Aspects of Bilingualism. Hornbeam Press, Columbia, S.C.

Shatz, M. 1977. On the development of communicative understandings: An early strategy for interpreting and responding to messages. In: J. Glick and A. Clarke-Stewart (eds.), Studies in Social and Cognitive Development. Gardner Press, New York.

Shatz, M., and Gelman, R. 1973. The development of communication skills: Modification in the speech of young children as a function of listeners. Monogr. Soc. Res. Child Dev. 38.

Smith, M. E. 1935. A study of some factors influencing the development of the sentence in pre-school children. J. Genet. Psychol. 46:182–212.

Stewart, W. A. 1962. Creole languages in the Carribean. In: F. A. Rice (ed.), Study of the Role of Second Languages in Asia, Africa and Latin America. Center for Applied Linguistics, Washington, D.C.

Walters, J. 1978. Variation in the requesting behavior of bilingual children. Paper presented to the Fifth International Congress of Applied Linguistics, Montreal, Canada.

Walters, J. 1979. A study of deference in the language use of Armenian speakers of English. Paper presented at the annual meeting of the American Education Research Association, San Francisco, Cal.

Weeks, T. E. 1971. Speech registers in young children. Child Dev. 42:1119–1131.

Weintraub, S. 1974. Sex differences in conversational style: Children's use of direct and indirect request forms. Unpublished manuscript, Boston University, Boston.

Williams, F., and Naremore, R. C. 1969. In the functional analysis of social class differences in modes of speech. Speech Monogr. 36:77–102.

Wolfram, W. 1969. A Sociolinguistic Description of Detroit Negro Speech. Urban Language series, No. 5. Center for Applied Linguistics, Washington, D.C.

chapter twelve

Pragmatic and Ethological Techniques for the Observational Assessment of Children's Communicative Abilities

Donald R. Omark

Assessment of children is a common and recurring phenomenon in American education. Placement in any sort of special program, bilingual class, remedial instruction, or the like, involves testing, even beyond the amount to which most children are subjected. The broader assessment tests are generally administered to children in their classrooms, and can certainly be frightening to a child who does not understand the instructions. For those children who fail the first round of group tests, the next level involves individual testing, generally in a special room, by a complete stranger who may or may not speak the language or even the dialect with which the child is familiar. Such test situations supposedly "standardize" the situation across subjects, as if they had no prior histories related to such experiences (e.g., being visited or not visited by strange social workers, or visiting doctors' offices versus a complete absence of such visits).

All of the types of tests discussed in the preceding chapters are so-called "objective" tests, which basically means that they are impartial to any particular problems the child may have. They generally have to be administered in strictly proscribed ways, with little encouragement or modification being permitted. Some of the language assessment tests recognize dialectical differences, but nonetheless the alternative responses permitted are usually narrowly defined (as other chapters indicate).

While some of the tests may be individually administered, they are in fact interested not in the individual per se, but only in the way the individual's scores compare with the mean of the population upon which the tests were normed. The normed population may, but generally does not, include the population where the child lives. Furthermore, the test items may bear little resemblance to anything the child has ever experienced before, either within his or her culture as an item, artifact, or experience (e.g., a telegram being delivered, father wearing a tie, or even the lawn being watered with a hose) or in the form presented in the test (e.g., a series of line drawings).

Finally, most tests are designed by test constructors based on some conceptualization of how the Anglo middle-class child passes through a series of developmental stages and sets of experiences (those which the test constructor faced and which subsequent research on the same group reaffirmed). From such experiences and research are the test items drawn. As one can begin to see, the typical test may be heavily loaded against children who come from a lower socioeconomic status (SES), are bilingual (actually monolingual in some other language), or are retarded in terms of language development. The first order of priorities for testers should be whether they are more interested in supposed group norms or whether they are really interested in accurately assessing individual abilities, so that each individual child can be placed within the program that will do the most good.

The second order of priorities involve the teacher and tester both. This is the disentanglement of language and intelligence. Equating language abilities with intelligence is an easy trap into which to fall. Personal experiences of this author have included both erroneously judging foreign students and having been erroneously judged when traveling abroad; such misjudgment is not an uncommon occurrence even for those who should know better. Virtually all IQ tests administered in the United States require language in standard English for their successful completion. Obviously, nothing can be gained from the administration of such tests to children with a different language, or from those with marked dialectical differences (cf. Omark, 1981). Any argument that the tests reflect the language of the classroom and are therefore valid are nonsensical; the language of the classroom can be changed much more easily than can the language of the child. Bilingual programs are attempting to do just that, as are programs that encourage minorities to go to college to become teachers. Teachers who speak the language of the child and come from the child's culture can do much to alleviate the feelings of alienation that result from mismatches between children and educational programs.[1]

---

[1] One should be aware of a paradox that can occur by simply placing minority teachers in classrooms without any further considerations of their attitudes. Some minority teachers have "passed" into the Anglo middle-class subculture. Their attitude is "I made it, and, hence, what I have acquired is also what the children should acquire." Such an attitude can obviously act counter to the purposes of bilingual education. It will be necessary to examine more than the surname or linguistic abilities of teachers for the creation of successful bilingual programs.

When tests are normed on populations and cultures different from those to which the child has been exposed, then the tests should be rejected as valid assessment instruments (Cole, 1975; Omark, 1981). Ultimately, the child who is about to be assigned to a special program has to be considered as an individual. This individual has to be tested within the child's environment if one is going to come to understand the child.

LINGUISTIC MEASURES: QUANTITATIVE VERSUS QUALITATIVE

Earlier linguistic measures were qualitative in that they relied upon a native speaker of a language (either the investigator or an informant) for details about how a language was structured. Most recently, quantitative data have been collected on the frequency of occurrence of various speech forms in different SES groups and across various racial populations (see Labov et al., 1968; Wolfram and Fasold, 1974). From such studies, predictions could be made about the *probability* of some speakers using a particular dialectical variant given information about their SES, locality, and race.

While such studies may provide information to teachers about what to expect from their students in terms of expected percentages of occurrences, the results frequently are presented in terms that can only have meaning to a trained linguist. For example, Shuy (1977) has presented an example from Labov of a rule for contraction in Black English Vernacular, which he constructs as follows:

$$\begin{bmatrix} +\text{voc} \\ -\text{str} \\ +\text{cen} \end{bmatrix} \to \phi \: / \: \begin{bmatrix} *\text{Pro} \\ \\ V \end{bmatrix} \begin{bmatrix} \\ \underline{} \\ \end{bmatrix} \begin{bmatrix} \underline{\text{Cl}} \\ \text{O} \\ -T \\ [*\text{nas}] \end{bmatrix} \begin{bmatrix} \alpha \: \text{Vb} \\ \beta \: \text{gn} \\ -\gamma \: \text{NP} \end{bmatrix}$$

This rule operates on a form in which the vowel has been reduced to a schwa; for example *he is* becomes he [αZ] with this rule making the form *he's*. More technically, the rule deals with the removal of a schwa, as in "Man, he runnin' fas'." While examples are readily understandable by school personnel, the more intricate rules are not apt to be understood by those already in the schools.

The results of linguistic, psycholinguistic, and sociolinguistic research endeavors should be important to teachers, testers, and test designers because they describe, or are beginning to describe, the range of dialects that children produce. What the child speaks is some indication of what he or she can understand. When there is no match among 1) the test instructions, 2) the permissible test responses, 3) the cultural items represented on the test, and 4) the child's own language and cultural experiences, there is little hope of determining *anything* about the child. Because 1, 2, and 3 above almost always are confounded (except for tests like the Del Rio (Toronto et al., 1975), which was developed for a specific population), one cannot even say that the child does not speak standard Spanish or English. He or she may even speak one or the other quite well but never have encountered the cultural objects presented on the test.

Tests that are short and quick, easy to score, and clearly differentiate between different kinds of children would obviously be desirable for any school program that has to test large numbers of children. Such tests may appear to exist, but as this book demonstrates, they may actually be rare. Also, such tests can now be seen to be based upon linguistic paradigms that have changed without a concomitant change in the tests themselves.

SPEECH ACTS

Shifting our perspective away from discrete point tests and the errors they produce then places us in a quandary about what to measure. The revolution or paradigm shift started by Chomsky meant a change from perceiving linguistic entities (phonemes, morphemes, words, etc.) as items that are learned in a behavioristic fashion through habit formation and drill. Eventually (and different from Chomsky) language came to be viewed as something that had variability (Labov, 1971) and a rule structure that the organism per force would acquire. Evolutionary theory would suggest that organisms are modified through naturalistic and social selection to be capable of acquiring that which it is most important for them to acquire (Washburn and Hamburg, 1965) and language certainly should be expected to be one human characteristic the acquisition of which is important.

Something more is needed if one is to assess the child's level of language development, and measure his or her progress in becoming an adequate speaker of one or more languages, than simple counts of whether or not the child can say 20 or 25 words in a language. What is needed is an assessment of the language capabilities of the child as he or she functions within his or her experiential world. Searle (1969; see Sridhar, this volume for the historical development preceding Searle) suggested *speech acts* as an appropriate level of analysis of linguistic communication. Within his framework there should be analytic connections among the notion of speech acts, what the speaker intends, what the hearer understands, and what the rules governing the linguistic elements are. If one records speech acts, then presumably one can begin to ask questions about the effectiveness of the speaker (e.g., could the child express what he or she meant to say), or the linguistic competence of the speaker (e.g., did the hearer understand what was said).

For example, suppose a child who normally speaks Spanish (L_1) directs an English comment to a peer. One could then ask the child in Spanish what the child meant to say (the intended meaning). The English form of the utterance could then be compared with its meaning as expressed by the child's more fluent expression in Spanish. The peer could then be addressed in the peer's most fluent language to see what the peer understood from the message. In that way one could test two individuals at the same time with regard to productive and receptive abilities while they engaged in some task, say building an object where they had to alternate turns in giving instructions as to what should be done next.

Such an approach would begin to tap what Searle labels as *illocutionary acts* (e.g., stating, questioning, commanding, promising). Unfortunately, there appear to be about 1,000 possible illocutionary acts (see Searle, p. 23, re: Austin); these range across "assert, warn, remark, comment, command, order, request, criticize, apologize, censure, approve, welcome, promise, object, demand, argue," to name only a few. Obviously, testing a child to see whether that child knows 20, 25, or even 150 words does not begin to tap whether the child can perform any of the 1,000 or more illocutionary acts. Equally obvious is the fact that the tester (whether teacher, teacher aide, school psychologist, or other personnel) could not begin to test whether the child was capable of all such illocutionary acts.

Let me expand Searle's approach slightly to illustrate what has been done in previous approaches to testing language and what could be done. Searle breaks down speech acts, or communicative acts, into three levels: *utterance acts*, *propositional acts*, and *illocutionary acts*. Utterance acts are the utterance of words; they may be just morphemes or single words, or they may constitute sentences. Most commercial tests are at this level: is the proper morpheme given in response to a picture stimulus; can the child say something about a picture, or construct an entire sentence? Frequently the test goes to the phoneme (or morpheme) level and looks for particular markers: was an [s] included at the end of plurals, and so forth.

With most tests, what was uttered need not strictly make sense. Suppose two children are shown a test item, meant to elicit the plural -*s* marker, with a picture of two dogs, and are asked, "What do you see?" One child can respond, "I see three dogs," and the other could respond, "I see two dog." The first child passes and the second does not. Most discrete point tests seem to be at the utterance act level of analysis. The tests investigate a variety of utterances and the question you have to ask yourself when evaluating the tests is whether this variety is broad enough and valid enough to capture the communicative competence of your children.

Searle's next level of analysis considers propositional acts. Here one would examine sentences to see if they performed their functions of referring and predicating. Do they contain a subject, object, and verb? Few tests work at this level. The task is no easier because an infinite variety of sentences can supposedly be produced. For example, considering the picture of the two dogs, one might elicit from children: "There are two dogs," "I see two dogs," "There be two dogs," "Two dog are there," "I two dogs see," and so on. Which do you count as correct and when? If you are dealing with a native Spanish or English speaker then subject, verb, object is the preferred order. But if the child comes from the Philippines (speaking Tagalog), then the order may be subject, object, verb. "I two dogs see" has the right words but the wrong order. Does the child pass or fail? Is he or she given more normal exposure or referred to a special program?

At the third level are illocutionary acts. These speech acts are performed by all of us everyday. The full range of these acts would be difficult to test. However, children obviously are not yet capable of performing the entire variety of such acts. Tests can be developed to tap some of the illocutionary acts that students can be expected to perform as they learn a new language or act in their native (L_1) language. Walters (1979a) suggests one approach, and provides illustrations for politeness forms that might be investigated. The pragmatic tests provided at the end of this chapter suggest other forms of illocutionary acts that might be recorded as examples of this type of speech act. It should be noted that developmental norms and local norms (see Toronto, 1981) need to be developed for any instrument that is used in the decision-making process.

Searle then adds a fourth level (from Austin) which he identifies as *perlocutionary acts*. He defines these as the "consequences or *effects* such acts have on the actions, thoughts or beliefs, etc. of hearers." For example, an effect might be to persuade, alarm, or get the hearer to do something. At this point in Searle's progression we have moved beyond the spoken word per se into an examination of the effect of communication. Examination of this effect has been labeled *pragmatics*.

Taking a pragmatic linguistic approach may be one way out of the dilemma of determining a child's particular problems. The tester receives a child who has *failed* the language tests, not only in one language but sometimes two languages. There must really be something wrong with that child—what else is one to think? The other way of thinking is to say that "we" have not yet been able to get a score on that child—what are we doing wrong? Unless a child is absolutely deaf, or mute, there should be some language there, so how do we find out how much there is and what it is?

The first problem is to sort out the population into at least two groups: those who can exhibit some communicative competence and those who really may have other problems. *Do not assume* that linguistic testing is such a refined area that *only* those children with problems will be readily identified—*that* is the major problem in bilingual education. Instead, assume that so far not enough is known about this child. All a test reveals is what a child can do; it does not reveal what a child cannot do. There are too many non-test-related reasons for a child's failure to respond to a test item (shyness, strange situation, strange format, etc., see Cole, 1975) for the lack of a response to be considered an incapacity on the part of the child. Until something is known about the child's language capabilities, nothing can be determined about any of the other capabilities of the child.

The clinical tester might start with some standard "bag of tricks" to get the child to relax and pay attention in what is presumed or known to be the child's home language. If something is elicited but it is still not evident into which group, normal or handicapped, the child should be placed, then some of the pragmatic tests might be used as described in Oller (1972, 1981) and Spolsky (1972) (further suggestions appear in Leonard et al. 1978). If the child remains uncooperative, the tester should stop testing because no further worthwhile information is apt to be obtained in the clinic.

Something different has to be done if a decision is to be made about the group to which the child should be assigned, and the additional nonlanguage testing required. In order to see what the child's natural language capabilities may be, the child has to be examined in his or her natural environment. There are two parts to this procedure; first, a determination of what will be recorded, and second, a determination of how the records will be collected. The next section will introduce some pragmatic factors that will provide some background for later descriptions of how and what to record.

PRAGMATICS

The field of pragmatics as it is developing within the disciplines interested in communication (anthropology, linguistics, psychology, and sociology) is not monolithic in structure. Any new field, or any new concept within a field, quickly acquires a multitude of definitions, all of which are suggested as *the* definition by different practitioners and researchers. So it is with pragmatics. Sridhar and Walters (Chapters 10 and 11, respectively, this volume) illustrate some of the current thinking about communication and its assessment. What follows are some brief additional statements about another view of pragmatics.

The pragmatic linguistic approach is interested in communication. Discrete point tests are interested in language. Language, as the tests, and the linguists until recently, have examined it stops with semantics. Actually most of the tests stop at lower levels.[2] All that they (the tests and most linguists) have been interested in is the word or the sentence as it appears—an abstract entity. If, however, you are interested in communication, then you are interested in the exchange that is occurring. To paraphrase Briere (1972), the speaker has some intent to communicate, and he or she attempts to communicate. The listener has some understanding of this intent and understands what is communicated, more or less. So, a message of some sort is conveyed from one individual to another. It can be a command, an instruction, a description, and so forth. One does not *catch* this "thing"—word or sentence—as it passes from one individual to another, but instead lets it complete its passage *to see what happens*.

As Bates (1976) says, "Within linguistic theory, the study of *language use* can be called "pragmatics'." One of the widely cited definitions of pragmatics is that of Charles Morris (1946), who divided linguistic science into three areas: 1) syntactics—the relations holding among signs, 2) semantics—the relations between signs and their referents, and 3) pragmatics—the relations between signs and their

---

[2] *Lower* is used here in the sense of being more reductionistic and particularistic. If you do *not* believe that the whole is the sum of its parts, then you would take the pragmatic approach.

human users. Bates points out problems with Morris's definition and says that "pragmatics is not simply another kind of sign relation, equivalent to syntactics and semantics. Pragmatics is the study of linguistic indices, and indices can be interpreted only when they are used. One cannot describe the meaning of indices—one can only describe rules for relating them to a context, in which the meaning can be found."

As suggested earlier, Searle carries this point a bit further and talks about the *intent* behind an utterance. The speaker has an intent in making a statement. A hearer perceives some intent in what the speaker says. The spoken words, and the way they are said, carry this intentionality from one person to the other.

Now, as a researcher, one can get hung up on all sorts of things: Was the original intent actually conveyed by the spoken word? Did the listener understand this intent? Did the listener understand the communication but not the intent? All of these questions (and more) are fine if one is doing research per se, but if one is interested in assessing a child's communicative abilities, one should not be sidetracked by such questions.

What has to be examined is the *effect* (perlocutionary effect) of the communication produced by the child. This is a slightly older principle in ethology (Altmann, 1967; Smith, 1977) as well as in linguistics (Austin, 1962; Searle, 1969; Walters, in preparation), and both fields seem to be rapidly converging. In animal ethology (which is the biological study of behavior and especially communicative behavior (Omark, 1980a)), the only way to see what was communicated was to look for the effect of one animal on another animal. One might see an apparent signal occurring, but if the other animal did not change its behavior then no communication could be recorded as having occurred.[3] If a child says something to another child (even if *you* do not understand what was said), then it still may be possible to assess what was communicated (and/or how well) by the change in behavior of the receiver of the signal.

To illustrate, one could see one child say to another, "Ab sitze, bitte," and see the other child immediately change from standing to sitting. Hence, One could easily recognize that a command had been given because there followed a complete change in behavior in the hearer. One could probably also identify, with some accuracy, the giving of instructions, passing of information, and requests for something, and certainly

---

[3] This approach has subsequently been extended to recognize the longer term effects of communication. There need not always be an immediate cause–effect relationship.

one could identify humerous remarks, all without knowing the children's language.[4]

PROBLEMS WITH ASSESSMENT IN A PRAGMATIC FRAMEWORK

There are, however, four basic problems in doing a pragmatic naturalistic study of a child's communicative behavior. The first problem is one with which both pragmatists and ethologists are coming to grips, and that is the effect that different settings can have on children's linguistic behaviors. A child may be silent in the classroom, quiet on the playground with new peers, talkative at home, and boisterous on the streets. Since the task of the tester is to determine if the child can communicate, this means that more than one setting may have to be examined. If one can find out all one needs in the testing situation or classroom, fine; but a child should not be labeled language deficient until the tester has maximized that child's chances to communicate.

A second problem interacting with settings are the social relationships in those settings. Offhand, the playground might look like a good place to collect speech samples. However, the playground is one place where dominance relationships among children manifest themselves. Within our research experience (Omark, Omark, and Edelman, 1975; Omark and Edelman, 1976; Parker and Omark, 1980; Omark, 1980b; Weisfeld, Omark and Cronin, 1980), some children at the lower end of the dominance hierarchy withdraw from interacting and consequently are very passive linguistically. The street or the home may provide different opportunities and the chance for different relationships. Eventually, of course, with some children one has to say, "That's enough watching—the child does not communicate." That may be why the child is at the bottom of the hierarchy. Until one watches, however, one cannot be sure whether a problem really exists.

One caveat: children have been observed from the United States (Omark, 1980b) to the Kalahari desert (Draper, 1980), and within at least some cultures boys are less verbal than girls. If a preponderance of boys are being sent for further testing, one needs to raise some questions

---

[4] A single instance of the occurrence of a particular behavior in one child folowing a verbalization by another child obviously only provides clues as to the nature of the interaction, especially if the observer does not speak the language. Probability statements, however, can be developed to show that, for example, from out of the five times a particular statement was made a particular response followed. The important point to investigate is whether a child can send or receive different kinds of speech acts, and each instance provides data.

about the initial testing procedures. Simply because boys are less verbally expressive, perhaps as a natural trait, should not lead them to be tested more frequently for problems related to communication. One of the purposes of the Scan technique (described later) is to put the tester in tune with the group with which he or she has to deal. It is suggested that distinct scores be kept for the boys and for the girls so that the child being tested is compared with others of the same sex.

There are any number of cultures where being verbally fluent is highly rewarded (e.g., some American Indian tribes, some African tribes, and adolescent Black American males). Some cultures put restrictions on females being verbal but encourage male verbosity, and some may support the reverse (Hymes, 1974). In any case, it is best to compare a child with his or her own sex and cultural group in order to determine communicative skills.

The third major problem is language. If one's task is to find out if the child *can communicate* in a way in which an effect can be seen in the "other's" change of behavior, then this can be done without knowing the language. Data that the author has collected in Switzerland and Ethiopia show that this is possible. School authorities, however, probably prefer data that are something like those derived from tests with which they are familiar (see Tymitz, 1981). One must not get hung up on language per se, but one might want to know how to score what was communicated. If so, the tester will either have to have some knowledge of the other language or will have to have an informant who can be trained to observe and score accurately. It may even be necessary to elicit the parents' aid before testing can proceed.

The fourth major problem is that of being an unbiased observer. A major reason for using tests is to objectify the determination of children's capabilities and problems. Clinical and/or educational training has the same goal of producing objective observers, interviewers, and testers. The snot-nosed, noisy, dirty little boy has to have the same chance of receiving a good score as the well-mannered, neatly dressed, quiet little gentleman. If the tester is now asked to move out of the clinical/educational setting, and away from discrete point test results, to a consideration of how an individual communicates with others in natural settings, then some means of objectifying this process has to be included. Subjective impressions should not be the sole basis for whatever happens to any child.

There would appear to be two ways around this problem. The first is to examine the child in relationship to the child's group. Clinical training has the same goal; a lot of children are seen (with problems) so that the tester begins to assess any child in relationship to the tester's past experiences. When a switch is made to a different cultural group, those past experiences with an Anglo middle-class population become largely or entirely superfluous. In essence, the tester has to be retrained, although this need not take as long as the initial training. All that is needed is a data base, and the Scan technique will help provide this. This technique will permit one to compare the "problem" child with the child's group to see if, in fact, the child's behavior is unusual or abnormal (assuming this group is of the same ethnicity). The focal child technique can help expand this data base.

The second way around this problem of objectivity is to identify a fixed set of behaviors that have to be scored. If every child is scored in the same way, then the tester cannot make one child appear worse than another because of some underlying bias. The sample scoring sheets discussed below provide the opportunity to score each child in a similar manner. Alternatively, one could develop a list of the more probable speech acts mentioned by Searle (1969, see Walters, in preparation). Still another approach would be to develop a score sheet from the developmental linguistic stages suggested by Prutting (1979). If any of these potential forms are used, corrections will have to be made for the particular language that is being used.

Pragmatics, and the naturalistic observation of speech acts, are relatively new within linguistics. As far as we know there are no commercial tests available that take this approach.[5] The examples suggested in this book should not be taken as a sole or exclusive approach. One should feel free to change any of the forms suggested here, but then use the new form consistently so as to avoid observer bias.

Peers, parents, and others can be observed as interactors with the child (in essence, as observers aiding you by serving as elicitors of speech). An example from your own experience, if you are a parent, will illustrate that such an approach works. If you have had young children (2–4 years of age), then you know that most of the time you understand what they are saying *or* what they are talking about; communication is occurring. A friend comes to visit, and the child talks to the stranger as he or she does to you. The friend nods at part of what the child says, then looks blank, turns to you, and asks what the child is saying. You then translate the child's utterances. As a clinical observer you are like the friend: some interactions can be recorded directly from your observa-

---

[5] Oller takes a different definition of pragmatics and suggests tests like the "cloze" technique and other approaches (1972, 1973).

tions, some need translation to make sense, and some may need a parent or someone else to aid in the interpretation of what is happening.

There is one problem with this approach. Parents become very good at understanding their children who have real speech and hearing problems. Peers on the street where the child lives may have less experience understanding the child, and peers on the school playground will have even less experience. One has to observe the child in different settings in order to decide if the child can communicate *effectively*. In essence, one moves toward the home setting to see if the child can communicate, and away from the home to test the effectiveness of the child in communicating with others.

TECHNIQUES OF NATURALISTIC OBSERVATION

This section describes a few techniques of naturalistic observation as a supplement to clinical observations and as an alternative to discrete point testing. Three methods are discussed, and suggestions are made about who, how long, where, when, and what to watch.

Hundreds of observational schedules have been produced, but fortunately all of these are derived from seven basic techniques, one of which should never be used (see Omark, Fiedler, and Marvin, 1976). These techniques were developed by ethologists, primatologists, and early child psychologists and educators who were interested in accurately recording the nonverbal behaviors of animals and children.

The three techniques that appear to be most directly useful for the sampling of children's linguistic abilities are: 1) the Focal Child, 2) Scan sampling, and 3) Matrix Completion techniques. The first involves a focus on a single child at a time. The second provides a measure of group behavior, such as an entire classroom. A modification of the third includes a particular way of recording data and a suggestion for which children need to be examined more closely, or which children might be paired together for clinical assessment.

Focal Child Sampling

In a focal child sampling technique, a single child is observed for an extended period of time (e.g., 10 minutes, 1 hour, all day) at repeated intervals (e.g., twice an hour, once a week) until an adequate sample of the child's behavior has been recorded. Everything that the child does that is of interest to the observer is recorded. The records of a child may then be compared with 1) later records on that child (i.e., to see what improvement or changes have occurred), 2) records on other children in the class (i.e., to see which children need more help or how the child compares with a sample from his group), 3) other research results (e.g., with Labov et al.'s (1968) findings on Black English) or on other groups, 4) the teacher's/tester's experience with other children in past years from the same school district, or finally, 5) the teacher's/tester's own linguistic background.

Since the assessment of language, rather than of nonverbal behavior, is the concern of this book, it should be noted that an observer need not always be present for the collecting of the desired information. For example, a tape recorder can be left in the home and the parent instructed in its operation and told when samples should be collected. If it is explained to the parent that it is important to know what the child says in order to teach the child more and help him or her, almost all parents will be cooperative.

Where the observations or recordings are made are extremely important if an adequate sample of linguistic behavior is to be collected. Variety in situations which might elicit different kinds of language samples would be preferred (see Walters, Chapter 11, this volume). For the teacher as tester the easiest set would be the classroom, the playground, and the home. A classroom can be manipulated in any number of ways, especially in the lower grades, with a house corner, a store corner, a make-believe enclosure, and even an English only corner. What the children do in each setting can then be observed and recorded. Such settings, once they have been used for a while, are sometimes even better than actually going to a store because the children are not inhibited by strange adults and can perform both the "seller and buyer" or "mother/father and child" roles. Even a child playing alone in such a setting will frequently verbalize one or more roles.

If a variety of settings can be sampled, then the child has been permitted the opportunity to produce or respond to a variety of speech acts.[6] In the classroom he or she can follow directions (here one might want also to record nonverbal behaviors rather than language as examples of communicative understanding rather than production). The child

---

[6] Nonverbal responses obviously cannot be recorded on audiotape, unless an observer is present and comments on the behavior. Videotape captures a broader range of verbal and nonverbal behaviors, but would be prohibitively expensive in some settings. A decision then has to be made as to the variety of behaviors that are to be recorded. The suggestion would be to use an observer or an audio tape recorder as availability or appropriateness to the situation dictates. For those extreme cases where it is difficult to make a decision, an observer *and* audio tape recorder may be necessary.

can also give answers, ask questions, request to go to the bathroom, etc. On the playground he or she can discuss feeling, give commands (during games), follow suggestions, defer to others, and so forth. At home the child can direct siblings, express wants, comply with instructions, perform tasks, tell about events, and interact with others socially.

Fifty speech acts collected across such a sample of situations, especially if the teacher makes creative use of the classroom, should be far more meaningful than the results provided by any "quickie" test. The tester can record not only the variety of words used, but also the completeness of sentences expressed and the variety of instructions to which responses have been made.

Clinical interviewing of a child would still be focal child sampling but without the naturalness suggested above. There may, however, be linguistic structures that have not occurred in the natural setting that necessitate a closer interaction with the child. To suggest a quiet, comfortable place for such interviewing may seem appropriate, but from the child's perspective these places may, in fact, be strange and threatening. *Within the classroom testing* might be preferable, especially if it can be done as part of classroom procedure. For example, the teacher or teacher aide takes the child to a table at the back to work on some materials in the course of which the necessary remarks are elicited. Since these procedures happen to all of the children, and happen repeatedly as progress is measured, it becomes a classroom routine. Classrooms with different kinds of "corners" or work centers could also be used to elicit different language structures.

Labov (1972) has demonstrated that very rich language samples can occur when peers interact. The clinical situation might therefore be modified to include more than one child, thus putting the children more at ease and willing to participate.[7] The tester might suggest "Pick a friend to help you," "Play a language game," or "Do_____" in order to provide a peer with whom the subject can interact.

If the tester wants complete samples of a child's verbal productions, then a tape recorder might be used. If the procedures are to become a classroom routine, the tape recorder should be openly displayed. It would also be helpful to let the children learn how to manipulate it; even 3-year-

---

[7] Friendships begin to occur as soon as children meet in groups, and dominance relationships (which can be both attracting and repelling in nature) become strong by first grade (Omark, Omark, and Edelman, 1975; Omark and Edelman, 1976; Omark, Fiedler, and Marvin, 1976). Such factors should be considered by the tester whenever children are paired to work together.

olds can operate the cassette models. If it becomes familiar enough, it can even be used to have the children tell stories for the rest of the class, which can then also be used for analysis purposes (see Day et al., Chapter 7, and Erickson, Chapter 1, this volume).

For data collection purposes, the tape has to be replayed later and appropriate recordings transcribed on some form. Depending on the detail desired, transcribing can range from a complete transcription to simply marking off items on a tally sheet. Use of a tally sheet obviously saves time because transcripts take three to four times as long to write as the actual recording time. However, the tally sheets should be open-ended rather than completely spelled out. This open-endedness permits the child to illustrate communicative abilities without this simply becoming another discrete point test. Samples collected from "normal" children of the child's same culture and sex should be used for comparative purposes. Oller (1973) suggests a scoring method for such data.

Scan Sampling

In this technique, in essence, a snapshot or picture is made of a child and then the observer moves on to take a similar snapshot of the next child. Since language has a temporal dimension little about what is being expressed can be determined by such a snapshot, even one a few seconds in length. What can be determined by briefly observing each child is whether or not he or she is vocal (as compared with classmates), what language the child is speaking, and where and with whom the child speaks that language. For example, by scanning an "open"-style bilingual classroom where it is, say, the "English hour," one can see how many students are following instructions. Over time one can see which students rarely speak one or even the other language. Also, one can see if there is any continuity in the language spoken during class, when the children go to recess, or frequent different parts of the room (e.g., a home or cooking center may elicit the native language). All of this provides a measure of what the group naturally produces.

A scan is meant to be quick; only broad categories as suggested above should be recorded. It can provide a profile of typical classroom behavior both inside and outside the classroom, and it provides identification of particular children who are shifting their use of language, as well as of those who are slower. In particular, if such samplings of the classroom are done two, three, or more times a day, it quickly indicates and validates those children who are nonverbal and who may be in need of additional help, either because of language retardation or because of related speech and hearing problems. The nonverbal child, who may have passed the discrete point tests, is frequently ignored because this kind of a child generally is not a behavior problem. However, this type of a child is the very one who may be in need of language remediation, and this observational technique can help identify that child.

A simple, dittoed tally sheet with all of the children's names listed down one side and columns indicating what linguistic behaviors are to be collected is all that is needed. A few lines drawn at the top can be used to record when the sample was collected and where (e.g., home, classroom, playground, etc.). If these sheets are to be used later to form pairs for focal child testing, then one column ought to be used to record with whom the child was interacting at the time the record was made.

A scan can be done on a classroom or a playground in less then 10 minutes, once one knows the children's names. It can indicate much about the linguistic and social states of the classroom, and about those children in need of further attention. A focal child sample followed by a scan, then another focal child sample, and so on, can be taken. In this way numerous data are obtained on the children of interest, while information on the verbal characteristics of the group is gained at the same time.

Matrix Completion

The third observational technique that may prove useful in language assessment is a measure of the interactions that occur between individuals. This technique was originally designed to measure who aggressed against whom, i.e., who was dominant and who was submissive in an encounter (see Strayer, 1980). It is a way of recording encounters with regard to a particular behavior. One makes a list of the children down the left-hand side of a sheet and also across the top of the sheet; columns and rows for each child are then ruled off to produce a matrix. What could be recorded would be items like who speaks Spanish or English to each other at the time each observation is made.

Such a sheet could be used to transcribe the data from either the focal child or the scan techniques, or it could be used as the primary recording instrument. Over time the sheet will indicate who interacts with whom and how, and can serve as the basis for later pairings of children for further clinical testing. Empty cells for the noninteractive or nonverbal children are readily apparent.

Who Should Be Watched

As suggested above, we watch the child whom the initial set of testing indicated was marginal. The focus of our attention should be on a single child (*the focal child*) during the observation period. The purpose of the observation is to hear and record the speech acts of that individual, in as much detail as possible. A linguist might be able to catch all of the bilabial fricative errors, and so forth, but a teacher or aide can put a question mark above the transcript indicating that something was not said quite right.

The child is, primarily, only going to speak when interacting with another, This interaction, of course, affects what and how something is said by the focal child. Hence, some minimal notes have to be made about the language environment of the child. If no one the child encounters talks English, then an observer is not going to gain much data on whether or not the child knows any English. It might be necessary to contrive some situations so that the child is placed in an English language environment (see Walters, 1979b).

The object of such manipulations, however, should be to make this environment as nonthreatening as possible, and not to return to the testing situation where the child has just failed. Some possible approaches might be to place the child in a situation where he or she has to deal with a peer who code-switches regularly, or with the teacher or aide who have been instructed to code-switch. This presents the opportunity for the child to do so, while permitting him or her to continue L_1 production if that is the child's choice. The point is that one has to get this marginal child communicating.

If no aide is available to help the tester understand the child's language, then the tester has to observe when the child attempts to communicate with others. What is recorded is the effect this communication has on these others. The more culturally isolated the child and the family are, the more the observations will have to be made in the home or on the street.

How Long to Watch

An important consideration is the length of time one can spend observing. Each school district will have to decide for itself how much time should be invested in assessing individual children's capabilities. Some balance needs to be made between cost, the fact that initial placement may well affect the next 12 or more years of a child's life, the differentials in cost between special versus normal placement, *and* the cost of potential court proceedings. The weight of the latter three factors suggests that a couple of hours of observational time, or more if parents, teachers, or aides are involved, would be appropriate.

Where possible, the suggestion would be to place the child in a bilingual classroom and not to immediately pursue clinical testing. Observations might then be conducted by the teacher, aide, or tester *in a systematic way* across the school year. Judgments could be made periodically and at the end of the year based upon progress the child has made, and such progress or lack of progress would be supported by hard data amounting to many hours of observation, rather than a 20-minute test normed upon some irrelevant population. Such a procedure would probably work best in the lower grades (say, K through 3).

With older children the observations should be done more quickly if problems are to be ameliorated before the child leaves school. The child might be placed in a bilingual classroom for a month or two while communication samples are collected. If observations are carefully scheduled, more than one focal child can be observed successively on the playground, in class, etc., while collecting scan samples in between focal samples. Twenty scans would probably be a minimum; the more that are collected the better will be the determination of how the older child's behavior compares with that of the child's group.

When to Record

The aim of any testing procedure is to provide an estimate of an individual's capabilities. A 20-minute test probably grossly underestimates anyone's abilities. The intent of the suggested naturalistic approach is to maximize this estimation. How good an estimation it will be depends upon how much time is spent in observation, in what settings it is undertaken, and what manipulations the tester can introduce. In turn, what is done depends upon what the school administration permits, but more than 20 minutes is obviously required.

An "estimate" means that one samples from the total set of behaviors that an individual is continuously producing (see Prutting, in preparation). The purpose of the proposed approach is not to obtain some "unbiased estimate" of what a child can do in an experimental setting, but rather to see if the child can speak Spanish or English, or whatever, and how fluently. This kind of an approach means that if very few speech acts appear in one setting (e.g., the classroom), then this fact should be noted and the observer should move on to other settings. Something can be recorded whenever and wherever the child speaks.

What to Observe

The process of communication is not carried on through a single medium or channel, but is multifaceted. One hears, sees, talks, touches, and smells, and one does each of these with different capabilities and intensities. Recording the verbalizations of a child will reflect only about half of what occurred in that child's interaction with another. Much of the message, and how well it was received, will depend upon the paralinguistic (prosody, stress, etc.) and nonverbal (behavioral) aspects of the communication.

Some of the nonverbal ways of acting and reacting may be quite universal. Anger, fear, surprise, disgust, sadness, happiness, or humor, and a few other facial gestures or emotions, have been found to be common in a wide variety of cultures (Ekman and Friesen, 1975, 1978). Consequently, when recording the effect a child has upon another, trust your reactions. What the child says to those who understand the child provides the clues as to whether the child can communicate. Requests from others for repetitions mean that the child is not effectively communicating, and such situations should be obvious in most languages. Responses by others versus requests for repetition or ignoring behaviors are clues in assessing the child's communicative competence.

INSTRUMENTS FOR TEACHER, PARENT, AND OBSERVER

In this concluding section three different approaches to identification of the language disordered child are described. The purpose of any test, observational process, questionnaire, etc., is to provide data points that can aid in the decision process relative to particular children. Discrete point tests or extensions of them (when properly normed locally and used appropriately) can provide the data necessary for decisions about many of the children. Ultimately, however, there are some children upon whom further data are needed; three sample cases are described below. It should be noted that these are just examples. The reader is encouraged to modify these examples as appropriate for the characteristics of the local population.

The Teacher

The teacher may be one of the first persons to feel that a particular child has a communicative problem. It is also the teacher of bilingual students to whom the problem is returned when no meaningful results are obtained through discrete point testing of a child. The form shown in Table 1 (developed by Karyn Gitlis, Tempe, Arizona[8]), as one example among many, provides a checklist that can be used by teachers to aid in

---

[8] Ms. Karyn Gitlis, Tempe Elementary Schools, P. O. Box 27708, Tempe, Arizona 85281.

The Parents

With the exception of the teacher, the people who spend the greatest number of waking hours with the child are his or her parents. Their concern for and information about the child are apt to be even greater than the involvement of the teacher, and they can be motivated to provide accurate information about the child.

The parent questionnaire, shown in Table 3, was developed by Bruce Tomblin, Richard Hurting, and Nancy Larsen.[9] As written, it is meant to be an instrument the parent uses to reflect back upon past verbal and behavioral characteristics of the child. The introductory paragraph to the parent could also be rephrased such that the parent considers and watches for over a period of a week or more.

This questionnaire is more language oriented than the sample form for the teacher shown in Table 1 (which could also suggest other problem areas). This questionnaire was designed to investigate the pragmatic uses of language. To quote Tomblin (1978), "in its most general sense pragmatics is concerned with the appropriate use of language in various communicative contexts." This questionnaire therefore examines some of the speech acts mentioned earlier in this chapter (Austin, 1962; Searle, 1969), in areas in which children might be expected to perform.

Developmental norms for this test are still in progress. In any case, local norms should always be developed for any test, especially where bicultural groups are present in the school system. For example, questions 6 and 11 may produce diametrically opposite results in Anglo versus American Indian or Puerto Rican populations. The pragmatics of the situation are quite highly dependent upon cultural factors. Local norms can be assembled easily by sending such a form home with every child at the beginning of the school year. The form should, of course, be in a language appropriate for the parents. The form could also be given by a bilingual aide when appropriate.

The results of the local norming procedure provide the comparative data against which each child can be examined. For instance, in question 1 you know that the first answer should be yes by the time a child is 2 and certainly by age 3. For 1(b) a 4-year-old may sometimes request things that a person cannot give, but by 6 to 8 years of age such requests should be rare, and so on. The child should developmentally pass through a series of stages where the child becomes progressively aware of the rules about communicative interactions with others. Children who have difficulty dur-

---

[9] Dr. Bruce Tomblin, Wendell Johnson Speech and Hearing Center, University of Iowa, Iowa City, Iowa 52242.

Table 3. A sample parent questionnaire on pragmatics

After carefully reading each question, check the answer that is most appropriate for your child. Many of the questions have several possible answers, so please consider each option carefully before checking the appropriate one. The information requested applies to your child's verbal interactions that have occurred within about the last 6 months. After completing the questionnaire, please return it as soon as possible. Thank you; your cooperation is appreciated.

1. Can your child ask you to *give* something or *do* something for the child?
   yes ___ no ___, if yes . . .
   (a) How often does your child ask you or other people for things compared to other children of the same age?
   much less often ___ as often as most other children ___ much more often ___
   (b) Does your child ask people for things that do not make sense, for example, something your child knows the person cannot give?
   hardly ever ___ sometimes ___ often ___
   (c) Who does your child direct questions to?
   one particular person ___ only people the child knows ___ whoever is present ___
   If only one particular person, who? (e.g., mother, father, sister, . . .)
   _____

2. Can your child understand direct requests or commands?
   yes ___ no ___, if yes . . .
   (a) How often does your child do what you ask?
   rarely ___ as often as most children ___ almost always ___
   (b) Whose requests does your child respond to?
   one particular person ___ only people he/she knows ___ whoever is around ___
   If only one particular person, who? (e.g., father, mother, brother, . . .)
   _____
   (c) What type of request does your child respond to?
   almost all requests ___ firm or repeated demands ___ fairly strong commands ___

3. Can your child verbally protest/complain?
   yes ___ no ___, if yes . . .
   (a) How often does your child protest/complain?
   hardly ever ___ as often as most children ___ more often than most children ___
   (b) Are your child's protests/complaints called for or justified?
   hardly ever ___ most of the time ___ always ___
   (c) To whom does your child protest/complain?
   one particular person ___ only people he/she knows ___ whoever is around ___
   If only one particular person, who? (e.g., mother, father, etc. . . . .)
   _____

4. Can your child say or act sorry?
   yes ___ no ___, if yes . . .

(continued)

(a) How often does your child say or act sorry?
hardly ever __ as often as most children __ more often than most children __
(b) When your child says he/she is sorry, is there usually a good reason? (i.e., how sincere are the apologies?)
hardly ever __ as often as most children __ always __
5. How often does your child use language to stand up for himself/herself (e.g., how often does your child defend himself/herself when being accused of doing something wrong)?
hardly ever __ as often as most children __ more often than most children __
6. Does your child interrupt conversations?
yes __ no __
(a) How often do such interruptions occur?
hardly ever __ as often as most children __ more often than most children __
(b) Who is interrupted? (you may check any or all)
mother __ father __ brothers or sisters __ peers __ company __
7. How often does your child ask you irrelevant questions where an answer is already known?
hardly ever __ as often as most children __ more often than most children __
8. Does your child frequently change the subject being discussed before a logical ending point has been reached?
hardly ever __ as often as most children __ more often than most children __
9. Does your child use gestures instead of speaking?
hardly ever __ as often as most children __ more than most children __
10. Does your child look at the listener when talking?
hardly ever __ as often as most children __ almost always __
11. Does your child look at the speaker who is talking to your child?
hardly ever __ most of the time __ almost always __
12. Can your child argue?
yes __ no __
(a) With whom does your child usually argue?
only one person but all of the time __ a few people but not often __ everyone but not often __ everyone all the time __
If only one person, who? (e.g., mother, father . . .) _____
13. Does your child take over conversations? (For example, does your child not let others have their turn when speaking?)
never __ sometimes __ almost always __
14. Is your child truthful?
yes __ no __ if yes . . .
(a) How often is your child truthful?
hardly ever __ sometimes __ almost always __
15. Does your child simplify his/her speech when talking to babies or very young children?
yes __ no __

(continued)

Table 3. *Continued*

16. Does your child thank people for doing things for him/her?
    yes ___ no ___ if yes . . .
    (a) How often does your child thank others?
        hardly ever ___ sometimes ___ almost always ___
17. Is your child bossy toward others, without considering their desires?
    hardly ever ___ sometimes ___ almost always ___
18. Can your child describe objects or events? (For example, can your child describe something that happened in school?)
    yes ___ no ___, if yes . . .
    (a) How often does your child describe things to you?
        hardly ever ___ sometimes ___ all the time ___
    (b) Are the descriptions successful?
        hardly ever ___ sometimes ___ almost always ___
    (c) Does your child seem to understand when you describe something?
        hardly ever ___ sometimes ___ almost always ___

---

ing interactions with others, particularly in their L_1 in the home setting, may have one or more other related problems. The results from the parent questionnaire can then be used to suggest which children need to be further examined by the teacher with the form shown in Table 1 and/or by the observer with the form in Table 4.

The last form (see Table 4) was initially developed by Joan Erickson and then revised for the purposes of this volume. It is a "pragmatic" instrument meant to reveal whether or not a child can function communicatively in more than one linguistic setting. At this point in any typical school's set of testing procedures the number of children upon whom data need be obtained should be minimal. Unlike the parent questionnaire, this observer form is meant to be used with just a few children; everyone cannot be observed!

As with the other forms, this sample form for observers is meant to be only an example and should be modified as needed. A Summary Section box might be included with such factors as 1) number of interactions, 2) number of children and/or adults involved, 3) number of initiated interactions, 4) number of responses made by others, and 5) number of utterances (which may be distinct from #3 because children sometimes talk without directing their speech toward a specific other). These categories were suggested by Walters (see Walters, Vega, and Crespo, 1978).

The simplest level of observational analysis could examine what conversational styles the child uses. A conversation is an exchange of information between two or more individuals. In order to carry on a conversation one has to make appropriate responses and recognize the rules of turn taking. Using a focal child technique, one might examine the following features:

1. Started a conversation.
2. Showed "listening" verbally or nonverbally.
3. Continued a conversation by answering, making a statement on the

Table 4. Sample speech act assessment for use by observers

Child's name: _____
Setting: _____
Others present: _____

In what follows the words provided in the speech act column are meant to elicit in the observer's mind a label that identifies a category for describing the child's speech. Sometimes more than one label, and/or examples in parentheses, are provided as an aid in further defining the speech act. The labels, or speech acts, are not listed in any particular order because various orderings are possible (e.g., alphabetical, functional, act–response). The final form used by the observer should be as simple as possible. The speech acts listed in the left-hand column might be checked off as they are observed and dates might be inserted in the right-hand column so that patterns of acquisition can be studied later.

Speech act   Date

1. Threatens/Warns ("I'm going to hit you.")
2. Requests
3. Questions
4. Agrees
5. Answers/Provides information
6. Commands/Directs ("Put that over there." "Give me that.")
7. Pleads
8. Bargains ("If you let me . . ., then I'll . . . .")
9. Greetings/Leavings
10. Suggests ("Let's play . . . .")
11. Politeness
12. Humor
13. Promises
14. Protests/Disagrees/Argues
15. Apologizes
16. Swears
17. Submits ("Uncle!")
18. Describes ("This car is fast.")
19. States ("I like to color things green.")
20. Other (*describe*)

same topic, or providing a verbal or nonverbal cue to the other to continue ("umm," nod of head, etc.).
4. Changed topic within a conversation.
5. Interrupted an ongoing conversation.
6. Produced an irrelevant comment that stopped a conversation or modified it drastically.
7. Appropriately ended a conversation.
8. Inappropriately ended a conversation (by leaving while the other was still talking, turning away, not responding, etc.).

As a guideline in assessing the above features, from hundreds of hours of preschool and grade school classroom observation in the United States and Switzerland about what might be expected, young children (2 to 4 years of age and possibly older if there are problems of different varieties) can be expected to exhibit items 5, 6, and 8, with some diminishing frequency as they get older. Items 1, 2, 3, 4, and 7 should increase, in that order, with increasing age. By first grade (6 years of age) a child should be able to produce item 3 when speaking to others in the same language. Cultural rules for conversations can be expected to differ so what the individual does has to be examined in terms of the culture. However, that the communication continues is the important point to observe.

Preschoolers frequently exhibit item 8, and hence this is not inappropriate behavior for them. Much of their conversation appears to be a simple "clueing-in" to the other of what the individual is thinking or doing. By 7 or 8 years of age such behaviors should be almost absent—the children can carry on a conversation and know the appropriate cultural rules. The occurrence of item 6 may take a bit longer to disappear because children's minds seem to be occupied with so many different thoughts that they want to express.

The purpose of this first, simplistic look at a child (particularly one engaging in a different language base from the observer) is to see if the child can in fact communicate with others in the child's own language. If communication can occur in a fashion appropriate to a child's age, then any other exceptionalities (e.g., mental retardation, speech handicaps, etc.) are contraindicated and the child should be perceived as normal even if the child has not yet learned the language used in school. What is obviously necessary in this set of observations is that the child be examined in situations where the child's "mother tongue" can be used.

The next, slightly more sophisticated set of focal child observations that might be examined are "feeling states" or "feeling styles." What might be observed here are both the child's behavioral expressions about the self and his or her expressions about and toward others. The reason for observing such factors can be twofold. First, observing such feeling states helps acquaint the observer with cultural nuances that may be different from those found in the observer's own cultural training. States which might be examined include:

1. Anger/hostility
2. Politeness/deference
3. Sympathy
4. Hurt/injured/depressed
5. Like/love
6. Dislike/hate
7. Happiness/joy
8. Curiosity/inquiry
9. Fear/distress
10. Surprise
11. Others (specify)

The second reason for observing these states is because they provide information about the observed child's well-being. The end purpose of any testing program is to provide a suitable program for the child, and part of the effectiveness of the program can be determined by the child's emotional behavior. Other factors can also be examined. For instance, a large part of a child's verbal and nonverbal behaviors will have emotional overtones. These are not always adequately captured by the speech acts listed in Table 4. The child's relationships with the peer group, as suggested earlier, may affect the kinds of data that can be obtained. If peers are to be jointly tested in a more clinical setting, then the above states might be recorded in matrix fashion to indicate which peers should be chosen. An example of such a form could be:

	Emotional states				
Peers	Anger	Politeness	Sympathy	Hurt	etc.
A					
B					
C					
D					
E					

Finally, speech acts can be recorded whenever and wherever they are produced. The purpose in recording speech acts is to see if the child can successfully communicate with others. For any child in a bilingual program, the sample speech acts assessment form (Table 4) might well be reproduced twice for each of the languages. The first language (home language or L_1) form represents how well established the child's capabilities are in L_1. The second form (English, L_2) can then become a measure of progress, as well as being an initial diagnostic instrument.

Speech acts, within L_1, follow some developmental sequence (Prutting, 1979, 1981). All of the speech acts indicated in Table 4 should be produced by L_1 learners in the 4- to 6-year range, and hence, for those children in strong command of an L_1 there should be no change over time. Given peer interaction factors, like dominance relationships (Omark, 1980b), some children may receive scores for items 1 and 6, but none for items 7, 8, and 10. The rest of the items would be expected to appear in one or more settings for a child dominant in L_1. If little more than items 9 (greetings) and 11 (politeness), and perhaps 3 (questions) and 4 (agrees), appear, it can be assumed that the child's dominant language is not L_1 (see Day, Chapter 9, this volume).

In contrast, items 3, 4, 9, and 11 are probably the first to appear during L_2 acquisition in the school-age child. The particular course of instruction in English as a Second Language (ESL) or other instructional techniques, the number of English-speaking peers, and so forth, will determine any actual order of acquisition. If dittoed sheets containing items like those in Table 4 were kept on a number of the potentially bilingual children, patterns of acquisition should soon become evident for any particular school program.[10] Testings of subsequent sets of children could then be examined in terms of this pattern to determine if the children are making suitable progress.

It should be stressed that most of the children coming to school have already acquired the cognitive and linguistic capabilities for producing these and hundreds of other speech acts. Given situations demanding communication (as in games played at recess with English-speaking peers), they will want to communicate their thoughts, ideas, desires, and so on. Their speech acts will be relatively simplistic at first (e.g., "Stop!" instead of "Stop bothering me!"; "Here" instead of "Throw the ball here"; "Paper?" instead of "Do you have a piece of paper I could borrow?").

The idea behind recording speech acts is to see if the child can communicate—can reveal the intentions desired—in a form that will cause an appropriate action or reaction in listeners. Sophistication comes with

---

[10] Starting at the beginning of the school year, dates could be entered after each item as the item was observed to be used spontaneously (e.g., during recess) by each child.

time, but if the potentials can be recognized then the child is striving to acquire appropriate communicative abilities. It is the child with broad gaps in the patterns who probably has problems and for whom appropriate educational programs need to be designed.

It was argued earlier that discrete point tests may fail to elicit particular features; all that the test can tell you is what the child can do, rather than what the child cannot do. An investigation of speech acts is designed to move the tester closer to the child's real world—to see what the child wants to do and is capable of doing. No a priori criteria are established for success or failure, but instead the observer can investigate the child's ongoing attempts to communicate. These attempts can then be compared with the capabilities of others from the child's own set of peers rather than with some set of hypothetical others who, in fact, bear little relationship to the child being observed.

CONCLUSION

Three different assessment forms, plus two other sets of possible observational material, have been described in this last section. This variety of material is meant to illustrate how the child can be viewed in different situations by different kinds of observers (teachers, parents, aides, etc.). Any of the forms can and should be modified to reflect the particular culture settings within which the child is being observed and tested. The child's capabilities relative to the child's group are probably the only realistic and fair measures that can be done. One has to be flexible when studying new and/or different populations, and all of these forms should be changed as seems locally appropriate.

Each of the forms has been designed with some particular task in mind by investigators working in particular settings. Feel free to modify them and design your own instrument. The earlier parts of this chapter discussed ways in which any observational instrument can be used in an unbiased fashion; these factors must be kept in mind. Any self-constructed instrument, with a bit of careful thought and careful local testing, should provide as much as or more useful information than any discrete point test.

REFERENCES

Altmann, S. A. 1967. The structure of primate social communication. In: S. A. Altmann (ed.), Social Communication among Primates. University of Chicago Press, Chicago.

Anderson, G., and Anderson, S. 1981. Issues in language assessment and exceptionalities in Native Americans. In: D. R. Omark and J. G. Erickson (eds.) The Bilingual Exceptional Child. Charles C Thomas, Springfield, Ill.
Austin, J. L. 1962. How to Do Things with Words. Harvard University Press, Cambridge, Mass.
Bates, E. 1976. Language and Context. Academic Press, New York.
Briere, E. 1972. Are we really measuring proficiency with our foreign language tests? In: B. Spolsky (ed.), The Language Education of Minority Children. Newbury House Publishers, Rowley, Mass.
Cole, M. 1975. An ethnographic psychology of cognition. In: R. W. Brislin, S. Lochner, and W. J. Lonner (eds.), Cross-cultural Perspectives on Learning. John Wiley & Sons, New York.
Draper, P. 1980. The interaction of behavior variables in the development of dominance relations. In: D. R. Omark, F. F. Strayer, and D. G. Freedman (eds.), Dominance Relations: An Ethological View of Human Conflict and Social Interaction. Garland Publishing, Inc., New York.
Ekman, P., and Friesen, W. 1975. Unmasking the Face. Prentice-Hall, Englewood Cliffs, N.J.
Ekman, P., and Friesen, W. 1978. The Facial Action Coding System. Consulting Psychology Press, Palo Alto, Cal.
Hall, E. T. 1969. The Hidden Dimension. Doubleday, Garden City, N.Y.
Hymes, D. 1974. Foundations in Sociolinguistics: An Ethnographic Approach. University of Pennsylvania Press, Philadelphia.
Labov, W. 1971. The study of language in its social context. In: J. A. Fishman (ed.), Advances in the Sociology of Language. Mouton Publishers, The Hague.
Labov, W. 1972. Language in the Inner City: Studies in the Black English Vernacular. University of Pennsylvania Press, Philadelphia.
Labov, W., Cohen, P., Robins, C., and Lewis, J. 1968. A study of nonstandard English of Negro and Puerto Rican speakers. Cooperative Research Project No. 3288.
Leonard, L. B., Prutting, C. A., Perrozi, J. A., and Berkley, R. K. 1978. Nonstandardized approaches to the assessment of language behaviors. ASHA, 20:371–379.
Linares, N. 1981. Communicative disorders. In: D. R. Omark and J. G. Erickson (eds.), The Bilingual Exceptional Child. Charles C Thomas, Springfield, Ill.
Morris, C. 1946. Signs, Language, and Behavior. Prentice-Hall, Englewood Cliffs, N.J.
Oller, J. W., Jr. 1972. Scoring methods and difficulty levels for Cloze tests of ESL proficiency. Mod. Lang. J. 56:151–158.
Oller, J. W., Jr. 1973. Discrete-point tests versus tests of integrative skills. In: J. W. Oller, Jr., and J. C. Richards (eds.), Focus on the Learner: Pragmatic Perspectives for the Language Teacher. Newbury House Publishers, Rowley, Mass.
Oller, J. W., Jr. 1981. Tests of bilingual children. In: D. R. Omark and J. G. Erickson (eds.), The Bilingual Exceptional Child. Charles C Thomas, Springfield, Ill.
Omark, D. R. 1980a. Human ethology: A holistic perspective. In: D. R. Omark, F. F. Strayer, and D. G. Freedman (eds.), Dominance Relations: An

Ethological View of Human Conflict and Social Interaction. Garland Publishing, Inc., New York.

Omark, D. R. 1980b. The Umwelt and cognitive development. In: D. R. Omark, F. F. Strayer, and D. G. Freedman (eds.), Dominance Relations: An Ethological View of Human Conflict and Social Interaction. Garland Publishing, Inc., New York.

Omark D. R. 1981. Genetically inferior or just different: Conceptualizations of the bilingual child. In: D. R. Omark and J. G. Erickson (eds.), The Bilingual Exceptional Child. Charles C Thomas, Springfield, Ill.

Omark, D. R., and Edelman, M. S. 1976. The development of attention structures in young children. In: M. R. A. Chance and R. R. Larsen (eds.), The Social Structure of Attention. John Wiley, & Sons, Inc. New York.

Omark, D. R., Fiedler, M., and Marvin, R. S. 1976. Dominance hierarchies: Observational techniques applied to the study of children at play. Instruct. Sci. 5:403–423.

Omark, D. R., Omark, M., and Edelman, M.S. 1975. Formation of dominance hierarchies in young children: Action and perception. In: T. Williams (ed.), Psychological Anthropology. Mouton Publishers, The Hague.

Parker, R., and Omark, D. R. 1980. The social ecology of toughness: In: D. R. Omark, F. F. Strayer, and D. G. Freedman (eds.), Dominance Relations: An Ethological View of Human Conflict and Social Interaction. Garland Publishing, Inc., New York.

Perrone, P. A., and Aleman, N. 1981. Educating the talented child in a pluralistic society. In: D. R. Omark and J. G. Erickson (eds.), The Bilingual Exceptional Child. Charles C Thomas, Springfield, Ill.

Prutting, C. A. 1979. Process: The action of moving forward progressively from one point to another on the way to completion. J. Speech Hear. Disord. 44:3–23.

Prutting, C. A. 1981. Assessing communication using a language sample. In: D. R. Omark and J. G. Erickson (eds.), The Bilingual Exceptional Child. Charles C Thomas, Springfield, Ill.

Searle, J. R. 1969. Speech Acts: An Essay in the Philosophy of Language. Cambridge University Press, Cambridge, Eng.

Shuy, R. 1977. Quantitative language data: A case for and some warnings against. Anthropol. Educ. Q. 8:73–82.

Smith, W. J. 1977. The Behavior of Communicating. Harvard University Press, Cambridge, Mass.

Spolsky, B. (ed.). 1972. The Language Education of Minority Children. Newbury House Publishers, Rowley, Mass.

Stewart, J. L. 1981. Communication disorders in the American Indian population. In: D. R. Omark and J. G. Erickson (eds.), The Bilingual Exceptional Child. Charles C Thomas, Springfield, Ill.

Strayer, F. F., 1980. Current problems in the study of human dominance. In: D. R. Omark, F. F. Strayer, and D. G. Freedman (eds.), Dominance Relations: An Ethological View of Human Conflict and Social Interaction. Garland Publishing, Inc., New York.

Tomblin, B. 1978. An outline of pragmatics. University of Iowa, Iowa City. (Mimeo.)

Toronto, A. S., Leverman, D., Hanna, C., Rosenweig, P. and Maldonado, A.

1975. Del Rio Language Screening Test (English/Spanish). National Educational Laboratories Publishers, Austin, Tex.

Toronto, A. S. 1981. Developing local normed assessment instruments. In: D. R. Omark and J. G. Erickson (eds.), The Bilingual Exceptional Child. Charles C Thomas, Springfield, Ill.

Tymitz, B. 1981. Evaluation of programs for bilingual exceptional children. In: D. R. Omark and J. G. Erickson (eds.), The Bilingual Exceptional Child. Charles C Thomas, Springfield, Ill.

Walters, J. 1979a. The perception of politeness in English and Spanish. Paper presented at TESOL Convention, Boston, Mass.

Walters, J. 1979b. Language variation in the assessment of the communicative competence of bilingual children: Evidence for the linguistic interdependence hypothesis. Paper presented at AERA, San Francisco.

Walters, J. In preparation. A speech acts approach to second language research. In: H. Trueba and G. Arakapadavil (eds.), Bilingual Education: A Search for Theoretical Foundations. Newbury House Publishers, Rowley, Mass.

Walters, J., Vega, C., and Crespo, O. 1978. Designs and guidelines for the evaluation of state bilingual problems. Illinois Office of Education, Chicago.

Washburn, S. L., and Hamburg, D. A. 1965. The implications of primate research. In: I. DeVore (ed.), Primate Behavior: Field Studies of Monkeys and Apes. Holt, Rinehart and Winston, New York.

Weisfeld, G. E., Omark, D. R., and Cronin, C. L. 1980. A longitudinal and cross-sectional study of dominance in boys. In: D. R. Omark, F. F. Strayer, and D. G. Freedman (eds.), Dominance Relations: An Ethological View of Human Conflict and Social Interaction. Garland Publishing, Inc., New York.

Wolfram, W., and Fasold, R. W. 1974. The Study of Social Dialects in American English. Prentice-Hall, Englewood Cliffs, N.J.

appendix A

Suggestions for Interviewing Children

Joan Good Erickson

Verbal interactions with children are sometimes difficult for adults who have had limited experience in this area. The following discussion provides general information and specific suggestions for interviewing children for the purpose of obtaining a communication sample.

When obtaining an expressive language/communication sample on a child, it is important to have an informal atmosphere. This informality is necessary even when conducting specific probes into a child's language structure (comprehension and production) or language function. Child interviewing, like indirect teaching, should be "characterized by interactions in which the environment and the encounters allow for latitude in the child's responses and interpretation of concepts" (Tymitz, 1977, p. 9).

There are several constraints inherent in an interview situation which may limit the child's verbal output. The interviewer should be aware that a child's interactions with adults, let alone strangers, will be less free than those with peers or persons familiar to the child. Differences in language use and complexity will also occur (Cazden, 1972a). Both first and second language learners show different discourse behaviors in child-child versus adult-child interactions (Ervin-Tripp and Mitchell-Hernan, 1976; Hatch, 1978). One reason for the differences is the adult's tendency to play a role of questioner which imposes restraints on conversational potentials. Another reason relates to perceived status and language level differences between the speakers. Awareness of these problems/limitations should help an interviewer modify his or her behavior and maximize the potential of obtaining information from a verbal interaction with a child.

The establishment of rapport is paramount for obtaining a language sample that represents a child's optimal output. The relationship of rapport to test results is especially important when the child is from a minority ethnic or lower socioeconomic status group. Cazden (1972a) presents a report on research conducted by Palmer who tested the mental ability of middle and lower class black children from Harlem. Testing was delayed, up to as many as seven sessions, until rapport was established. Results indicated few significant differences in the mental ability between the two socioeconomic groups. Extensive work done by Labov also indicates the negative effects of the test situation on obtaining language samples from minority children. Further information on sampling and analyzing the spontaneous speech of children is provided by Cazden (1972a, 1972b).

In order to maximize the potential for establishing rapport with a child, an interviewer must be aware of his or her perceptions of conversational roles and attitudes toward children. A "clinical interview" with a child should be couched in three basic premises. First, it is important to view the child as a person who has something worthwhile to say and the potential for sharing it with an interested listener. Second, the child deserves the same conversational rights as an adult—not answering, answering with incomplete utterances or ellipses, directing the conversation, interrupting, and so forth. The final premise is that if the interview is not going well, it is the interviewer's and not the child's responsibility. It may be that the interviewer is talking *at* rather than *with* the child or that he or she is interrogating rather than conversing. One of the basic problems may be that the interviewer does not present verbal and nonverbal behavior that indicates listening, including interest in what the child says, which circularly brings us to the first point.

Information on obtaining expressive language samples has been suggested by Lee (1974) and Hubbell (1977). Interviewing principles with regard to children and adolescents are presented by Finch (1968). A clinical interview can also be used for probing specific linguistic skills. Walters (Chapter 11, this volume) presents activities with puppets that can be used for evaluating a child's ability to perform various speech acts. Informal activities with toys or pictures can be used to explore a child's understanding of various morphological markers and syntactic structures (Bellugi-Klima, 1969; Leach, 1972). Suggestions for and problems to avoid in obtaining a communication sample through a clinical interview are presented below.

USEFUL SUGGESTIONS

1. Before interviewing the child, ask the teacher or parent about areas of conversation that might stimulate the child and be related to his or her personal orientation (e.g., a pet, toys, a favorite television

show, cultural holidays, his or her birthday, vacation). Use these as starters or work around to them.
2. Use materials suitable to the age or level of functioning of the child. For example, for preschoolers, actual toys usually produce more speech than pictures of toys. Toys that have moving parts, as well as at least one broken toy, are good stimulus materials. In general, books, toys, and brightly colored pictures are especially useful for kindergarten and elementary school children.
3. Consider the physical characteristics of the situation. It should lend itself to a naturalistic interaction rather than a structured situation such as two interactors seated formally at a table.
4. Present the child with a few items and allow for freedom of selection. When the child has made a choice, watch what he or she does with it and use the activity as a basis for conversation. If the child does not talk, make general statements such as "I wonder what's happening," "What does it make you think of?", "I'm interested in your story about the picture." Avoid questions such as "Do you want to (or can you) tell me about that picture?" for which the child has the right to answer "No."
5. If statements or questions produce no response to stimulus items, demonstrate what you require of the child. For example, take a toy yourself and play with it, telling about what you are doing and personalize your account using an imaginary situation. Engage the child in the game as soon as possible and begin to prompt indirectly (e.g., make your car crash into the child's car and ask what happens next).
6. When the child choses a picture and does not respond to questions, demonstrate how to talk about a picture (e.g., "This is a bad rabbit who ran away from home. He forgot to take any clothes or food with him. Luckily these two children found him and looked after him. Here's another picture. You tell me about this one"). If you have any indication of the child's language comprehension, suit your input to a level that you are confident he or she can follow, keeping in mind that if it is too simplistic you will be providing a model of what you expect from the child.
7. If you show a series of pictures depicting a sequence and then require the child to tell you the story, remove the pictures while he or she tells the story, since this will reflect a more integrated account from the child's viewpoint.
8. Vary the situation. Try to obtain a sample with the child playing a

game such as keeping house, then building something, then playing with toys, etc. Interview indoors and outdoors and at the child's home when possible.
9. Vary the listener/interaction. It might be helpful to interview two children at the same time and encourage peer interaction. Observe the child with a parent or sibling and, if possible, obtain a sample from home while the child is engaged in some activity with a family member during the daily routine.
10. Record what you say (or other interviewers say) as well as what the child says in order to evaluate the utterances as related to another speaker. With these data one can gain insight into the child's comprehension as well as conversational skills.
11. Combine tape-recording an interview with writing down the child's utterances as accurately as possible. In some instances it also may be helpful to echo the child so there are no questions later when transcribing from the tape. Keeping verbal (on tape) or written notes as to items or situations that stimulated the child's utterances will also be helpful.

PROBLEMS TO AVOID

1. Avoid asking very specific questions that elicit yes/no answers or questions typically resulting in one word responses (e.g., "What's that?" ("A horse"); "What is it doing?" ("Running"); "What do you see?" ("A fork"); "Do you have one of those?" ("Yes/No")).
2. Avoid asking the child to tell a very familiar story that is known by heart or involves a lot of repetition of sentences (e.g., *Goldilocks and the Three Bears*).
3. Be aware of the limitations of your stimulus materials as far as vocabulary and syntax are concerned. For example, a doll house limits the child to furniture vocabulary, and action pictures limit the child to the present progressive tense.
4. Modify your statements so they do not lock the response set. For example, asking "What is he doing" will probably elicit gerund form responses; questioning may only give you samples of declaratives and not allow the child to demonstrate the use of interrogatives; conversation related to materials present may never allow an opportunity for the child to generate past tense markers; talking about single items limits the potential use of plural markers.
5. Realize that reinforcement techniques could condition the child to produce stereotypic and repetitious responses.

6. Do not present only boy-like or girl-like toys or pictures, but allow for choice in that children will vary in their interest and background of experience.
7. Do not be concerned by silences to the point of filling in the gaps with your own verbal output. The focus is on obtaining a language sample of the child rather than of the interviewer.

In general, a well conducted clinical interview can reveal a great deal of information about the child's language form and function. If you wish to evaluate your own interviewing skills, you can do so by analyzing the same corpus according to the quantity and quality of your language usage and the potential effect it had on the child's conversation.

REFERENCES

Bellugi-Klima, U, 1969. Some language comprehension tests. In: C. S. Lavatelli (ed.), Language Training in Early Childhood Education. University of Illinois Press, Urbana.

Cazden, C. B., 1972a. Child Language and Education. Holt, Rinehart and Winston, Inc., New York.

Cazden, C. B., (ed.) 1972b. Language in Early Childhood Education. National Association for the Education of Young Children, Washington, D.C.

Ervin-Tripp, S., and Mitchell-Kernen, C. (eds.). 1976. Child Discourse. Academic Press, New York.

Finch, J. 1968. Interviewing Children and Adolescents. Macmillan, New York.

Hatch, E. 1978, Discourse analysis, speech acts, and language acquisition. In: W. C. Ritchie (ed.), Second Language Acquisition Research: Issues and Implications. Academic Press, New York.

Hubbell, R. D. 1977. On facilitating spontaneous talking in young children. J. Speech Hear. Disord. 42:216–231.

Leach, E. 1972. Interrogation: A model and some implications. J. Speech Hear. Disord. 37:33–46.

Lee, L. 1974. Developmental Sentence Analysis. Northwestern University Press, Evanston, Ill.

Tymitz, B. S. 1977. The relationship of differentiated teacher/learner interactions on teacher's frame of reference in understanding children's cognitions and behaviors. Unpublished doctoral dissertation, University of Illinois, Urbana.

appendix B

Rules for Calculating Mean Length of Utterance in Morphemes for Spanish

Nicolás Linares

The rules for calculating the mean length of utterance (MLU) for Spanish-speaking children were devised for use in a dissertation study (Linares, 1975) pertaining to the language of preschool Spanish-speaking children. An edited version is reprinted here with the author's permission. Once a language corpus is obtained for a child (see Erickson, Appendix A), the following procedure can be used to compute the MLU.

GENERAL PROCEDURES

1. Transcribe the recording of the child's sample of utterances. Number or mark each utterance for later ease in separating them. Mark echolalic utterances with an "e," keeping in mind that semi-echolalic utterances (those that have some changes) are considered spontaneous.
2. Start the corpus selection by eliminating the first 15 spontaneous (nonecholalic) utterances.
3. Select and count the next 100 utterances that are consecutive, intelligible, and spontaneous. Include repeated utterances.
4. Count the morphemes in each utterance following these guidelines:
   a. Count how many free morphemes appear in the utterance whether correctly inflected or not.
   b. Count interrogative words as one morpheme, giving credit for the question morpheme, except when they are inflected in which case add another point for the inflection.
   c. Consider the contractions *del* (*de el*), *della* (*de ella*) as having two roots and thus count as two morphemes.
   d. Do not count fillers like *ah, eh, porque si, porque no, ajá*.
   e. Count compound words, proper names and ritualized reduplications as single words (for example *Juan Pérez, cumpleaños, subibaja*).

. Do not count memorized dialogues, songs, or stereotypic responses.
  g. Determine how many bound morphemes (inflections) appear in the utterance. According to the rules suggested below, count only correct inflections and if the child gives evidence of knowing the alternative inflections for the particular root.
5. Add the free morphemes and the bound morphemes in *each* of the utterances.
6. Add the morphemes in *all* of the 100 utterances.
7. Divide the total number of morphemes in the 100 utterances by 100.
8. The quotient is the MLU value for the child.

RULES FOR COUNTING BOUND MORPHEMES

1. Nouns
   a. Gender: Count as one morpheme the generic ending *-a* (feminine) or *-o* (masculine) only when the root can have different generic endings. For example, the noun *gat-o* (cat + masculine + singular) counts as two morphemes (one for the root *gat* and one for the masculine inflection *-o*); however, the noun *luz* (light + no gender + singular) counts as one morpheme because it has no gender and thus nouns like *luz-a* do not appear in Spanish.
   b. Number: Count as one morpheme the plural ending *-s* (for singular ending in vowel) or *-es* (for singular ending in consonant). Singulars are not given points because the child is not adding morphemes to them. For example, the noun *gat-a-s* (cat + feminine + plural) counts as three morphemes (one for the root *gat*, one for the feminine inflection *-a*, and one for the plural inflection *-s*); and the noun *flor-es* (flower + no gender + plural) counts as two morphemes (one for the root *flor* and one for the plural inflection *-es*).
   c. Diminutives: Count as one morpheme the diminutive endings *-it-* and *-cit-* as in *carr-it-o* or *pece-cit-o*.
   d. Augmentatives: Count as one morpheme the augmentative ending *-ot-* as in *cas-ot-a*.
2. Adjectives
   a. Gender: Count as one morpheme the generic ending *-a* (feminine) or *-o* (masculine) only when the root can have different generic endings. For example, the adjectives *alt-o* (tall + masculine + singular) counts as two morphemes (one for the

root *alt* and one for the masculine inflection -*o*); however, the adjective *grand-e* (big + no gender + singular) counts as one morpheme because it has no gender, and thus adjectives like *grand-a* do not appear in Spanish.

    b. Number: Count as one morpheme the plural ending -*s* or -*es*. Singulars do not count because the child is not adding morphemes to them. For example, the adjective *alt-o-s* (tall + masculine + plural) counts as three morphemes (one for the root *alt*, one for the masculine inflection -*o*, and one for plural inflection -*s*); The adjective *azul-es* (blue + no gender + plural) counts as two morphemes (one for the root *azul* and one for the plural inflection -*es*).

    c. Superlatives: Count as one morpheme the superlative ending -*isim*- or -*im*- For example, the adjective *car-íisim-o* (very expensive + superlative + masculine + singular) counts as three morphemes (one for the root *car*, one for the superlative inflection -*isim*-, and one for the masculine inflection -*o*); and the adjective *paupérr-im-o* (very poor + superlative + masculine + singular) counts as three morphemes (one for the root *pauperr*, one for the superlative inflection -*im*-, and one for the masculine inflection -*o*).

    d. Diminutives: Count as one morpheme the diminutive endings -*it*- and -*cit*- as in *chiqu-it-o* or *precio-cit-o*.

    e. Augmentatives: Count as one morpheme the augmentative ending -*ot*- as in *grand-ot-a*.

3. Adverbs

Count as one morpheme the adverbial ending -*mente*. For example, the adverb *fácil-mente* (easi-ly) counts as two morphemes (one for the root *fácil* and one for the adverbial inflection -*mente*).

4. Pronouns

    a. Gender: Count as one morpheme the generic ending -*a* (feminine), -*o* (masculine), or -*o* (neuter) only when the root can have different generic endings. For example, the pronoun *mí-o* (mine + a masculine possessed object + singular) counts as two morphemes (one for the root *mi* and one for the masculine inflection -*o*); however, the pronoun *se* (a form of the copula + no gender + no number) counts as one morpheme (for the copula *se*).

    b. Number: Count as one morpheme the plural ending -*s* or -*es* only when the root can have singular number. Singulars do not count because the child is not adding morphemes to them. For

example, the pronoun *nosotr-o-s* (we + masculine + plural + no singular number) counts as two morphemes (one for the root *nosotr* and one for the masculine inflection *-o*); and the pronoun *usted-es* (you + no gender + plural) counts as two morphemes (one for the root *usted* and one for the plural inflection *-es*).
   c. Prepositional case: Count as one morpheme the prepositional ending *-sigo*, *-migo*, or *-tigo* when added to the root *con*. For example, the pronoun *con-tigo* counts as two morphemes (one for the root *con* and one for the prepositional case inflection *-tigo*).
5. Articles
   a. Gender: Count as one morpheme the generic ending *-a* (feminine), *-e* (masculine), and *-o* (neuter) only when the root can have different generic endings. For example, the article *l-a* (the + feminine + singular) counts as two morphemes (one for the root *l* and one for the feminine inflection *-a*); however, the article *el* (the + masculine + singular) counts as one morpheme (for the root *el*) because the root *el* cannot be inflected to any other gender.
   b. Number: Count as one morpheme the plural ending *-s*. Singulars do not count because the child is not adding morphemes in them. For example, the article *l-o-s* (the + masculine + plural) counts as three morphemes (one for the root *l*, one for the masculine inflection *-o*, and one for the plural inflection *-s*).
6. Prepositions, Interjections, and Conjunctions
   Count as one morpheme because they are not inflected in the Spanish language.
7. Verbs
   Verbs in Spanish can take combined inflections related to the mood, tense, number, and person. To devise a system for counting all the different inflections present in verbs uttered by a child would seem like an extremely laborious task. An unusual intuition for the Spanish language and a great amount of time would be required from the examiner doing the MLU calculation to accomplish a thorough job. Few persons possess those two qualifications. Because of these facts, the writer recommends that, in general, decisions be based on your intuitions about Spanish, although specific examples are given below. When scoring a Spanish verb, first decide whether or not it is conjugated in the particular utterance; then examine whether the verb is correctly conjugated in *all* inflectional aspects in the particular utterance. Determine if the verb is or is not an infini-

tive (inflected with -*ar* or -*er*), a participial (inflected with -*do*), or a gerund (inflected with -*ndo*). In addition, consider whether the verb (root) can take various different inflections (suffixes). Then apply the following scoring system:

a. When the verb is correctly used in *all* inflectional aspects, is not an infinitive, participial, or gerund, and the root *can* take various inflections, count it as having five morphemes (one for the root, one for the number inflection, one for the person inflection, one for the tense inflection, and one for the mood inflection).

b. When the verb is not conjugated, count it as having one morpheme (for the root).

c. If the root cannot take various inflections, count it as having one morpheme (for the root).

d. When the verb is correctly used in only *some* of the inflectional aspects, count it as having 2.5 morphemes (one for the root and 1.5 for whatever other inflections might be correct).

e. If the verb has an ending like -*ar*, -*er* (infinitive), -*do* (participial), or -*ndo* (gerund), count it as having two morphemes (one for the root and one for any of these inflections).

These rules for counting morphemes can be expatiated as the user becomes familiar with the system. Of primary importance is that the corpus be representative of the child's language ability and that the scoring system be consistently applied.

REFERENCE

Linares-Orama, N. 1975. The language evaluation of pre-school Spanish-speaking Puerto Rican children. Unpublished doctoral dissertation, University of Illinois, Urbana.

appendix C

An Annotated Bibliography on the Communication Assessment of the Bilingual Child

Kathryn Kutz Scott

The Bilingual Act of 1974 requires that the educational needs of children who speak primarily a language other than English be met. PL 94-142 (Education for All Handicapped Children Act), which requires that school districts provide appropriate education for handicapped children ages 3 to 21, further highlights the importance of nondiscriminatory testing. For bilingual educators, school psychologists, speech-language pathologists, and others involved in the evaluations of these children, these two pieces of legislation provide a great challenge. Ordinary testing is difficult enough, but testing of the bilingual child adds new problems; for example, to be valid each test must be nonbiased and nondiscriminatory. Given that most tests on the market were originally developed for white English-speaking middle-class children, new tests and procedures must be developed that take into consideration the bilingual child's linguistic and cultural heritage. In the American school system, various bilingual and/or bicultural combinations exist: Spanish/Standard English (SE), Japanese/SE, Chinese/SE, and so on. Adequate bilingual communication assessment must include all of these combinations and other less common languages.

The purpose of these 140 annotated references is to provide a guide to relevant research in the area of bilingual communication assessment of the preschool through high school child. The majority of the references are journal articles written within the past 10 years or documents easily obtained through the Educational Resources Instruction Center (ERIC) by writing to: ERIC Document Reproduction Service, Computer Microfilm International, P. O. Box 190, Arlington, Virginia 22210. Only four books have been cited as references. The reader will find in Cazden's book a thorough introduction to the subject of child language and educational needs. Jakobovits' book takes a look at variables affecting second language acquisition from a psycholinguistic perspective. Oakland's book on the assessment of minority children provides a practical approach to developing diagnostic-intervention strategies for minority children as well as a discussion of several tests and test development considerations. Tobier's book, a collection of writings on the instruction of bilingual children is an informative resource book for beginning teachers in bilingual education. The majority of the references deal specifically with the assessment of language skills. Other areas covered include the determination of language dominance and culture-free test development.

The bibliography was compiled both through a manual search of recent journals and through several computer searchers. Three data banks were tapped: the Educational Resources Instruction Center (ERIC), Language Abstracts (LABS), and Human Resources Abstracts (HRA). The ERIC abstracts are in public domain; however, the other two are covered by copyright laws, and permission to use the abstracts here is gratefully acknowledged. After each reference in the bibliography a source note is given which indicates the author or editor, the initials of the data bank's abstractor, and the data bank. An example follows: Erickson/XX-ERIC Summary. On the other hand, if the summary statement was written by the compiler of this appendix, her initials are used—KKS.

This appendix should provide interesting reading material to those professionals who are pursuing greater knowledge of the communication assessment of the bilingual child.

Anastasi, A. 1968. Culture fair testing. In: N. E. Gronland (ed.), Readings in Measurement and Evaluation. Ch. 31, pp. 280–286. Macmillan, New York.

The rationale behind culture-fair testing is to use the commonalities displayed by different cultures while eliminating those parameters that differ between cultures, e.g., language, literacy levels, and culturally loaded content. The degree of cultural fairness depends upon how well these parameters can be controlled. There will be differences in the design, content, and factors measured between the various culture-fair tests. Questions are raised about the extent to which cultural differentials should be eliminated and the effect such elimination may have upon the tests' validity in certain situations. (KKS Summary)

Bain, B. 1975. Toward an integration of Piaget and Vygotsky: Bilingual considerations. Linguistics 160:5-20.

The unprejudiced study of human development reveals the urgent need for a more integrated understanding of that phenomenon. On the one hand, in the works of Jean Piaget we have a detailed and concise map of the biologically rooted process of maturation in its evolution toward epistemic competence. On the other hand, in the works of Lev Vygotsky, we have a penetrating analysis of how specific cultural-historical conditions give unique direction and meaning to that evolution. Theoretical integration of these two works in spirit or in kind would provide a more balanced view of the developing child, one more in keeping with empirical and phenomenological evidences. The purpose of this paper is to offer a small insight into a possible direction which such a theoretical integration might take by presenting two studies on the course of development when children are raised and schooled in a bilingual manner. Bilingual and unilingual Canadian children were tested in problem-solving tests and on portrait sensitivity tests. Evidence was obtained which suggested heavy correlation between the language education matrix the child grows up in and the developments of his epistemic competences. (HA-LABS Summary)

Balinksy, W. L., and Peng, S. S. 1974. An evaluation of bilingual education for Spanish-speaking children. Urban Educ. 9(3):271-278.

This study investigated the cognitive achievement of 32 first-grade and 22 second-grade children who were enrolled in bilingual education programs. Results indicated that the children were benefiting from the placement, particularly in mathematics which required the least amount of English skills. It is also suggested that the use of standardized tests in English is an inappropriate approach to classifying the students. The authors conclude that bilingual education has a postive influence on children's achievement. (KKS Summary)

Barabas, J. 1973. The Assessment of Minority Groups: An Annotated Bibliography. (ERIC Document Reproduction Service No. ED 083 325)

The materials cited here represent information on such diverse but interrelated areas as: methods of assessing achievement, intelligence, personality factors, and attitudes; effects of testing of self-concept and employment opportunities; prediction of academic success; reliability and validity of specific tests; criticisms of the methods and use of assessment for educational placement and diagnosis; culture free and culture fair tests; performance differences on tests between majority and minority groups. (ERIC Summary)

Baratz, J. 1969. A bidialectal task for determining language proficiency in disadvantaged children. Child Dev. 40(3–4):889–901.

Lower-middle class and black children, both classified as 'disadvantaged', were given a repetition task test involving standard and non-standard English sentences. The results indicated that the white children performed better on standard English sentences and black children on nonstandard English sentences. The interaction of age and grammatical features was also significant for both groups. The results clearly indicate that there are two dialects involved in the education of black children, that black children are, generally, not bidialectal, and that there is ample evidence of interference from their black dialect when they use standard English. The author concludes that language assessment of disadvantaged black children must involve measures of their knowledge of standard English. (Author Summary) (Reprinted by permission; copyright © 1969 by the Society for Research in Child Development, Inc.)

Bass, B. M. 1975. Oral English Language Assessment of First Grade Children in Bilingual Bicultural Education: Emphasis on Phonology and Syntax. (University of Florida Microfilms No. 77-51)

The purpose of this study was to develop a reliable instrument that could be used by teachers and staff in Colorado to assist in the assessment of oral English language, particularly the syntax and the phonology of first-grade children in bilingual bicultural education (BBE). The study also related the scores of the instrument to seven variables; intelligence, age, language spoken in the home, ethnicity, number of siblings, kindergarten attendance, and sex. Subjects were 78 first graders in BBE programs in Colorado during the 1974–1975 school year. Children were tested using the Bass Sentence Repetition Task (BSRT) and the Peabody Picture Vocabulary Test (PPVT). Correlation analysis showed that intelligence, language spoken in the home, and ethnicity were correlated to the BSRT pronunciation score at the .01 level, and the variables of intelligence and home language were significant at the .05 level to the BSRT structure score, with the sex variable at the .01 level. Multiple regression analysis showed intelligence, measured by the PPVT, to be contributing factor to the measure of English pronunciation and oral structure, as measured by the BSRT. The number of siblings is considered a contributing factor in the prediction of oral English structure. (Author/JM–ERIC Summary)

Ben-Zeev, S. 1976. The influence of bilingualism on cognitive development and cognitive strategy. Papers Reports Child Lang. Dev. 12:39–46.

Language is learned through adjustment to cognitive conflict by mechanisms similar to those used in general cognitive development. An intense degree of cognitive conflict will result in a greater understanding of language by the child. Bilingualism involves an intense degree of cognitive conflict. The two studies in this paper test the hypothesis that language acquisition is enhanced by cognitive conflict. Two groups of Hebrew-English bilingual children were chosen from metropolitan areas in the U.S. and Israel. Comparison monolingual groups were tested in Israel (Hebrew) and the U.S. (English). The 98 Ss, ranging in age from 5:5 to 8:5, were from highly educated families. The Ss were tested individually and orally. Results from the Symbol Substitution Test (SST) (bilinguals performed at a significantly superior level) and the Morphological Generalization Test indicate that bilinguals have a highly analytical grasp of syntax. This supports the contention that bilinguals have a highly developed sense of system understanding. Other tests used in this study were the Matrix Transportation and the Ravens' Matrices. In Study II, the hypothesis in Study I was tested to see if it would apply to a different combination of languages from much lower economic and educational level families. Spanish and English were the test languages. One hundred eighty-eight Ss were chosen from the inner city of Chicago. Age range was the same as in Study I and the Ss were again tested orally and individually. Both bilingual and monolingual groups in this study had extreme vocabulary deficits and basic grammatical deficiencies. While the total scores of the two groups on the SSI were the same, the bilinguals made fewer errors of a primitive, global type. (JA–LABS Summary)

Berry-Luterman, L., and Bar, A. 1971. The diagnostic significance of sentence repetition for language impairment. J. Speech Hear. Disord. 36:29–39

The procedure of sentence repetition, described in this study, would seem to provide a valuable, simple tool to assess the linguistic performance of a language-impaired subject. It enables the performance of each individual subject to be compared with his own previous production. It provides a means for observing and analyzing any shift in production under the other two conditions which the subject may make. As such, the procedure enables the interviewer to examine and assess the grammatical performance and to infer or hypothesize about each subject's linguistic competence. Further recommendations might involve the comparison of children who are culturally disadvantaged with those diagnosed as language-impaired. A possible difference might be the former's ability to shift production when a correct model is presented for repetition. Another implication might involve the possible correlation of a subject's ability to produce structures in the sentence repetition task with test scores on various standardized language tests. (Author Summary)

Bickson, T. K. 1974. Minority Speech as Objectively Measured and Subjectively Evaluated. (ERIC Document Reproduction Service No. ED 131 135)

Spontaneous speech performance of ethnically diverse children was investigated by linguistic measures and teacher evaluations. Interview data was collected from 144 elementary school children, comprising equal white, Chicano, and black subsamples evenly divided among lower and higher grades. Speech evaluators were 60 white teachers. Analyses focused on whether minority children were, or were perceived as, linguistically deficient compared with white age mates. Measures indicate that minority speech performance equalled or excelled white performance, but teachers heard it as significantly inferior. Two points are noted: (1) Teachers did not hear Chicano-black speech differences which appeared in the objective measures, sugesting that their inability to discriminate properties of unfamiliar speech styles partially accounts for differences between objective and subjective outcomes. (2) The very regular patterning of minority evaluation and the reversal of age trends from objective to subjective measures, suggest that ethnic stereotyping was also at work in the results. The extent to which teacher unresponsiveness to minority ability in the younger grades is related to absence of objective performance gains in the older grades is not assessed here. However, it is held that there are many links between speech performance style and school success. (Author/AM-ERIC Summary)

Bouton, L. F. 1975. Meeting the needs of children with diverse linguistic and ethnic backgrounds. Foreign Lang. Ann. 8(4):306-316.

Meeting the needs of the multilingual student population at King Elementary School posed a challenge. An English as a Second Language (ESL) program met only some of those needs; to meet others, the school adapted the goals and principles of bilingual education. While English was the basic language of the school, non-English speakers were given language arts, tutoring in other subject areas in their native language, and ESL instruction. At the same time, native

English speakers studied a 2nd language. Intercultural education was also emphasized, with the focus on the cultural background of the children and their teachers. Evaluation of the program showed that these students did as well on standardized tests as children from the entire school district, that they were more willing to accept children speaking a different language, and that their parents felt the program was successful. As a result, King School was opened to any child in the district for whom there was room. (HA-LABS Summary)

Boyd, P. 1975. The development of grammar categories in Spanish by Anglo children learning a second language. TESOL Q. 9(2):125-135.

The purpose of this study was to investigate the hypothesis that 2nd language learning in children is similar to 1st language learning. The subjects were 12 Anglo 2nd graders in the Spanish Immersion Program in Culver City, CA. Two Spanish morphology tests, the Bilingual Syntax Measure, an oral storytelling measure, a repetition task, and a reflexive elicitation task were used to elicit speech. Spontaneous speech was also recorded, and 5 hours of teacher language were taped in the classroom. A detailed error analysis was performed on the elicited natural speech data. Results indicated that subject-verb number and person agreement, adjective-noun gender and article-noun gender were tenacious morphological problems. Object pronoun omission (40%) and misuse (20%), and the expression of tense (18%) were other problem areas. The low frequency of object pronouns (4%) and tenses other than present in the teacher input data was suggested as a reason for the children's problems in these areas. Overall, the study found similarities between 1st and 2nd language development data, but the differences in order of acquisition of structures tended to disconfirm a strong version of the $L_1 = L_2$ hypothesis, which would claim that the acquisition order and learning strategies shown in 2nd language acquisition would be identical to those shown in 1st language acquisition. (HA-LABS Summary)

Breland, H. M., and others. 1973. Cross-cultural Stability of Test Items: An Investigaton of Response Patterns for Ten Socio-cultural Groups with Exploration of an Index of Cross-cultural Stability. Final Report. (ERIC Document Reproduction Service No. ED 115 682).

Over 14,000 high school seniors were studied with respect to sociocultural differences on cognitive test item responses. Six different cognitive tests and ten different groups were analyzed. The tests were: vocabulary, picture-number, reading, letter groups, mathematics, and mosaic comparisons. The groups were: American Indians, Blacks, Mexican Americans, white Northeastern, white North Central, white Southern, white Western (ERIC Summary)

Briere, E. J. 1963. Phonological testing reconsidered. Lang. Learn. 17(3-4): 163-171.

This paper was a report on an experimental investigation of various methods of testing perception and production in phonology. From the standpoint of perception, it was found that an AX paradigm probably measures the subject's bias for responding "same" or "different" rather than test a particular phonological category. On the ABX paradigm (or the XAB) as would be expected, it was found that it is easier to make correct responses when the "X" is like the immediately adjacent sound, regardless of the phonological category being tested. It was suggested that the ABX paradigm may measure short-term memory and not ability to perceive or produce a given phonological category. The prediction of difficulties made on the basis of a theoretical contrastive analysis of Spanish and English was found to be considerably less than 100% accurate. The problem of accurate judging of responses made on production tests was also investigated. It was found that untrained judges on a short task have a higher degree of correlation of judgments than do trained judges on longer tasks. It was suggested that these confounded variables (training and length of task) should be further investigated experimentally. (Author Summary)

Brière, E. J. 1972. Are we really measuring proficiency with our foreign language tests? In: B. Spolsky (ed.), The Language Education of Minority Children. Ch. 14, pp. 182-192. Newbury House Publishers, Rowley, Mass.

If we hope to be able to give minority children or anyone else good language education, we need to have valid and reliable methods of measuring language proficiency. To decide whether someone needs instruction in a language or how successful a particular program has been, we need to be able to test how competent a child is in one or more languages. There are numbers of tests that claim or are believed to do just this. In this article, Eugene Briere points out the theoretical and practical weaknesses of the tests that are currently available. (Editor Summary)

Briere, E. J. 1973. Cross-cultural biases in language testing. In: J. W. Oller, Jr., and J. C. Richards (eds.), Focus on the Learner: Pragmatic Perspectives for the Language Teacher. pp. 214-230. Newbury House Publishers, Rowley, Mass.

Briere takes up some of the linguistic and sociocultural aspects of tests in general. His discussion carries us well beyond the testing of context-level coding operations in a second language situation. The functional validity of tests which employ language and procedures that may be appropriate for middle-class white Americans may be entirely inappropriate for children from other sociocultural backgrounds. Biased tests convey important relationship information to the child. They say that his world, in some sense, is inappropriate. It is in this manner that culturally biased tests are "criminal" in their effects. The problem is crucial with such tests because they lead to false conclusions about "mental ability" and related skills of the child and they ultimately contribute to a definition of the child as inferior. These falsehoods must inevitably lead to decisions that will significantly limit the opportunities available to the culturally different child in a hostile educational setting. (Editor Summary)

Brown, M. E., and Zirkel, P. A. 1977, Emerging Instrumentation for Assessing Language Dominance. (ERIC Document Reproduction Service No. ED 144 410)

This paper offers a two-step review to be used in designing dominance assessment plans and in determining appropriate instrumentation. The first step provides a classification system of dominance instruments according to testing specificity and strategy. The second step suggests criteria by which such instruments can be evaluated and selected. Selected dominance assessment instruments are categorized in a three-way descriptive matrix. The global/specific dimension distinguishes instruments which tend toward generic screening of gross language behavior from those which tend toward a refined classification of specific language indicators. Within the global and specific modalities, oral and aural performance subclasses are designated. The third dimension consists of four major strategies: rating, home interview, indirect, and parallel instruments. Specific examples of instruments are given to clarify how the classification matrix operates. Criteria for evaluating and selecting tests include examinee factors relating to developmental and cultural appropriateness, administrative and logistic factors, and psychometric considerations. A sample evaluation of Burt's Bilingual Syntax Measure is provided. (CLK-ERIC Summary)

Bryen, D. N. 1976. Speech-sound discrimination ability on linguistically unbiased tests. Except. Chil. 42(4):195-201

Traditional testing practices are considered by some educators as discriminatory against minority groups. In response to this problem, a particular language ability—speech sound discrimination—was assessed from a bilingual rather than a standard English perspective. Three parallel forms of speech sound discrimination (standard English, black English, and Spanish) were each administered to a sample of lower socioeconomic group white, black, and Puerto Rican children. The results indicated that each language group did best on the discrimination form that most closely approximated the phonological structure of its language. Also, there were no significant differences in speech sound discrimination ability among the 3 groups when performances across all language forms were considered. Implications for educational assessment are discussed (HA-LABS Summary)

Cardenas, J. A. 1976. Lau Remedies Outlined. (ERIC Document Reproduction Service No. ED 125 148)

The understanding of two principles is important if school districts are to develop comprehensive plans responsive to the *Lau v. Nichols* remedies specified by the Department of Health, Education, and Welfare (HEW) in ways that both adhere to the spirit of the *Lau* decision and allow the school district to develop coherent educational programs for all students. First, it should be understood that the remedies are minimal and that they have been drawn to adhere to the narrowest legal interpretation on the basis of the most promising current knowledge and thought relating to the education of children of limited English-speaking ability, and cannot require bilingual, multicultural programs for all children. Second, an acceptable plan must include realistic time-outcome expectations; a plan can be rejected for projecting unrealistic expectations. The development of an elementary-level compliance plan calls for four phases: student identification, student language assessment, analysis of achievement data, and creation of program offerings. The process at the secondary level is the same except that program offerings can include a wider array of options. A sample community language survey form is included. (Author/IRI-ERIC Summary)

Carlisle-Zepeda, V., and Saldate, M. 1978. And who assesses the bilingual teacher's language proficiency? Educ. Leadership 35(4):318–321.

Describes the rationale and design of the Zepeda/Saldate Spanish Language Proficiency Exam developed at the University of Arizona for use in evaluating the language proficiency of applicants for bilingual/bicultural teacher education programs. (JG-ERIC Summary)

Carringer, R. 1974. Creative thinking abilities of Mexican youth. J. Cross-Cultural Psychol. 5(4):492–504.

To examine the relationship of bilingualism to the creative thinking abilities of Mexican youth, four subsets from the Torrance Tests of Creative Thinking were administered to Spanish-English coordinate bilingual and Spanish monolingual Ss from two private high schools in Torreon, Coahuila, Mexico. It was hypothesized that the Spanish-English coordinate bilinguals would score significantly higher on the dependent measures of figural fluency, figural flexibility, figural originality, verbal fluency, verbal flexibility, and verbal originality than the Spanish monolinguals. A multivariate analysis indicates that the main effect of language group was significant in favor of the bilinguals. Neither the main effect of sex nor the interaction effect was significant. Univariate analysis indicates that the dependent measures of verbal flexibility, verbal originality, and figural originality were significant at the .05 level in favor of the bilinguals and the dependent measures of figural fluency was significant at the .01 level in favor of the bilinguals. (HA–LABS Summary)

Carrow, E. 1972. Auditory comprehension of English by monolingual and bilingual preschool children. J. Speech Hear. Res. 15(2):407–412.

The auditory comprehension of English by 30 monolingual and 30 bilingual children, ages three years, 10 months, to five years, nine months, from low socioeconomic areas in Houston, Texas, was compared. The monolingual children obtained significantly higher mean scores than the bilingual children. Analysis of errors indicated that the linguistic areas in which the scores of monolingual children were significantly higher than those of bilingual children were nouns, pronouns, plurality of nouns, and noun phrases with two adjective modifiers. (Author Summary)

Carrow, E. 1974. A test using elicited imitations in assessing grammatical structure in children. J. Speech Hear. Disord. 39:437–444.

Elicited imitation was used to obtain performance data on the grammatical system of 475 children, ages 3-0 to 7-11. The procedure attempted to provide an instrument which is valid and reliable while at the same time easy to administer and score without extensive training or knowledge of linguistics. Grammatical categories included are articles, adjectives, nouns, pronouns, demonstratives, conjunctions, verbs, negatives, contractions, prepositions, and adverbs. Results demonstrate reliability and validity as well as test usefulness in specific analysis of grammatical constructions. (Author Summary)

Cartier, F. A. 1968. Criterion-referenced testing of language skills. TESOL Q. 2(1):27–32.

After defining the term, criterion-referenced testing, the author explains the advantages and disadvantages of this type of language testing. A section of the paper covers the developmental procedures for this type of test. (KKS Summary)

Cazden, C. B. 1972. Child Language and Education. Holt, Rinehart & Winston, New York.

A review of a work on child language and education, which clears up misunderstanding concerning the concepts of "linguistic deprivation" and "cultural deprivation" with remarkable clarity, though this is not the sole aim of the book. After the introduction, the first chapter deals with the nature of language. It is followed by four chapters dealing with language development, developmental processes, and environmental assistance. The next group of chapters deals with language differences and language use: dialects and bilingualism, communication styles, and the role of language in cognition. The final chapter contains thoughts on oral language education. An appendix describes methods for analyzing child language from spontaneous speech and from tests. Chomsky's linguistic theory underlies most of the research discussed although the book's concept of communicative adequacy is somewhat removed from Chomsky's. Communicative competence includes a knowledge of the social world and its rules as well as knowledge of language. The appropriateness of Chomsky's linguistic model for sociolinguistic purposes is questioned. The overview of the research findings is masterly. In discussing the differences between Black English and Standard English, the work of Labov is drawn from. The various chapters are praised for their extreme readability and lively account of recent child language research. (RG–LABS Summary)

Cervantes, R. A. 1974. Problems and Alternatives in Testing Mexican American Students. (ERIC Document Reproduction Service No. ED 093 951)

The problems of standardized tests with regard to Mexican American students, particularly "ethnic validity," are reviewed. Inadequate norm group representation, cultural bias and language bias are purported by the author to be the most common faults of standardized tests. Suggested is the elimination of standardized testing as a principal means of individual or minority group oriented educational program assessment. Researchers and educators are reminded that Mexican Americans represent a complex, heterogeneous group affected in varying degrees by mixtures of culture and values and that their unique multivariate socio-cultural and linguistic characteristics must be recognized and accounted for. Alternatives suggested and discussed are: the use of criterion-referenced tests, use of culture free tests, use of "balanced" research and program evaluation methodology, sensitive interpretation of test data when the use of tests is unavoidable and the development and use of culture-specific and dialect-appropriate measures. (Author/ERIC Summary)

Cohen, A. D. 1976. Assessing the English Speaking Skills of Bilingual Children. (ERIC Document Reproduction Service No. ED 122 556)

Discussed are problems to consider and possible techniques to use in assessing the English speaking skills of bilingual children. Reviewed is literature on the reasons for differences in ease of acquisition of English speaking skills among bilingual children (such as personality variables) and on inadequacies of existing language assessment instruments. Six means of assessing English speaking skills among nonnatives (such as the Bilingual Syntax Measure) are described briefly, and four suggestions for assessment (such as use of an eclectic approach) are offered. (LS–ERIC Summary)

Conrad, E. E., et al. 1976. Children's Language Assessment-Situational Tasks. (ERIC Document Reproduction Service No. ED 126 153)

The CLA-ST was developed to collect language samples within a normally operating classroom. A cassette was used and it is broken into three segments: 1) "mystery bag" with household objects, 2) eight picture cards, 3) children are left alone. (Author/YMG–ERIC Summary)

Council for Exceptional Children. 1973. Exceptional Children Conference Papers: Early Childhood Education. (ERIC Document Reproduction Service No. ED 078 631)

Five conference papers consider a bilingual kindergarten program, language assessment and development, a nursery school program for retarded children, instructional materials for handicapped children, and a comparison study on social status for bilingual exceptional children, respectively. The bilingual kindergarten program is described as a total learning system with three major components comprised of staff development materials (teacher manuals or filmstrips), the instructional model (sensory, motor, and language skills training in 12 units), and parent involvement. Suggested for children's language assessments are standardized scales, informational observations, and reports from persons close to the child; and offered for remediation are teacher techniques for an ongoing program. Emphasized in a free nursery school program for mentally handicapped children, 3- to 7-years-old, are development of a positive self-concept; and motor, self-help, language, sensory, and cognitive skills through art activities and creative movement. Approximately 23 teacher-made instructional materials for training parents of preschool handicapped children are presented in a lesson format, which gives the name of toy, time to make material, skill to be developed, material needed, procedure, use, and a space for trial evaluations. Results of a study using sociometric techniques to compare 20 bilingual (French and English) Ss with 42 primarily English speaking Ss, 8- to 15-years-old, in a special class in New Brunswick, indicate that the status among peers of the bilingual Ss did not differ significantly from the status of the English speaking Ss. (MC-ERIC Summary)

Crane, R. 1977. Hispanic Student Achievement in Five Learning Areas: 1971–75. (ERIC Document Reproduction Service No. ED 138 414)

Data on the achievement of 9-, 13-, and 17-year-old Hispanos in school in the areas of social studies, science, mathematics, career and occupational development (COD), and reading were collected between fall of 1971 and spring of 1975. Results were examined in relation to the achievement levels of students in the nation as a whole and those of black and white students. Representing a cross-section of typical schools across the country, the sample consisted of 75,000 students, of which about 2,500 answered a given question. Results were reported by age, region (Northeast and West), sex, and level of parental education. Among the results were: Hispanic achievement was consistently below that of the total national age population and of white students; Hispanic achievement was often closer to national levels than black achievement; the achievement of male Hispanos was consistently closer to national levels than that of females on the science items; and students who reported that one parent had at least graduated from high school were closer to the national level than those who reported that neither parent had graduated. Appended are: definitions of national assessment Hispanic-reporting categories, special analyses of reading items, statistics of the achievement of the white and black groups in each area; and proportion of Hispanic students within the national assessment samples. (NQ-ERIC Summary)

Dall, A. L. 1973. Infant Development Through Enriching Activities at Home. (ERIC Document Reproduction Service No. ED 101 851)

This final report contains narrative information and statistical data on the 3-year Infant Development through Enriching Activities (IDEA) program. The project was designed to increase the potential for academic success of high-risk, low-income children by promoting motor, social and language development through home intervention. Approximately 450 Mexican-American children, ages 1–5, were included in the program. Feedback from weekly home visits and from pre- and post-testing was used to determine the mothers' and children's progress. Narrative information is presented in a question-answer format accompanied by data tables. Statistical information on parents, children and other project aspects make up more than half of the report. (SDH–ERIC Summary)

Darlington, R. C. 1973. Is Culture-fairness Objective or Subjective? (ERIC Document Reproduction Service No. ED 080 601)

The search for a satisfactory objective definition of a culture-fair test is doomed to failure, except in the special case in which different cultural groups have the same mean scores on the criterion variable to be predicted by the test. In the general case, it can be shown that no test (except one with the rare quality of perfect validity) can meet all the criteria reasonably expected of a "culture fair" test. The search for an objective definition of culture fairness must therefore be replaced by a subjective judgment of the degree of validity a tester is willing to sacrifice in order to select more or fewer members of certain cultural groups. (Author/ERIC Summary)

Day, R. R., and others. A standard English performance measure for young children. The Standard English Repetition Test (SERT). (ERIC Document Reproduction Service No. ED 111 175)

In view of the fact that the teaching of Standard English has high educational priority in American schools, and that its use as the medium of instruction makes it a vital skill for nonstandard speakers, the present paper reports on an investigation of the Standard English performance of young children from minority groups in which Standard English is not a primary language. The investigation technique described is that of elicited imitation, whereby the child is simply asked to repeat sentences containing grammatical features observed to show variation. Previous use of this technique and its advantages and disadvantages are discussed. The test itself appears in two forms, each one containing 15 sentences taken from recordings of natural speech. It is administered individually to children whose mean age is 5.5 years, by an adult tester, and recorded. Native speakers of English should perform better on the test, and the scores should improve with age, that is, further exposure to Standard English. The results confirm these predictions, thus demonstrating the validity of the test. Specific results are given for tests given to Mexican-American and Pima children, and to Hawaiian-Creole speaking children, the results from the latter being the most detailed. (CLK–ERIC Summary)

DeAvila, E. A., and Duncan, S. E. 1976. A Few Thoughts about Language Assessment: The *Lau* Decision Reconsidered. Paper prepared for the Conference on Research and Policy Implications of the Task Force Report of the U.S. Office of Civil Rights. Southwest Educational Laboratory, Austin, Tex.

The *Lau* decision is considered in relationship to the issues involved in language assessment approaches facing professionals in school districts as well as on the national level. Forty-six currently available language tests are discussed in regard to phonology, morphology, syntax, and semantics. The authors conclude that both linguistic and sociolinguistic factors must be considered when assessing the language of bilingual children. (KKS Summary)

Drew, C. J. 1973. Criterion-referenced and Norm-referenced Assessment of Minority Group Children. (ERIC Document Reproduction Service No. ED 092 438)

Traditional norm-referenced measurement has received criticism concerning cultural unfairness. Responses to such accusations primarily have consisted of new instrumentation aimed at a culture-fair assessment. Little response has addressed a conceptual standpoint concerning issues of purpose and use of test results. Although many have turned to criterion-referenced measurement to avoid the problems of non-referenced evaluation, cultural bias is not necessarily eliminated in this framework. (ERIC Summary)

Drumwright, A., Van Natta, P., Camp, B., Frankenburg, B., and Drexler, H. 1973. The Denver articulation screening exam. J. Speech Hear. Disord. 38(1):3–14.

This report describes the development of an articulation-screening test for economically disadvantaged children. The test is unique in that it was designed for use by trained nonprofessional workers. Thirty-four sound elements were administered to over 1500 Anglos, blacks, and Mexican-Americans two and one-half to six years of age. They varied significantly on the production of four sounds, which were eliminated from further study. In their production of the remaining 30 sounds, no significant differences were noted among cultural groups or betwen males and females. Age normative data in pronunciation of the 30 sounds were combined for all three cultural groups and displayed in a percentile rank format for each age category. Validation studies using nonprofessional screeners established the fifteenth percentile as the cutoff point for referral of abnormal children. Test-retest reliability was 0.95. Application of the test to large populations of children and use of nonprofessional screeners are discussed. (Author Summary)

Ebel, R. L. 1975. Constructing Unbiased Achievement Tests. (ERIC Document Reproduction Service No. ED 120 290)

The approach characterizing this study of bias in tests of educational achievement is stated to be reflective and philosophical rather than experimental and statistical. Its concern is with operationally definable areas of learning and indicators of achievement rather than with the hypothetical latent traits that are presumed by some to influence or determine test performance. A brief discussion of emotionality in test bias, that also considers the seriousness of the problem, is followed by comments on bias in selection testing. The meaning of bias in achievement tests is discussed next, together with other topics such as: bias in the test itself, the problem of reading difficulty and linguistic difference as a possible source of bias, non-standard English speakers, language specificity in achievement, test bias and test validity, constructing unbiased achievement tests, operational definition versus construct validation, appearance versus reality in test validation, the correctness of operational definitions, and a discussion of two propositions advanced to support the suggestion that criterion-referenced tests minimize bias. Issues discussed throughout the paper are noted to suggest that bias in tests of educational achievement is quite improbable. The a priori assumption that an achievement test is essentially unbiased is considered more reasonable than the assumption that it is biased. (Author/AM-ERIC Summary)

English Teaching Information Center. 1974. Language Testing, with Special Reference to English as a Foreign Language. Specialized Bibliography. (ERIC Document Reproduction Service No. ED 113 951)

This bibliography is divided into four main sections. The first section cites bibliographies dealing with language testing, while the second and third sections deal with books and articles in the same area. A fourth section lists test distributors' catalogues. Entries include publications from many countries. (ERIC Summary).

Evans, J. 1976. Identification and Supplementary Instruction for Handicapped Children in a Regular Bilingual Program. (ERIC Document Reproduction Service No. ED 123 891)

Early identification and supplementary instruction for the Mexican American child who is also handicapped are essential. The purposes of the Ability Development Programs are to identify the child with existing and/or potentially handicapping conditions, to develop and test supplementary materials, and to determine the efficacy of supplementary instruction within the regular bilingual classroom. In the first project for four-year-olds, completed in 1975, 40 out of 99 children enrolled had some type of problem, 29 severe enough to interfere with learning. Following five months of supplementary instruction, the experimental group out-performed the comparison group not receiving supplementary instruction and were learning at the level of non-handicapped peers. In the second project for five-year-olds, scheduled for completion in 1977, materials for continuous observation and supplementary instruction on a lesson-by-lesson basis are in initial development stages. Materials developed for these projects include "Supplementary Activities for Four-Year-Olds," "Observation-Action-Activity Cards for Five-Year-Olds," two teacher manuals, "Working with Parents of Handicapped Children," and "How to Fill Your Toy Shelves without Emptying Your Pocketbook"; and two assessment instruments, the "Spanish/English Language Performance Screening" (S/ELPS) and the "Observational Checklists for Referral" (OCR). Development and evaluation data for the S/ELPS and OCR are reported as well as the results of the completed project with four-year-olds. (Author/ERIC Summary)

Evard, B. L., and McGrady, H. J. 1974. Development of Local Language Norms for Papago Indians, Mexican-Americans, Blacks, and Anglos. (ERIC Document Reproduction Service No. ED 105 732)

The development of local norms using the Illinois Test of Psycholinguistic Abilities was part of a larger study, the purpose of which was to identify the percentage of Arizona school children having a handicap. The first step in this part of the project, which involved screening for communication disorders, was the selection of tests to identify language disorders. Step 2, the development of criteria for identifying the disorder, raised the question of when such a disorder should be considered pathological and when it should be considered an identifying feature of some dialect of English. The main question, however, was whether a test developed for one population is valid when administered to another. The Auditory Association and Grammatical Closure subtests of the ITPA were administered to a random selection of subjects representing the Arizona public school population. Subgroups differences appeared chiefly across ethnic boundaries. From this it is concluded that a test is valid for a specific group only if relevant norms have been developed for that group. The local norms and other statistics on the study are tabulated at the end of the report. (AM-ERIC Summary)

Fredriksen, N. 1976. How to Tell if a Test Measures the Same Thing in Different Cultures. (ERIC Document Reproduction Service No. ED 131 093)

A number of different ways of ascertaining whether or not a test measures the same thing in different cultures are examined. Methods range from some that are obvious and simple to those requiring statistical and psychological sophistication. Simpler methods include such things as having candidates "think aloud" and interviewing them about how they solved the problem, and techniques such as using pantomine or moving pictures to give instructions. Another approach is to make the tests different in such a way that they measure the same construct—so that they are functionally equivalent. The variety of approaches that require statistical methods include analysis of covariance, comparing test performances at the level of the test items (e.g., comparing item difficulties), item characteristic curve theory, factor analysis, and a construct validity approach. An understanding of the psychological processes involved in performing the tasks involved in taking a test item, or performing an experimental task in a laboratory, is prerequisite to making judgments as to whether a test is measuring the same thing in two cultures. The methods described provide ways to improve the understanding of such processes. (ERIC Summary)

Fulton, M. W. 1971. Adult Evaluation of Child Language. (ERIC Document Reproduction Service No. ED 123 924)

Analysis of adult evaluation of children's linguistic output provides a basis for elaboration upon the work of McNeill (1970) and Brown (1970). When limited to the uttered words of a child paired with an utterance spoken at an earlier time, adults cannot judge the relative age of the children making those utterances; in fact, their predictions of language maturity do not rise substantially above the level of chance. When restating what the children's deviant utterances mean in the absence of context, most adults retain the original vocabulary and word order and supply functors to make grammatical sentences appropriate to typical childhood interests; with context supplied, functors are added to produce well-formed simple sentences appropriate to the circumstances. (Author/ERIC Summary)

Garza, S. G. 1976. Language Assessment Identifying LESA's. (ERIC Document Reproduction Service No. ED 144 415)

Numerous instruments used by school districts to assess language dominance are not designed to determine either language dominance or proficiency. Nor do they yield sufficient data for appropriate program placement. One example of such an instrument is the Del Rio Language Screening Test (DRLST), designed to screen children of three to seven years of age who may require special education programs, and not bilingual education programs. It is recommended for use with students in the following language groups: (1) English-speaking Anglo-Americans; (2) predominantly English-speaking Mexican Americans; and (3) predominantly Spanish-speaking Mexican Americans. The test is not designed to test language dominance; it is designed to diagnose disorders in language performance. In conclusion, it is not recommended that school districts use this measure to identify students for placement in bilingual-bicultural programs. Rather, this test should be used in connection with bilingual special education programs. (Author/AM-ERIC Summary)

Genishi, C., and Chambers, R. 1977. Informal assessment of the bilingual child. Lang. Arts 54(5) 496–500.

Several techniques for conducting an informal assessment of bilingual children are described. It is suggested that these results could be used to supplement formal test results. (KKS Summary)

Gezi, K. 1974. Bilingual-bicultural education: A review of relevant research. Cal. J. Educ. Res. 25(5):223–239.

A six month survey of significant studies in bilingual-bicultural education and practitioners interested in this field. Specifically, research studies reviewed focused on the following areas: (1) mental abilities, achievement and attitude of bilinguals as compared to monolinguals; (2) difference between Anglo individuals and non-Anglos in achievement, self-image, problems and programs in bilingual-bicultural education. The evidence seems to be mixed and the results are difficult to interpret. The inability of many researchers to separate the socio-psychoeconomic variables from the linguistic and cultural factors has contributed to the confusion in their results. (AA–LABS Summary)

Gil, S. 1975. PAL Measures Language Dominance. (ERIC Document Reproduction Service No. ED 125 153)

The Primary Acquisition of Languages Oral Language Dominance Measure (PAL) developed by the El Paso Independent School District determines a child's structural proficiency in English and Spanish and measures language dominance to aid in placing pupils in bilingual programs. PAL consists of four components, including an examiner's manual containing directions for administering and scoring the test, a picture book containing three cartoon-type pictures used in administering the test, a scoring book containing the English questions and spaces for recording and scoring the child's responses in English, and a scoring booklet containing the Spanish questions and spaces for recording and scoring the child's responses in Spanish. PAL is administered to one child at a time by a bilingual person who has undergone special training. When scoring is completed for all children, language dominance is established by converting the English and Spanish scores into language levels. Each child is then classified as Spanish dominant, bilingual, or English dominant. PAL is an economical instrument that provides valuable information on levels of language proficiency; however, it does require specialized training, particularly for the scoring process. (Author/JG–ERIC Summary)

Gil, S, 1976. BSM Assesses Linguistic Proficiency in English/Spanish. (ERIC Document Reproduction Service No. 125 152)

This paper answers a series of questions concerning the Bilingual Syntax Measure (BSM): what it is, who it is designed for, what it consists of, how long it takes to administer the test, who should administer it, where the BSM should be given, how to conduct the assessment, and how to score the test. The paper concludes that, overall, the BSM can be useful for diagnosing a student's strengths and weaknesses in the basic structures of a language, for student placement, and to measure the degree of student has maintained or lost certain basic structures. The measure offers instructional suggestions for each level. (Author/ERIC Summary)

Golub, L. S. 1975. English syntax of Black, White, Indian, and Spanish-American children. Elem. School J. 75(5):323–334.

The written syntax of intermediate grade minority and white children is evaluated and compared. These differences are listed and implications for teachers are provided. (KKS Summary)

Goodman, K. S. 1969. Language Difference and the Ethno-centric Researcher. (ERIC Document Reproduction Service No. ED 030 107)

The author lists steps for constructing a research study

guaranteeing "statistically significant results when comparing two populations which differ linguistically." Many of these steps are direct quotations from typical research reports—choose a control group as much like yourself as possible; assume your own dialect is standard; encode all directions, questions, and answers in your own dialect; judge responses as correct only if they are properly stated in your dialect; use experiences drawn from the control (your own) group; follow a rule of thumb: if something is important to you it is important; judge all data as deviation from the control group: you are the norm, all else is deficiency. This facetious model for research is based on a "total fiction" that language can be judged on a single norm and that "language difference and language deficiency are synonymous." Every child achieves a basic mastery of his dialect well before beginning school and can express anything important to him to the people in his speech community. He speaks his dialect grammmatically: if he didn't, he couldn't be understood since grammar is the system of language and all language is systematic. Because "all people are ethno-centric," we build our stereotypes out of differences between ourselves and others. We need objective humility for effective research, not "elitist" views. (ERIC Summary)

Goodrick, H. C. 1975. Distractor Efficiency: A Study into the Nature of Distractor Efficiency in Foreign Language Testing. (ERIC Document Reproduction Service No. ED 122 613)

The aim of the research in question was to investigate the efficiency of various classes of distractors used in multiple-choice vocabulary question testing. Much of the quality of multiple-choice questions relies on the extent to which incorrect choices tempt the student. The study attempted to discover whether the effectiveness of distractors could be quantified and a rank order of preference could be established for population samples of different levels of English proficiency. The study, involving 1200 Arabic-speaking students of English, found a consistent order of preference and some puzzling questions. It was found that a definite hierarchy of distractor efficiency exists in terms of discrimination and, particularly, potency. All groups demonstrated a preference for distractor types, but there was an uneven agreement in discrimination. In addition, the most popular distractors were not necessarily the most discriminating. Differences between populations of varied proficiency were greater than between groups from different geographical locations. (Author/ERIC Summary)

Gray, T. C. 1975. A Bicultural Approach to the Issues of Achievement Motivation. (ERIC Document Reproduction Service No. ED 124 639)

This study examined (1) the incentive for achievement motivation of female and male Mexican American and Anglo American children and (2) the relationship between language behavior, as a possible indicator of acculturation, and modes of achievement motivation. A questionnaire type scale was developed to provide a viable assessment measure that is relevant for bicultural children who must learn to deal with the two sociocultural worlds of home and school. The Bicultural Achievement Motivation Scale (BAMS) contains 52 items and provides a general assessment of the motive to achieve. Four scales permit the assessment of the preferred mode of achievement; i.e., Achievement for Self and Achievement for Others within two achievement settings, Academic (competitive) and Home (noncompetitive). The scales permit assessment of the absolute as well as the relative strength of each motive and the identification of a bicultural child who exhibits a strong preference for both modes. In order to assess intracultural variability among Mexican American children, a Language Usage Index was developed and used as a possible indicator of degree of acculturation. All of the tests were developed in both English and Spanish versions. The subjects consisted of 480 fourth and sixth grade Mexican American and Anglo American students in three dispersed districts. (Author/JM-ERIC Summary)

Greene, J. F., and Zirkel, P. A. 1974. The use of parallel testing of aural ability as an indicator of bilingual dominance. Psychol. Schools 11(1):51-55.

A report of a study investigating differences in the performance of Spanish speaking children on alternate forms of the Oral Vocabulary subtest of the Inter-American Test of General Abilities in Spanish and English that may be due to practice effect, language level, and chance errors of measurement. The instrument was administered in opposite language order to 148 Spanish speaking first graders in a large Connecticut city who were randomly divided into two groups. Analysis of variance procedures indicates that their language level had a significant effect in favor of the Spanish version, but that practice effect and interaction were not significant factors. The difference in language level is attributed to the sample rather than the instrument. The standard error of difference between the Spanish and English scores was three points. Thus, if a child is equally proficient in both languages, the chances are 2:1 that the difference in his two test scores will be less than 3.00, and 19:1 that this difference will be less than 5.88. Parallel tests of ability in two languages may be used as indicators but not absolute measures of language dominance. (AA-LABS Summary)

Guilliams, C. I. 1975. Item-analysis of Amerindian and Chicano Responses on the Vocabulary Scales of the Standard-Binet (LM) and Wechsler Batteries. Final Report. (ERIC Document Reproduction Service No. ED 111 878)

Chicano and Amerindian vocabulary scale responses from the Stanford-Binet (LM) and Wechsler Intelligence Scale for Children were item-analyzed for 1,009 subjects. The response patterns differed both by ethnic group and test, as well as by age. The most common, and recurring, pattern found was "level-of-difficulty" gradient inconsistencies. The item-analysis method employed in this report was that of the covariance matrix where the sum of the matrix is the total-test's variance; vocabulary scale totals here, for both the SB-LM and the WISC. Tribes sampled were Navajo, Apache, and a group of subjects with mixed-tribal backgrounds designated "called Indian." Most of the protocols that could be analyzed on the vocabulary scales were pulled from the testing-course files at Arizona State University; other protocols were obtained from the reservations mentioned above. In the epilogue, based on the findings, it is suggested that bilingual programs similar to those being used in Texas' NIE funded program for the coming academic year be adopted for other large minority groups whose primary language is not either English or Spanish. (Author/ERIC Summary)

Harrera, D. 1973. Puerto Ricans in the United States: A Review of the Literature. (ERIC Document Reproduction Service No. ED 108 488)

This bibliography of 2,155 items is a resource book intended for educators. It provides up-to-date information on current advances in bilingual education as well as information on the historical, economic, sociological and anthropological aspects of Puerto Ricans, Mexican Americans and other minority groups. Emphasis is on testing, cognitive style and teacher training. Many of the entries are annotated. Part 1 is a listing of other bibliographies. The entries in part 2 are concerned with the Puerto Rican child in the American educational system. This section deals with the child's socioeconomic and sociocultural characteristics, intelligence and cognitive development; measurement of the child's self-concept, socialization, language competence and scholastic achievement; special educational programs for Puerto Ricans and other non-English speakers; educational materials for teachers; and teacher training and attitudes. The entries in part 3 deal with the Puerto Rican experience on the mainland. The topics covered here include demographic studies and migration patterns, the psychological adjustment of migrants, sociological and anthropological studies of communities, and the group's experience as it is portrayed in Anglo and Puerto Rican literature. Part 4 is a bibliography of unpublished materials. (Author/AM-ERIC Summary)

Harrison, H. W. 1975. Final Evaluation Report of the Harlandale Independent School District's Bilingual Education Program, 1974-1975. (ERIC Document Reproduction Service No. ED 111 557)

Comprised of pre-K-6 and LLD (Language Learning Disability) classrooms, the program is designed to provide bilingual education for pupils who have limited English speaking ability. There are 1,612 pupils from 7 elementary schools and 1 junior high school. Program objectives are to: 1) prevent their educational retardation by instructing them in Spanish while developing their command of English; 2) enhance their understanding and cognitive development in both languages; 3) give them the advantage of becoming literate in both languages; and 4) instill a knowledge of and pride in their bicultural heritage. Project components are: development of and revision of curriculum materials for bilingual classes, bilingual instruction in grades pre-K-6 and LLD, staff development, and parental and community involvement. However, this report deals with the instructional component. This 1974-75 evaluation report discusses the text results from the: Peabody Picture Vocabulary Test, Boehm Test of Basic Concepts, School Readiness Survey, Comprehensive Test of Basic Skills, Prueba de Lectura (Spanish reading test), Bilingual Education Program Test in Social Studies and Science (a copy included in the appendix), Projected Self-Concept Inventory, and Wide Range Achievement Test. These tests were administered on a pre- and post-test basis; both English and Spanish versions were administered. (ERIC Summary)

Harrison, H. W. 1975. Final Evaluation Report of the San Marcos Consolidated Independent School District's Bilingual Education Program, 1974-1975. (ERIC Document Reproduction Service No. ED 111 556)

The program is primarily designed to provide bilingual education for pupils in grades K-6, with limited English-speaking ability. Due to parental requests, approximately 16 percent monolingual English-speakers have been accepted into the program. Of the 529 children enrolled in the program, 89 percent have Spanish surnames. Objectives for the Mexican American pupils are to: 1) prevent their educational retardation by instructing them in Spanish while developing their command of English; 2) enhance their understanding and congitive development in both languages; and 3) instill a knowledge of and pride in their bicultural heritage. Objectives for Anglo pupils are to: 1) give them the opportunity to become bilingual and literate in 2 languages and 2) broaden their outlook and enhance their understanding of other peoples. Program components are: development of and revision of curriculum materials for bilingual classes, bilingual instruction in grades K-6, staff development, and parental and community involvement. This 1974-75 evaluation report deals only with the instructional component. Discussed are the results from the: Peabody Picture Vocabulary Test, Boehm Test of Basic Concepts, Comprehensive Test of Basic Skills, Prueba de Lectura (Spanish reading test), Bilingual Education Program Test in Social Studies and Science (given in the appendix), and Projected Self-Concept Inventory. (ERIC Summary)

Harrison, H. W. 1976. Final Evaluation Report of the San Marcos Consolidated Independent School District's Bilingual Education Program, 1975-1976. (ERIC Document Reproduction Service No. ED 125 837)

Comprised of 27 classrooms from grade levels 1-6, the program was primarily designed to provide bilingual education for pupils with limited English speaking ability. However, due to parental requests, almost 16% monolingual English-speakers were accepted into the program. Of the 717 pupils participating in the program 84.6% were Mexican American. Goals for the Mexican American pupils were to: prevent their educational retardation by instructing them in Spanish while developing their command of English; enhance their understanding and cognitive development in both languages; give them the advantage of becoming literate in both languages; and instill a knowledge of and pride in their bicultural heritage. Goals for the other pupils were to: develop understanding and respect for both cultures; develop oral communication skills in both languages; and develop reading and written communication skills in both languages. This report discusses the test results from the: Psychomotor

Skills Learned and Demonstrated—Mexican games, songs, and dances; Boehm Test of Basic Concepts; Prueba de Lectura (Spanish Reading Test); Projected Self-Concept Inventory; and Comprehensive Test of Basic Skills. Both English and Spanish versions of these tests were administered on a pre- and post-test basis. Comparisons of the achievement test results for grades 1–5 are included. (NQ–ERIC Summary)

Harrison, H. W. 1976. Final Evaluation for "The Forgotten Southside," Harlandale Independent School District's Bilingual Education Program, 1975–1976. (ERIC Document Reproduction Service No. ED 125 836)

Comprised of 60 pre-K–6 classrooms, the program was designed to provide bilingual education for pupils who have limited English speaking ability. Program objectives were to: prevent their educational retardation by instructing them in Spanish while developing their command of English; enhance their understanding and cognitive development in both languages; give them the advantages of becoming literate in both languages; and instill a knowledge of and pride in their bicultural heritage. During 1975–76, there were 1,726 pupils from 10 elementary schools and 2 junior high schools enrolled in the program. This evaluation report discusses the test results from the: Peabody Picture Vocabulary Test; Bilingual Syntax Measure; Boehm Test of Basic Concepts; Prueba de Lectura (Spanish Reading Test); Social Studies Units and Packages; Projected Self-Concept Inventory; Psychomotor Skills Learned and Demonstrated— Mexican music, songs, and dances; and Comprehensive Test of Basic Skills. Both English and Spanish versions of these tests were administered on a pre- and post-test basis. These tests indicated that continuing bilingual education resulted in higher performance. (NQ–ERIC Summary)

Hasayan, E., and others. 1975. Elicited Imitation in Second Language Learners. (ERIC Document Reproduction Service No. ED 125 254)

Three groups of subjects were tested in an elicited imitation study. These were 8-year-old, 11-year-old and adult native speakers of Arabic who were learning English as a second language. The subjects were asked to repeat sentences of seven different grammatical structure types. Previous research with 4-year-old native speakers of English (Smith, 1973) has found that three of the structures were easy to repeat (Type A structures) while four were difficult to repeat (Type B structures). In the present study, a similar difference in the repeatability of A and B structures was found for the youngest subjects, but there was no such difference for the adults and only a moderate difference for the intermediate group. The pattern of results suggested that this was not a function of differences in the subjects' English-language backgrounds, but represents a developmental difference in the ability of second-language learners to repeat certain grammatical structures. The theoretical reasons for the variability in repetition difficulty for the different structure types were considered. (Author/ERIC Summary)

Helmer, S. 1977. Demonstration of Assessment of Language Dominance of Spanish-Speaking Bilingual Children. (ERIC Document Reproduction Service No. ED 144 417)

Assessment of the Spanish-speaking bilingual child's language dominance is essential to bilingual education, but to date there is no universally accepted way of doing this. There are many tests on the market which purport to measure language dominance and achievement, and which involve various criteria and methods. This paper describes four tests, each of which can be useful in contributing to an overall assessment of language dominance. The Bilingual Syntax Measure defines language in terms of phonemes, and is designed to measure oral proficiency in English and Spanish. The Dos Amigos Verbal Language Scale measures language development in English and Spanish separately. The James Language Dominance Test is designed to assess active and passive language dominance of kindergarten and first grade Mexican American children. The Pictorial Test of Bilingualism and Language Dominance measures oral vocabulary for both Spanish and English, as well as phonological, morphological, and syntactic development in both languages. (AM–ERIC Summary)

Hickey, T. 1972. Bilingualism and the measurement of intelligence and verbal learning ability. Except. Child. 39(1):24–28.

The problems involved in the use of the Peabody Picture Vocabulary Test for evaluating intelligence and verbal learning ability of Mexican-American preschoolers are presented. Evaluation methods used with this population are discussed. The problems inherent in relying on approaches that are not analogous to the context of a particular handicap are provided. (KKS Summary)

Hofmann, T. R. 1974. Levels of Competence in Oral Communication. (ERIC Document Reproduction Service No. ED 123 869)

A set of levels of useful oral competence in a second language are proposed, and a revision in its structure is shown that can make it applicable to first language and to passive-bilingual situations.

Unlike many other scales of bilingualism, it integrates oral expression and oral comprehension into a single scale without losing validity. Its distinctions are gross enough to be easily perceived and easily tested for, to be objective and reliable, and to be easily interpreted in terms of ordinary experience. In addition to developing this scale, several principles about language competence and its measurement are discussed: 1) skills with the oral language and the written language are logically independent of each other, though they are correlated in many populations. 2) Although it is obvious that language competence is not a dichotomous property, it is also not a single continuum, as it has often been described. Oral competence includes at least two independent dimensions, comprehension and expression. 3) Levels of competence in oral expression and comprehension can be combined, however, based on their utility in communication. 4) Because of this interconnection, they can be interleaved together into a single scale of competnce. (Author/ERIC Summary)

Hollomon, J. W. 1976. A practical approach to assessing bilingualism in young Mexican-American children. TESOL Q. 10(4):389–402.

This article presents a practical approach to assessing bilingualism in children entering school. It includes the general aim of bilingual assessment, and an overall approach, which includes a method of selecting subjects, the use of socio-linguistic survey, and tests for measuring bilingual communicative competence. It also suggests variables to be included in the analysis of data, as well as some limitations of the tests discussed. (Author Summary) (Reprinted by permission of Teachers of English to Speakers of Other Languages.)

Hollomon, J. W. 1977. A conceptual approach to assessing bilingualism in children entering school. TESOL Q. 11(4):389–399.

The author argues that the insight provided by traditional methods of assessing bilingualism in children entering school has often been achieved without a variety of perspective. He calls for a conceptual approach and presents the problem to be solved. The essay continues by describing the Information-Eliciting Question Instrument, which is designed to reveal the conceptual baseline of bilingual children, including the question forms and concepts revealed in their verbal responses in two languages. The author says that the investigator using this approach is faced with: a) using the Instrument to develop parallel information-eliciting questions in two languages, arranged in an ascending order of conceptual difficulty; b) administering the questions to a sample of bilingual children entering school, in order to determine if they can grasp each question, decode the information elicited, and structure appropriate verbal responses; and c) determining the extent to which the children can use their two languages to verbalize baseline concepts. (Author Summary) (Reprinted by permission of Teachers of English to Speakers of Other Languages.)

Hollomon, J. W., and others. 1975. Eliciting Covert Mental Operations, Concepts and Oral Language Skills in Young Bilingual Children. (ERIC Document Reproductive Services No. ED 138 123)

The purpose of this investigation was to design and test an information-eliciting question instrument in order to determine whether the structures in the verbal responses of young Mexican-American, bilingual children entering school would reveal the covert mental operations, concepts and oral language skills elicited. The basic objective was to make an in-depth study of such problems as the relationship between language and thought (how the bilingual child uses his thought as content for his language and how he uses his language to structure his thought), language interference (mixing and code-switching), and fluency. The study was therefore limited to 6 Ss (3 kindergarteners and 3 first graders, including 3 boys and 3 girls, ages 6–7). The instrument consisted of 112 (56 parallel) questions in both English and Spanish. The results suggest that the instrument: 1) accounts for the language and thought components it elicited; 2) offers a different approach to the study of bilingualism in children entering school; and 3) reveals the match or mismatch between the language and thought processes already acquired by the Ss and those required for academic success with school-related tasks. In addition, the results dispel the view that a young bilingual child's initial ability or inability to experience academic success in school is primarily a language problem. (Author/CFM–ERIC Summary)

Jacobson, R. 1975. Semantic Compounding in the Speech of Mexican-American Bilinguals: A Reexamination of the Compound-Coordinate Distinction. (ERIC Document Reproduction Service No. ED 115 112)

This paper reports on a study done at the University of Texas at San Antonio to examine the extent of compoundness or coordinateness with respect to the language use of Spanish-English speaking bilinguals in the Southwest. The long-range purpose was to delve into the more theoretical issue of the kinds of bilingual functioning. The discussion is divided into the following sections: 1) the compound-coordinate dimension—the history of the study of this concept and the difficulty of defining the distinction between compound bilinguals and coordinate bilinguals; 2) acquisitional and societal patterns—how the place and manner of the acquisition of the two languages affects the degree of compoundness or coordinateness; and 3) description and analysis of the data—the subjects, the instruments used, and the results, which are summarized in tables appended to the report. The experiment suggests that: 1) UTSA Chicanos fall, by and large, into the category of compound bilinguals, 2) their compoundness is a result of a fairly high degree of acculturation into the dominant society, and 3) the diglossic behavior of the older generation is in the process of changing into a more random-bilingual one in the younger generation. (Author/TL-ERIC Summary)

Jakobovits, L. A. 1970. Foreign Language Learning: A Psycholinguistic Analysis of the Issues. Newbury House Publishers, Rowley, Mass.

This book presents a psycholinguistic perspective on the numerous variables affecting second language acquisition. Age, background, aptitude, attitude, motivation, and cultural environment are some of the variables discussed. Also examined in this book are the linguistic, psychological and physiological factors affecting second language acquisition. Instructional procedures, testing methods, and problems are described. The final chapter provides a review of relevant research. (KKS Summary)

Jarvis, F. 1975. Testing for Meaning and Communication in the Foreign Language Classroom. (ERIC Document Reproduction Service No. ED 123 886)

Testing in foreign language classrooms is characterized by excessive preoccupation with the student's ability to manipulate small grammatical features, while testing of communication is conspicuously absent. Furthermore, current testing is often done for the purpose of generating labels for students or for their post-instructional performance. This paper suggests that evaluators add another purpose: to discover what they know already and what they don't know yet. Testing of communication of meaningful context, with focus on all four language skills, should also be added. In this paper, test items exemplifying these concepts are contrasted with traditional test questions. Although the incorporation of these concepts in foreign language testing will not radically change the status quo, perhaps it will promote the development of students who are more capable of communicating with other human beings, and help them to become more knowledgeable, sensitive, self-actualizing and fully functioning individuals. (ERIC Summary)

Jones, A. R. 1970. Oral Facility in Bilingual and Monoglot Children. Pamphlet No. 18. (ERIC Document Reproduction Service No. ED 121 108)

The oral communication skills of bilingual students in Wales were examined in a study reported in this paper. Oral facility was treated according to five indices: quantity and quality of words in the oral responses, time taken to complete the response, length of pauses and number of corrections and repetitions. Pictorial frames provided a visual stimulus. Three standard tests were used to measure intelligence and English and Welsh attainment. The sample included 291 children aged 10–12 grouped according to socioeconomic class, "Welshness" of linguistic background and type of school. It appeared that middle-class children achieved higher on the standard tests than working-class children, but showed no differences in Welsh oral facility and differed in English oral facility only in the quality index. The main differences in oral facility are between linguistic-background groups, rather than socioeconomic classes. The more Welsh or English in the child's background, the lower the quality of oral reponses in the other language. The language of instruction in school and the emphasis on written or oral work in teaching also affect scores. Care should be taken in selecting both the medium and the method of instruction. (ERIC Summary)

Kennedy, G. 1972. The language of tests for young children. In: B. Spolsky (ed.), The Language Education of Minority Children. Ch. 13, pp. 164–181. Newbury Publishers, Rowley, Mass.

To find out something about its pupils and their progress, schools use tests. Standardized tests are widely used in the belief that they are a fair and reliable method of recognizing educational achievement. But most standardized tests are written in English and have been standardized with native speakers of English. This means that children whose native language is not English are often classified as being educationally retarded or of low intelligence. In this paper, Dr. Kennedy analyses in some detail the way that tests are often unsuitable for young children and for nonnative speakers of English. (Editor Summary)

Kessler, C. 1972. Syntactic contrasts in child bilingualism. Lang. Learn. 22(2):221–223.

Contrasts in the simultaneous acquisition of two languages in bilingual children support the theory that languages share deep structures and that differences derive from language-specific rules. Twelve bilingual children, age six to eight, participated in a study of the sequencing and rate of acquisition for late-developing syntactic structures. Comprehension tests examined linguistic competence over a wide range of structures. A statistical analysis provided the basis for interpreting the general pattern of acquisition; case grammar gave the framework for the linguistic analytic. Empirical evidence points to a parallelism in the acquisition of shared structures. Differences reflect language contrasts. If one assumes that first and second language learning are qualitatively the same processes, the sequential order in which the bilingual child acquires the structures of his two languages may have significance for the adult learner of English and for the development of TESOL materials. (LABS Summary)

Lambert, W. E. 1974. A Canadian experiment in the development of bilingual competence. Can. Mod. Lang. Rev. 31(2):108–116.

For many Canadians, acquiring the country's second language is an urgent matter. In the past 10 years, there has been a rapid change in language policy at both federal and local levels of government. Bilingualism is now a prerequisite for advancement at the federal level. Experimental French "immersion" classes were begun at St. Lambert Elementary School in 1965. Vocabulary and French comprehension skills have been used in a direct native language approach in kindergarten. In first grade, reading, writing, and arithmetic are introduced in French; in second grade, two half periods of English are introduced each week. The approximate time in min. per week devoted to each subject in French and/or English in grades two through seven is illustrated in table form. Every attempt is made to have native speakers teach. The students' progress has been compared each year with control classes of French children taught in French and English children taught in English. A battery of individual and group tests, achievement tests, science and math, listening, and speaking tests are administered. The results after seven years indicate that the experimental students can read, write, speak, understand, and use English as well as the students taught in English. In addition, they have all the same skills in French in a way that English students in a French second language program never do. These students have mastered the basics of French phonology, morphology, and syntax. They are not yet balanced bilinguals, but such a goal is realistic and can be achieved. (JH–LABS Summary)

Levy, B., and Cook, H. 1973. Dialect proficiency and auditory comprehension in standard and Black nonstandard English., J. Speech Hear. Res. 16:642–649.

A dialect proficiency task and an auditory comprehension task (stories and questions) were administered to 32 black second graders. Half of the subjects received the auditory comprehension task in black nonstandard English; the other half received the task in standard English. Subjects were asked to identify the race of the speakers and how well they liked the stories and speakers. Performance was significantly better on the questions in the standard treatment. Within treatments, there was a positive correlation between dialect proficiency and auditory comprehension. The subjects correctly identified black speakers but tended to misidentify standard speakers. The results are discussed in terms of a "difference" vs. a "bicultural" model of dialect proficiency and achievement. (Author Summary)

Linares-Orama, N., and Sanders, L. J. 1977. Evaluation of syntax in three-year-old Spanish-speaking Puerto Rican children. J. Speech Hear. Res. 20(2):350–357.

The performance of 30 normal and 30 language-deviant three-year-old Spanish-speaking Puerto Rican children was compared on two measures of linguistic proficiency. They are mean length of utterance, following a scoring procedure adapted for Spanish speakers by the primary investigator, and Lee's Developmental Sentence Scoring procedure adapted for Spanish by Toronto. Results indicated that both methods of language assessment were sensitive to age and language status differences within the three-year age range. Accordingly, they can be usefully employed in research investigations to equate subjects on a linguistic basis, and in the clinical evaluation of small differences in the language maturity of preschool Spanish-speaking Puerto Rican children. (Author Summary) (Reprinted by permission of the authors; supported by the Ford Foundation, University of Puerto Rico and University of Illinois)

LoCoco, V. G. M. 1976. A Comparison of Three Methods for the Collecting of L_2 Data: Free Composition, Translation and Picture Description. (ERIC Document Reproduction Service NO. ED 125 250)

Three methods for second language data collection are studied and compared: free composition, picture description and translation. The comparison is based on percentage of errors in a grammatical category and in a source category. Greater variation was found for some error categories between free composition and description and the translation task. (Author/MG-ERIC Summary)

Luft, M., and others. 1977. Development of a Test Instrument to Determine Language Dominance of Primary Students: Test of Language Dominance (TOLD). (ERIC Document Reproduction Service No. ED 141 393)

The objective of this study was to develop a highly reliable instrument for primary grade students which was relatively culture free and could accurately identify each child's dominant language. In addition, it should provide normative data regarding the child's fluency in his two most predominant languages. This test, known as the Test of Language Dominance, was simultaneously developed in English, Navajo, Spanish, Yupik and Zuni. Items which did not indicate satisfactory statistical rigor during the pilot test phase were removed or modified. The test is divided into Part I (receptive verbal ability) and Part II (expressive verbal ability). Part I, which features progressive item difficulty, is group-administered to children who respond by marking one picture out of the four which the administrator describes. Part II is individually administered with each student naming as many things as he can in a given domain in one minute. The test must be administered by a person fluent in both of the languages being assessed. Standardized directions are provided; scoring is objective and extremely simple. In pilot testing, run with over 1000 students, test reliability was .75 in English and .94 in other languages. The validated version of the TOLD has now been translated into 15 additional languages. (Author/MV-ERIC Summary)

Lutz, M. 1967. The Development of Foreign Language Aptitude Tests: A Review of the literature. (ERIC Document Reproduction Service No. ED 119 487)

Early language aptitude tests were generally tests of ability in English or work-sample tests in the target language or an artificial language. Recent work has involved various correlational studies and factor analyses to determine what factors correlate most with success in foreign language learning. Approaches include: 1) correlations of several language aptitude tests with the U.S. Air Force Schools English Comprehension Level Tests to study English learning ability in foreign students; 2) a predictor study using the vocabulary and paragraph reading sections of the Pennsylvania State College Academic Aptitude Examination; and 3) a study involving work-sample tests and artificial languages. Factor analytic studies seem of greater relevance now, to analyze and measure abilities constituting language aptitude. A study by Gardner and Lambert analyzed 24 variables of language skills and mental abilities and identified four as indices of second language skills. A study by Pinsleur, Stockwell and Conrey concluded that verbal intelligence and motivation were the main success factors. The Modern Language Aptitude Test consists of five subtests concerning number learning, phonetic script, spelling clues, words in sentences and paired associates. Reviews of the MLAT indicate that it is probably the most effective available, but criticize certain aspects. (CHK-ERIC Summary)

Martin, F. N., and Hart, D. B. 1978. Measurement of speech thresholds of Spanish-speaking children by non-Spanish-speaking clinicians. J. Speech Hear. Disord. 43(2)255-262.

This study investigated the feasibility of a prerecorded speech threshold procedure that was used in a picture-pointing format, and was administered to Spanish-speaking children by non-Spanish-speaking clinicians. The derived Spanish word list was compared for equivalency to English spondees on a group of billingual adults. The test, administered to 16 children ages three to six years, resulted in good agreement between SRT and pure-tone average. The test was found to be feasible, rapid, and reliable. (Author Summary)

Martinez-Bernal, J. A. 1972. Children's Acquisition of Spanish and English Morphological Systems and Noun Phrases. (Georgetown University Microfilms No. 72-34)

In this experimental study for developing a bilingual diagnostic language test, findings in English and Spanish about monolingual language acquisition were used in designing materials to investigate the bilingual language acquisition (English and Spanish) of children five to eight years old in Tucson, Arizona. Attention was focused on acquisition of the morphological systems and of noun phrases of varying degrees of length and complexity. Results indicated that both the linguistic content and the testing techniques were appropriate for children of this age, and that errors could be classified with a combination of data about native language acquisition and contrastive analysis. The research materials show that it is feasible to use psycholinguistic research techniques to study language development of bilingual children in a school setting. The subjects appear to be acquiring both English and Spanish in substantially the same way as children who are monolingual in each language. Neither language seems to be a "second" language for these subjects. (Author/DI-ERIC Summary)

Matluck, J. H., and Mace-Matluck, B. J. 1975. Language and culture in the multi-ethnic community: Spoken-language assessment. Mod. Lang. J. 59(5-6):250-255.

A problem in testing is that one individual who may be just as knowledgeable in a certain area as another individual may nevertheless answer incorrectly on a test because of faulty language control. Another consideration is the student's interpretation of the test item—an interpretation based on the student's view of reality as shared by his native cultural patterns. English-speaking Americans notice physical and speech differences (i.e., vocabulary, morphology, phonology, and suprasegmentals) of foreign speakers. However, our observational powers are less sharp in sociolinguistic areas. We tend to rely (often falsely) on certain universals in human experience, to the extent that we assume these manifestations of sensation are roughly the same in all cultures. These differences must be considered in assessment situations. Examples of cultural and linguistic bias are presented. Other areas of concern in test development are content and supporting materials. Although the skills of identifying, classifying, quantifying, negating, and showing relationship are apparent in all languages, the manifestations often differ. Conventions in art also differ from culture to culture. The MAT-SEA-CAL Oral Proficiency Tests are designed to measure audiolingual proficiency in the native language and in English. The unique design of these tests provides for a profile of the student's ability to handle each concept and of his areas of strength and weakness in both languages. (LF-LABS Summary)

Matluck, J. H., and Mace-Matluck, B. 1975. The Multilingual Test Development Project: Oral Language Assessment in a Multicultural Community. (ERIC Document Reproduction Service No. ED 119 498)

This paper discusses a series of oral proficiency tests in six languages developed under the auspices of the Center for Applied Linguistics and the Seattle Public Schools District. The prototype is an English Test, totally oral, for use in grades K-4, designed to: a) determine the child's ability to 1) understand and produce the distinctive characteristics of spoken English, 2) express known cognitive concepts, 3) handle learning tasks in English; and b) provide placement and instructional recommendations for alternate programs such as special English instruction and bilingual education. Comparable tests with similar objectives were then developed in Cantonese, Mandarin, Tagalog, Ilokano, and Spanish, reflecting some of the largest of the forty non-native-English-speaking groups in Seattle schools. Development of the tests was based on identifying basic learning concepts that children must handle in order to perform in a school setting. The grammatical manifestations of a language that a child must handle to perceive or to communicate these concepts were then determined. The construction of the tests and scoring methods, are discussed, as well as cultural and linguistic differences encountered in the preparation of the tests. (Author/ERIC Summary)

Matluck, J. H., and Mace-Matluck, B. 1976. The MAT-SEA-CAL Instruments for Assessing Language Proficiency. (ERIC Document Reproduction Service No. ED 129 877)

The Multilingual Test Development Project, recently completed in Seattle, Washington, has yielded a series of comparable oral proficiency tests in six languages designed for use with elementary school children, K–6. Extensive field-testing of the English, Spanish, Cantonese, Mandarin, Tagalog, and Ilokano tests was conducted with a research sample of several thousand students, both in the metropolitan area of Seattle and in several of the large migrant centers of eastern Washington and southern Idaho. This paper describes the project, reports on the preliminary findings, and focuses on the problems encountered and the solutions devised in attempting oral language assessment in a multilingual community. Both the findings and the research design will have implications for educational planning and program development by school districts throughout the country and for further research in these areas. (Author/BW–ERIC Summary)

Matthews-Bresky, R. J. H. 1972. Translation as a testing device. Eng. Lang. Teach. 27(1):59–65.

The author discusses the use of translation as a means of testing grammatical and structural items. The argument is presented that translation when used in conjunction with other methods is a "pedagogical tool" that should not be totally disregarded. Specific classroom testing examples are provided. (KKS Summary)

Mazeika, E. J. 1977. The Description of an Instrument to Assess the Receptive Language of Monolingual or Bilingual (Spanish/English) Children 12 to 36 Months of Age. (ERIC Document Reproduction Service No. ED 144 411).

This paper describes an instrument used to assess the receptive language of children. The bilingual child is tested first in the non-dominant language. When the ceiling is reached in the non-dominant language, the tester switches to the dominant language. (The ideal situation would be to give the test in one language one day, then repeat the test in the other language some days later. However, the logistics of testing young children and other factors make this alternative less practical.) The test consists of three parts: 1) Parent's Report; 2) Vocabulary; and 3) Performed Task. In the Parent's Report portion, the child is given 12 tasks to perform such as turning off the light, saying bye-bye, etc. This portion is designed to gather data and to provide a setting in which the child can observe the friendly interaction of the mother and the tester. The vocabulary portion consists of four parts: 1) identification of four common items which are found in the home; 2) identification of objects from the test kit; 3) identification of two similiar objects; and 4) identification of objects by use. The third portion (Performed Task) consists of 47 items in which the child should demonstrate that he/she understands the instruction for each task. (CFM-ERIC Summary)

Mazon, M. R., and McRae, S. C. 1975. Bilingual Education: Oral Language Assessment as a Prerequisite. (ERIC Document Reproduction Service No. ED 104 137)

This is an interim report on the first year of a five-year Spanish/English, bilingual/bicultural education program in Pueblo, Colorado, for grades K-4. The program is based on the premise that realistic language instruction begins with an assessment of each student's oral proficiency in both languages. The teacher should then develop this proficiency, before reading instruction begins, to bridge the gap between the informal spoken language of the child's home and the formal language of school. To do this, teachers must understand the process of language learning, the differences between oral and written language, and language varieties and functions. The "Gloria and David Oral Language Assessment: Spanish/English Version" was administered to determine oral language dominance and to profile each student's language skills for use as a basis for individualized instruction. The report includes statistics on program enrollment; language assessment materials and data; outlines of inservice workshops; an evaluation of the program to date; and recommendations for instruction, development of objectives, relative emphasis on the first and second languages, community involvement, program coordination, and staff needs. (CK-ERIC Summary)

Mecham, R. J. 1975. Enhancing environments for children with cultural linguistic differences. Language, Speech, and Hearing Services in Schools 6(4):155-160.

There are three syndromes surrounding the social attitudes toward minority groups and their speech: 1) the Caucasian syndrome, that all substandard speech is bad, 2) the minority culture syndrome, that minorities need to preserve their cultures and languages, 3) the educators' syndrome, that all minority children are inferior. The first and third must be counteracted and the second empathized with. The result of these syndromes is that testing of minority children for speech abilities is often impossible since few standardized tests have been constructed. This makes it difficult for speech pathologists to determine to what extent speech difficulties are the result of second language problems and what methods to use in remediating those difficulties. Bilingual programs need to be improved and educators better informed on the difficulties minority children face and how they can be alleviated. (TL-LABS Summary)

Merino, B. J., and Politzer, R. L. 1977. Toward Validation of Tests for Teachers in Spanish/English Bilingual Education Programs. (ERIC Document Reproduction Service No. ED 143 708)

This memorandum reports the validation of the SCRDT Tests for Teachers in Spanish/English Bilingual Education Programs. The tests, which are designed for elementary and secondary teachers and aides, measure knowledge of methods used in teaching English as a second language (ESL), teaching Spanish as a second language (SSL), and teaching reading in Spanish; and they measure proficiency in standard Spanish and acquaintance with the non-standard varieties of Spanish found in the southwestern United States. The results of a scale designed to measure teachers' attitudes toward varieties of Spanish used in the Southwest are also reported. The tests, the attitude scale, and a questionnaire covering the language use patterns, personal history, professional preparation, and expertise of the participants were administered to 83 teachers and 64 teachers' aides working in bilingual education programs in 31 schools at 3 sites in the Southwest. At all three sites teacher and aide scores on proficiency in standard Spanish had a significant positive relation to pupil gains; scores on the ESL, SSL, and Spanish Reading Methods tests did not. (Author/MV-ERIC Summary)

Morgan, E. R. 1975. Bilingualism and Non-verbal Intelligence: A Study of Test Results. Pamphlet No. 4. (ERIC Document Reproduction Service No. ED 117 959)

This report discusses the relationship between bilingualism and mental development of bilingual children. After a review of the relevant literature, a specific study is described. The linguistic background of 648 children from 29 schools, age 10 through 12 inclusive, was measured with the Welsh Linguistic Background Scale. General intelligence was assessed with three nonverbal tests: Raven's Progressive Matrices, Daniel's Figure Reasoning Test and the Non-Verbal Test No. 2 of the National Foundation for Educational Research. Objectives were to: 1) determine which of the nonverbal tests was the most independent of linguistic background and hence most suitable for intelligence testing in mixed language areas, and 2) describe the relationship between linguistic background and test scores. Conclusions are that: 1) none of the tests used is completely suitable for evaluating Welsh-speaking children if the results are to be compared with those of English-speaking children; 2) Welsh-dominant bilingual children scored consistently lower than English-dominant children; 3) a correlation exists between test performance and degree of bilingualism; 4) the location of a community accentuates the influence of bilingualism; 5) occupational levels and socioeconomic status must be considered when interpreting test scores; and 6) Raven's Progressive Matrices is the most independent test. (CLK-ERIC Summary)

Mukhergee, A. K., and others. 1976. Measurement of intellectual potential of Mexican-American school-age children. (ERIC Document Reproduction Service No. ED 138 034)

Described is the development of an ethnologically unbiased test for proper classification of Mexican-American elementary students. It is explained that of the 14 subtests drawn from standardized and nonstandardized tests and administered to 122 Anglo and Mexican-American children (7-9 years old), only five were found to be insignificantly correlated with ethnic background. It is reported that these five subtests along with two additional tests (Haptic Memory and the Peabody Picture Vocabulary Test) were then administered to 297 Mexican-American Ss, and that the results were used to produce a profile of intellect. Educational implications of the test include screening, placement, and differential diagnosis of strengths and weaknesses. Descriptions of the seven subtests are appended. (CL-ERIC Summary)

Nelson-Burgess, S. A., and Meyerson, M. D. 1975. MIRA: A concept in receptive language assessment of bilingual children. Language, Speech, and Hearing Services in Schools 6(1):24-28.

Because large numbers of children in California come from bilingual or monolingual Spanish homes, Standard English language assessment tests often fail to distinguish language disorders and delays from language differences. An attempt was made to develop a receptive language screening device to determine the bilingual dominance configuration and to assess vocabulary recognition skills. A corpus of lexical items representing 1st words taught to and learned by Mexican-American/Chicano toddlers was obtained. The words were represented by large, clear pictures in a test named MIRA, an acronym for Mexican-American Inventory of Receptive Abilities, and the Spanish word for "look." Support for field work efforts in determining language norms for multicultural communities is emphasized. (AA-LABS Summary)

Northwest Regional Educational Laboratory. 1976. Oral Language Tests for Bilingual Students: An Evaluation of Language Dominance and Proficiency Instruments. (ERIC Document Reproduction Service No. ED 129 099).

This publication represents the first attempt to address the problem of adequate evaluation processes for testing language dominance and proficiency in bilingual education. It is produced by individuals intimately acquainted with the fields of language testing and bilingual education. Issues in language testing as well as its history are discussed. Evaluation criteria are established for tests: measurement validity, examinee appropriateness, technical excellence, and administrative usability. The following tests are described: 16 commercially available tests; 6 tests undergoing development or testing; and 2 tests used for experimental purposes. A final section provides a concise evaluation of these 24 tests according to the above-mentioned criteria. An appendix lists test development efforts in Chamorro, Cherokee, Crow, French, Marshallese, Miccosukee, Navajo, Papago, Samoan, and Yup'ik. (Author/AM-ERIC Summary)

Oakland, T. (ed.). 1977. Psychological and Educational Assessment of Minority Children. Brunner/Mazel, New York.

This book of readings provides a highly equitable and practical approach to developing diagnostic-intervention services for minority children. It spans every area of application—from initial referral and actual intervention to follow-up services to meet the specific needs. It identifies the significant practices as well as various professional, legal, social and ethical issues involved. It also focuses on attaining the basic goals of assessement, to advance children's healthy development and to enable those reponsible for it to make the best decisions as to how to do it. (Editor Summary)

Office of Education (DHEW), Washington, D.C., Bureau of Research. 1971. Test Bias: A Bibliography. (ERIC Document Reproduction Service No. ED 051 312).

This bibliography, which lists selected articles, research reports, monographs, books, and reference works related to test bias, is limited to material which deals directly with the question of test bias—such as research reports or commentaries. References listed cover the period from 1945 to the present and are grouped under two main headings: General Education References and Employment References. (ERIC Summary)

Oliveira, A. L. 1972. Barrio test of verbal abilities (form A). Educ. Leadership 30(2):169-170,

A new intelligence test for Spanish-speaking students in the Rio Grande Valley, Texas is described. The test can be administered by teachers and other school professionals. (KKS Summary)

Oller, J. W., Jr. 1971. Dictation as a device for testing foreign language proficiency. Eng. Lang. Teach. 25(3):254-259.

This paper reports data supporting the use of dictation as a technique for testing foreign language proficiency. Correlations between the dictation and the other parts of the examination were found to be significant at the .001 level of confidence. Oller also presents a short theoretical discussion of the processes involved in taking dictation. (KKS Summary)

Oller, J. W., Jr. 1973. Cloze tests of second language proficiency and what they measure. Lang. Learn. 23(1):105-117.

Data from a wide variety of sources are cited in support of the cloze technique as a global measure of language proficiency. Cloze tests as measures of readability, reading comprehension, quality of translations, pragmatic expectancies due to textual illustrations, attitudes, and ethno-linguistic background are discussed. In second language applications of the cloze procedure the effects of variations in difficulty, scoring methods, and the language used are considered. Analyses of response types and frequencies are examined. Correlations with external criteria and other theoretical considerations suggest that short term memory constraints are invoked by the cloze procedure. It is argued that such constraints are limitations on *competence* rather than mere *performance*. It is claimed that cloze tests tap this underlying competence. (Author Summary)

Oller, J. W., Jr. 1973. Discrete-point tests versus tests of integrative skills. In: J. W. Oller, Jr., and J. C. Richards (eds.), Focus on the Learner: Pragmatic Perspectives for the Language Teacher. pp. 184-299. Newbury House Publishers, Rowley, Mass.

In this paper, Oller agrees with the thesis that tests which aim at specific points of grammar are less effective as measures of communicative competence than tests that require the integration of skills. The latter type of test most closely parallels the communicative use of language. (Editor Summary)

Oller, J. W., Jr., Atai, P., and Irvine, P. 1974. Cloze, dictation, and the Test of English as a Foreign Language. Lang. Learn. 24(2):245-252.

The Test of English as a Foreign Language (TOEFL) was taken by 159 non-native speakers of English in Tehran, Iran. They also took a cloze test and two dictations. The former was scored for both exact and contextually acceptable responses. A correlation of .94 between the two methods recommends the exact method for non-native teachers of ESL and concurs with the result of a study by Stubbs and Tucker (1974). Cloze scores correlated with the combined dictations at .75. Cloze scored by either method was more highly correlated with the TOEFL total score (.79, acceptable word method; .78, exact word method) than was the combined dictation (.69). Confirming earlier research by Darnell (1968) and Oller and Conrad (1971), both cloze and dictation correlated better with the Listening Comprehension than with any other sub-section of the TOEFL. This tends to confirm the suspicion that the Listening Comprehension section, which is a highly integrative and pragmatic task, is more valid than other sections of the TOEFL. On the whole, Listening Comprehension, cloze, and dictation were more highly correlated with each other, and with the remaining part scores on the TOEFL than the latter were with each other. This last fact provides strong support for integrative testing procedures. (Author Summary)

Oller, J. W., Jr., Bowen, J. D., Dien, T. T., and Mason, V. W. 1972. Cloze tests in English, Thai, and Vietnamese: Native and non-native performance. Lang. Learn. 22(1):1-15.

A passage in English was translated into Vietnamese and Thai, and a passage in Thai and one in Vietnamese were each translated into English. Speakers of English (35 subjects), Thai (122), and Vietnamese (115) were tested on the cloze passages in their native languages, and the Thais and Vietnamese, all of whom had studied English as a foreign language (EFL) for at least six years, were tested in the English passages. Response types of natives and non-natives were compared. Native speakers in contrast to non-natives made almost no responses which failed to conform to at least some of the contextual constraints in the cloze tests. The errors of natives were not only fewer but tended to be different in type. Mean scores for native speakers on the originals and translations revealed that carefully translating a passage from one language into another yields cloze tests of approximately equal difficulty in both languages. Item analyses, and K-R (20) measures of reliability ranging from .80 to .98 indicate considerable internal validity for the cloze tests used with non-natives. A comparison of items (on the English passages only) by the grammatical category of the response(s) most frequently employed by natives, item facility for natives and non-natives, and the determinacy of items stated in terms of the number of different correct responses given by native speakers, showed little obvious interdependence among these variables. The context of items was apparently much more important than any other single variable contributing to item difficulty. (Author Summary)

Oller, J. W., Jr., and Conrad, C. A. 1971. The Cloze technique and ESL proficiency. Lang. Learn. 21(2):183-195.

The variety of fill-in-blank test known as the "cloze" procedure is discussed as a device for teaching and testing ESL proficiency. Research with native speakers and the sparse literature available concerning studies with non-native speakers are explored briefly. An experiment is conducted to attempt to partially determine the discriminative power of a cloze test (scored by the exact-word method) and its validity as a device for measuring ESL skills. Students in beginning, intermediate, and advanced ESL along with two control groups of native (ENL) speakers (freshmen and graduates, respectively) are tested. Differentiation of levels of proficiency among the ESL groups seems adequate, but ENL freshmen are not significantly distinct from advanced ESL students though they are significantly inferior to ENL graduate students. The cloze test correlates best with the dictation (.82) on the *UCLA ESLPE 2C*, and next best with the reading section (.80): multiple correlation with all sections is .88. It is concluded that the cloze method is a very promising device for measuring ESL proficiency. (Author Summary)

Pascale, J., and Jakobovits, S. 1971. The Impossible Dream: A Culture-free Test. (ERIC Document Reproduction Service No. ED 054 217)

The study reviewed the formats and psychometric rationale of several alleged culture-fair tests. Advantages and disadvantages of each instrument were examined and implications for compensatory education were discussed. (Author/ERIC Summary)

Paulston, C. B. 1977. Linguistic Aspects of Emigrant Children. (ERIC Document Reproduction Service No. ED 144 340)

The language problem of emigrant children has two major aspects: 1) concern for mother tongue maintenance; and 2) concern that the children are not learning the second language, which is the official language of the host country. The first is primarily the concern of the family, whereas the second is the concern of the entire community. Massive school failure on the part of emigrant children has brought about federal legislation mandating bilingual education programs. Research done with Finnish students in Swedish schools and French-speaking students in English-language schools in Canada show that the students who do better in their mother tongue also do better in the second language and in other academic courses. The evidence for the importance of mother tongue development seems overwhelmingly clear, and in the United States, as in Europe, the educational consequence is, or should be, bilingual education. The goal of bilingual education programs, stable bilingualism, makes them vital parts of any educational program. The assessment of the efficacy of bilingual education, however, varies widely, and there is a widespread difference of opinions on its aims and objectives. One of the best indicators with which to evaluate these programs is the drop-out rate, not a psychometric assessment of the students' language skills. (CFM–ERIC Summary)

Politzer, R. L. 1975. Initial Language Acquisition in Two Bilingual Schools. (ERIC Document Reproduction Service No. ED 126 725)

The study reports the results of the analysis of Comprehension-Production Test in the kindergarten of two bilingual schools (L-1 English/L-2 French, L-1 Spanish/L-2 English) in the San Francisco Bay area. The tests used covered 14 formal contrasts of English. Parallel tests for Spanish and French were developed by translating the English test. Tests were administered in L-1 once at the beginning of the school year and in L-2 three times at regular intervals during the year. Various types of analysis are presented: 1) Correlations between L-1 and L-2 scores; 2) Correlations between Comprehension and Production scores; 3) Significant rank order of difficulty of the 14 contrasts in L-1 and L-2; 4) Determination of a) significant differences between Comprehension and Production scores, b) significant gains made in L-2 during the year, c) significant differences between L-1 scores at the two schools, d) significant difference between L-2 scores at the two schools. The main conclusions advanced are that 1) in spite of an overall similarity between factors accounting for difficulty in first and second language acquisition, interference from L-1 cannot be ruled out as playing a role in early childhood L-2 acquisition. 2) Comparative studies of second language acquisition can furnish an empirical basis for psycholinguistic and perhaps also linguistic theory. (Author/ERIC Summary)

Politzer, R. L., and McKay, M. 1975. A pilot study concerning the development of a Spanish/English oral proficiency test. Biling. Rev. 2(1&2):112–137.

Studied were production measurements in Spanish and English, according to the following requirements: extension of present efforts beyond the primary grades to higher levels; relative ease in scoring; insuring comparability between the 2 languages so that imbalance in favor of either could be measured; and giving of dominance information by domains. The method involves submitting 8 pictures with scenes illustrating various nouns and verbs; Ss were asked "What is this?" and "What are they doing?" The same pictures were used for English and Spanish versions of a text. Forty-one bilingual Spanish speaking students took part in the testing. Dominance analysis showed considerable bias in favor of Spanish over English among the Ss. Better scores were achieved by those who reported speaking either English or Spanish with friends, than by those who reported that they spoke both; the highest Spanish grammar score was made by those who spoke English with their friends. Difficulties in deciding what to use as the standard of correct Spanish are cited as a caveat in interpreting the results and an obstacle in devising similar tests. (SK–LABS Summary)

Prutting, C. A., and Connolly, J. E. 1976. Imitation: A closer look. J. Speech Hear. Disord. 41:412–422.

This paper explores the effectiveness of elicited imitation in clinical assessment and remediation procedures. A critical review of the literature dealing with the role of elicited imitation in language acquisition as well as the use of elicited imitation clinically is presented. Conclusions drawn from the review indicated that the effectiveness of employing elicited imitation for assessment and remediation purposes is not clearly defined. (Author Summary)

Purnell, R. F. 1973. Portuguese-English Bilingual Test Development (Providence, Rhode Island, FY 1973). Final Report. (ERIC Document Reproduction Service No. ED 101 581)

This report discusses the work accomplished during fiscal year 1973 by the Providence Portuguese-English Bilingual Test Development Project, the purpose of which was to develop a series of ability tests useful to Portuguese-English programs. English as a second language (ESL) and Portuguese as a second language (PSL) achievement test videotapes were revised and produced in final form. Procedures for providing empirical information about the reliability and validity of the achievement tests were established and implemented. Four activities for fiscal year 1974 were recommended: 1) improved versions of the aptitude tests and a user's manual are to be prepared; 2) teachers are to be trained in the use of the test; 3) a training tape is to be produced for the administering of the aptitude tests and for the collecting of the second-stage data; and 4) reporting of the analyses of the data should be incorporated into the manuals. An appendix contains sample items from the ESL and PSL aptitude and achievement tests. (AM-ERIC Summary)

Ramirez, A. G., and Politzer, R. L. 1975. The acquistion of English and the maintenance of Spanish in a bilingual education program. TESOL Q. 9(2):113-124.

Achievement in English appeared to be unrelated to the maintenance of Spanish in bilingual children. An oral proficiency test (English and Spanish versions) was administered to Spanish-surnamed children in kindergarten, first, third, and fifth grades in a bilingual education program. (KKS Summary)

Robinson, G. L. 1975. Linguistic Ability: Some Myths and Some Evidence. (ERIC Document Reproduction Service No. ED 126 689)

"Linguistic ability" is a widely misused term in foreign language literature. This confusion prompted an investigation into language aptitude testing, the specific goals of which included determining: the distribution of language aptitude across ability range; the validity of Pimsleur's suggestions of combined verbal and auditory scores; and whether students are generally consistent in their pattern of scoring. On the first day of the investigation, 160 students at a high school in the Sydney suburbs completed a questionnaire requesting information about language background and interests. On the second day 151 of the students (9 were absent) took the Pimsleur Language Aptitude Battery. The data yielded the following findings, among others: 1) interest is more important than I.Q. or any other component of language aptitude in FL election and perceived difficulty; 2) evidence does not support use of a combined "verbal" and "auditory" score; and 3) students are not consistently "above average," "average," or "below average" in language potential. These and other findings reveal the importance of individualized instruction and the dangers of overgeneraliztaion in FL instruction. This in turn assumes a commitment to the principle of equal opportunity for students in New South Wales. (Author/AM-ERIC Summary)

Rodriquez-Mungia, J. C., and Pereira, I. 1972. List of Testing Materials in English as a Second Language and Spanish. (ERIC Document Reproduction Service No. ED 084 917)

This booklet presents a list of testing materials in English as a second language and Spanish. Among the information included are the name and description of each test, the test level, the address of the publisher, and the known uses. Forty-three tests are discussed. (SK-ERIC Summary)

Rueda, R., and Perozzi, J. A. 1977. A comparison of two Spanish tests of receptive language. J. Speech Hear. Disord. 42(2):210–215.

Twenty Spanish-speaking Mexican-American children were administered the receptive portion of the Screening Test of Spanish Grammar (STSG) and the Spanish version of the Test of Auditory Comprehension of Language (TACL). The correlation obtained between the two tests was not statistically significant. The correlation obtained between 24 syntactical items common to both tests was also not statistically significant. The probable reasons for the nonsignificant correlations obtained are discussed. In addition, a detailed critique of the Spanish version of the TACL is presented. (Author Summary)

Sanchez, R. 1976. Critique of oral language assessment instruments. J. Nat. Assoc. Bilingu. Educ. 1(2):120–127.

This article proposes that assessment of communication ability must consider the speech events and linguistic patterns that are familiar to the student. Additional considerations are that one use evaluation approaches that recognize the speech community from which the child comes and that assess both linguistic comprehension and expression. (KKS Summary)

Sassenrath, J. M., and Maddux, R. E. 1973. The factor structure of three school readiness or diagnostic tests for disadvantaged kindergarten children. Psychol. Schools 10(3):287–293.

Diagnostic tests were administered to determine which children need help with certain conceptual, perceptual, and auditory skills. An attempt is made to provide some factor structure information on the following tests: School Readiness Survey, Auditory Discrimination Test, and the Illinois Test of Psycholinguistic Abilities. The tests were administered to 98 children (52 boys and 46 girls) from disadvantaged neighborhoods enrolled in kindergarten. Of the Ss, 43 were bilingual for English and Spanish. The results of the study are presented in table form, and they indicate that the Illinois Test does not measure what it purports to; namely, specific cognitive abilities. Suggestions for further studies are included. (DL-LABS Summary)

Seliger, H. W., and Whiteson, V. 1975. Contextualizing laboratory administered aural comprehension tests. System 3(1):10-15.

An experimental test for evaluating the aural comprehension of non-English speakers who were candidates for admission to an English department at an Israeli university is described. The test consisted of a dialogue with 25 intermittent pauses for responses by examinees. The dialogue was presented on tape with the accompaniment of white noise at the 3 dB level electronically added to the voice track. The experiment had 3 goals: (1) to test the reliability of the above type of aural comprehension test; (2) to develop a language test consistent with current findings about what to test in evaluating FL proficiency; and (3) to develop a test that would correlate with other measures of FL proficiency while providing a more economical means of measuring such proficiency. Ss were 65 adult non-native speakers of English. (AA-LABS Summary)

Silverman, R. J., Noa, J. K., Russell, R. H., and Molina, J. C. 1976. Oral Language Tests for Bilingual Students: An Evaluation of Language Dominance and Proficiency Instruments. Center for Bilingual Education, Northwest Region Educational Laboratory, Portland, Ore.

This pamphlet provides objective and comprehensive evaluations of 20 oral language tests that can be used in the assessment of bilingual students. General information of the theory of language testing is also included (KKS Summary)

Silverman, R. J., and Russell, R. H. 1977. The Relationships among Three Measures of Bilingualism and Their Relationship to Achievement Test Scores. (ERIC Document Reproduction Service No. ED 140 632)

Before a bilingual program can be set up, students who are potential candidates for such a program must be identified. A study was made to investigate the interrelationships of three commonly used measures of "language dominance": the Language Facility Test (LFT), the Home Bilingual Usage Estimate (HBUE), and the Teacher Judgment Questionnaire (TJQ). The population for this study included 1,799 students in grades 1-12 from three school districts in Washington State. The results indicate that the three measures do not have a high degree of interrelationship and that based on this set of data, one measure will not serve as a substitute for the others. When examined from a content analysis perspective, it is not totally surprising that the three measures are not perfectly related. Each looks at students' language usage from a somewhat different perspective. However, the fact that the results from each measure purport to indicate the "language dominance" of students implies that the results from the measures should converge. In the present study the results from the three instruments do not converge. Three possible explanations may account for the findings: (1) the study itself may be limited, given the small sample sizes and some lack of control in the administration and scoring of the instruments; (2) the instruments themselves may be faulty; (3) the problem may reside in the construct "language dominance" itself. (Author/CFM-ERIC Summary)

Simon, A. J., and Joiner, L. M. 1974. Adapting the Peabody Picture Vocabulary Test for use with Mexican children. (ERIC Document Reproduction Service No. ED 102 201)

The effectiveness of test adaptation based on item selection and reordering of a Spanish (Mexican) version of the Peabody Picture Vocabulary Test (PPVT) was examined. Translated forms were administered to a sample of Mexican students. One item from each pair (A and B) was selected and reordered using a priori rules. The revised instrument was administered to a new cross-validation sample. Findings confirmed the cost effectiveness of this technique for improving reliability and validity over simple translation or the creation of completely new items for populations of different culture and language. (Author/ERIC Summary)

Slager, W. R., and Madsen, B. M. (eds.). 1972. Language in American Indian Education: A Newsletter of the Office of Education Programs, Bureau of Indian Affairs, United States Department of the Interior. (ERIC Document Reproduction Service No. ED 069 166)

This issue of the 1971-72 series on "Language in American Indian Education" contains articles on bilingual education and the testing of language skills. The first, "The language of the Sioux," is a bibliographic essay dealing with the studies that have been made to date of the Sioux language and its dialects. A Title 7 bilingual education project at Loneman Day School in Oglala, South Dakota, and a Title 1 bilingual education program in the Bethel Agency, Juneau Area, Alaska, are reported. Other articles examine means teachers use to evaluate their students' progress in English. They include: 1) "Testing Language Skills," 2) "Common Errors in Constructing

Multiple Choice Items," and 3) "The Language of Tests for Young Children." A section on Indian languages contains a story in Papago and a sample of the Cree materials presently being developed by the Title 7 bilingual project on the Rocky Boy reservation in Montana. An information exchange section concerning Indian education is also included. (RL-ERIC Summary)

Spolsky, B. 1973. What does it mean to know a language, or how do you get someone to perform his competence? In: J. W. Oller, Jr., and J. C. Richards (eds.), Focus on the Learner: Pragmatic Perspectives for the Language Teacher. pp. 164-176. Newbury House Publishers, Rowley, Mass.

In this paper, Spolsky considers some of the theoretical issues which have important implications for techniques of language testing. In particular the distinction between competence and performance proposed by Chomsky is seen to have serious consequences for methods of measuring proficiency as well as for teaching practices. Spolsky contends that this distinction brings into question the technique of testing which concentrates on one point of grammar at a time. (Editor Summary)

Spolsky, B., Murphy, P., Holm, W., and Ferrel, A. 1972. Three functional tests of oral proficiency. TESOL Q. 6(3):221-235.

A description of three experimental tests that attempt to measure communicative competence. The Spanish-English Dominance Assessment Test was developed to permit assignment of six- and seven-year-old children to appropriate streams in a New Mexico school with a bilingual education program. The Navajo-English Dominance Interview, also intended to be used with six year olds beginning school, was used to validate teacher ratings in a study of Navajo language maintenance. The Oral Placement Test for Adults is an experimental instrument to place non-literate adults in appropriate levels of an ESL program. The three tests display certain common principles in developing usable functional tests. Each is closely tied to the practical situation for which it was prepared and is intended to be used by relatively untrained testers with the simplest possible materials. Results are gross, classifying rather than ranking students, but this is appropriate to the goals. (LABS Summary)

Stafford, K. R., and Milam, D. 1970. Types of Bilingualism and Performance of Navaho Children in School, Phase I. Final Report. (ERIC Document Reproduction Service No. ED 044 702)

The purposes of this first phase of a proposed two-phase study were 1) to collect necessary baseline data for the completion of the total two-part study, and 2) to note the effect on school achievement of one year's instruction in English given to kindergarten Navaho-speaking monolinguals. The following groups from the Window Rock–Ft. Defiance schools were selected: kindergarten Navaho-speaking monolinguals, kindergarten compound bilinguals (Navaho-English), kindergarten Navaho-speaking monolinguals who received one year's concentrated instruction in English, first-grade Navaho-speaking monolinguals, first-grade English-speaking monolinguals, and first-grade compound bilinguals. Measures of intelligence and achievement were obtained. Analysis of variance and Sheffe's technique were used to test for differences in order to meet the second objective of this project. Aside from getting baseline data and finding expected differences (e.g., English-speaking monlinguals scored higher in achievement than Navaho-speaking monolinguals), the most promising discovery was the positive influence of instruction in English on school performance. In light of this, it is important to determine the long-term effects of early concentrated English instruction in a school setting. (Author/AMM–ERIC Summary)

Stephens, M. I. 1976. Elicited imitations of selected features of two American English dialects in Head Start children. J. Speech Hear. Res. 19:493–507.

Three measures were used to check the bidialectal imitative facility of 100 black, white, and Spanish-speaking Head Start children. In general, blacks and Spanish-speaking subjects performed more accurately on black English markers than on Standard English markers and whites, the reverse. When the children did make an error on the feature marker they usually substituted the opposing dialectal marker. Blacks and Spanish-speaking subjects were more apt to be accurate on the total sentence when it was given in black English. Several explanations are offered for group similarities and differences. (Author Summary)

Sullivan, A. R. 1973. Issues in Assessing Multi-cultural Youth. Its Implications for Teachers. (ERIC Document Reproduction Service No. ED 115 621)

There has recently been an increasing awareness that the United States is a culturally diverse nation. Many people have seen this diversity as a divisive force and have therefore adhered to the melting pot theory. Everyone comes out of a melting pot the same. Consequently, 1) intelligence tests have been devised that are only relevant to the experiences of nonminority children; 2) schools have refused to offer bilingual education to Chinese, Mexican, and other children whose first language is not English; 3) courts have only recently considered offering bilingual translation of court proceedings; and 4) teacher training has rarely included anything that would focus a potential teacher's attention on the needs of culturally different children. In fact, many white teachers come to teaching with unfortunate prejudices against nonwhite children, as was shown by a study in which white female undergraduates consistently gave less praise, encouragement, or attention to black junior high students regardless of whether they had been told these students were gifted or nongifted. Intelligence tests are particularly susceptible to cultural bias; furthermore, they are limited in their ability to assess a child's real potential. The Dove Counter Balance Intelligence Test was created to help psychologists and others think about and design tests that recognize varieties of cultural experience and the different usages of language among different ethnic groups. (An example of this test is included.) (CD-ERIC Summary)

Swain, M., and others. 1974. Alternatives to Spontaneous Speech: Elicited Translation and Imitation as Indicators of Second Language Competence. (ERIC Document Reproduction Service No. ED 123 872)

Elicited imitation occurs in an exepimental situation during which subjects are requested to repeat a model sentence constructed so as to include specific desired grammatical structures. Elicited translation involves giving subjects a sentence in one language and asking them to say the same thing, but in another language; elicited translation may work from native language to second language or vice versa. This study finds both methods useful as indicators of second language competence. Imitation taps both comprehension and production; data obtained through imitation may be interpreted to determine the stage of acquisition of a given structure. Translation also taps aspects of second language competence, although additional investigation is needed into the translation process itself and into other variations of the translation task. (Author/ERIC Summary)

Symes, D. S. 1975. A Description and an Analysis of Tests for the Bilingual Child. (ERIC Document Reproduction Service No. ED 128 359)

Because of the recent *Lau* vs. *Nichols* decision by the Supreme Court, school districts will be looking for various instruments to determine language functionality in bilingual students. Nine tests are reviewed: the Leiter International Performance Scale (LIPS), the Michigan Oral Language Productive Tests Structured Response, the

Michigan Oral Language Productive Test, the El Paso Public School Oral Language Dominance Measure, the Bilingual Syntax Measure, three Functional Tests of Oral Proficiency, the Oral Placement Test for Adults, and the Skoczylas Bilingual Tests and Measures. Each is described briefly, and its strengths and weaknesses are listed. (BW-ERIC Summary)

Taylor, T. H. 1969. A Comparative Study of the Effects of Oral-Aural Language Training on Gains in English Language for Fourth and Fifth Grade Disadvantaged Mexican-American Children. (ERIC Document Reproduction Service No. ED 041 252)

The study reported in this dissertation was conducted with the cooperation of the San Antonio Independent School District as part of the Language Research Project (formerly the San Antonio Language Research Project), Department of Curriculum and Instruction, the University of Texas. (For the author's descriptive abstract of the project, see AL 002 445.) Chapters in this document are 1) Introduction; 2) Review of Related Literature; 3) Description of Research Design, Procedures and Data Analyses; 4) Statistical Analyses of the Hypotheses; 5) Summary, Limitations, Conclusions and Recommendations. Appendixes contain 1) Prerecorded instruction for students who were tested; 2) Sample of Sanborn sound tape record; 3) Visual presentation of testing procedure; 4) Scoring sheet; and 5) Rating form supplied teachers in order to determine relationship between numerical scores and teacher ratings. A bibliography concludes the work. (AMM-ERIC Summary)

Taylor, T. H. 1970. English Language Proficiency for Fourth and Fifth Grade Spanish-Speaking Children. (ERIC Document Reproduction Service No. Ed 040 391)

An experimental program designed to develop oral language (English) was started in the San Antonio Independent School District in 1964 and included 28 first grade classrooms of culturally deprived urban Spanish-speaking children. Classrooms were designated as Oral-Aural English, with intensive English one hour daily; Oral-Aural Spanish, with intensive Spanish one hour daily; and non Oral-Aural (which was merged with O-AE and O-AS after two years). Ott's study, 1967, showed superior gains made by the experimental groups in the first grade, but these findings were not predictive of continued superiority through the intermediate grades. The author's study (her doctoral dissertation, University of Texas at Austin, January 1969, of which the present paper is an abstract) was designed to analyze the cumulative effects of instruction on children receiving continuous treatment over a period of years. Conclusions remain unexplained as to why the scores of children receiving Spanish treatment excelled the other treatment groups when the criterion was English proficiency. A possible reason is that hearing one's own language amplifies the phonemic and syntactical contrasts between English and Spanish, thus making it easier for Spanish speakers to learn English. (AMM-ERIC Summary)

Terry, C., and Cooper, R. L. 1969. A note on the perception and production of phonological variation. Mod. Lang. J. 53(4):254-255.

This study investigated the difference between auditory perception and verbal production of the phonological variation between Spanish and English as evaluated by Puerto Rican subjects. Although perception was not generally related to the relative frequency of production, some items were related to three criterion variables. The authors suggest that some perception items which are easy to administer might be used in language surveys. (KKS Summary)

Tobier, A. (ed). 1974. Teaching Bilingual Children. City University of New York, New York: (ERIC Document Reproduction Service No. ED 095 100)

In his brief introduction, the editor states that this collection of writing is intended to assist the understanding of a child's language development as he masters his mother tongue. It is especially for teachers just beginning in bilingual education. The predominance of essays on the experiences of Spanish-speaking people in this collection is because these writings are more readily available and not that they are thought more valid than other material. Included in this collection are a strategy for bilingual education, an essay on learning to read in a bilingual context, an excerpt from the U.S. Commission on Civil Rights report entitled "Toward Quality Education for Mexican Americans," an essay "A Framework for Implementing Bilingual Education," excerpted from a report by the National Puerto Rican Development and Training Institute and other pieces that represent the experiences of students and teachers. (JA-ERIC Summary)

Toronto, A. S. 1976. The Influence of Parents' Income, Education, and Culture on Language Performance of Children in a Texas Border Town. (ERIC Document Reproduction Service No. ED 122 624)

A bilingual language test was constructed and standardized on 384 children in three groups: Spanish-speaking Mexican-Americans, English-speaking Mexican-Americans, and Anglo-Americans. The three groups' scores were significantly different. Data on parents' income and education was obtained and compared to the children's test performance. No significant differences in scoring were found between different income or educational levels. This indicates that the group scoring differences may have been due to cultural or testing variables not related to income or education. (Author/ERIC Summary)

Toronto, A. S. 1976. Developmental assessment of Spanish grammar. J. Speech Hear. Disord. 41(2):150–171.

The Developmental Assessment of Spanish Grammar (DASG) provides a language analysis procedure for Spanish-speaking children similar to the Developmental Sentence Scoring (DSS) procedure in English. The DASG is not an attempted translation of the DSS but was developed independently, taking into consideration the present knowledge of Spanish language acquisition. The purpose of the DASG is to evaluate the language of children with deficient grammatical skills in Spanish and to serve as a model for structuring Spanish language therapy. Proposed syntactic hierarchies for the following six grammatical categories are presented: indefinite pronouns and noun modifiers, personal pronouns, primary verbs, secondary verbs, conjunctions, and interrogative words. Weighted scores are assigned to groups of structures within the hierarchies and are used to score Spanish sentences children use spontaneously in conversation with an adult. The DASG was standardized on 128 Spanish-speaking children between the ages of 3.0 and 6.11 years. Norms and reliability measures are presented. (Author Summary)

Trepper, T. S. 1975. A Comparison of English and Spanish Verbal Facility of Mexican-American Children. (ERIC Document Reproduction Service No. ED 121 547)

Fifty poverty-level Mexican bilingual children in first and fourth grade were tested for verbal facility in both English and Spanish to determine which language was dominant at the initial grade level and an advanced grade level. In East Los Angeles almost all of its students lived in the same Federal housing project, thus ensuring low income status and reasonable homogeneity in terms of language and culture. Students were individually given the Peabody Picture Vocabulary Test in both English and Spanish by a bilingual member of the community who was not informed as to the purpose of the testing. Since some of the Spanish stimulus words were not meaningful for this particular region and dialect, bilingual educators from the community helped to substitute stimulus words for the less appropriate ones. If form A was given in English, then form B was given in Spanish. This variable was counter-balanced as was the order of the language used. Results indicated there was no significant difference between verbal facility scores in English and Spanish at either the first or fourth grade level. This indicates that placement into bilingual programs without assessing language dominance may be a mistake. (Author/ERIC Summary)

Upshur, J. A. 1973. Context for language testing. In: J. W. Oller, Jr., and J. C. Richards (eds.), Focus on the Learner: Pragmatic Perspectives for the Language Teacher. pp. 200–213. Newbury House Publishers, Rowley, Mass.

Upshur considers the functional uses of language skill in total educational settings. On the basis of an analogy with information processing systems, several ways in which tests constitute decision making procedures in educational programs are illustrated. Upshur's paper also serves to make clear the important and intimate interrelations between teaching, learning and testing. (Editor Summary)

Upshur, J. A. 1973. Productive communication testing: Progress report. In: J. W. Oller, Jr., and J. C. Richards (eds.), Focus on the Learner: Pragmatic Perspectives for the Language Teacher. Newbury House Publishers, Rowley, Mass.

Upshur reports on the promising approach to the testing of productive communication skills. He also focuses on the practical and theoretical differences between discrete-point tests and tests of integrative skills. (Editor Summary)

Vasquez, J. 1972. Measurement of intelligence and language difference. Aztlan 3(1):155–163. (ERIC Document Reproduction Service No. ED 078 793)

The measurement of intelligence and language differences among Chicano children are discussed in relationship to translated and nonverbal tests. (KKS Summary)

Yen, M. C. L. 1976. The Issues in the Measurement of Bilingual Language Dominance. (ERIC Document Reproduction Service No. ED 121 853)

This paper deals with measurement of language dominance at the early-childhood level using a rating scale to help bilingual programs with student classification and placement. Some of the assumptions unique in the measurement of language dominance are discussed and applied to the validation procedure on a Spanish/English language dominance scale which is under drastic revision. The instrument was developed for children whose home language may be Spanish, and is designed to be individually administered by a bilingual tester. Part 1 is administered in Spanish and Part 2 in English. The screening discriminates among children in three categories; those preferring English, those preferring Spanish, and bilingual children. The instrument was given to 30 four-year-old Mexican-American children attending three day care centers in the summer of 1974. Teachers' judgments and test results were compared to determine validity, resulting in a coefficient of .86. The test–retest and the rater's reliability coefficients were quite high, which may indicate that the test manual was clearly written, the categories were well defined, and the children performed consistently on this variable. It may be concluded that this is a reliable instrument for four-year-old Mexican-American children at the testing site. (RC–ERIC Summary)

Yousef, F. S. 1968. Cross-cultural testing: An aspect of the resistance reaction. Lang. Learn. 43(3–4):227–234.

This paper is based on a classroom experience that showed the need of teaching American culture before attempting to teach American literature meaningfully to foreigners. The students in this learning situation were the Middle-Eastern employees of an American organization in the school year 1966–1967. The teachers found out the students interpreted literature in terms of their own native culture. Many times, a behavioral pattern had opposite meanings in American and Middle Eastern cultures. Consequently, a course in American culture was taught. In objective quizzes, whenever the questions on American behavioral patterns came directly from the book and were of a general nature, the students did well. But when the questions related to everyday-life situations, the students unconsciously answered according to their own native behavioral patterns. Such answers revealed intense, vehement resistance to the target culture, due to prejudice and mistrust of the foreign behavioral codes. The students' work careers depended on their school records. The answers to quiz questions were reliable. Gradually, the students' responses showed less resistance to the target, cultural patterns of behavior. (Author Summary)

Zirkel, P. A. 1974. A method for determining and depicting language dominance. TESOL Q. 8(1):7–16.

A description of a practical model for determining and depicting language dominance, given the general nature and needs of bilingual education programs in the United States. The use of parallel tests of aural ability is explained to indicate initially the language dominance of children who, for example, are otherwise commonly classified as "Spanish-speaking" or "bilingual" based upon surname. The results can be organized for placement of programmatic purposes into a continuum, for Spanish—to English—dominance. However, this unidimensional representation does not permit differentiation of ability level with each language. For example, a "balanced alingual" child, who is equally deficient in each language, is represented at the same point on the continuum as a "balanced bilingual" child, who is natively proficient in each language. Thus, a two dimensional representation is proposed elevating the left side of the continuum into a vertical plane so as to form a two dimensional matrix. This model allows for the distinct depiction of various dominance configurations in order to plan programs effectively according to bilingual dominance and proficiency. Several such linguistic and programmatic patterns are discussed. (HA-LABS Summary)

Zirkel, P. A. 1976. The whys and ways of testing bilinguality before teaching bilingually. Elem. School J. 76(6):323-330.

For a bilingual program to succeed, it is essential that a precise assessment of students' language dominance be made. Complete mastery and literacy in two languages is an unrealistic expectation—placement of a student on a continuum of speaking and listening skill is preferable. Fishman's "domain" concept is applicable to the child who is Spanish dominant at home but English dominant at school. Surname surveys can be grossly imprecise because of mixed marriages or misinterpretation of a name's origin. Assessment of language dominance is evaluated by use of rating scales, like Dailey's Language Facility Test. However, special bilingual examiners would need to first establish testee rapport; self-rating would only be effective for older students. In the *Aspira* legal agreement, the New York City Board of Education is committed to develop an assessment system to cover listening, speaking, reading, and writing abilities in Spanish and English. An English pilot instrument and battery for skills measuring has been developed on a small scale, and the Spanish version is being worked on (Polemeni, A. et al, Rating Scale of Pupils' Ability to speak English, 1974, and Language Assessment Battery, 1975, New York: Board of Education, 1975.). (MA-LABS Summary)

Zirkel, P. A., and Greene, J. F. 1974. The validation of parallel testing of aural ability as an indicator of bilingual dominance. Psychol. Schools 11(2):153-157.

There is a need to determine the degree of language dominance in students classified as bilingual, particularly Spanish-speaking students; thus a study was conducted to test the validity of picture-type parallel tests of aural ability as a measure of aural language dominance. Its relationship with various criterion measures and length of residence in the continental United States was explored. The Oral Vocabulary subtest (OV) of the Inter-American Test of General Abilities was used, and concurrent data on lingual dominance was gathered for each pupil in the sample using the Hoffman Bilingual Background Schedule and a language dominance rating scale. General agreement between the OV difference scores and the results of the criterion measures suggests that parallel testing of aural ability is a promising, practicable technique for assessment of language dominance of Spanish-speaking students in the early grades. (JM–LABS Summary)

Ziros, G. I. 1976. Language interference and teaching the Chicano to read. J. Read. 19(4):284–288.

In focusing on Chicano language and reading skills development, educators often seem to think that bilingualism is a detriment to learning English. The difficulties experienced by the Chicano in learning English have been broadly described as "interference." Carter (see Mexican Americans in School: A History of Educational Neglect. New York: College Entrance Board, 1970) and others report that the prevailing attitude among educators on interference is that it must be eradicated by eradicating Chicano Spanish. This attitude must be called into question. Although Chicanos do experience interference on the phonological and morphological levels, there is little evidence to support the idea that this interference is a detriment in learning to read English. Several research studies indicate that interference on the syntactic level is not apparent. For example, when socioeconomic variables were controlled, bilinguals who were allowed to develop both languages fully performed better on verbal and nonverbal intelligence tests. One of the main problems in bilingualism research and research on Chicanos' ability to learn to read English is disregard of socioeconomic variables. When this variable is controlled, the Chicano uses syntactic patterns basic to standard English, and displays a syntactic style consistent with socioeconomic status. Thus, the assumption which has influenced the adoption of many educational strategies related to the bilingual—that the Chicano's command of Spanish interferes with his ability to learn to read English—is not correct. Teacher attitudes toward nonstandard dialects, in particular toward syntactic style, and the teaching must be further investigated. There should be a move away from examining phonological and morphological differences and a move toward focusing on the semantic component. (AA-LABS Summary)

Index

Achievement and learning rates, 63–64
Acquisition of language
 first language, see First language acquisition
 second language, see Second language acquisition
 sequences in adults and adolescents, 61–63
 sequences in children, 59–60
Adults and adolescents
 error analysis, 60–61
 rates of learning and achievement, 63–64
 sequences of acquisition, 16–63
African languages, word coinage, 69–70
Age
 bias in language tests, 125–127, 215
 critical period hypothesis, 61, 69, 91–92
 English consonant phonemes, 83–84
 language variation as function of age of addressee, 230–231
 in learning phonology, 95
 optimum age for learning foreign language, 91–92
 second language acquisition, 92
Allophones
 identification of, 80–81
 obligatory, 90
Analytic and Gestalt speech, 207
Arabic language problems, 50–51
Arizona Articulation Proficiency Scale (Barker-Fudala, 1970), 86
Articles, usage errors, 54
Articulation
 dialectal variations and disorders of, 85–86
 errors, 84
 manner and place of, 78
 see also Phonological assessments; Phonology
 tests, 85–87
  availability of, 96
  in child's dominant language, 77, 96
  for phonological assessment, 85–87
 Spanish-dominant child, 88–89
Aspira Consent Decree, 38, 122
Assessment of communicative competence, 7–11, 208, 239
 analysis of function with supportive information, 16–18
 assumptions, 7
 collecting communication samples, 12–13, 107–111
  informants, 12
  interactors, 12
  settings, 12
 conceptualizing communicative abilities, 111
 considerations, 7–9
 definition, 1
 functional procedures, 11–14
 general model for assessment, 9–11
 historical perspectives, 2–4
 language function, 11–14
  analyzing samples, 13–14
 multi-informational approach to, 10, 17
 overview, 1–24
 pedagogical applications, 16–17
 by professionals, 17–18
 see also Observational assessment; Tests and testing
Assimilation, phonological processes, 81, 84
Austin Spanish Articulation Test, 88
Avoidance strategies, 51–52, 69–70

Basic Inventory of Natural Language (BINL) (Herbert, 1974), 211; (Herbert, 1977), 166–169
 general description, 166
 procedure, 166–167
 reliability and validity, 167
 reviewers comments, 168–169
Behaviorist school of psychology, 129
Belgium, language problems, 35
Biases
 observational assessment, 259–261
 test, 125–127, 215
Bibliography, 297–358

Bilingual bicultural programs, 17
Bilingual education
  case studies, 92
  federal legislation, 6
  tests for identifying children in need of, 213–214
Bilingual Index of Natural Language (Herbert, 1977), 16
Bilingual Syntax Measure (BSM) (Burt, Delay, and Hernandez, 1975), 16, 59, 211–212
  critiques of, 62, 172–175
  elicitation instrument, 62
  general description, 169
  procedure, 169–171
  reliability and validity, 62, 171–172
  reviewers comments, 141–142, 172–175
  sequences of acquisition, 61
Bilingualism
  assessing degree of, 36–39
  balanced bilinguals, 36–37
  bibliography, 7, 297–358
  classification system, 28, 30–34
  compound bilinguals, 30–31
  compound-coordinate bilinguals, 31–33
  concepts in, 25–41, 111
  coordinate bilinguals, 31–32
  definition, 2, 26–27, 34–35
  diglossia and, 34–36
  incipient, 27
  language assessment and, 25–41
  language dominance and, 33–34, 36–39
  language proficiency and, 37–38
  literature on, 25–26
  monolingual speakers and, 29, 30
  semantic differential technique, 32–33
  sociological factors and, 3, 25–26, 39, 236–237
  speed of response on various tasks, 32–33
  subordinate bilingualism, 31
  theories describing, 26–30
    Bloomfieldian, 26, 30, 36
    ideal mastery criterion, 29, 30
    sociolinguistic factors, 30
    strong and weak, 26
    stylistic changes and, 29–30
  usage in society, 236–237

BINL, see Basic Inventory of Natural Language
Black English, 85, 226, 251
  phonological differences, 85
Blacks, IQ test scores, 107
Boehm Test of Basic Concepts (Boehm, 1971), 144–151
  general description, 144
  procedure, 144–145
  reliability and validity, 145–148
  reviewers comments, 148–151
BSM, see Bilingual Syntax Measure

CA, see Contrastive analysis
Canada, language problems, 35
Case studies on bilingual development, 92–94
CEEB, see College Entrance Examination Board
Chinese language problems, 50–51
Chinese-speaking children, sequences of acquisition, 59–60
Chomskyan linguistic theory, 2–4, 122
Cloze procedure, proficiency testing, 124
Code-switching and code-mixing, 3, 211, 214, 226, 266
  contextual factors, 237–238
  as function of setting and addressee, 238–239
  principle of least effort, 70, 237
  relevance of, 238
  as variation in language use, 237–238
Coding system, 13
College Entrance Examination Board, Listening and Reading Tests, 189
Communication assessment, see Assessment of Communicative competence
Communication diagnostician, 17
Communication strategies, 68–70
  avoidance, types of, 51–52, 69–70
  economy principle, 70, 237
  native language transfer, 69, 94
  overelaboration, 69
  overgeneralization, 52–53, 69
  prefabricated routines, 69
  reliance on word order, 70
Competence

communicative, 10, 115, 208, 239
    see also Assessment of communicative competence
  integrative tests for measuring, 179-197
  language, 215
  testing, 120, 122
Conceptual approach
  children's capabilities, 99-103
  communicative abilities, 111
  contrastive analysis, 48-49
Consonants
  chart of English, 79
  clusters, 81
    simplification, 84
  final consonant deletion, 84
Contextual factors, 214-215, 221-247
  assessment procedures, 11-12, 239-244
  bilingual usage in society, 236-237
  categories of, 229
  code-switching, 237-238
    as function of setting and addressee, 2348-239
    as variation in language use, 237-238
  definitions, 221-223
  experimental studies, 229-235
  language acquisition and, 206-207
  language assessment and, 239-244
    experimental technique with puppets, 240-243
  language variations and, 224, 229-235
    as function of age of addressee, 230-231
    as function of setting and topic, 226, 235, 237
    as function of sex of speaker and addressee, 231-235
  linguistics, philosophers and, 221-223
  measuring functional language use, 38-39
  psycholinguistic investigations, 226-229
  relevance in study of language, 221-223
  review of literature, 222-247
  see also Assessment of communicative competence
  sociolinguistic rules and, 225-226

sociological approaches, 223-225, 236-237
  variation among bilinguals, 235-239
Contrastive analysis (CA), 43-52, 90
  apriori and *aposteriori,* 45, 50
  conceptual approach to, 48-49
  Contrastive Structure Series, 45-46
  counter arguments, 49-52
  criticisms, 45-46, 90
  equivalence of languages, 46-47
  learners' strategies and, 67-70
  methodological hybrids, 56-58
  pedagogical implications, 47-48
  phonological assessment and, 90
  phonological development in second language, 94
  for prediction of errors in second language acquisition, 70
  predictive value of, 56, 70
  research tool, 47-48
  strong and weak versions, 43-45
  syntax and semantic analysis, 43-52
Conversational acts, 3, 276-278
  contextual factors, 221
  conversational implicature, 203-205, 207, 222
  cooperative principle, 203
  cultural rules for, 276-278
  evaluating, 13
  maxims of, 203-205
  role of setting, topic and participants, 236-237, 243-244
  speaker-hearer relationships, 236-237
Creative construction theory of language, 59, 61, 65
Critical period hypothesis, 62, 69
  critical age for learning second language, 91-92
Critical similarity measures, 71
Cultural differences
  assessing communications, 8
  in language tests, 125-127
  observational assessments, 259

Data, collection and analysis, 17
  see also Samples and sampling
Del Rio Language Screening Test (Toronto et al., 1975), 5, 252
Descriptive ability, 211

Developmental sequences
  age range and, 83-84
  assessing, 14-16
  in English, 82-84
  first language acquisition, 82-84
  psycholinguistic studies, 211
  in Spanish, 87-88
Diacriticalmarks, 78
Diagnosis of areas of difficulty, 57
Dialectal considerations, 8-9, 17, 224
  contextual factors, 236
  phonological assessment and, 85
  of Puerto Rican Spanish, 88
Difficulties in learning
  contrastive analysis and, 44-45
  diagnosis of areas of difficulty, 57
  hierarchy of difficulties, 44-45, 71, 90
  student's perception of difficulty (SPD), 56-57
Diglossia, 236
  and bilingualism, 34-36
  definition, 34
  formal and personal use of language, 34
Directives, 222-223, 228
  responses to, 229
Discourse analysis, 3
  frameworks for, 205-206
  see also Conversational acts
Discrete point tests, 5, 101, 121-122
  based on structural approach, 129=130
  Boehm Test of Basic Concepts (Boehm, 1971), 144-151
  definition, 129
  dissatisfaction with, 179, 281
  Dos Amigos Verbal Language Scales (Critchlow, 1974), 134-137
  James Language Dominance Test, 130-133
  limitations, 129-130
  Short Tests of Linguistic Skills (Fredrickson and Wick, 1976), 137-144
  Test of Auditory Comprehension of Language (Carrow, 1973), 151-159
Dominance, language
  bilingualism and, 33-34, 36-39
  current tests, 5, 38, 130-133
  measuring functional language use, 38-39, 243
  pragmatic considerations, 213-214
  Dos Amigos Verbal Language Scales (Critchlow, 1974), 134-137
  general description, 134
  procedure, 134-135
  reliability and validity, 135-136
  reviewers comments, 136-137
Drop outs, 101
Dutch language problems, 48-49, 92

Eastern Europe, language problems, 35
Economy principle, language acquisition, 70, 237
Educational systems
  effect of standard tests, 99-100, 111
  placement of children, 38, 122, 126
  planning programs, 39
  tracking systems, 100
Elicitation of spontaneous speech, 209, 211-212, 215-216
  through observation, 215-216
  recording, 215-216
  use of puppets for, 239-243
English as a second language (ESL)
  assessment approaches, 5
  developmental or functional aspects, 5
  teachers of, 1
  see also Second language acquisition
English language
  articulation tests, 85-87
  Black English, 85
  developmental sequences in, 82-84
  Standard American English, 85
  syntax and semantic analysis, 48-49
Environment, sequences of acquisition and, 62, 235-236
Equivalence or compatibility of languages, 46-47
  cross-linguistic equivalences, 47
ERIC system, 7*n*
Error analysis, 43, 56, 57-58
  adult and adolescent errors, 60-61
  articulation errors, 84
  classification of identified errors, 52, 54-55
  contrastive analysis and, 43, 51,

53–54
developmental errors, 53, 59
fossilizable linguistic phenomena, 53
frequency ratio, 55
identification and isolation of errors, 54
interference from first language, 49–50, 58, 60
interlingual errors, 53, 57, 60
lack of explanatory power, 55
learners' difficulties revealed by, 53, 70
learners' strategies and, 67–70
local and global errors, 58
methodological hybrids, 56–58
mistakes and, 53
phonological assessment and, 91
second language acquisition, 70, 89
students perception of difficulty (SPD), 56–57
syntax and semantic analysis, 3, 52–55
transfer, 90
weaknesses and problems with, 54–55
ESL, *see* English as a second language
Ethnocentrism, 118
Ethological techniques, 1
observational assessments, 257
European educational systems, 100
Evaluating language assessment tests, 115–128, 129–161, 163–177, 179–197
age and cultural bias, 125–127
current issues, 121–125
reliability, 118–121
see also Discrete point tests; Integrative language tests; Quasi-integrative approaches
validity, 115–118

Far Eastern non-Indo-European languages, sequences of acquisition, 62
Feature contrast processes, 87
Federal legislation, 5–6
Fine arts skills, 102
First language acquisition, 2, 3, 82–89
contextual factors, 206–207

developmental sequences
in children, 59–60
in English, 82–84
in Spanish, 87–88
dialectal considerations, 85
hierarchies or natural sequences, 60
negations, 64–65
"ordering-theoretic" or "tree" method, 59
patterns of, 280
phonological processes, 84–85
testing for articulation disorders, 85–87
in Spanish dominant child, 88–89
Fisher-Logemann Test of Articulation (1971), 86
Fisher-Logemann Test of Articulation Competence Manual (1972), 89
FLS, *see* Functional Language Survey
Fluency, definition, 4
Focal child sampling technique, 261–264
Foreign Service Institute (FSI) Oral Interview, 180–187
general description, 180–181
procedure, 181–184
reliability and validity, 186–187
reviewers comments, 184–186
Form, assessing language form, 14–16
French
error analysis, 60
Savignon Communicative Competence Tests, 187–189
and simultaneous acquisition of English and, 92
FSI, *see* Foreign Service Institute
Functional language, 10
assessing, 11–14
development of, 39–40
examples of, 38–39
integrative tests, 179–180
measuring, 36–39
bilingual proficiency, 39–40
context of situation and, 38–39
Parent/Teacher Observation of Functional Language Ability, 22–24
see also Competence
tests for, 122–123
Functional Language Survey (FLS) (Walberg, Valdes and Rasher, 1978), 213–214

Generalizations, 208
  overgeneralizations, 52, 53
    errors, 91
    learner's strategies, 69
German language
  simultaneous acquisition of English and, 92
  syntax and semantics, 48-49
Global language proficiency, 121
  tests of, 122-123, 125
Goldman-Fristoe Test of Articulation (1972), 86
"Grammar of expectancy," 124
Grammatical Structures of English and Spanish, The (Stockwell, Bowen, and Martin, 1965), 44-45
Greek-speaking children, order of acquisition, 62

Habit formation theory, 58
Harmony processes, 87
Hearing disorders, 272
  tests of, 151-159
High/Scope Instruments (Bond, Epstein, and Matz, 1977), 192-194
  description, 192-193
  procedure, 193-194
Historical perspectives, assessing communication, 2-4

Identification of language disordered child, 268-272
  checklist for, 260
Identity hypotheses, acquisition stages, 65
Illocutionary acts, 223, 253-254
Ilyin Oral Interview (IOI) (Ilyin, 1976b), 189-192
  description, 189-190
  procedure, 190
  reliability and validity, 191-192
  research needs, 194-196
Imperatives, 229
Implicature, conversational and logical, 204, 222
India, language problems, 35
Individualized assessment approach, 102

  See also Observational assessment
Indo-European languages, sequences of acquisition, 62
Institute of Communicative English, Catholic University, Puerto Rico, 185, 186
Integrative language tests, 10-11, 125, 179-197
  Foreign Service Institute (FSI) Oral Interview, 180-187
  High/Scope Instruments (Bond, Epstein, and Matz, 1977), 192-194
  Ilyin Oral Interview (IOI), 189-192
  needs for research, 194-196
  quasi-integrative approaches, 163-177
    Basic Inventory of Natural Language (Herbert, 1977), 166-169
    Bilingual Syntax Measure (BSM) (Burt, Dulay, and Hernandez-Chavez, 1976), 169-176
    Oral Language Evaluation (Silvaroli and Maynes, 1975), 163-166
  Savignon Communicative Competence Tests (Savignon, 1972), 187-189
Intellectual impairment, 272
Interactional Sociolinguistics, 205
Interferences
  error analysis, 52
  native language, 44, 65, 94
  source of error in target language, 49-50, 56
Interlanguage hypothesis, 91, 94
International Phonetic Alphabet, 78
Interrogatives, 229
  language acquisition study of, 64-67
Interviews and interviewing
  clinical, 10-11
  focal child sampling, 263
  Ilyin Oral Interview (IOI), 189-192
  oral, 120, 122, 189-192
  problems to avoid, 288-289
  suggestions for, 285-289
  for testing language competence, 120, 122
IOI, *see* Ilyin Oral Interview
IQ tests, 107, 250
Israeli acquisition of English, 65

James Language Dominance Test
(James, 1975), 5, 130–133
general description, 130–131
procedure, 131–132
reliability and validity, 132–133
reviewers' comments, 133
Japanese language
perceptual strategies, 67–68
relative clause formation strategies, 50–51
SOV (subject-object-verb) language, 68

Kiel Project on language acquisition, 65
Korean-speaking children, 61

Language
assessing communications, 7–11
considerations, 7–9
cognitive orientation, 2
continuously evolving process, 108, 110
first, *see* First language acquisition
function in contrast to form, 2–4
functional, 10–14
grammatical analysis, 3, 44–45
historical perspectives, 2–4
psycholinguistic interpretation, 2
second, *see* Second language acquisition
see also Speech acts; Pragmatics, 2–3
Language acquisition
analytic and gestalt speech, 207
conversational implicature, 203–205, 207, 222
relevance of context in, 206–207, 221
see also First language acquisition; Second language acquisition
Language arternation and descriptive ability, 211
Language aptitude, 118
Language assessment
communicative error analysis, 57–58
contextual factors and, 239–244
emphasis on communicative competence, 115, 208
evaluating tests, 115–128
age and cultural bias, 125–127
current issues, 121–125
reliability, 118–121
validity, 116–118
game-like endeavors, 144
linguistic measures, 251–252
observational assessment and, 243, 248–284
see also Observational assessment
oral proficiency tests, 179–197, 208–209
panic approach, 6–7
pragmatics and, 199–219
puppets, use of, 239–243
tests, *see* Tests and testing
Language Cognition Test (LCT) (Stemmler, 1967), 209
Language dominance, *see* Dominance, language
Language Facility Test (Dailey, 1968), 209–210
Language functions, *see* Functional language
Lateralization, 62, 91
LCCE, *see* Limited communicative competence in English
LCI, *see* Length-Complexity Index
LCT, *see* Language Cognition Test
Learning strategies, 212
achievement and rates of, 63–64
adolescents and, 62
adults, 64
communication and, 68–70
from EA and CA research, 67–70
perceptual strategies, 67–68
Length-Complexity Index (LCI), 15–16
LES, *see* Limited English-speaking children
LESA, *see* Limited English-speaking ability
LFT, *see* Language Facility Test
Limited communicative competence in English (LCCE), 1*n*
Limited English-speaking ability (LESA), 1*n*
Limited English-speaking children (LES)
assessment of communication skills, 1, 4–7, 10
Linquistic analysis

Linguistic analysis—*continued*
  analytic and gestalt speech, 207
  assessing bilingual children, 8
  context and language acquisition, 206-207, 221
  frameworks for discourse analysis, 205-206
  maxims of conversation, 203-205
  quantitative versus qualitative measures, 251-252
  speech acts, 201-203
Listening comprehension, tests of, 124, 272

Mathematic skills, 102
Matrix completion, observational technique, 265
Mean length of response (MLR), 14
Mean length of utterance (MLU), 15
  Spanish and other languages, 15, 291-295
Meaning
  intended and implied, 222
  pragmatic or contextual, 200
Metalanguage, 57
Mexican-American children
  Dos Amigos Verbal Language Scales, 134-137
  James Language Dominance Test, 130-133
  Language Facility Test, 209-210
  Test of Auditory Comprehension of Language, 151-159
Michigan Picture Language Inventory (Lerea, 1958), 5
MLAT, *see* Modern Language Aptitude Test
MLR, *see* Mean length of response
MLU, *see* Mean length of utterance
Model of assessing communication, 9-11, 249-284
Modern Language Aptitude Test (MLAT), 189
Morphemes
  acquisition studies, 60, 62-63
  system for scoring Spanish utterances, 15, 291-295
Motivation to learn language, 118
Mutual Problem-Solving Test (MPST), 192-194

National Consortia for Bilingual Education, 95
Negation studies, acquisition of second language, 64-65
Non-English proficient (NEP), 1*n*
Northwestern Syntax Screening Test (Lee, 1969), 4
Norwegian-speaking children, development of negation, 65-66
Nutritional problems, 272

Observational assessment of communicative abilities, 243, 249-284
  alternative to discrete point testing, 261
  bias of observers, 259-261
  conversational styles, 276-278
  cultural differences, 259, 270-273
  effect of settings, 258-259
  ethological techniques, 257
  "feeling states," 278-279
  identification of language disordered child, 268-272
  checklist for, 269
  instruments for teacher, parent, and observer, 22-24, 268-281
  checklist used by teachers, 268-272
  parent questionnaire, 273-281
  used by observers, 276-281
  linguistic measures, 251-252 256-258
  modifying, 281
  nonverbal responses, 262
  objectivity problem, 259-260
  by peer groups, 260-261
  pragmatic linguistic approaches, 256-258
  problems with assessment, 258-261
    being unbiased, 259-261
    effect of settings, 258-259
    language problem, 259
    social relationship of settings, 258
  quantitative versus qualitative, 251-252
  reasons for failure, 270
  sex differences, 258-259
  speech acts, 252-256
  techniques of, 261-268

focal child sampling, 261-264
length of time for, 266-267
for marginal children, 265-266
matrix completion, 265
recording verbalizations, 267
Scan sampling, 260, 264-265
what to observe, 267-268
Oral Language Evaluation (OLE) (Silvaroli and Maynes, 1975), 16, 163-166
general description, 163
procedure, 163-164
reliability and validity, 164
reviewers' comments, 165-166
Oral Language Evaluation (OLE) (Silvaroli, Skinner, and Maynes, 1977), 212-213
Oral proficiency tests, 123, 179-197
Foreign Service Institute Oral Interview, 180-187
High/Scope Instruments, 192-194
Ilyin Oral Interview, 189-192
need for research, 194-196
review of literature, 208-209
Savignon Communicative Competence Tests, 187-189
Order of acquisition, 62, 66
reliance on word order, 70
"Ordering-theoretic" or "tree" method, 59
Overelaboration, use of, 69
Overgeneralization, 52, 53
errors, 91
learner's strategies, 69
Overviews
assessing communication, 7-11
assessment considerations, 7-9
general model for, 9-11
assessing English as first or second language, 4-7
assessing language form, 14-16
assessing language function, 11-14
analyzing samples, 13-14
collecting communication samples, 12-13
assessment of child's communication ability, 1-24
historical perspectives, 2-4

Paraguay
bilingualism in, 236-237

Spanish and Guarani speech, 35, 236-237
Parents
language sample collection by, 12-13
observational assessments, 22-24, 260-261, 273-281
questionnaires, 273-276
Parents/Teacher Observation of Functional Language Ability, 22-24
communication functions, 23
conversational styles, 22
observer impressions, 23-24
Pathologists, speech-language, 1
Peabody Picture Vocabulary Tests (Dunn), 4, 239
Pedagogical techniques, 57
for contrastive analysis, 47-48
Peer groups, 279
observations by, 260-261
Perceptual strategies, 67-68
Persian language problems, 50-51
Phonemes
articulation tests, 86
distinctive features, 81
identification of, 80-81
optional, 90
Phonetics
description of consonants and vowels, 78-80
diacritical marks, 78
manner and place of articulation, 78
notation systems, 78-80
stops and fricatives, 78
transcribing sounds, 78
voicing, 78
Phonological assessments, 77-98
acquisition of first language, 82-89
developmental sequences in English, 82-84
developmental sequences in Spanish, 87-88
dialectal considerations, 85
English articulation tests, 85-87
phonological processes, 84-85
testing for articulation disorders in Spanish dominant child, 88-89
acquisition of second language,

Phonological assessment—*continued*
  89–96
  research on phonological development, 92–95
    testing for phonological proficiency, 95–96
    theories, 89–91
  assimilation, 81, 84
  bilingual child, 95–96
  phonetics, 78–79
  phonological analysis, 80–81
  proficiency testing, 96–97
  study of sound systems, 78–82
    distinctive features, 81
    phonetics, 78–80
    phonological analysis, 80–81
    suprasegmental phonology, 81–82
    syllable structure, 81
Phonological processes
  assimilation, 81, 84
  consonant cluster simplification, 84
  final consonant deletion, 84
  first language acquisition, 84–85
  Phonological Process Analysis (Weiner, 1979), 86
  substitution, 84
Phonology
  age differences in learning, 95–96
  analysis, 80–81
  contextual variations, 226
  contrastive distribution, 80
  definition, 80
  distinctive features, 81
  phonemes and allophones, 80–81
  phonetics, 78–79
  proficiency testing, 95–96
  rates of learning and achievement, 63
  study of sound systems, 77–82
  suprasegmental features, 81–82
    stress, intonation, and juncture, 81–82
  units of rhythm, 82
Placement of children in educational programs, 38, 122
  cultural bias, 126
  tests used for, 179, 208
PLAT, *see* Productive Language Assessment Tasks
Politeness, development of, 228–229
Pragmatics and language assessment, 2, 199–219
  application to language assessment tests, 2, 11, 122, 207–214, 254
  Basic Inventory of Natural Language, 211
  Bilingual Syntax Measure, 211–212
  collecting speech samples, 215–216, 285–289
  Functional Language Survey, 213–214
  Language Cognition Test, 209
  Language Facility Test, 209–210
  Oral Language Evaluation, 212–213
  research needs, 214–216
  revision behaviors, 214–215
  Storytelling Task, 210–211
  context and language acquisition, 206–207
  conversational implicature, 199, 203–205, 207, 222
  definition, 199–200, 256–257
  direct and indirect speech acts, 201–203
  discourse analysis, 205–206
  implications of recent developments, 214–216
  maxims of conversation, 203–205
  observational assessments, 256–258
  politeness, development of, 228–229
  research needs and, 199–200
  role in language dominance, 213–214
  transmission of meaning, 199–200
Prefabricated routines, learner's strategies, 69
Preschool children, assessing language development, 14–15
Productive Language Assessment Tasks (PLAT), 192–194
Proficiency in language
  bilingualism, 37–39
    functional language assessment and, 39–40
  evaluating language assessment tests, 115–128
  oral testing, 123, 179–197
  phonological tests, 77, 95–96
  Savignon Communicative Competence Tests, 187–189
  testing, 123–124
    cloze procedure, 124

global proficiency, 121, 125
  see also Tests and testing
Psycholinguistic studies, 9
  contextual factors, 226-229
  developmental, 211
  recent research, 227-229
Psychology, behaviorist school, 129
Puppets for language assessment tests, 239-243

Quasi-integrative approaches, 163-177
  Basic Inventory of Natural Language (Herbert, 1977), 166-169
  Bilingual Syntax Measure (BSM), 169-176
  Oral Language Evaluation (Silvaroli and Maynes, 1975), 163-166
Questions
  acquisition stages for, 64-65
  developmental sequences, 66-67
  Wh-questions, 66
  yes/no, 66
  see also Interrogatives

Recording speech acts, 13, 262, 267-268
  spontaneous speech, 215-216
Redundancy utilization, 124
Relative clauses, formation strategies, 50-51
Reliability
  coefficients, 119-120
  definition, 118-119
  estimated, 120-121
  evaluating language assessment tests, 115-128
  rational equivalence, 120
  standard error of measurement, 119
Remediation programs
  articulation tests for diagnostic and prognostic use, 87
  error analysis and, 53
Research
  phonological assessment, 82-89, 92-95
  second language learning, 6, 77, 89, 92-95
Revision behaviors and studies in pragmatics, 214-215

Rules
  with contextual factors, 224
  ignorance of restrictions, 53

Samples and sampling, 107-111
  analyzing, 13-14
  collecting communication samples, 12-13
    informants, 12
    interactors, 12
    settings, 12
  elicitation of natural speech, 209-210
  use of puppets, 239-243
  focal child sampling, 261-264
  Parent/Teacher Observation of Functional Language Ability, 22-24
  recording, 13-14
  scan sampling, 259, 264-265
  size of sample, 99, 107-111, 117
  "statistically significant" changes, 108-109
  validity of tests and, 117
  spontaneous versus elicited, 60, 62-63
Savignon Communicative Competence Tests (Savignon, 1971), 187-189
  description, 187-188
  procedure, 188-189
Scan sampling, 259-260, 264-265
School dropouts, 101
Science skills, 102
Scoring tests
  bias on part of scorer, 123
  language assessment tests, 120-121
Second language acquisition, 2-3
  adult compared to child, 58-63, 71
  age for acquiring, 90-92
  creative construction theory, 58-59
  developmental sequences, 71
  difficulty of adults and adolescents in, 89
  education can continue while learning second language, 102
  error analysis and, 49, 58-67
    acquisition stages for various structures, 64-67
    adult and adolescent errors, 60-61

Second language acquisition—*continued*
  adult and adolescent sequences of acquisition, 61-63
  child errors, 59
  child sequences of acquisition, 59-60
  rates of learning and achievement, 63-64
  evaluation of methods, 70-71
  interference from first language, 65
  interlanguage hypothesis, 91
  interrogatives, 64-65
  morpheme acquisition studies, 62-63
  order of acquisition, 62
  phonological development, 92-95
  sequences of, 61-63
    adults and adolescents, 61-63
    children, 59-60
  stages for various structures, 64-67
  testing for phonological proficiency, 77, 95-97
  use of native-language structures, 58-59, 89-90
Second Language Oral Production English (SLOPE) test, 61-62
Semantics, *see* Syntax and semantic analysis
Sentence usage, 16
  acquisition stages for various structures, 64-67
  contextual meaning, 200-201
  deep structure, 200
  speech acts and, 201-203
  transformation rules, 200
Settings and topics, 236
  language variation as function of, 235
Sex differences
  contextual factors and, 231-235
  observational assessments, 258-259
Short Tests of Linguistic Skills (STLS) (Fredrickson and Wick, 1976), 95, 137-144
  general description, 137
  procedure, 138-141
  reliability and validity, 141
  reviewers' comments, 141-144
Simplification and communication strategies, 70
Situational context, 205
SLOPE, *see* Second Language Oral Production English test
Sociolinguistic factors, 3
  bilingualism and, 30
  contextual factors and, 223-226
Sound systems, 78-82
  criteria for determining when acquired, 82
  distinctive features, 81
  phonetics, 78-79
  phonological analysis, 80-81
  suprasegmental phonology, 81-82
Spanish
  articulation tests, 88-89
  Bilingual Syntax Measure, 169-176
  calculating MLU in morphemes for, 15, 291-295
  developing national tests, 105-106
  developmental sequences in, 87-88
  Dos Amigos Verbal Language Scales, 134-137
  Test of Auditory Comprehension of Language, 151-159
Spanish-speaking children
  article usage errors, 54
  Cuban-dominant child, 88
  dialect variation, 88-89
  error analysis, 61
  grammar tests, 56
  Puerto Rican dialects, 88
  sequences of acquisition, 59-60, 61, 62, 87-88
SPD, *see* Students perception of difficulty
Spearman-Brown Prophecy Formula, 147
Special education, federal legislation, 6
Speech acts, 2-3, 199-203, 211, 223, 225
  analytic and gestalt speech, 207
  assessment for use by observers, 276-281
  contextual factors, 226
  developmental sequence, 280
  direct and indirect, 201-203
  illocutionary acts, 223, 253-254
  linguistic context, 223
  observational assessments, 252-256
  perlocutionary acts, 254-255
  propositional acts, 253-254
  recording/categorizing, 13
  utterance acts, 253-254

Speech disorders, 272
  assessment in dominant language, 96
Speech patterns, 111
Speech samples, *see* Samples and sampling
Speed of response of bilinguals, 32–33
Statistical procedures, tests and testing, 5, 99, 102, 108
STLS, *see* Short Tests of Linguistic Skills
Storytelling Task (Cohen, 1975), 210–211
Strategies
  communication, 68–70
  learners', 67–70
    see also Learners strategies
  perceptual, 67–68
Structural approach to language learning, 5, 14–16
  acquisition stages for various structures, 64–67
  discrete-point tests, 129–130
  to language testing, 121
Students' perception of difficulty (SPD), 56–57
Substitution, phonological processes, 84–85
Surface structure analysis of English, 14–16
Syllable structure processes, 81, 87
Syntax and semantic analysis, 43–75, 199–200
  contrastive analysis, 43–52
    apriori and *aposteriori*, 45, 50
    conceptual approach, 48–49
    criticism of, 45–46
    in defense of, 49–52
    equivalence of languages, 46–47
    pedagogical implications, 47–48
    strong and weak versions, 43–45
  error analysis, 3, 52–55, 58–67
    acquisition stages for various structures, 64–67
    adult and adolescent errors, 60–61
    adult and adolescent sequences of acquisition, 61–63
    child errors, 59
    child sequences of acquisition, 59–60
    rates of learning and achievement, 63–64
    second language acquisition and, 58–67
    support for, 52–54
    weaknesses and problems with, 54–55
  learner's strategies
    communication and, 68–70
    economy principle, 70, 237
    native language transfer, 69, 94
    overelaboration, 69
    overgeneralization, 69
    perceptual strategies, 67–68
    prefabricated routines, 69
    reliance on word order, 70
    types of avoidance, 69–70
  methodological hybrids, 56–58
  tests, 3n, 4–5

Teachers
  of English as a Second Language, 1, 3
  observational assessments by, 268–272
  checklist for, 269
Templin-Darley Test of Articulation (1960), 86
Terminology, 1, 3
  biases in definitions and, 4
  variability in, 4
Test of Auditory Comprehension of Language (Carrow, 1973), 5, 151–159
Test of Syntactic Abilities, 3n
Tests and Testing
  achievement, 105
  age and cultural bias, 125–127
  alternative strategies, 111
  articulation tests, 85–87
  assessing communications, 7–11
    considerations, 7–9
    model for, 9–11
  assessing language function, 11–14, 121–125
  based on contemporary theory, 9
  cloze procedure, 124
  conceptualization of bilingual children, 99–103
  children's capabilities, 99–103
  construction of, 99, 103–105
    based on linguistic and psycho-

Tests and testing—*continued*
    logical theory, 99
    design of, 103
    nationally normed tests, 105–107
    populations for norming national tests, 106–107
    sample size, 107–111
    weighted against minority populations, 106
    for diagnostic and placement purposes, 208
    discrete point tests, *see* Discrete point tests
    elicitation of spontaneous speech sample, 209, 211–212, 215–216
    ethnic differences, 101–102
    evaluations of, 103, 110, 115–128
    in-depth evaluations, 9*n*
    functional language ability, 122–123
    of global proficiency, 125
    incorrect placement of children, 6, 126
    integrative, 10–11, 125, 179–197
    see also Integrative language tests
    IQ, 107, 250
    language assessment tests, 115–128
    large-scale testing, 127
    learning theory approach, 101
    limitations, 103, 126–127
    linguistic and psychological theory, 99, 122
    matching questions to child's capabilities, 99
    measures of central tendency, 239
    new approaches to, 103
    nonstandardized approaches, 110–111
    normative data, 6, 105–107
        locally normed tests, 110
        tests for developing, 99–113, 209–210
    observational assessment, 249–284
    oral interviews or compositions, 120, 122
    oral proficiency, 123, 208–209
    Parent/Teacher Observation of Functional Language Ability, 22–24, 268–281
    for phonological proficiency, 95–96
    population being tested, 99, 100, 104, 107–111
    pragmatics and language assessment, 122, 207–214
    proficiency testing, 123–124, 208–209
    purpose of, 99–100
    quasi-integrative approaches, 163–177
    recognizing individual differences, 102–103
    relevancy of, 104–105
    reliability, 6, 103, 118–121
    research needs, 6
    reviews of, 5
    sample size, 107–111
    scoring, 104
    selection of, 9, 115–116
    sex differences, 101–102
    for speech disorders, 96
    statistical procedures, 5, 99, 102, 108
    structuralist approach, 121
    translations of, 115, 126
    validity, 6, 103–104, 116–118
Title VII Bilingual Projects, 95, 159
Topics and settings, contextual factors, 226, 235, 237
Transfer of native language, 69, 94
    errors, 90
Transmission of meaning, 199–201

Utterances
    application of pragmatics, 208
    calculating MLU in morphemes for Spanish, 291–295
    mean length of utterance (MLU), 175
    relevance of, 203–204

Validity in language testing, 6, 103–104, 116–118
    concurrent or correlational, 117
    construct, 118
    content, 117–118
    criterion-referenced, 117
    face validity, 116
    sample size and, 117

Variation in child's language
  as function of age of addressee, 230–233
  as function of setting and topic, 226, 235
  sex differences and, 231–235, 258–259
Vocabulary tests, 4–5
Vowels, chart of English, 80

Wales, language problems, 35
Wechsler Intelligence Scale for Children (WISC), 135–136
Word coinage, 69–70
Word order, reliance on, 70
Written compositions for testing language competence, 120, 122